P9-AOT-691

Justice James Iredell

JAMES IREDELL
1751–1799

Associate Justice,
United States Supreme Court
1790–1799

Justice James Iredell

Willis P. Whichard

CAROLINA ACADEMIC PRESS
Durham, North Carolina

TAO

Library of Congress Cataloging-in-Publication Data

Whichard, Willis P.
  Justice James Iredell / Willis P. Whichard.
    p.   cm.
  A revised and redacted version of thesis (S.J.D.) — University
of Virginia. Includes bibliographical references and index.
  ISBN 0-89089-971-1
  1. Iredell, James, 1751–1799. 2. Judges — United States —
Biography. 3. United States. Supreme Court — Biography.
  I. Title.

KF8745.I72 W48 2000
347.73'2634 — dc21
[B]   00-036105

CAROLINA ACADEMIC PRESS
700 Kent Street
Durham, North Carolina 27701
Telephone (919) 489-7486
Fax (919) 493-5668
www.cap-press.com

Frontispiece and front of jacket: engraving of James Iredell by Albert Rosenthal, cour-
tesy North Carolina Collection, University of North Carolina Library at Chapel Hill.
Back of jacket: Chowan County Courthouse, Edenton, North Carolina, courtesy
North Carolina Collection, University of North Carolina Library at Chapel Hill.

Printed in the United States of America

To the memory of
WILLIS G. WHICHARD
*My father, who gently guided me into the career in law
he had wanted for himself*

and

WILLIAM H. BOBBITT
*My mentor and friend, who was, like Iredell, an important
part of the North Carolina judicial tradition.*

Contents

IV
THE MAN

Illustrations follow page 136

Acknowledgments

This book is a revised and redacted version of an S.J.D. dissertation done at the University of Virginia. G. Edward White was my advisor, and I am especially grateful to him for consistent availability, assistance, encouragement, and support. Charles McCurdy and Calvin Woodard, the other members of my graduate committee, also contributed meaningfully to the endeavor.

In addition to Professors White, McCurdy, and Woodard, the following professional historians have read and commented on the manuscript at various stages: Warren H. Billings, Don Higginbotham, Herbert A. Johnson, William E. Leuchtenburg, John V. Orth, William S. Powell, and William S. Price, Jr. Maeva Marcus, editor of *The Documentary History of the United States Supreme Court*, granted me an interview as I began my work on Iredell's life on the federal circuits. She both contributed to my perspective and referred me to sources I might otherwise have overlooked. I had similar conversations, with similar results, with Peter G. Fish, Professor of Political Science at Duke University, who is writing a history of the United States Court of Appeals for the Fourth Circuit. They all have my gratitude for contributing significantly to the endeavor; the responsibility for its final form is, of course, mine alone.

The directors and staffs of the archival repositories involved could hardly have been more helpful. Debra Blake, Earl Imes, Donna Kelly, Russell Koontz (later at Duke also), Ed Morris, George Stevenson, and others assisted me at the North Carolina State Archives. Donna DiMichele, Bill Erwin, Tony Jenkins, Linda McCurdy, and Pat Webb were cheerful and helpful during my encampment at the Manuscripts Department, Duke University. H.G. Jones, Bob Anthony, David Moltke-Hansen and their staffs at the North Carolina Collection and the Southern Historical Collection, the University of North Carolina at Chapel Hill, were indispensable to my efforts. Gerard Gawalt assisted me at the Library of Congress; John Vandereedt, at the National Archives; and Shelley Dowling, at the United States Supreme Court Library. At Lewes, England, Iredell's birthplace, I had help from Mrs. Colin Brent of the Sussex County Records Office and from Susan Bain, Joyce Crow, and Ken Dickens of the Sussex Archeological Society. Pansy Alderman Elliott, president of the James Iredell Association, Inc., and Linda J. Eure, site manager of the James Iredell House, facilitated my efforts in Iredell's American hometown of Edenton, North Carolina.

The support of Louise H. Stafford, librarian to the North Carolina Supreme Court, and her staff, has been truly essential. Lolly Gasaway of the University of North Carolina Law Library and Janine Denson of the Duke University Law Library helped by facilitating long-term loans of books. The Duke Law Library and the Davis Library at the University of North Carolina at Chapel Hill provided me with carrel space at various stages of the endeavor.

Others who have assisted with various aspects of the detail work include: Elizabeth Armstrong, Pam Britt, Fred Jones, Leslie Laufer, Tracy Lischer, Robert Long, Lisa Lukasik, Joan Magat, Lynn Marshbanks, Jill Moore, Susan Owens, Julie Rischer, Elizabeth Davenport Scott, Mary Spear, and Beth Tillman.

When I have worked at home, my wife, Leona, and our now-grown daughters, Jennifer and Ida, have been tolerant of my scattered books and papers. They have also been generally uncomplaining while their husband/father passed time with his late-eighteenth-century friends that he might otherwise have spent with them.

Finally, while it perhaps goes without saying, my greatest debt is to my subject. James Iredell has been consistently good company through over twelve years of episodic research, reading, writing, and revising. He lived an interesting and significant life and left a reasonably extensive record of it. As his biographer, I hope I "have him right." To the extent that is possible, I believe I do; to the degree that I may have failed, I take comfort in the thought that "[h]istorical biography, after all, is an interpretive art, not an exact science."[1]

Author's Note

The Iredell papers are located mainly in the North Carolina State Archives, Raleigh; the Manuscripts Department, Duke University, Durham; and the Southern Historical Collection, the University of North Carolina at Chapel Hill. Many have been published in the two-volume work by Griffith J. McRee (1857–58), the two-volume set by Don Higginbotham (1976), and the multi-volume *Documentary History of the United States Supreme Court* (in progress, six volumes to date). For the reader's convenience, I have cited published sources when available, while noting the content parenthetically.

Judged by modern standards, Iredell and his contemporaries used excessive capitalization and punctuation as well as archaic or abbreviated forms of spelling. To enhance readability, I have conformed capitalization, punctuation, and spelling to modern custom. Except where expressly indicated by the use of brackets, in no instance have I intentionally altered the words themselves or their significance in the context in which used, though I may occasionally have failed to translate with total accuracy the virtually inscrutable handwriting Iredell and his contemporaries sometimes employed.

A Very Affecting Death

G EORGE WASHINGTON DID NOT ATTEND FUNERALS. PERHAPS THE DEMANDS OF THE PRESIDENCY WERE TOO GREAT, OR THE POLITICAL PROBLEMS IN SELECTING AMONG SO MANY TOO SEVERE, TO PERMIT IT. WHATEVER THE REASON, HIS POLICY WAS NOT TO GO. But this one was different. Tobias Lear, the deceased's husband, was the president's senior and most-trusted aide. Originally employed to tutor Martha's grandchildren, he had long since penetrated Washington's veneer of formality and become like family. In April 1790, when Lear had married his longtime inamorata, the president had been present. The bride and Martha Washington soon became inseparable, as Polly Lear attended the first lady as assiduously as her husband did the president.

Only two days before Polly's death in July 1793, the president noticed that she was ill. West Indies trading ships had brought mosquitos to the infant nation's capital, and with them, the yellow fever. Before the autumn frosts, over five thousand Philadelphians would join twenty-three-year-old Polly Lear in premature graves.

Polly's was "a very affecting death," and not surprisingly, her rites attracted the luminaries of the Washington era to Philadelphia's Christ Church, among them the pallbearers her anguished husband had selected. As the grieving president watched these notables convey the youthful remains to an untimely tomb, he saw among them his feuding secretaries of state and treasury, Thomas Jefferson and Alexander Hamilton; his secretary of war, Henry Knox, himself still mourning the death of a son; and three whom he had appointed to federal judgeships: Richard Peters of Pennsylvania, a district court judge; James Wilson, also of Pennsylvania, an associate justice of the Supreme Court; and James Iredell of North Carolina, the junior justice of that Court as initially constituted.[1]

The prominence of the forty-one-year-old North Carolinian in this esteemed assemblage reflected the relative egalitarianism of the infant American experiment. The rigid class structure of his native England likely would have precluded the attainment of similar status by this grandson of an unremarkable clergyman and son of a failed merchant. But this was a new country and a new age, and ironically, the dire family circumstances that had thrust responsibility upon the youth, suddenly and prematurely, had worked to his advantage.

The oldest of five surviving children of Francis Iredell, a merchant of Bristol, England, and his wife, the former Margaret McCulloh of Ireland, Iredell sailed to the New World in 1768, at age seventeen, to be King George III's comptroller of customs in the northeastern North Carolina village of Edenton. Family poverty impelled his voyage. In 1766 his father suffered a paralytic stroke that forced his retirement from the mercantile business. Even while healthy, the elder Iredell fared poorly. According to his brother Thomas, he was weak and wanting in enterprise and ambition. As a result, he and his family soon experienced penurious circumstances.

Fortunately, felicitous family connections enabled Francis to survive and produced remunerative positions for three of his sons. Margaret Iredell's uncle, Henry McCulloh, and his son, Henry Eustace McCulloh, aided the eldest son, James, in securing the comptroller's post at Edenton. The position was thought to be "genteel, requir[ing] little or no duty," to pay adequately, yet to allow time for other business. Notwithstanding James' lament that he was "pressed by the narrowness of [his] income, which occasion[ed] very disagreeable difficulties in [his] situation," the emoluments from the office allowed him to assist his family of origin in England throughout his early years in America.[2]

As predicted, the job also left time for other pursuits — among them, a fervent courtship with Hannah Johnston, sister of Samuel Johnston, his law teacher and probably Edenton's most respected and influential citizen. Iredell's letters and diary entries for this period exemplify the flowery language in which eighteenth-century men verbalized their ardor, proposed marriage, and sought permission therefor. His union with Hannah in July 1773 failed to diminish the suitor's fervor, for years later he continued to express his affection for her with near equal grandiloquence.

While Iredell's nomadic lifestyle as lawyer and jurist often strained the relationship, the marriage proved durable and appears to have been generally happy. It was childless for over twelve years but then produced four children, three of whom survived: Annie (b. 1785), James (b. 1788), and Helen (b. 1792). They, too, suffered from their father's frequent, often prolonged absences, yet the father-offspring associations could hardly have been more affectionate.[3]

Iredell's love for spouse and family was not unrivaled, however, for through these years he courted learning as ardently as he had wooed Hannah. While most men of that era passed their days in fields and forests, not libraries, Iredell was perhaps foremost among "a respectable proportion of the men in the colony who cultivated both the arts and the sciences." His brother-in-law, Samuel Johnston, had probably the best library in the province in that period, containing books on a wide variety of subjects, and Iredell patronized it. His pre-American Revolution reading included history, literature, and classical authors such as Livy, Horace, and Virgil. He apparently became familiar with *Cato's Letters*, for his revolutionary-period political essays reflect themes developed there. His voluminous correspondence contains frequent literary allusions and other reflections of his extensive scholarship.[4]

Iredell's zealous pursuit of worldly culture did not preclude a serious commitment to matters metaphysical. He was devoted to the Anglican church, in which his grandfather was a clergyman, and his spiritual interests clearly surpassed mere formal, organized religion. The church was also one of many outlets for his always-active social life.[5]

Iredell's comptroller position also allowed him leisure for the study of law. Samuel Johnston was his mentor, and Johnston's tutelage prepared the youthful emigrant for a professional practice in which he acquired both a reputation as a superior lawyer and more business than he reasonably could handle.

As a lawyer, Iredell participated as counsel for the plaintiff in *Bayard v. Singleton*, a 1787 North Carolina suit that was among the first American cases to apply the doctrine of judicial review of the constitutionality of legislative enactments. He was a cogent and vigorous advocate of the theory, supporting it first in a pre-*Bayard*, pseudonymous letter addressed "TO THE PUBLIC" from "AN ELECTOR," and later in a post-*Bayard* missive to Richard Dobbs Spaight, a champion of legislative supremacy.

While practicing his profession, Iredell was a model of the lawyer-public servant. His adopted state of North Carolina benefited from his service as a member of a commission to prepare statutes for its new government, draftsman of its initial court bill, one of its first three superior-court judges, its second attorney general, an original trustee of its university, and the initial revisor of its statutes. The country joined the state in profiting from his more-significant exertions in behalf of the American cause in the Revolution and the adoption of the federal Constitution.

Iredell came to the revolutionary cause reluctantly, yet became the leading essayist in his region in support of independence. His treatise "Principles of an American Whig" predates, and bears unmistakable traces of consanguinity with, the American Declaration of Independence. His papers convey a sense of life in North Carolina in the Revolutionary War period, one of considerable personal consequence for him in that it brought temporary severance of his ties with his family of origin in England and disinheritance by a wealthy bachelor uncle who heartily disapproved of his disloyalty to the mother country.

Following the Revolution, Iredell was the foremost advocate in his state of adoption of the proposed federal Constitution. While financial limitations barred his being a delegate to the Philadelphia convention, he corresponded regularly with the North Carolina delegates, and this correspondence unfolds the progress of the convention. He then inaugurated the first public movement in North Carolina in favor of the proffered document and maintained a busy pen as an essayist urging the birth of the new government. In particular, he responded seriatim to George Mason's eleven objections to the Constitution, drawing national attention to himself in the process.

When delegates convened in Hillsborough, North Carolina, to consider ratification, Iredell was the floor leader for the Federalist forces. After the convention refused to ratify the Constitution, he continued to promote it. He and William R. Davie, later the founder of the University of North Carolina, published the convention debates at their own expense and distributed them widely. Iredell persisted in applying his considerable talents as a political essayist to the cause of the new government. He joined other Federalists in circulating petitions requesting a second ratification convention. When the Federalist cause finally triumphed in North Carolina, he was widely recognized as a principle architect of its victory.

The bereft president who would join the pallbearers at Polly Lear's graveside rewarded these efforts by appointing Iredell to the original United States Supreme Court, where he served for almost a decade. While there, he had intimate associations with George Washington, John Adams, and their administrations; and both on and off the bench, he was their vigorous, highly partisan defender. He also served as a chronicler of important events and personalities during these years.

Ordinarily, treatments of Supreme Court justices devote considerable attention to the cases in which they participated, particularly to the opinions they wrote. With Iredell, this is impossible. The Court's caseload was so low during his tenure that the justices went to the capital only twice annually to hear arguments. They apparently did not always reduce their opinions to writing. As a consequence, in his near decade on the Court Iredell wrote opinions in only a handful of reported cases. Of these, only *Chisholm v. Geor-*

gia (1793), in which as the lone dissenter he supported the result that ultimately prevailed through adoption of the Eleventh Amendment to the federal Constitution, merits expansive consideration.

Instead of sitting together at the capital to decide cases, the early justices logged mile after mile riding the federal circuits, hearing appeals from the federal district courts in some instances, but mainly serving as the primary federal trial courts for several categories of cases. The life, Iredell bemoaned, was one of "perpetual traveling and almost a continual absence from home, [and was] a very severe lot."[6] The justices thus were in the vanguard of efforts to alter or remove this onerous duty; Iredell, who was the most severely affected because he most often traveled the harshest circuit, the Southern, was their leader. The attempts were unsuccessful, however, and Iredell thus spent a considerable portion of the last near decade of his life traveling the circuits and doing the work of the circuit courts.

As with the cases, surviving information on this work is somewhat sparse. Iredell as correspondent and chronicler, more than as jurist, makes biographical consideration of this aspect of his life feasible. Such treatment thus perhaps accords more with the early-American travel genre of literature than with typical judicial biography and resonates more of the general life of the period than of the era's jurisprudence.

General biographical treatment of this early American jurist-traveler is attainable, however, and long neglected. Many years ago, Hugh T. Lefler, probably the foremost disciple of Clio of his time who specialized in North Carolina history, lamented the vacuum in full biographical treatment of the state's leaders. "In the field of biography," he wrote,

> where one might expect to find the greatest interest and perhaps the largest number of books, one encounters the most frustration. The plain fact is that most North Carolina leaders, in all areas of activity, have simply not been studied.... Time will permit me to list only a few leaders who merit study and, perhaps, full-length books.

The initial name on Lefler's attendant list was "James Iredell, distinguished judge and 'letter writer' of the American Revolution."[7]

To view Iredell merely as a North Carolina leader slights him severely, for during much of his life he was a truly national figure. This, though, renders the void Lefler correctly perceived still more enigmatic. The narrative that follows addresses this void thematically, briefly considering its subject as a professional and focusing more extensively on his roles as statesman and jurist. It concludes by considering aspects of the man himself: his family relations, slave ownership, friends, finances, religion, and general humanity.

As a statesman-jurist, Iredell should perhaps be remembered foremost as a consummate Federalist who retained an abiding (to some, counterintuitive) commitment to the residual sovereignty of the states. At a time when the modern Supreme Court is accused of verging on reinstating the Articles of Confederation,[8] yet many still fret over a perceived erosion of state powers, a consideration of Iredell's life and work may have uncommon relevance. The story is as old as the American republic, but it has pertinency as current as the Clinton impeachment proceedings and the Supreme Court's 1998–99 Term.

I

The Professional

The study of the law qualifies a man to be useful to himself, to his neighbors, and to the public. It is the most certain stepping stone to public preferment in the political line.

—*Thomas Jefferson*

CHAPTER 1

That Amusing Study, The Law

N MID-CAREER, IREDELL TOLD A FRIEND: "THAT AMUSING STUDY, THE LAW, IS MY PRINCIPAL EMPLOYMENT." HE COULD HAVE SAID THE SAME MUCH SOONER, FOR WHILE WE KNOW LITTLE OF HIS CHILDHOOD, WE KNOW THE LEGAL PROFESSION BECKONED HIM EARLY. EVEN BEFORE Iredell left England as a teenager, Henry Eustace McCulloh, a cousin who aided him in securing the Edenton customs post, advised him to expect success at the bar in "a most growing country." Early in his American experience another cousin, Margaret Macartney, foresaw that he would be a great figure in the law and anticipated his rendering gratuitous services to her.[1]

Roscoe Pound lists Iredell among early American leaders who implanted in the colonies a legal tradition in which the English Inns of Court had trained them.[2] No evidence supports this assertion. Iredell's formal legal education appears to have commenced in Edenton—a former capital of the province, then of the colony—a locale which at the time remained a focal point of professional, political, social, and cultural life in colonial North Carolina. His legal studies began soon after he arrived there, and he pursued them intensely, berating himself when he strayed from contemplating Sir Thomas Littleton's *Tenures* into losing at billiards.[3]

Iredell's law teacher, Samuel Johnston, was already probably Edenton's leading citizen and was later to be North Carolina's governor, one of its first United States senators, and his pupil's brother-in-law. The student copied his tutor's arguments and pleas; he attended the courts and noted the arguments made there. His texts were Matthew Bacon's *Abridgement*, Sir Edward Coke's *Institutes*, and Sir William Blackstone's *Commentaries*. The latter particularly impressed the young scholar. Having read Johnston's copy, he desired his own and asked his father, and later a friend, to procure a set for him in England. "No one can possibly read [Blackstone]," he wrote, "without infinite pleasure and improvement."[4]

A 1760 North Carolina statute required that superior-court judges examine prospective attorneys on both substantive and procedural law. The judges certified successful applicants to the governor for licensing; a certificate of good character from a justice of the inferior court of the candidate's home county was also necessary. The initial license restricted practice to the inferior courts; a further commendation and licensure was requisite to unrestricted practice in all courts of law and equity.

Iredell apparently passed the oral examination and secured suitable commendations with ease. On December 14, 1770, on the recommendation of Chief Justice Martin Howard, Governor William Tryon issued the nineteen-year-old aspirant a license to practice in the inferior courts. The newly accredited attorney took the prescribed oaths on December 19th before Thomas Jones, the clerk at Edenton. In less than a year, on November 26, 1771, Governor Josiah Martin granted him an unrestricted license. He took the prescribed oath at the 1772 April Term before his preceptor, Samuel Johnston.[5]

Then, as now, the vocation Iredell entered was much maligned. His uncle, Thomas Iredell, wished him success, but termed the legal profession "dangerous to virtue in all countries, but more especially in your colony, where persons can with so much ease qualify themselves for its practice." Many lawyers were properly called pettifoggers, he thought, and were "very pickpockets, [whose] company and example carry contagion along with them."

The craft had internal critics as well. Archibald Maclaine, Iredell's professional contemporary, blamed a perverse public for encouraging the "profligate character[s] at the bar" while "uniformly [opposing] every man of abilities and virtue."[6]

Late-eighteenth-century North Carolina lawyers endured hardships greater than mere adverse public opinion. They traveled widely, and travel conditions were markedly harsh. Streams rose rapidly, often becoming impassable until flooding subsided. Eastern North Carolina roads, those Iredell traveled the most, contained deep ruts, fallen trees, swampy causeways, and barely passable bridges. Many were mere paths, poorly marked; most were lonely and desolate. On his 1791 southern tour, George Washington noted that the road from New Bern to Wilmington, North Carolina, "passes through the most barren country I ever beheld."

Horseback, the common mode of travel, was uncomfortable and fatiguing. Saddlebags provided little room for provisions, and horses' backs afforded no protection from inclement weather. Iredell rode in rain, found road guts passable solely by swimming, and reached creeks traversable only by canoe.

Accommodations, too, were often poor. A coeval traveler in North Carolina reported "bad accommodation, . . . bad company and attendance, and . . . everything disagreeable in the extreme." Washington found eastern North Carolina inns and houses indifferent, providing well for neither man nor horse. Iredell would rest in "a poor miserable hovel" one night and inconveniently share a bed with Samuel Johnston another; he consistently experienced sleep deprivation from execrable lodgment. "We had a most cursed night at Relfe's," he once related, "devoured by insects all night, not a wink of sleep, and scarcely alive in the morning." Finding "an exceeding good house to rest in" was less common.[7]

Occasional desolation was an inevitable byproduct of this always nomadic, often solitary existence. Iredell constantly thought of home and longed to be there, occasionally acknowledging outright homesickness. The sojourner's refrain, "I am heartily tired of this cursed place," characterized his communications.[8]

Extensive overhead was a further byproduct. Though meager, lodging was expensive. "Monstrous" costs for room and board offset even propitious legal fees. Horses had to be maintained or hired; Iredell's own proper grooming and attire were high-priced essentials.[9]

Financial deficiencies in the practice enhanced the distress from high overhead. Iredell at times attended indifferent courts and saw no prospect of money. "Thanks, sir, are but a poor reward to a lawyer," a client once wrote him, "[but] I have nothing else at present to send you." A life so harried should be more profitable, Iredell thought, and he regretted leaving Hannah "in so unprovided a situation."[10]

Competition for business sometimes occasioned the indifferent revenues. Other lawyers "smuggled up" the more lucrative cases, submitting, in Iredell's view, "to methods to obtain such business that those of honor and principle disdain." Even when fees were plenteous, inflation threatened their sufficiency, and the practitioner feared depreciation between receipt and expenditure.

A one-year suspension of suits to aid inflation-ridden debtors was not the befitting solution, however. When the General Assembly adopted this expedient, Iredell joined other lawyers in maintaining that it was denying them a livelihood. He also scribed for Edenton citizens a document instructing their representatives to end the suspension. The law was no longer necessary, as it was a temporary measure bred by the unusual scarcity of money, which the circulation of paper currency had alleviated. Indeed, it was unreasonable from the outset, Iredell argued, causing delay in the ascertainment of debts and loss of proof from such intervening causes as the death of witnesses.[11]

Hazards and privations notwithstanding, Iredell clearly enjoyed his work. Early in his career, he reported an evening consultation that left him "greatly refreshed," as he always was "after doing business." A speech impediment that would have diverted less-intrepid aspirants from the legal profession failed to deter him. Instead, he tended toward flamboyance, causing Samuel Johnston, even well into Iredell's career, to reprimand him for his intemperate manner of speaking. Recollections of his mentor's reproof, Iredell said, "frequently check rising passionate expressions, and if any except me, I instantly reproach myself." Hannah, too, admonished him on professional temperament; and late in his career as a practicing lawyer, he was yet hoping "to mend a little every day."[12]

His economic complaints notwithstanding, Iredell was a successful lawyer, ultimately acquiring more business than he could well handle. "I am like the lawyer described by Horace who is beset with clients almost at each crowing," he bemoaned. The work fatigued him and kept him from home, so much so that he resolved to reject new business. It required his "constant attendance," precluding visits to his native England. Still, he proudly informed kinsmen there that the work suited his inclinations and that few American lawyers were exceeding his success in it.[13]

Such achievement enhanced Iredell's heedfulness of his growing professional reputation. He was "treated with great distinction," he said, and was "satisfied with the general opinion entertained of [his] conduct." He appeared to be "of some consideration," and his name was "a little in vogue." He considered the esteem in which he was held highly flattering.[14]

As he neared the end of his practice in the late 1780s, Iredell had clients at least as distant as Petersburg, Virginia. His spreading reputation appears to have engendered higher fees, for William Hooper, his professional compatriot, informed a prospective Iredell client to expect to pay well to secure his services. In his home county his considerably more-frequent employment by plaintiffs than by defendants indicates that the local populace favored him over other attorneys, since the initial choice belonged to the plaintiffs.[15]

Samuel Johnston, confident that his pupil would attain such success, advised him early in his career not to "give up [his] prospect of making money in the law for any place less than such a one as the Chief Justice's or one of the first offices in the Country." Thus heartened, Iredell developed a general practice characteristic of the period. Among other endeavors he tried admiralty suits, drafted wills, administered estates, resolved land disputes, and sought death-sentence commutations.[16]

Nonlitigation work for lawyers appears to have been sparse in the 1770s and 1780s. Original wills and deeds of the period seldom display the hand-writing of members of the bar, suggesting that most were homedrawn by lay draftsmen. Iredell's surviving account books, which cover 1783–84 partially and 1785–89 in detail, reveal only 212 requests for out-of-court opinions, five wills, thirty-two land-related instruments (deeds, leases, mortgages), and nine miscellaneous services. Litigation and dispute settlement constituted the major part of his practice, which appears illustrative of the profession at the time. Even charges unrelated to pending lawsuits appear litigation oriented, many of his private opinions being directed to whether an actionable wrong had been committed.[17]

Iredell did little criminal work after his brief tenure as state attorney general (*see infra* Chapter 3). Civil actions to recover specific possessions or for personal injury or property damage constituted most of his litigation practice. The significance of such work, at a time when ownership of property largely determined social and political status, can scarcely be overstated. His efforts involved not just the settling of accounts, but also the economic, political, and social standing of his clients.[18]

Both in the colonial period and under the new state government, North Carolina adopted the rigid English system of common-law pleading, in which selection of the proper writ for a cause of action was essential to avoid a dismissal. Throughout Iredell's practice, he relied principally upon "trespass on the case." The greater portion of these actions was in assumpsit, which involved unpaid accounts, oral contracts, or simple notes for debt. A few actions were for slander and interference with relationships, also within this form of action. Most, though, involved unfulfilled commercial transactions or disputes over the ownership or value of property.

"Debt," in which a plaintiff sought recovery of a specified sum a defendant had agreed to pay, was the second most frequent cause of action. While these actions would seem to include many of the trespass-on-the-case suits on notes and contracts, by the late 1760s these representations of debt were largely under seal and actionable in covenant. Many of Iredell's debt actions were to enforce a conditional bond, which usually required payment of a certain sum or product (naval stores, pork, corn, etc.) by a set date, perhaps providing for a penal sum upon the debtor's failure timely to comply.[19]

Professional fees, like commercial debts, were often paid in products. Iredell was compensated in this manner, as well as with coin, paper money, and promissory notes.[20]

During and after the American Revolution, Tory persecution spawned a distinctive kind of legal work for Iredell. A 1777 act of the North Carolina

General Assembly required absentee landowners to return to the state and attain citizenship by October 1, 1778, or lose their property. One 1779 act implemented confiscation, while another named sixty-eight individuals whose estates were expressly expropriated—among them, Iredell's cousin, Henry Eustace McCulloh (49,150 acres), and his friend, Sir Nathaniel Dukinfield (6,842 acres). Iredell vigorously represented McCulloh and others whom he considered real British subjects with no allegiance to North Carolina or who had been unavoidably outside the state. He petitioned the General Assembly for a restoration of McCulloh's property, and he and McCulloh corresponded over a period of years pending the legislature's ultimate rejection of the request. McCulloh considered Iredell's work "masterly," and Iredell regarded the takings as "unjust." "The spirit of the country at present is not a liberal one," he ruefully informed the client, who considered his property "wickedly and cruelly torn from [him]."[21]

Dukinfield fared somewhat better, receiving £3,000 at three and one-half percent interest in semiannual installments over an eight-year period. A petition partly in Iredell's hand appears to have produced no legislative action on behalf of Dukinfield's mother, Margaret Pearson, who was also named in the Confiscation Act.[22]

Iredell appears to have been scrupulously honest and principled in his dealings with clients. Early in his Supreme Court service, a former client accused him of accepting a fee but failing to appear in court for him. Iredell carefully defended himself against the charge, explaining that he had relegated his cases to "the two first [best] lawyers in the state," Alfred Moore and William R. Davie, who had promised to appear for his clients, and to Hannah's recently licensed nephew. While thus acquitting himself, he nevertheless promised to refund the fee because the client had "paid another to Col. Davie." "I would under no circumstances retain a fee from any client," he said, "after his having had to pay again to another lawyer."[23]

He could also be kind and generous, providing *pro bono publico* services to the poor long before bar associations gave awards for such favors. A destitute prospective client sought uncompensated representation from him, hoping he would be motivated by "the principles of natural justice" to "save a worthy woman & two lovely children from inevitable want & destruction." Even after he ceased to practice his profession, a woman "treated barbarously" by her father secured him as an unrecompensed mediator as "another proof of the friendship" he had always shown her.[24]

CHAPTER 2

The Fundamental, Unrepealable Law

T HE CONFISCATION OF TORY PROPERTY IN NORTH CAROLINA SPAWNED THE CASE OF *BAYARD V. SINGLETON*, THE MOST SIGNIF- ICANT CONTROVERSY IN WHICH IREDELL PARTICIPATED AS COUNSEL AND ONE THAT MARKED A CONFLUENCE OF HIS PRIVATE and public personas. The action remains noteworthy as one of the early American skirmishes over the then-nascent concept of judicial review; one scholar considers it "[t]he clearest pre-Constitution case involving review power."[1]

A 1785 North Carolina statute sought to protect purchasers of expropriated estates and their heirs and assigns "from expensive and vexatious lawsuits" brought by "the obnoxious and disqualified persons" specified in the confis- cation acts and those claiming through them. Titleholders under lawfully con- ducted confiscation sales were deemed "not liable to answer" such suits; courts were to dismiss the actions, charging the costs to the plaintiffs, upon the defendants' presentation of motions or affidavits accompanied by deeds from confiscation commissioners showing *prima facie* title in the defendants. Seek- ing unmistakable clarity, the General Assembly provided that the statute ap- plied notwithstanding "any law, usage or custom to the contrary."[2]

The 1776 North Carolina Constitution established the right to a trial by jury in all controversies respecting property. This provision, the Constitution declared, "ought to remain sacred and inviolable [and]...never...be violated on any pretence whatsoever." The palpable contrariety between this directive and the act for quieting confiscated titles virtually assured a clash between the legislative and judicial branches of the fledgling state government.[3]

Samuel Cornell of New Bern was the wealthiest merchant in colonial North Carolina. He had served on the Royal Council, which functioned as the upper house of the colonial assembly, as a higher court (usually chancery), and as a board of advice and consent to the chief executive. Such men, prosperous and politically successful under the old regime, tended to be loyal to it; Cornell was a Loyalist, living and dying a British subject.

When Cornell returned from two years in England in December 1777, he was not allowed to land in New Bern unless he took the legislatively prescribed oath to the new government, which he refused to do. Correctly anticipating confiscation of his property, Cornell deeded it to his wife and daughters before departing North Carolina for exile in New York. The property was later confiscated and sold nevertheless; the proceeds from the sale of Cornell's house paid the expenses of the North Carolina delegates to the Continental Congress.[4]

Spyers Singleton, like Samuel Cornell, was a New Bern merchant. He, too, was politically active, serving under the new government as a justice of the peace, a member of the General Assembly, and a member of the Council of State (after previous unsuccessful bids). At a confiscation sale, Singleton purchased property Cornell had conveyed to his daughter, Elizabeth Cornell Bayard. Her attempts to recover the property in 1786–87 led to Iredell's enshrinement as perhaps the foremost early-American exponent of the concept of judicial review.[5]

Iredell was an avid supporter of the American cause in the Revolution, and as attorney general under the new state government, he vigorously prosecuted treason and disloyalty cases (*see infra* Chapters 3, 4). The excesses of the Revolution's aftermath appalled him, however, particularly the confiscation acts and practices. One suspects his involvement in a protest his friend Archibald Maclaine and others filed against the original Confiscation Act in 1777. The language is thoroughly Iredellian, including the assertion that the Act "is a violation even of the forms of justice, and as an unconstitutional law, is nugatory." In 1783, four years before *Bayard v. Singleton* was decided, Iredell decried "the most wanton injury … done to individuals" by the acts, and he deplored still more the disgrace to the national character from their express violations of provisions of the peace treaty with Britain. If the depredations continued, he said, "this will not be a country to live in, and … they must deeply wound the feelings of every man of sensibility and honor." The laws, he later said, sacrificed "every principle of decency and justice," and "no consideration under heaven" would induce him to participate in their execution.[6]

Iredell accordingly often represented Tory clients who were attempting to retain or regain their property. The physical beating Wilmington lawyer Archibald Maclaine sustained while defending an accused Tory in Bladen County, North Carolina, vividly illustrates the contemporary unpopularity of such representations. Iredell observed that he and Samuel Johnston, too, were "looked upon by the patrons of violence with a hateful eye" for their opposition to anti-Loyalist "outrages."[7]

While Iredell's position on confiscation thus is clear, his actual role in the *Bayard* litigation is not. As attorney general, he had represented the state in contending successfully, contrary to his personal convictions, that the Cornell properties were subject to seizure. Interestingly, Singleton, having leased Cornell property, was the defendant in that action. When Singleton later purchased the property from the confiscation commissioner, his interest and the state's became allied.

When Samuel Johnston subsequently filed ejectment actions for the Cornell family, including Elizabeth Bayard, Singleton employed former governor Abner Nash as lead counsel. He also retained Iredell and other leading attorneys, however — ostensibly to represent him, but in reality apparently to quiet them — leaving the Cornells to choose from less-skilled advocates. Singleton claimed he had nothing to fear because he and his associates had "silenced" Archibald Maclaine, Iredell, and William Hooper. They apparently had also silenced Alfred Moore by retaining him as well.

Maclaine, however, would not be hushed; he returned the retainer and wrote Singleton that although he had deprived him of a fee, he would not seal his lips. Hooper, by contrast, thought he was indeed muffled. Iredell's response, like his part in the case, is unclear. The original court dockets do not reflect him as attorney for the plaintiffs. There is some evidence that he indeed appeared pursuant to his retainer from Singleton; in a memorandum that is undated but clearly postdates the case, Iredell stated: "I was present during the... trial (having received a retaining fee... *on behalf of the purchasers under the act*, though particular circumstances prevented my being fully engaged)." A statement by William R. Davie, who was associated with Samuel Johnston for the Cornell interests, also suggests that Iredell was not with them as lead counsel for the plaintiffs. Davie justified a continuance of the case on the ground that he was engaged in public service and Johnston was unprepared; had Iredell also been lead counsel, a continuance for those reasons would seem unnecessary. Finally, an entry in Iredell's fee book shows him almost simultaneously representing Singleton in at least one other case in the same court.[8]

Only the official report of the case contradicts the foregoing, showing Iredell, with Johnston and Davie, as counsel for the plaintiffs.[9] Speculation that Iredell changed sides without criticism because of his immaculate reputation, or that he avoided ethical reproof by returning any retainer from Singleton and appearing *pro bono* for the plaintiffs,[10] is just that. While equally speculative, the theory that his appearance may have been as a "friend of the court" is more plausible.[11]

If Iredell's was indeed an *amicus* argument, the fact that he was an early and cogent advocate of judicial review of the constitutionality of legislative acts, the formidable issue at stake, was undoubtedly responsible. Samuel Johnston likely influenced the younger lawyer in this regard. Johnston viewed a constitution as a charter that both established and regulated a government. It was to be obeyed, he argued, and laws repugnant to it were void. The Constitution, he urged, defined the powers of the legislature; if one assembly took the first step beyond those designated powers, the next might go further, and another further still, "till at last the barrier will be entirely destroyed." Because the legislature could not be the judge of its own usurpations, the principle of judicial review was logically implicit in his polemic.[12]

Johnston's pupil held similar but more explicit views. Four years before *Bayard*, Iredell had defined a republic as a form of government in which "the law is superior to any or all the individuals, and the constitution superior even to the legislature, *and of which the judges are the guardians and protectors*."[13] While *Bayard* was pending, he forcefully amplified his analysis in a pseudonymous letter addressed "TO THE PUBLIC" from "AN ELECTOR."

The problem, Iredell posited, was how to impose restrictions on the legislature to guard against the abuse of unlimited power. Such power was not to be trusted to any man or body of men. The British Parliament had provided an ominous example of the abuse of omnipotent power. Americans, when free to form their own government, had decisively expressed their sentiments against such.

The power of the legislative Assembly, he continued, was undoubtedly limited and defined by the Constitution. The Assembly itself was a creature of the Constitution. The people had chosen to be governed by constitutional principles only, and the Assembly had no more right to obedience to its pronouncements on other terms than did any other earthly power.

While a law of the state, the Constitution differed from legislative enactments. It was the fundamental law, which the legislature could not repeal and from which it derived all its power. While one legislative act could repeal another, a legislative act could not repeal the Constitution, in whole or in part. Any act inconsistent with the Constitution therefore was void and could not be obeyed without disobeying the superior law.

The judiciary, Iredell concluded, thus had authority to intervene and determine whether a legislative act was warranted by the Constitution. This authority resulted inevitably from the Constitution and the judicial office, the judges being servants of the whole people, not just of the Assembly.[14]

North Carolina had no formal appellate court until the legislature established the Court of Conference, predecessor to the modern Supreme Court, in 1799. The court in *Bayard* consisted of the state's three judges — Samuel Ashe, Samuel Spencer, and John Williams — sitting together as an informal court of conference. There can be little doubt that Iredell's "TO THE PUBLIC," which was published in a New Bern newspaper on August 17, 1786, was intended to influence both this court and public opinion. There can be equally little doubt that it succeeded.

The court was painfully conscious of the delicate nature of the task with which it was confronted by Abner Nash's motion to dismiss. It attempted without success to coax a settlement, expressly noting that it had endeavored in vain to avert "a disagreeable difference" between the state's legislative and judicial powers. Ultimately, however, its reluctance to dispute the legislature had to yield to its duty to the public derived from the oaths of its members. The state Constitution, it said, provided all citizens a right to a trial by jury on decisions affecting their property. If the legislature could excise that right, it was without constraints, and a legislative dictatorship could ensue. It could then take a defendant's life without a jury trial or any trial at all. Its members could grant themselves life tenure or transmit their seats to their male heirs in perpetuity.

No legislative act could alter or repeal the Constitution, however. Such action, the court observed, would destroy the legislature itself, for the Assembly was a creature of the Constitution. Because the Constitution was the fundamental law of the land, and the Confiscation Act was inconsistent with it, the Act had to "stand as abrogated and without any effect." In "TO THE PUBLIC," Iredell had written similarly. Such an act, he had said, is "void, and cannot be obeyed."[15]

These words ultimately rang somewhat hollow to Elizabeth Bayard, who received her jury trial but lost the case because her father had been an alien and thus incapacitated from holding the property.[16] The aftermath of the decision saw the judges, too, less than ecstatic, as the legislature continually postponed their request for a pay increase to offset depreciation in the value of their salaries.[17] It was small consolation that they had made history by sitting on one of the first American cases to declare a legislative act unconstitutional.[18]

Resolution of the question in *Bayard* did not end Iredell's explication of the review doctrine. Richard Dobbs Spaight — earlier, chair of the state House committee before which complaints against the *Bayard* judges were presented; now, a delegate to the Philadelphia Constitutional Convention; and later, governor of North Carolina — articulated to Iredell the concerns of the concept's skeptics. While acknowledging that many legislative enactments had been both unjust and repugnant to the state Constitution, he denied that courts were empowered to declare them void. Nothing in the Constitution granted them that authority, he argued, and it would be absurd and improper to do so. "[N]o judiciary," he said, "ought ever to possess [such powers]." If it did, the judges, rather than the legislature, would govern, combining legislative and judicial functions. Corrupt judges could then set aside every law; personal and property rights would be subject to their whims. Spaight dangled before Iredell the reverberative question: If the judiciary checks and controls the legislature, who performs this function as to the judiciary?[19]

Iredell responded posthaste and at some length. The imperfection of man, he contended, dictates choices between evils. The Constitution, as the fundamental, written law, must be the groundwork of all authority. It must be obeyed by rejecting an act inconsistent with it, or else an act not authorized by the people, to which they thus owe no obedience, must be followed. When an act is brought before the judges, then, "they must, unavoidably, determine one way or the other." If the legislature abolished trial by jury in criminal cases, for example, the court must obey either the Constitution or an act inconsistent with it. The exercise of the power is unavoidable, for "the judges cannot wilfully blind themselves."

While the power is subject to abuse, Iredell continued, this is unlikely, for judges are oblivious neither to public opinion nor to the fact that the legislature sets their salaries. The danger thus, he said, is "chimerical." The judges' reticence in *Bayard* had demonstrated to Iredell the improbability of a court declaring a statute unconstitutional if it could possibly avoid it. "In all doubtful cases," he concluded, "the act ought to be supported: it should be unconstitutional beyond dispute before it is pronounced such."[20]

"Aratus" and "Horatius" continued to trumpet Iredell's defense of judicial review. Whether Iredell was the pseudonymous author of these offerings is uncertain.[21] It is certain, however, that the foregoing essays, clearly attributable to him, predated Alexander Hamilton's more renowned *Federalist Papers* treatises expressing similar views.

Hamilton, also a conspicuous advocate of plenary judicial power, dealt first with the authority of courts to declare void any law at variance with a state constitution. "[E]very act of a delegated authority contrary to the tenor of the commission under which it is exercised," he wrote, "is void"; thus, "[n]o legislative act ... contrary to the constitution can be valid." Were it otherwise, he postulated, the servant would be above the master and the people's representatives superior to the people themselves.

Hamilton then spoke of the proposed federal judicial system and its jurisdiction over state legislation repugnant to the new Constitution. Restrictions on the authority of state legislatures would be of no avail, he asserted, without some constitutional method of enforcing the observance of them. The plan of the Philadelphia Convention placed several prohibitions on the states, but some effectual power in the government to restrain or correct infractions of the prohibitions was essential if they were to be scrupulously regarded. Only two courses were conceivable: a direct negative on the state laws or authority in the federal courts to overrule those in manifest contravention of the articles of union. The Convention preferred the latter, Hamilton said, as would the states.[22]

Scholars have considered Iredell's analysis superior even to Hamilton's, viewing it as the clearest, most straightforward and integral exposition in the literature on judicial review.[23] His explanation of the doctrine, a present-day scholar writes, "accurately foreshadowed virtually all subsequent judicial discussions of the issue in the early Republic." "No Justice of the Supreme Court—including Chief Justice [John] Marshall—has ever written more comprehensive and sophisticated analyses of the issue," he concludes.[24] The Iredell-Spaight correspondence, an earlier writer states, reflected the best arguments of the time for and against the power—Spaight's position according with the prevailing theory of legislative supremacy, and Iredell's setting a standard for the future.[25]

Both Spaight and William R. Davie, who was co-counsel for Elizabeth Bayard, were delegates to the Philadelphia Convention that proposed the federal Constitution. Through them and perhaps through delegates from other states that had faced the question, the convention undoubtedly knew of the new standard and of Iredell's role in raising it.[26]

It is equally almost beyond cavil that when the United States Supreme Court ensconced judicial review as a fundamental principle of American law, its justices were conversant with Iredell's views. The Court decided *Marbury v. Madison* sixteen years after *Bayard v. Singleton*. Alfred Moore, co-counsel for the defendant in *Bayard*, then held the Supreme Court seat that had been Iredell's. While Moore missed portions of the *Marbury* proceedings and sat silently when the decision was announced,[27] it is virtually inconceivable that he would not have referred his colleagues to both the *Bayard* case and his predecessor's essays. He also could have cited Iredell's later statements to the 1788 North Carolina convention that considered ratification of the proposed federal Constitution. In addressing the Supremacy Clause, Iredell there said that Congress was to be obeyed only when it had not exceeded its authority and that a law not warranted by the Constitution "is barefaced usurpation."[28]

Like Alfred Moore, John Marshall was almost surely acquainted with Iredell's thought. He was probably cognizant of *Calder v. Bull*, where Iredell reiterated the premise that a legislative act violative of constitutional provisions is "unquestionably void."[29] A comparison of Marshall's language in *Marbury*[30] with Iredell's earlier discourses enhances the credence of this thesis.

On constitutions as borders of legislative power, Marshall said in *Marbury*: "The powers of the legislature are defined and limited; and that those limits may not be mistaken, or forgotten, the constitution is written."[31] Iredell had written similarly, though more cryptically: "[T]he power of the Assembly is limited and defined by the Constitution."[32]

On constitutions as fundamental law, voiding all repugnant edicts, Marshall declared in *Marbury*: "[W]ritten constitutions . . . [form] the fundamental and paramount law . . . , and, consequently, . . . an act . . . repugnant to the constitution is void."[33] Earlier, Iredell had affirmed: "[T]he Constitution is . . . the *fundamental* law, and unalterable by the legislature. . . . For that reason, an act of Assembly, inconsistent with the constitution, is *void*."[34]

On courts as the final arbiters of constitutionality, Marshall scribed in *Marbury*: "It is emphatically the province and duty of the judicial department to say what the law is. . . . [T]he court must determine which of these conflicting rules [constitution or statute] governs the case. This is of the very essence of judicial duty."[35] Iredell had antedated him, saying: "The judges . . . must take care . . . that every act of Assembly they presume to enforce is warranted by the constitution. . . . This is not a usurped or a discretionary power, but one inevitably resulting from the constitution of their office."[36]

Following *Bayard*, "Horatius" hoped "the virtuous and spirited conduct of the judges will deter [the legislature], *forever*, from attempting to pass any unconstitutional law."[37] History has proven him overly optimistic. It has also, however, confirmed Iredell, who was possibly the penman, as "one of the most cogent advocates" of judicial review[38] and as a superior lawyer — second, if to anyone in his region and time, only to his preceptor, brother-in-law, and close friend, Samuel Johnston.[39]

II

The Statesman

It is our business to bring the dispositions that are lovely in private life into the service and conduct of the commonwealth.

— Edmund Burke

CHAPTER 3

Sufferings in the Public Service

P UBLIC SERVICE WAS MORE THAN A SUBSIDIARY STRING TO IRE-
DELL'S LEGAL BOW. A PARADIGM OF THE LAWYER-PUBLIC SERVANT,
HE CONTINUOUSLY CONTRIBUTED HIS SUPERIOR LEGAL TALENTS
TO THE WELFARE OF HIS COMMUNITY AND STATE.

Following adoption of the North Carolina Constitution of 1776, the Fifth
Provincial Congress appointed a commission, with Iredell as a member, to revise and present to the General Assembly such statutes previously in force in
the state as were consistent with the genius of a free people and the form of
government the free people of North Carolina had now adopted. The General Assembly implemented most of the proposals; continuity was characteristic. The province had first declared the common law in force in its government in 1711. The new state reenacted this provision in 1777, and
subsequent case law defined the applicable common law as that in force in
England when the Declaration of Independence was signed. The extant legal
system was adapted to the new situation, with the former statutory and common law continuing in effect except as otherwise specified.[1]

The eastern North Carolina planter aristocracy and other Whigs strongly
opposed popular election of judges, favoring an independent judiciary with
life tenure. Popular election, Samuel Johnston told Iredell as the Fifth Provincial Congress considered and rejected such a proposal, was absurd and would
produce "numberless inconveniences."[2] The 1776 Constitution ultimately
empowered the legislature to elect judges who would hold office during good
behavior, subject only to impeachment. It implicitly authorized the Assembly
to erect courts and set salaries for their officers.[3]

In 1777 Iredell drafted and presented a bill to establish the state's initial
court system. The measure preserved the old judicial districts; the courts

were to meet twice annually in each of the previously established court towns, with one judge constituting a quorum except in limited situations requiring two or more. The plan deviated little from the pre-Revolution system.[4]

Iredell's bill provided for three superior-court judges. When the first were elected, Iredell was among them. The others were Samuel Ashe of New Hanover County and Samuel Spencer of Anson County. Iredell related reasonably well to Ashe, a man of ardent disposition and deep conviction. He deplored Spencer's lack of both legal knowledge and proper courtroom demeanor, however. Spencer quarreled frequently with his fellow judges, causing John Williams, Iredell's successor, once to swear never to sit with him again.[5]

Unlike Spencer's, Iredell's appointment received the approbation of his colleagues. Though youthful and relatively new at the bar, he had impressed his compeers with his ability, integrity, and knowledge. Archibald Maclaine hoped the promotion would prove as suitable to Iredell as it was to his friends and the public. William Hooper termed the appointment "the first honors the State can bestow"; Iredell in this position, he said, "even for a short period," would reduce his fatigues in the practice and induce him to open his law books anew.[6]

Hooper's parenthetical "even for a short period" proved prophetic. Life as a judge was even more strenuous than that as a practicing attorney. Twice annually the judges rode the full circuit of the state's court towns (Wilmington, New Bern, Edenton, Halifax, Hillsborough, and Salisbury) for four-month periods, sitting ten days in each district. The travel fatigued Iredell. Arrangements were often inconvenient, leaving him to pen his missives home from a crowded courtroom. Loneliness was his constant companion, causing him to long to move homeward "with all imaginable expedition" when a court ended. The legal ignorance and lack of judicial decorum of Iredell's fellow judges enhanced the unpleasantness of his task and prompted a contemporary to write, upon learning of his intent to resign, "I feel much for the honor of the bench."[7]

Iredell tendered his resignation to Governor Richard Caswell on June 13, 1778, after completing only one circuit. With characteristic self-deprecation, he expressed misgivings about his qualifications for the position but attributed his assumption of it to a perceived duty to affirm his allegiance to the new government. The governor accepted the resignation reluctantly, doubting that he could find a replacement of equal ability and commitment. In his one circuit Iredell had largely perused old lawsuits to determine which remained viable, thereby preparing the courts to try cases at the next term.[8]

Shortly, Iredell was prosecuting as the state's attorney for Chowan County and again practicing law at the various county courts in his area. His absence from significant public service was brief, however, for the following year he became North Carolina's second attorney general. Waightstill Avery, the first, had resigned; and Thomas McGuire, a New Hanover County lawyer and holder of numerous lesser offices, had declined the appointment. Governor Caswell had informed Iredell that if McGuire refused, he would recommend Iredell for the interim position and was confident the Council of State would confirm. The Council indeed approved, and both houses of the General Assembly then elected the Edentonian to the permanent position on November 20, 1779. A grateful Iredell thanked Abner Nash, speaker of the Senate, for this "mark of distinction" and pledged to devote himself zealously to promoting the welfare and prosperity of a people to whom he was greatly attached.[9]

Iredell's appointment to another position of public trust again met with general approbation. Nash conveyed to him the Senate's confidence in his ability and dedication. William Hooper wrote that the leading citizens of his area viewed Iredell as "a capital acquisition to our courts" and thought criminal offenders would now receive due but dispassionate and unbiased punishment. Iredell perceived himself the recipient of extreme civility and attention and general satisfaction with his initial conduct in the office.[10]

As attorney general, Iredell traveled twice annually the same circuit he had as a jurist. The office functioned as a single, statewide district attorney now would, prosecuting criminal offenders in the superior courts. Avery, Iredell's predecessor, had been remiss in performing these duties. He attended few sessions of court and, according to Iredell, failed to heed his business. Perhaps as a consequence, he suffered a high acquittal rate, especially in treason cases.

Iredell attained a higher conviction rate. Still, he both succeeded and failed in prosecuting criminal defendants charged with such common crimes as horse theft, robbery, burglary, grand larceny, murder, and passing counterfeit money. In November 1779, he secured judgments of death in five capital cases, three for horse theft and two for robbery; he acknowledged, however, that the governor probably would commute two of the sentences.[11]

Like Avery, Iredell suffered a high acquittal rate in treason and disloyalty cases. Postindependence legislative assemblies deemed the punishment of significant political dissent important to the internal security of the new state. They accordingly required proof of allegiance from persons of dubious loyalty. Those refusing so to pledge could be ordered to leave the state, and their property not sold within three months of deportation was forfeited to the state. These assemblies also enacted the crimes of high treason (aiding or con-

spiring to aid enemies at war with the state or the United States) and misprision of treason (supporting an enemy in various ways). Conviction for treason
invoked a mandatory death penalty and confiscation of the offender's estate;
for misprision of treason, a sentence of imprisonment for the duration of the
war and confiscation of one-half of the offender's estate.[12]

In historical context, such measures were not altogether irrational. Large
numbers of North Carolinians were Tories during the Revolution, while others were neutral or equivocal. Still others objected to the new state's wartime
measures such as conscripted military service and constraints on political expression. This state of public opinion enhanced the difficulty of Iredell's
prosecutorial task. While the requisite two-thirds majority of a grand jury
might grant his requests for true bills of indictment, securing petit juries that
would unanimously convict was difficult.[13]

Iredell's disinclination to reduce offenses to lesser crimes contributed to
his losses in these political prosecutions. His successor, Alfred Moore, was
more successful, probably at least in part because he often pursued lesser
charges initially. Jury nullification was reasonably foreseeable from the divergence in public opinion, and this made Moore's the more realistic prosecutorial perspective.[14]

A perceived need to prove his own loyalty to the Revolution and the new
state government may explain Iredell's zeal in prosecuting political dissidents.
Shortly before independence, and for reasons admittedly pecuniary, Iredell
seriously contemplated returning to England. Patriotic considerations ultimately impelled his decision to stay, and he cast his lot with the American
cause quite thoroughly. He nevertheless continued to fret over a concern that
others questioned his allegiance. Years later he avowed that he would have declined the superior-court judgeship, because of his inadequate knowledge of
the law, but for the considerations that until then he had not "had a fair opportunity to avow my principles" and that his declination might have been attributed to "unworthy motives." Whatever the reason for his vigorous prosecution of these treason and disloyalty cases, the high acquittal rate no doubt
disappointed Iredell.[15]

Sensitivity to perceptions of his patriotism also affected the timing of
Iredell's resignations from public office. He resigned his judgeship, he said,
only after the French alliance in 1778 enabled him to do so "with decency";
and he took umbrage with Governor Caswell for the governor's failure to inform the General Assembly as to his proclaimed motives. He likewise resigned as attorney general, he professed, only when Cornwallis' capture left
him free to do so without censure, in order to "repair the sufferings my poor
circumstances had received in the public service." "I have lately suffered so

much, both in pocket and health by my office," he declared, "that I have [ten-dered my] resignation. . . . I have yet reaped little of the fruit of [the office], and the fatigue and incessant application it requires is too much for me."[16]

Distress of pocket likewise prompted Iredell repeatedly to decline impor-tunings toward legislative service, pleading irreconcilable conflicts with his law practice. An attempt to accommodate his situation by altering the time the Assembly convened was unavailing, merely moving the inconvenience, Iredell explained, to a different season. He actively followed events in the state As-sembly, however, and counselled legislators who shared his governmental goals, especially for the judicial system. He was directly involved in many leg-islative matters in the 1780s, and legislative enactments of the period reflect his covert activities.[17]

Court reform was a matter of particular interest. Iredell joined most state leaders of the time in advocating a court of equity, and the 1782 General As-sembly responded by giving the superior-court judges equity jurisdiction. He also championed independent appellate courts with no original jurisdiction. "Men are commonly careful enough to correct the errors of others," he said, "though seldom sufficiently watchful of their own, especially if they have no check upon them." North Carolina did not establish independent appellate courts until long after Iredell's death, however.[18]

In 1787 the North Carolina General Assembly appointed Iredell the sole commissioner to revise and compile the legislative acts of the late province and the state. Iredell persuaded the printers of the revisal to move from New Bern to Edenton so that he could direct their work at every stage. The com-pilation, still known as "Iredell's Revisal," was completed in 1791, after Iredell had assumed his Supreme Court duties. He transmitted it to Gover-nor Alexander Martin with typical modesty, noting his concern that "the dis-advantages under which [it] was compiled have occasioned it to be too liable to censure."[19]

The Assembly also elected Iredell to the Council of State, an advisory body to the governor, in 1788 and 1789. He was its president in 1788.[20]

While Iredell was interested and enmeshed in public affairs generally, ed-ucation was a particular concern for him. He served as an original trustee of the University of North Carolina, the nation's first operative public institution of higher education. The University's charter provided that a trustee's re-moval from the state created a vacancy; Iredell thus resigned when he moved to New York upon his appointment to the United States Supreme Court. He maintained an interest in the institution, however, and continued to promote it outside the state. His pedagogic commitment was not restricted to higher education; he served as a trustee of lower-school academies in the North Car-

olina towns of Edenton and Hillsborough as well, actively recruiting faculty
for the Hillsborough facility. These early experiences prompted him to mar-
vel at the benefits of universal education when he ventured northward as a
Supreme Court justice and to approve heartily when "gentlemen" combined
their resources to sponsor a Harvard education for a "poor man's son... [of]
uncommon genius and propensity to learning."[21]

The foregoing inventory would fully satisfy the average yen for public
achievement. It represents the less-significant aspects of Iredell's pre-Court
public career, however. He is remembered primarily, not for these contributions, but for his efforts on behalf of the American cause in the Revolution and
the adoption of the federal Constitution.

CHAPTER 4

An Open and Eager Part in Rebellion

ARLY IN IREDELL'S AMERICAN EXPERIENCE, HIS WEALTHY BACHE-LOR UNCLE, THOMAS IREDELL, COUNSELLED HIM: "[T]HE LESS YOU MEDDLE WITH POLITICS THE BETTER. AS YOU ARE A KING'S OFFICER, STAND NEUTER AT LEAST." HAD IREDELL HEEDED THIS advice, he likely would have been lost to history. As expressed by North Carolina's last royal governor, Josiah Martin, he instead took "an open and eager part in rebellion." In the process he made significant contributions to the political debate of the period, earning the appellation "one of the ablest of the Founders."[1]

Anglo-American tensions predated Iredell's assumption of the customs post at Edenton in 1768. The customs service itself was unpopular throughout America because of its enforcement of the taxes the 1767 Townshend Act had levied. In Boston, where Iredell landed upon his arrival in America, friction between merchants and customs commissioners had already required royal authorities to send troops.[2]

Still earlier, North Carolinians had protested both taxes perceived as unjust and the customs service's enforcement of them. In 1764 their Assembly denounced the Sugar Act as contrary to the people's inherent right and exclusive privilege to levy their own taxes. In 1765 Judge Maurice Moore, one of the colony's leading young political figures, condemned the Stamp Act for its taxation without representation; he also debunked the concept of "virtual representation" of the colonies by the whole House of Commons. That year, too, some five hundred citizens assembled at the Wilmington courthouse to burn in effigy a fellow townsman who supported the stamp tax. A somewhat smaller crowd later burned the colony's stamp officer in effigy and forced his resignation.[3]

25

In 1766, upon the seizure of two merchant sloops for violation of the Stamp Act, men of the Cape Fear area organized the Sons of Liberty and swore to prevent the operation of the Stamp Act entirely. They broke into the home of customs collector William Dry, forcibly removed the sloops' papers, and ultimately coerced release of the vessels. They then forced customs comptroller William Pennington from Governor William Tryon's home, but only after the governor accepted Pennington's resignation in order to avoid an indignity to a Crown officer. Still not satisfied, they required Pennington to swear never again to issue stamped paper in North Carolina unless the people willed it.[4]

Iredell thus did not assume an easy task when he became the King's customs officer at Edenton. His personal qualities facilitated his acceptance and integration into his new community, however. He was in no danger, his wife assured his brother Arthur in England as independence approached, because he was "too much respected and loved"; everyone, she said, highly esteemed him because of his "good sense and goodness of heart."

Influential connections eased the transition as well, foremost among them Samuel Johnston and Joseph Hewes. As noted, Johnston was Iredell's law teacher and brother-in-law. Hewes, an Edenton merchant and political figure, had been engaged to another Johnston sister, Isabella; her death shortly before their wedding date left Hewes so bereft that he never married, but he remained close to the Johnston family, including Iredell. These men, together with William Hooper (lawyer, provincial legislator, and representative in three continental congresses), had an impact in moving the youthful customs officer toward support for the cause of American independence.[5]

Probably in deference to Iredell's official position, his immediate family appears to have exercised some constraint in embracing the rebel cause. In 1774, when Edenton women signed resolutions supporting the First North Carolina Provincial Congress, which resolved to boycott certain British products, Hannah Iredell's name was not on the list. Names of her Johnston sisters and sisters-in-law were. The resolution drew considerable attention in the British press. In an oft-quoted letter to James, his brother Arthur wrote from England:

> Pray are you become patriotic? I see by the newspapers the Edenton ladies have signalized themselves by their protest against tea drinking. The name of Johnston I see among others; are any of my sister's relations patriotic heroines?... The Edenton ladies, conscious... of... superiority on their side,... are willing, I imagine, to crush us into atoms by their omnipotency; the only security on our side to

prevent the impending ruin...is the probability that there [are] but few places in America [that] possess so much female artillery as Edenton.[6]

Iredell's uncle Thomas continued to admonish him regarding the hypersensitive nature of his official post. "I am concerned to find you so full of politics," he wrote in 1775: "[T]hey can be of no use to you as a King's officer at the head of the customs in the province you live in. The people of America are certainly mad."

In retrospect Iredell convinced himself that, like his wife, he had done nothing to betray his official position. Following the peace, he defended his conduct, averring to his uncle: "In regard to my official character, I was scrupulously careful, so long as the least vestige of a British government remained, to do nothing inconsistent with it. But afterwards, I thought myself as much at liberty to choose my side as any man."[7]

While Iredell's retrospective defense of his comportment was dubious and self-interested, he indeed came reluctantly to the ironic stance of a King's servant promoting rebellion against the Crown. As late as June 1776, the month before America declared independence, he stated that an honorable reconciliation with Great Britain remained "the first and most earnest object of every man's wish and attention." A continuing connection with the mother country, he said, "in spite of every provocation, would be happier for America for a considerable time to come than *absolute independence.*"

Iredell's correspondence in the months immediately preceding these declarations conveys the profound disinclination of partisans on both sides to see the British-American rupture come to finality. Archibald Neilson, secretary to North Carolina's royal governor and a regular Iredell correspondent, viewed the impending dissolution with horror. Iredell's British cousin, Henry Eustace McCulloh, joined him in wishing and praying for a speedy reconciliation and remained confident that "America in general" abhorred the idea of independence. William Hooper prayed that heaven would yet "check [Britain's] approaching ruin, restore her to reason [and] to the affection of her American subjects." Iredell himself believed a large majority of Americans would oppose independence "till every shadow of a hope of reconciliation is vanished," and he wished the British could know how devoutly the most zealous American patriots wished and prayed "for this most happy event." Still, he was prepared for independence if it became necessary to America's safety.[8]

A dispute with the Crown over colonial court laws produced what was probably Iredell's first political article and marked him as the literary leader of the North Carolina Whigs. Under the last royal governor, Josiah Martin, North Carolina political leaders attempted to secure the right to attach property of debtors who had never been in the province. British merchants did business in the colony through agents without appearing personally, and British citizens owned land there but never visited it. This produced hardship for North Carolina creditors, thus forced to pursue debt collection in British courts.

In 1768, the year Iredell emigrated to North Carolina, the provincial legislature established a system of courts and provided that creditors could proceed against debtors who had never been to the colony. In 1773 the Assembly renewed the provision despite written disapproval from the Crown. The governor rejected it, however, and the Assembly reenacted it but suspended its effectiveness while awaiting the Crown's pleasure. As expected, royal disapproval was forthcoming.

Thus, the province was essentially lacking in civil courts (inferior courts were open, but the superior courts were closed), lawyers were without business, and creditors were without collections. The King instructed the governor that he must create courts himself, and the governor issued commissions for special terms of oyer and terminer. The Assembly refused to fund them, however, and passed a court bill containing the royally loathed attachment provision. The governor again rejected the provision and prorogued the legislature. Fortunately, the governor and the legislature had agreed on an inferior-court bill, but North Carolina continued with only a partial judicial system until it became a sovereign state. Controversy over the court system agitated North Carolinians and thereby promoted the colony's revolutionary fervor more than any dispute except parliamentary taxation.[9]

In response to a defense of the governor's new courts by an anonymous correspondent in the New Bern *North-Carolina Gazette*, Iredell, writing pseudonymously as "A Planter," began to etch his political essays across the pages of history. He disputed the notion that the governor's commission and instructions were "the foundation of our political constitution." To bind the people with rules and instructions locked in the governor's strongbox, he wrote, was inconsistent with the very idea of liberty. The constitution of the country, he attested, was founded on the provincial charter, which could be viewed as the original contract between the Crown and the colony's inhabitants. The repeal of the immediate court laws, he argued, simply revived former ones; and the commissions for courts of oyer and terminer, if legal on any basis, must be so on principles other than royal prerogative. "The law of discretion," his polemic concluded, "is the law of tyrants, and can never be admitted in any free state."[10]

William Hooper correctly perceived Iredell as the pseudonymous "Planter" and acknowledged that "[e]very man who thinks with candor" was indebted to him. Hooper and Samuel Johnston led the next two assemblies in supporting attachments and resisting appropriations for the governor's courts of oyer and terminer.

By the spring of 1774, Johnston and House Speaker John Harvey were threatening to call a provincial congress to sit independently of the governor and the Royal Council. The Congress met in New Bern on August 25, 1774. A meeting of freeholders from Edenton and Chowan County preceded it by three days. The Congress passed resolutions, which Iredell probably drafted, claiming entitlement to all liberties and privileges of British subjects; resolving that British revenue acts were arbitrary, unjust, and destructive of natural rights and privileges; and vowing to wear goods manufactured in America and avoid purchase of British wares or manufactures to the extent possible. The First Provincial Congress then also claimed the rights of Englishmen "without diminution or abridgement"; resolved that no subject should be taxed without his consent, personally or through representatives; and determined not to trade with Great Britain or with any colony that, or individual who, refused to execute this plan.[11]

While this First Provincial Congress disaffirmed the powers of Parliament over the colonies in circumscribed respects, it failed to define the constitutional relationship between the colonies and the mother country. As the delegates appointed to the First Continental Congress grappled with this problem in Philadelphia, Iredell issued his next major political tract, "To The Inhabitants of Great Britain," addressing the "attempt in your Parliament to exercise a supreme authority over us." Parliament was not entitled to any such authority, he asserted; and the colonists preferred freedom to any benefits offered "by a humiliating tenure." If Parliament had sovereign dominion, the colonists were bereft of liberty and property; if it had absolute authority, that was the very definition of slavery.

Notwithstanding his admiration for Blackstone, Iredell considered the principle of parliamentary sovereignty enunciated in the *Commentaries* erroneous in representing the American legal condition as that of conquered subjects. Liberty, Iredell avouched, was everyone's right, and happiness of the governed, the object of all government. A policy that provided for the happiness of one part of the empire while neglecting that of others was wrong, and the British would be fatally deceived if they thought the Americans would patiently bear any hardships imposed upon them.[12]

Whether Iredell's participation in the revolutionary movement remained furtive at this point is unclear. By the spring of 1775, however, Josiah Martin,

North Carolina's royal governor, clearly knew of his ties with the Whigs. The governor's secretary, Archibald Neilson, with whom Iredell corresponded regularly on the mounting crisis, also knew. As early as February 1775, Neilson told Iredell, "People here [New Bern, the capital,] talk of your being very warm." By this time, Iredell's brother Arthur in England must have suspected his complicity with the rebel patriots as well, for in April 1775 he wrote: "What are you Americans about? For God's sake if you are determined to destroy your own peace, don't break in upon ours too."[13]

Though the governor knew of Iredell's involvement, he did not retaliate against him as he did against other Whigs. Iredell retained his port position and appears not to have been intimidated by the governor's actions against others and knowledge of his activities. Albeit quietly, Iredell worked with the Chowan County Committee of Safety, which implemented a policy of nonimportation with Britain and stimulation of local manufactures. He supported the Committee's dispatch of a sloop with provisions to Boston. He attended the Second Provincial Congress in New Bern as an unofficial correspondent for his Edenton political associates, who would not, he said, "go uninformed of anything... material." He joined twenty-six other Edentonians in employing a rider to bring news and intelligence regarding "the present critical times" from Suffolk, Virginia; while most subscribers pledged five shillings, Iredell pledged ten.[14]

Although Iredell maintained a preference for compromise of the imperial discord, he did not preclude independence if all hope of reconciliation vanished. On the contrary, his next literary offering, "The Principles of An American Whig," apparently written in late 1775 or early 1776, bears unmistakable traces of consanguinity with the then-imminently forthcoming American Declaration of Independence. The following select language from the two discourses is illustrative.

Familiar words of the Declaration affirm a divinely granted human right to the pursuit of happiness. "Principles" correspondingly declaims "[t]hat mankind were intended to be happy, at least that God Almighty gave them the power of being so, if they would properly exert the means he has bestowed upon them."

The Declaration avers that governments are instituted to secure the rights to life, liberty, and the pursuit of happiness, and that when government becomes destructive of these ends, the people may alter or abolish it. "Principles" proclaims, similarly,

that government being only the *means* of securing freedom and happiness to the people, whenever it deviates from this end, and their freedom and happiness are in great danger of being irrevocably lost, the government is no longer entitled to their allegiance, the only consideration for which it could be justly claimed or honorably pledged being basely and tyrannically withheld.

Prudence dictates that long-established governments should not be changed "for light and transient causes," the Declaration attests, but when "a long train of abuses and usurpations" evinces a design for absolute despotism, a duty arises to establish a new government. With considerable affinity, "Principles" maintains that

> many dutiful applications and much forbearance...ought to be shown before [subjects of government] arrive at the last stage of opposition, because it being an evil incident to the form of government they have acknowledged, they ought patiently to bear it until it proceeds so far as to interfere with the great law of common happiness nature has ordained for all mankind, and to which all men have a right ultimately to refer their political situation.

Finally, like the Declaration, though in less detail, "Principles" recites perceived British abuses against the colonies, including the Stamp Act, other duties and taxation, and the dispatch of troops to Massachusetts.[15]

Though apparently a precursor of Jefferson's more-illustrious Declaration, and equally fervid, "Principles" did not decree Iredell's irrevocable commitment to the American cause. More or less contemporaneously with its composition, he seriously contemplated a return to England for financial reasons. Joseph Hewes forwarded Iredell's letter in this regard to General George Washington, but the letter went unanswered. This did not disappoint Iredell, he subsequently informed Hewes, for he had abandoned thoughts of going home. Patriotic considerations clearly impelled his decision to stay. He was, he said, "impatient to be attached to my friends in the noblest of all causes, a struggle for freedom." While maintaining hope for reconciliation, his primary attachment was to America, and he would so opt if forced to choose.[16]

Coeval sectional events savoring of independence perhaps influenced Iredell's decision. Shortly before, the Chowan County Committee of Safety had encouraged home manufacture of articles formerly imported from England by offering incentives to make wool and cotton cards, linen and woolen cloth, and steel "fit for edged tools." The Mecklenburg County Committee of Safety had passed resolves favoring independence. North Carolina's Third Provincial Congress had begun a military organization, issued currency, and elected and instructed delegates to the Continental Congress. The success of a small band of patriots in the Battle of Moore's Creek Bridge had given hope and confidence to North Carolina Whigs and enhanced the desire of many for independence.

Still, to suggest that Iredell opted for the expected victor would be inaccurate and unfair, for at this juncture the success of the American cause remained dubious. Samuel Johnston, who considered the prospects for independence dim unless France and Spain joined the colonies' struggle, praised Iredell's decision but questioned his judgment. He would never have recommended the choice, he told Iredell, because of the uncertainty of America's fate. "[O]ur prospects are at this time very gloomy," he opined.[17]

In this admixture of hope and gloom, of nostalgia for ancient ties mingled with visions of a new world, Iredell cleared his last ship and closed his books as port collector in April 1776. When he later made his final entry, "No Duties in July 1776--accounts then to close," his hope for a reconciliation with England was, if not dead, at least comatose.

Yet when Iredell inscribed his next political essay in June 1776, he still did not foreclose some form of mutual accommodation with Britain. While conceding that the prospects were poor, he prayed unsuccessfully that his analysis of the origins of the controversy and his recommendations for restoring harmony would assist in persuading England to alter its recent colonial policies. While it is not known which of Iredell's essays in this period were published, and their impact is thus largely inscrutable, this one is believed to have been widely circulated in manuscript form.[18]

Though apologetic for the length of his treatise, Iredell reviewed the events since the Stamp Act that had brought the empire to a state of impending dissolution. He was simply defending the rights of human nature against the attacks of tyrants, he asserted; and he did so for a people guilty only of an ardent love of liberty. Americans, he stated, would have been slaves, ruined in fortune as well as liberty, had they not resisted the act. The Crown's "hankering" for revenue propelled the colonists to critical self-examination of their freedom, he said; for if a penny could be raised in this manner, a million could, and liberty would thereby be destroyed. Duty demanded that a free country resist both "the palpable abuse of an acknowledged power" and "the arrogant usurpation of a new one."

Destruction of British tea thus was an act of patriotism, he continued, albeit perhaps carried to excess. English outrage led to punitive responses designed to deter other colonies, but the colonists rejected the notion that liberty was more necessary or important in Europe than in America. They thus refused to acknowledge in Parliament "an indiscriminate power of legislation," he maintained, and resisted rules that threatened their liberty.

Drawing upon his juridical expertise, Iredell then selected from the coercive acts for special criticism the bill for the Impartial Administration of Justice. The provisions for trials of soldiers and royal civil officials in colonies other than their own, as well as in England, drew his ire as exceptionally inimical to liberty. Liberty, he believed, had no stronger guardian than trial by jury; and the locale of such a trial was critical to its efficacy, for only a person's neighbors were equipped to assess both his character and that of the witnesses.

Liberty, indeed, was the only goal of the American exertions, he claimed; once freedom was attained, a return to "the most entire and cordial connection" with the mother country was desired, notwithstanding despair over her conduct and disproportionate punishments. Independence, Iredell said, was mentioned only "with horror and indignation." A "just and constitutional connection" remained the preferred alternative for America despite Britain's provocations, but if such could occur only upon terms of dishonor, and independence became necessary to America's safety, it would have his ready assent.[19]

When Iredell finished this essay, the American colonies were moving swiftly toward independence. Shortly before, Samuel Johnston, then presiding over North Carolina's Fourth Provincial Congress in Halifax, had written the young essayist that the House had adopted the Halifax Resolves (April 12, 1776), the first colony authorization for independence. The Resolves empowered North Carolina's delegates to the Continental Congress in Philadelphia to vote for independence and the formation of foreign alliances, reserving to the colony the right to enact its own constitution and laws. In June 1776, the month in which Iredell penned this essay, the vestry of his church, St. Paul's in Edenton, formally denied any right in Parliament to regulate the internal policies of the colonies. Its declaration recited, creed-like: "We ... do solemnly profess, testify and declare that we do absolutely believe that neither the Parliament of Great Britain, nor any member or constituent branch thereof, have a right to impose taxes upon these colonies, to regulate the internal policy thereof." Nine days later Joseph Hewes, who had presented the Halifax Resolves to the Continental Congress, informed Iredell that he expected independence to pass by a large margin. "I suppose we shall take upon us a new name," Hewes concluded.

Following adoption of the Declaration of Independence, Iredell continued to excoriate the government of his native land for "mismanagement, villa[i]ny, and perfidious ambition." Britain's was "the most tyrannical and bloody" of governments, a correspondent rejoined.[20]

As the new nation focused on the war to secure its freedom from this perceived tyranny, Iredell was not among the men-at-arms. While subjecting all persons ages sixteen to fifty to the military draft, North Carolina law permitted the hiring of substitutes. Iredell so opted, engaging Levi Horton to serve in his stead.[21] He promoted the effort by other means, however, becoming a clearinghouse for correspondents on the progress of the hostilities and continuing to discourse for the cause of independence.

On the date America declared autonomy from Britain, John Johnston, Iredell's brother-in-law, wrote Iredell of the repulsion by only one hundred Americans of three British ships that were trying to land troops at Charleston. Soon afterward, Iredell reported the expeditious forwarding of powder and alluded to various wartime skirmishes. The response to his letter mentioned the Indian uprising in Western North Carolina, and the recipient subsequently depicted for Iredell the state of British and American manpower, noting that the British had dispatched their entire artillery to America. Another correspondent wanted Iredell to share any important news with him. He viewed his request as superfluous, however. "You will be led to it by every consideration involving charity and a disposition to please," he concluded confidently.[22]

Internal politics intruded briefly on the war effort in the fall of 1776, causing Iredell to revert to his status as an essayist. Samuel Johnston was hardly a British sympathizer. The last royal governor, who denounced Johnston's "bent to democracy...manifested upon all occasions," had removed him from the post of deputy naval officer for North Carolina for using the position "to embarrass instead of aiding [the royal] government." Yet in the election for delegates to a fifth provincial congress, Johnston, who had served ably in four such congresses, was defeated. William Hooper lamented the vanquishment as depriving the Congress of "the most able head in North Carolina and as good a heart as God ever made"; it was, he said, the greatest example of ingratitude that ever marked a people.

Strangely, the more-radical Whigs were simultaneously labeling Johnston a Tory and burning him in effigy. This combustion spawned probably the most-caustic script ever to flow from Iredell's quill. Again writing pseudonymously, now as "A Rioter," Iredell flayed Johnston's extremist detractors even more harshly than he had the British government: They were sworn enemies to all gentlemen, possessing neither honor nor virtue. Neglect of mental prowess, in their view, was the surest route to understanding; and the most ignorant in appearance were in fact the most knowledgeable. These fanatics imputed all difficulties to gentlemen, found the public interest too troublesome to attend to, considered the property of others theirs if at all useful to them, and confidently viewed their own opinions as beyond reproach. The thought that a person might function from virtue alone was so foreign to them, Iredell alleged, that they would consider one so acting a madman. Figuratively donning the garb of such a "rioter," Iredell concluded:

I think that man alone a Whig, who has sagacity enough to mind his own interest, resolution enough to plunder his neighbors, who views the storm coolly at a distance, and discovers his principles by getting honestly drunk and abusing gentlemen.

... [O]ur affairs would prosper much better if gentlemen who read and consider too deeply for us were totally banished from all public business, and if those who neither read nor think at all (and consequently cannot injure us by the excess of those practices) were intrusted with the management of our present arduous concerns.

All the above I verily and truly believe, and G—d A—y D—n all those who differ from me.[23]

Iredell soon refocused externally, penning his essay "To his Majesty George the Third, King of Great Britain, & c." in February 1777. This text contains copious facts and arguments vindicating the Revolution. "Severe and painful" was the task of the rebel apologist who felt compelled to renounce his allegiance to the Crown and to disown his native country. Independence, he reprised, had been a subject broached with abhorrence and indignation. But the allegiance of Americans to the King was that of a free people, not that of "despicable slaves" to a tyrant. They required only liberties previously enjoyed, but they found altogether astounding the "stupendous claim" of a right to bind them "in all cases whatsoever." Such encroachments on privilege, Iredell averred, violated both the Constitution and the very concept of justice.

The Crown's provocations could be catalogued simply: rejection of petitions, refusal to discuss claims, hiring of foreign troops, and excitation of Indians and slaves to violence. The royal concept of freedom was equally evident: the "liberty" to be governed by distant tyrants who were ignorant of the locals' situation, unconnected with their interests, uninfluenced by their opinions, and had multiple ignoble motives to oppress and injure them. These, at least, the apologist concluded, were the "fervent sentiments" of a subject turned enemy, but one who wished "to be as little so as the indispensable safety of America (which it is his duty to support) will suffer him to be."[24]

When the General Assembly required an oath of allegiance to the state, with expulsion as the penalty for noncompliance, Iredell and Samuel Johnston were among the first to subscribe. Six months later Iredell assumed his superior-court judgeship. Following English legal tradition, he charged grand juries with assertions of patriotism containing strong expressions of devotion to America. A specimen of his rhetoric in this context survives, thanks to a resolution of the Edenton grand jury requesting its publication. The charge, the resolution vouches, vindicates independence by arguments from "un-alienable rights" and "incontestable facts."

Resuming in this charge his form as an essayist, Iredell again registered various British misprisions: foreign troops hired to slaughter an unoffending people, Indian scalping knives employed, and domestics armed for indiscriminate massacre. Independence came reluctantly but inevitably, he reprised, as Britain went from extreme to extreme pending a fatal and final severance prompted solely by a passion for liberty. Again exhibiting consanguinity with the Declaration of Independence, he asserted that ever since the Glorious Revolution in England, it had been "almost a settled axiom...*that all government was instituted for the good of the people, and that when it no longer answers this end, and they are in danger of slavery, or great oppression, they have a right to change it.*" Struggle had always preceded liberty, he concluded ardently, and this obliged liberty's beneficiaries to maintain and support it.[25]

When Britain extended an olive branch in mid-1778, sending commissioners to America bearing conciliatory offers, Iredell was not mollified. The Americans' only sin, he now asserted, was to resist serfdom to a power claiming authority bounded only by the moderation it chose. Americans had confined themselves to "respectful petitions and remonstrances" only to be rebuffed with "haughtiness and insult."

Sarcasm poured from his splenetic pen as he noted that "the only remission" was Lord North's scheme to allow Americans to choose the method of raising revenue for England and to retain any surplus. Iredell excoriated Britain's excitation of slave insurrection—an especially deplorable tactic, he flayed, in light of Britain's refusal to allow Virginia to prohibit the slave trade because Britain found it profitable. The mother country's conduct of the war, he further scathed, would make savages blush; and she should not expect that after her long denial of reasonable requests, followed by an unjust war, Americans would repent. "[T]he most brilliant offers," Iredell wrote defiantly, should now be rejected, for "when subjects have once drawn their sword against their sovereign, it ought never to be sheathed." He signed contumaciously, "A Man Who Despises Your Pardons."

This vehemence toward the British found private as well as public expression. While traveling the court circuit, Iredell joined in reproaching a Tory for his "insolent...conversation and sly slanders." He reported the man duly reproved and humbled as a consequence.[26]

The privations of the Revolutionary War did not alter the young essayist's ardor for the patriots' cause. He dutifully informed Hannah of the preliminaries of the late-1780 Battle of King's Mountain, noting that the enemy had been stalled a long time at Charlotte. "There is a spirit rising," he wrote, "not easily to be quelled."

Throughout 1781 Edentonians lived under constant threat of enemy attack. In an attempt to render themselves less vulnerable, they dumped their cannon into the bay; they also fled the town, carrying their property with them, to escape enemy attacks. Jean Blair, Hannah Iredell's sister, recorded damage to Iredell's desk in the process:

> The furniture is very much hurt already and I am afraid will be much more so before it is all safely housed in Windsor. There are two boats full gone and still a great deal left. They could not take in Mr. Iredell's desk nor mine belonging to the bookcase, though they attempted it and have damaged them very much. Mr. Iredell's more than mine, for which I am very sorry, but he made them too heavy with the books in the drawers and did not leave his key to take the drawers out when they were moved.

Soon thereafter, Blair also reported the English within thirty miles and their boats in Edenton Bay. Still, Samuel Johnston questioned the flight, believing defense of the town less risky and less expensive, notwithstanding the dangers. Iredell refused Hannah's entreaty to come to Windsor, her new locale, as he felt honor-bound to attend court as long as the judges did. "In times of tranquility some liberties may be taken," he told her painfully, "but not in these." It was "the next thing to hell to live in a country conquered by force of arms," a correspondent opined to Iredell, but he "hope[d] to live to see the Americans a free and happy people."[27]

Conventional atrocities of warfare prevailed. British troops reportedly abused women and assigned Negroes to plunder for provisions. When Hillsborough was pillaged, William Hooper's household possessions were taken, save a few Mrs. Hooper had secreted. "My library," Hooper told Iredell, "except as to law books, is shamefully injured, and above 100 valuable volumes taken away." "What vexes me most of all," Hooper continued, "is that they have broken several sets..., where the volumes were so necessarily dependent on each other as to make what remains useless lumber."

Traitors to the American cause bore the brunt of vengeance, and some met a violent fate. Several who had planned to join Lord Cornwallis near New Bern reportedly were executed, at least one by hanging. Barter became the means of exchange, as North Carolinians yearned for the return of money as the trade for goods.[28]

Only a fortuitous illness saved Iredell from probable capture and possible assassination by the British. While en route to Hillsborough as state attorney general in September 1781, Iredell was detained in Granville by a severe fever. Had he arrived in Hillsborough on schedule, he probably would have shared the fate of Governor Thomas Burke and others whom David Fanning and a party of Tories captured and made prisoners of war. According to Iredell, the party stayed in town well into the night, "rifling and plundering and doing a good deal of mischief, and then carried off their prisoners and booty, making even the Governor walk on foot."

Capture of the governor apparently was part of a general British plot to take important patriot leaders; two had already been seized and had died from maltreatment. Governor Burke ultimately escaped, attributing his flight to fear of assassination and the apparent futility of his pleas for protection. Iredell, who initially viewed his illness as a "great misfortune," subsequently considered it "far otherwise," and friends who had "trembled for [his] fate" came to rejoice "at [this] very opportune sickness."[29]

As the fortunes of war shifted to favor the colonies, the correspondence of the period assumed a more-positive tone. In September 1781 Samuel Johnston informed Hannah Iredell that the war should soon be so distant that she could return to Edenton from her exile in Windsor. Soon thereafter, Pierce Butler (South Carolina legislator, future United States senator, and longtime Iredell friend) told Iredell he could now occupy his home without British disturbance for the duration of the war; peace, Butler thought, would certainly come by spring. When peace at length arrived a year and a half later, Butler considered it quite necessary because of the exhausted state of the country's finances and the disquietude and "distressed situation" of its army. Away in Hillsborough when the peace came, Iredell speculated that Edentonians were rejoicing about this "most glorious affair." From Wilmington, he later reported its inglorious features:

> [T]he proclamation of the cessation of hostilities was read in form by the sheriff, and the town was finely illuminated in the evening. Unluckily, though, upon the discharge of cannon, a similar accident happened as at Edenton. A man who was drunk and careless was wounded in such a manner that he has ever since been in the most miserable condition, and his life is despaired of.[30]

The cessation of hostilities did not end Iredell's public service related to the effort and its aftermath. On August 1, 1783, Edenton citizens adopted resolutions, which Iredell drafted, calling for fulfillment of the peace terms, support of public credit, and gradual redemption of public debts. They also sought measures to guard against evils they feared from return of those who had joined the British "in the time of our distress."

The following month Edentonians submitted instructions to the Chowan County representatives, again in Iredell's script, seeking a fund for the payment of public debts, promotion of national unity as the foundation of future security, and adequate power in a federal government to procure this objective. The authority of the Congress should be enhanced, they resolved, for the Union could not survive without vesting adequate power in this institution. Finances should be ordered properly, free trade promoted, and foreign trade encouraged. The act suspending suits and executions should be repealed, the judges and the attorney general paid liberal salaries, and an alternate time set for the annual meeting of the General Assembly to accommodate planters and lawyers.

Finally, Edentonians wished that General Washington's letter of June 8, 1783, an appeal to Americans on the eve of victory to avoid losing the peace, be "most zealously attended to." Americans, the general had warned, stood at a crossroads; the eyes of the world were upon them, they were on "political probation," and they could give purposive "tone" to the federal government or idly watch as the Confederation crumbled. It was, said Washington, "yet to be decided whether the Revolution must ultimately be considered as a blessing or a curse...[and] with our fate will the destiny of unborn millions be involved."[31]

Just as public responsibilities endured for Iredell following the war, so, too, did personal consequences from the rebellion and his participation in it. The war years temporarily severed his ties with his family of origin in England. Mail, the only method of communication, became unreliable. Iredell's brother Arthur claimed to have sent him multiple letters during the war but doubted they had reached Carolina; Iredell acknowledged receipt of only one, and that only a year before the peace. Following the war Iredell informed his uncle Thomas that he was again receiving communications from his mother and his brother Arthur, "though...many have miscarried"; he fervently hoped "the same cause" had precluded word from the uncle. Whether Iredell had corresponded regularly with family members overseas is unclear but improbable. He told his brother Tom that "the hazard attending any letters during the war" had discouraged him from writing.

Notwithstanding Iredell's own failure to correspond, his family members' equivalent post-war laxness disappointed him severely, for he had contemplated frequent missives from them "as one of the greatest blessings peace... could bring." Perhaps attributing the scarcity of dispatches to their disdain for his role in the colonial revolt, Iredell commenced a rationalization of his revolutionist conduct. He repeatedly claimed that he had not dishonored his position as a Crown servant in that he had taken no part in the rebel cause until long after the colonies declared independence, "when no vestige of the British

Government was left, and I thought every man had a liberty to choose his side."[32]

Clearly, Iredell either experienced faulty recollection or engaged in rank dissembling. Although he held no elective or appointive office before independence, as an essayist he had supported the rebel cause with unsurpassed zeal. Equally clearly, he missed the principal target of his flings at expiation. He "seemed to be out of his [rich uncle's] books," his brother Arthur, who would inherit the uncle's estate in his stead, informed him; Thomas Iredell had "conceived the most rooted disapprobation" of Iredell's public conduct, and he appeared immovable.

Iredell did not surrender the legacy passively. He plied his uncle with defensive letters, conceding that ardent passion had perhaps led to "an indiscreet attachment to some subjects of public concern" and "some imprudence" but reiterating that his timing was honorable and his conduct principled. Indeed, he asserted, there could be no more-cogent proof of his sincerity than his voluntarily risking life, property, and cherished relationships over "feelings too powerful to be resisted." "My conscience," he concluded, "does not reproach me."[33]

The explication went for naught, as Iredell's uncle disinherited him and devolved the estate upon his brother Arthur. While the estate inventory was substantially diminished at Thomas Iredell's death in 1796, the residue clearly was not inconsequential, for Arthur spent much of the remainder of his life in Jamaica attending his hereditary acquisitions.[34]

The court of history may well judge Iredell's pleas to his obstinate uncle both fawning and mendacious. It was not his finest hour, as avarice spawned a rendition of his fervor for the American cause that was at best incomplete and at worst positively inaccurate. This fervor came naturally, though, to a man taught as a child to revere the principles of the English Revolution of 1688. "I imbibed . . . from my infancy almost a strong attachment to Whig Revolution Principles," he told his uncle; as a consequence, he did not consider an oath of allegiance binding in all circumstances. "I know of no other principles upon which the Revolution in 1688 can be defended," he said.

Iredell held tenaciously to the contract theory of government. The contract at issue in the Revolution was the charter of the colony; the parties were the British Crown and the people of the colony. The Parliament, which was not a party to the contract, was sovereign in England, but this sovereignty did not extend to the American colonies. Government existed to maintain the happiness of the people governed, and when it violated its contract with the people, becoming malevolent rather than beneficent, the people rightfully withdrew their allegiance to it.[35]

Iredell assimilated these convictions both from his youthful tutelage on the English Revolution of 1688 and from the general ambience of the Carolina Colony of his early adulthood. Adherence to them in the cauldron of imperial disintegration cost him a legacy but earned him an enduring place in the history of his adopted country.

CHAPTER 5

Ablest Defender of the Constitution

I N THE AFTERMATH OF THE MILITARY PHASE OF THE REVOLUTION IN NORTH CAROLINA, FORMER GOVERNOR ABNER NASH, THEN A DELEGATE TO THE CONTINENTAL CONGRESS, WROTE IREDELL FROM PHILADELPHIA THAT AMERICA WAS PREPARED FOR PEACE BUT NOTHING ELSE. Time has vindicated Nash's assessment. "The new nation suffered from an understandable insecurity of identity," an eminent twentieth-century historian concludes:

> Older nations were secure on this score in their common ethnic, or religious, or linguistic, or political heritage. Some nations could lay claim to unity in several of these important sources of identity and a few in all of them. The American nation could claim unity in none of them.[1]

Iredell next applied his knowledge and talent to addressing this observed vacuity in the political heritage category. In so doing, he enhanced an already secure place in history, as the former English subjects confronted the necessity of establishing a government for their infant nation. Their initial effort, the Articles of Confederation, proved an inadequate instrument for effective governance, particularly in the areas of commerce and trade regulation. The states retained ultimate sovereignty, including all power not expressly delegated to the Congress; the central government thus was largely impotent when confronted with problems of national dimension.[2]

Iredell was among North Carolina leaders dissatisfied with the Articles' deficiencies and receptive to major reform. Years later, he aptly summarized the problems. The Articles sufficed when war with a common enemy engendered national unity, he asserted, but not when "selfish and contending interests"

imperiled the gains of war. The consequences were ruinous: public debts unpaid and unprovided for, commerce languishing, agriculture discouraged,
disunion and jealousy prevailing, dissolution and anarchy threatening. The
magnitude of the resultant danger, he concluded, "alarmed all considerate
men."[3]

Consequently, "considerate men" convened in Philadelphia in May and
June 1787, ostensibly to revise the Articles but ultimately to form and adopt a
new constitution. Iredell's relative poverty apparently precluded his attendance; North Carolina's delegates communicated with him regularly, however.
William R. Davie soon solicited Iredell's views on national executive and judicial powers as applied to the states and on national regulation of trade. He
would trouble Iredell frequently, he warned, and would expect his opinion
"without reserve"; indeed, until forbidden by Convention rules imposing secrecy, Davie had expected to seek Iredell's perspective on all important questions. Richard Dobbs Spaight, another delegate, exchanged missives with
Iredell on the nascent doctrine of judicial review of the constitutionality of legislative acts. Hugh Williamson also wrote Iredell from Philadelphia, noting the
slow progress of the Convention and encouraging Samuel Johnston's mem-
bership in the next General Assembly to promote the Convention's measures.[4]

These dispatches kept Iredell abreast of the Convention's progress. On
July 8, 1787, Williamson attributed delays to diverse interests yet unreconciled. Two weeks later, he was more sanguine, viewing as within reach both
the outlines of a system of governance and a September adjournment. By early
August, Davie, too, considered the borders in place and foresaw tedium
rather than difficulty ahead. Spaight soon joined the refrain, like Williamson
anticipating a September termination. Every "man of reflection," he said,
craved a strong and efficient national government to surmount the extant federal frailty and the tyranny of the states.[5]

Williamson and Spaight had gauged the timetable accurately. On September 17, 1787, the Convention agreed to the proposed Constitution and transmitted it to the Continental Congress, which ordered the Convention's report
sent to the state legislatures for submission to ratification conventions. George
Washington, as president of the Convention, forwarded copies of the Constitution itself to the state legislatures via the governors.[6]

Even before the Convention completed the plan, it became an issue in
North Carolina politics, embroiling Iredell involuntarily. General Assembly
elections were held in August 1787, while the federal Convention still met.
Because the ensuing session would confront the Convention's measures, the
election aroused considerable interest. Iredell unknowingly became a partici-
pant when two friends nominated him as a candidate from Edenton one day

before the election. He had written earlier that while no one was more conscious of the critical situation or more disposed to assist, he was too unpopular to win; his support for returning refugees who had left the country during the Revolution had, he thought, cost him weight and influence and caused him to be viewed with suspicion. Accordingly, he would not solicit votes or use any "electionary arts" to carry a "bare election" by a people who lacked confidence in him and held views contrary to his.

This assessment proved accurate, for he lost the election to another Federalist candidate, Stephen Cabarrus. Cabarrus had declared that he would offer himself only if Iredell declined to. The manner in which the election was conducted, particularly the opening of a tavern for Iredell voters, satisfied Cabarrus that Iredell himself was not involved. Iredell assured him of that, deploring the "open house . . . kept on my account" and proclaiming confidence that the "accidental conflict" would not alter the positive sentiments each held for the other. The unwilled nature of his candidacy notwithstanding, Iredell, ever polite and thoughtful, thanked his principal promoter and requested that he express the candidate's gratitude to his unidentified supporters. While somewhat feebly rationalizing his uncountenanced actions, the supporter assured Iredell that the request would be honored.[7]

Although neither a delegate to the Convention that proposed the federal Constitution nor to the state Assembly that called the ratification convention, Iredell rendered perhaps the most outstanding of his many patriotic services in the ratification effort. Like an anonymous writer of the period, he harbored no illusions about the difficulty of the task, knowing well that "some of our farmers have not books and will not read or think: yet they will talk and judge and condemn." Still, he thrust himself vigorously into the debate, thereby earning posthumous tribute as "the ablest defender of the Constitution."[8]

Iredell appears to have launched the first public movement in North Carolina in favor of the proposed new charter of government. On November 8, 1787, Chowan County citizens gathered at Edenton to instruct their legislators to convoke a ratification convention forthwith and to convey ardent approval of the proffered Constitution. Iredell drafted the preamble and resolutions.

Iredell also penned an address presented four days later by the foreman of the grand jury for the Edenton District, extolling the Constitution and urging appointment of a convention to consider it. The address acknowledged the necessity of a strong and permanent union of the states to ensure safety and liberty. It reprised the problems of disunion under the Articles and urged maximal respect for a tendered charter devised by so able a collection of statesmen. The unanimity of the states assembled in Philadelphia, it urged, augured well for a surrender of subordinate local interests to the greater general good.

The address relished in the new Constitution a felicitous admixture of authority with liberty. Amendatory provisions would allow alteration without civil war, it naively presupposed, and the general provisions would promote strength in union and render America an asylum for the world's oppressed. An early ratification convention was accordingly exhorted, lest Americans lose both their own happiness and the respect of mankind.[9]

Iredell's pen was seldom idle in these days of birthing the new government. The Antifederalists focused their ire on the lack of a bill of rights in the proposed Constitution. Even Thomas Jefferson, in particularizing to James Madison his complaints about the document, lamented primarily "the omission of a bill of rights providing clearly & without the aid of sophisms" for a lengthy sequence of civil liberties. "[A] bill of rights," Jefferson avouched, "is what the people are entitled to against every government on earth, general or particular, & what no just government should refuse or rest on inference."

It was not Jefferson, however, but his fellow Virginian George Mason who next impelled Iredell to his inkstand. Mason, "[u]sually gruff and given to strong views on most subjects" but also one of the best minds of his generation in Virginia's public life, had issued the battle cry, "There is no Declaration of Rights." According to Madison, Mason feared "the dangerous power and structure of the Government, concluding that it would end either in monarchy, or a tyrannical aristocracy; which, he was in doubt, but one or the other, he was sure." This "alarm bell he barely tinkled at the Philadelphia convention [became] a rallying point for those critics of the constitution who shared Mason's thought that the whole plan had serious flaws." The *New-York Journal* and the *Philadelphia Independent Gazetteer* ran critical essays, and opponents everywhere hoisted Mason's muster call, "There is no Declaration of Rights," as they groused that the Federalists were "hustling the ratification conventions forward at an indecent pace."[10]

At the federal Convention Mason refused to sign the Constitution, and he published eleven objections to it. Writing under the *nom de plume* "Marcus," Iredell assumed the task of answering Mason, stating first the "OBJECTION" and then the "ANSWER."

Mason initially lamented the absence of both a declaration of rights and the secure retention of the common law. Iredell rejoined that declarations of rights had arisen from usurpations by the English Crown. A constitution like the one proposed, clearly delineating the Crown's power to act, would have rendered such declarations superfluous — as unnecessary, Iredell opined, as a judge who orders a man hanged superimposing strong admonitions that he not be decapitated. As to the common law, the proposed Constitution simply retained its benefits, except as expressly altered, until modified legislatively.[11]

Mason next bemoaned the proposed House of Representatives. It provided only the shadow of representation, he argued, and thus would emanate in uninformed lawmakers, constituents lacking confidence, and laws made in ignorance of their consequences. Iredell gave this objection short shrift; the alteration from 40,000 to 30,000 constituents per representative, he believed, largely removed it.

Mason's objections to the powers of the Senate were more substantial. They would destroy balance, he predicted, and permit usurpations of the people's rights and liberties at will. To Iredell, such fears were "chimerical." While senators (then to be elected by state legislatures) would not directly represent the people, they would represent the people's representatives. The "most popular, or confidential" persons thus were the likely appointees, and there were checks upon their abuse of power: staggered elections; the requirement of House concurrence; and particularly six-year terms, since members could fulfill their ambition for continued service only "by acting agreeably to the opinion of their constituents." Further, some of the powers, such as that of confirming ambassadors, were a check upon the president. The power to try impeachments must lie somewhere, and the Senate was as secure a repository as any. "The argument as to the possible abuse of power," Iredell sagely observed, "will reach all delegation of power, since all power may be abused when fallible beings are to execute it."[12]

Mason's demurrer to the judicial article evoked a more-terse response. To Mason's charge that the federal judiciary would absorb and destroy the state systems, Iredell replied that the federal courts would lack jurisdiction except where the Union was concerned. Evoking a metaphor from astronomy, he likened a state judiciary to "a satellite waiting upon its proper planet: That of the Union, like the sun, cherishing and preserving a whole planetary system."[13]

Mason's fifth objection and Iredell's response were more expansive. The president lacked a constitutional council, Mason moaned, "a thing unknown in any safe and regular government." He thus would not get proper information and advice; he would be directed by minions and favorites, become a tool to the Senate, or have a Council of State arise from the principal department heads. Absence of a constitutional council, Mason argued, had spawned improper appointive power in the Senate and a disquieting general fusion of executive and legislative functions. This void also sired the vice-president, a supernumerary whose duties as Senate president dangerously commingled executive and legislative powers and gave one state an unnecessary and unjust preeminence over others.

The British Privy Council was Mason's model, Iredell conjectured in response, and its members served at the King's pleasure; if this was the paradigm, minions and favorites could still govern the president. Senate control over the executive was greater than that of the peers in England over the Crown, for peers served at the Crown's pleasure, while the president would be selectively impotent without Senate concurrence. The British system nevertheless modeled limited commingling of executive and legislative prerogatives. The executive could be manipulated by a council as readily as by the Senate, and the Convention plan made him as independent as proper precaution permitted. Again mirroring the wisdom of the ages, Iredell observed: "Whether the President will be a tool to any persons will depend upon the man, and the same weakness of mind which would make him pliable to one body of control would certainly attend him with another."

Mason's notion that a Council of State might arise from the principal department heads did not disturb Iredell. The Cabinet Council, composed of the principal officers of departments, was the only council really consulted in England, he said, and the Privy Council only gave formal sanction to that body's previous determinations. The president would not receive the opinions of his principal officers informally over dinner, he continued, but in writing with "[n]o after-equivocation [to] explain it away." Fawning thus would be minimized and the president better enabled to judge than from informal opinions less carefully rendered by a larger number of officers. Again recounting universal truth, Iredell affirmed that the evil "of the possible depravity of *all public officers* is one that can admit of no cure, since in every institution of government the same danger in some degree or other must be risked." "[I]t can only be guarded against by strong checks," he continued, "and I believe it would be difficult for the objectors to our new Constitution to provide stronger ones against any abuse of the executive authority than will exist in that."

Finally, Iredell thought the selection of a vice-president, chosen in the same manner as the president, a proper means to avoid delay in filling a vacant presidency. He viewed Mason's concern over a possible advantage to one state in casting Senate votes as trivial and unworthy of the spirit of amity and nationalism essential to the country's salvation. No system could ensure precise equilibrium of power for all states, he concluded, and such jealousy and distrust should be subordinated to the noble prospects national unity offered.[14]

Mason next protested the president's untrammeled power to grant pardons for treason, thus permitting him to pardon even those he had furtively enticed to criminal activity and thereby preventing discovery of his own guilt. In response, Iredell appealed to necessity. A power to pardon had to repose somewhere in every government, he contended, because there would often be persons whom circumstance entitled to "a merciful interposition." Every executive power in America possessed this authority, he asserted, and Mason's concern thus was "the most chimerical apprehension that can be entertained." Foretelling modern intelligence apparatuses, Iredell postulated the need for spies in wartime. Only the president may know of their secret but useful services, he suggested, and he thus should be empowered to exercise mercy to obliterate their supposed misprisions. The likelihood of abuse of such power, Iredell concluded, was too remote to merit withholding it.[15]

Mason protested that by declaring treaties the supreme law of the land, the Constitution vested an exclusive legislative power in the executive and the Senate. Iredell defended the provision as inevitable. When the treaty-making power is exercised, he posited, the result should be binding on those who delegated authority for that purpose. Were this not so, he queried, "what foreign power would trust us?" He met Mason's proposal for consent by the House of Representatives "where it could be done with safety" with a further query: How could the safety question be resolved except during pending negotiations? Only the president and the Senate could make that judgment, he asserted; and if they determined that consultation with the House was risk-free, they did not need a constitutional provision to permit it.[16]

Iredell then confronted Mason's attack on the clause authorizing Congress to enact laws "necessary and proper" to implement the powers expressly granted. Mason predicted a parade of horrors: monopolies in trade and commerce, new crimes, unusual and severe punishment — in short, extension of the legislative power "as far as [Congress] shall think proper." Absence of provisions for freedom of the press and trial by jury in civil cases, and against standing armies in peacetime, also perturbed him.

Iredell retorted somewhat protractedly. Responding generally, he argued that the enumerated powers would be useless without the capacity to legislate upon them. No human body, including the Constitutional Convention, could foresee and provide for all future contingencies; subsequent general legislation must address such. With or without express contrary provisions, Congress could usurp rights; no mere "parchment stipulations" could forestall such tyranny. The Convention could only be "answerable for the propriety of the powers given, not for the future virtues of all with whom those powers may be intrusted."

Responding specifically, Iredell argued:

First, the provisions denying preference to the ports of one state over those of another, and granting citizens of each state all privileges and immunities of those in the several states, were inconsistent with any monopoly in trade and commerce.

Second, Congress' power to define offenses and prescribe punishments applied only to cases within the Union's legislative power. These were restricted to the areas of counterfeiting, piracy and felonies on the high seas, offenses against the law of nations, and treason. Congress could enforce its acts in these areas only with appropriate penalties, and without such penalties, the express powers would be useless and legislative regulation thus absurd.

Third, many state constitutions contained declarations, adopted from the English Bill of Rights of 1688, against cruel and unusual, or unusual and severe, punishments. The terms were too vague to admit of clear definition, and the Convention could not have enumerated all possible penalties they might fit. Such a provision thus would have been useless and possibly dangerous, and its omission was not a fault.

Fourth, liberty of the press was "a grand topic for declamation," but there was no restraint on it. If Congress did more than grant authors exclusive publication rights for a limited time, its action would be without warrant from the Constitution, and it would be answerable as for any other act of tyranny.

Fifth, even in common-law courts, civil jury trials resolved only factual disputes, and other methods resolved even some of these. Chancery and admiralty courts had no juries, and state practices differed widely. A general provision for trial by jury in all civil cases thus would only generate confusion over how to proceed. It was a proper subject for future legislation, and given its popularity, political expediency would force Congress to grant the right in appropriate cases.

Sixth, any danger from a standing army in peacetime was outweighed by its obvious necessity. Without such, at the onset of war "the enemy...would be prepared; we not." So glaring was the absurdity of waiting until an invasion had occurred to make ready to resist it that Iredell wondered how respectable men could "be led away by so delusive an idea."[17]

Iredell gave cursory treatment to Mason's ninth objection, that "[t]he state legislatures are restrained from laying export duties on their own produce." While convenient for the regime imposing them, Iredell responded, such duties did not merit advocacy as though the state's "very being" depended upon them. A tax by an exporting upon a nonexporting state, he argued, would have been an unwise source of discord.[18]

Mason's tenth objection drew a more-impassioned rejoinder. "The general legislature," Mason expostulated, "is restrained from prohibiting the further importation of slaves for twenty odd years, though such importations render the United States weaker, more vulnerable, and less capable of defense." Iredell again grounded his defense in necessity. South Carolina and Georgia, considering the slave trade of continuing utility to them, probably would not have agreed to the proposed Constitution without this provision. The states that had imported slaves "till they were satisfied" could not "with decency" have insisted that those states relinquish advantages they already enjoyed. "Our situation," Iredell concluded, "makes it necessary to bear the evil as it is."

While thus defending the provision, Iredell, a slave owner, issued a clarion utterance that the slave trade was indeed a deplorable evil. It had existed too long "for the honor and humanity of those concerned in it," and he would rejoice in its prohibition. The "interests of humanity" would be advanced by its proscription twenty-odd years hence, but for the interim, he conceded, the matter must repose between God and individual consciences.[19]

Mason's final objection was that the national and state legislatures were prohibited from enacting *ex post facto* laws, which he thought necessity and the public safety sometimes required. Mason had joined other delegates to the Constitutional Convention in opposing the prohibition of such laws on the ground that it was unwise to constrain the states from enacting retroactive legislation in civil cases. This expansive meaning of *ex post facto* obtained widely until the Supreme Court rejected it in favor of the view limiting application of the concept to the criminal law (*Calder v. Bull*, 1798).

This demurrer reactivated Iredell the jurisprudent. His ideas of liberty differed from Mason's, Iredell rejoined, so much so that he considered this prohibition one of the most-valuable features of the proposed charter. Such laws, while sometimes convenient, he said, were never necessary and had been the instruments of gross tyrannies. The clause was "worth ten thousand declarations of rights"; a person could be secure, he argued, only when he knew the innocent conduct of one day could not become the "guilt and danger" of another.[20]

Having answered Mason's objections, Iredell closed with a resonant plea for the proposed government. Mason had gloomily forecast its evolution from a moderate aristocracy to either a monarchy or a corrupt, oppressive aristocracy. A very different entity would emerge, Iredell confidently prophesied, if his answers to Mason were "in general solid." Its strength and its subjects' liberty would be novelties in world history. The country could not expect to move from convention to convention until all possible objections were removed; it was in a critical period which could not be neglected with impunity. The proposed system, viewed objectively, could withstand even the most-stringent scrutiny. Any flaws could be corrected at leisure, while the advantages were simultaneously enjoyed. Justice, order, and dignity would supplant "anarchical confusion," and industrious exertions would generate recovery from war and produce an "independent, great, and prosperous people."

The alternative, Iredell concluded, was grim. If his countrymen continued their captious wrangling over trifles, listening to a small minority rather than the "first men" in the country who merited their confidence, they would cause exultation for their enemies and dejection for their friends. The honor, glory, and prosperity within easy reach would be gone forever.[21]

John McLean, a Norfolk printer, soon informed Iredell of his plans to shelve other less-worthy political tracts in order to publish "Answers." The *State Gazette of North Carolina* advertised the publication "To all Friends of the Federal Constitution." Distribution appears not to have been restricted to Virginia and North Carolina, however. The document preceded the majority of the *Federalist Papers*, and it thus attracted national attention.

While Iredell had written pseudonymously as "Marcus," his anonymity apparently was short-lived. David Witherspoon, the son of John Witherspoon, a signer of the Declaration of Independence, informed him: "[Y]ou were very soon known to be the author, by what means I do not know." Witherspoon was quite sanguine about the effect "Answers" would have: Every reader would conclude that the objections to the Constitution were unfounded.

It would not be that easy; a colossal struggle for men's minds still loomed. But "Answers" was influential in the Federalist effort; and its author, for whom a still-greater exertion lay ahead, became favorably known in all Federalist sections.[22]

CHAPTER 6

Acknowledged Leader for Ratification: Prefatory Skirmishes

A S IREDELL PENNED HIS "ANSWERS" TO MASON, NORTH CAR-
OLINA WAS MOVING TOWARD A RATIFICATION CONVENTION.
ARCHIBALD MACLAINE, A WILMINGTON LAWYER AND A LEADING
FEDERALIST, CONVEYED DOUBTS ABOUT IREDELL'S ELECTABILITY
as a delegate in his own town or county and suggested that he seek a seat from
Brunswick. William Hooper was more sanguine about their friend's prospect
for local approval: Unless the devil had become a "uniform inmate of the
souls of the voters," Iredell's election from Chowan was certain. From whatever borough, though, Hooper thought Iredell had to be in the convention.

Iredell was indeed elected from Edenton, leaving another leading Federalist, William R. Davie, elated and confident that his colleague faced no danger
in his town or his county. Davie was disquieted, however, because his own
neighbor in Halifax, Willie Jones, remained "perfectly anti-federal" and
prompted doubts about adoption of the Constitution.

For the moment, Iredell ignored this skepticism. He thanked his supporters and pledged to execute the trust zealously and faithfully. Overmodestly
pleading abilities incommensurate with his ambition to serve, he reiterated his
fervid support for the proposition before the convention. The "security of
everything dear," he said, hung on approval of the recommended charter. In
supporting it, he would find comfort in knowing he spoke the sense of his
constituents. The closer it was examined, he opined, the greater would be the
Constitution's rate of approval and the more likely the conclusion that it provided "the only probable means of safety."[1]

Governor Richard Caswell's message to the fall 1787 session of the General Assembly had adverted mainly to a file endorsed "Papers respecting the Federal Convention." The two houses had met jointly and adopted resolutions providing for selection of delegates to a state convention to consider the Constitution, to assemble in Hillsborough on the third Monday in July 1788. Battle lines were already forming, as Thomas Person, a leading Antifederalist, objected to the joint session and attempted to prevent action on the proposal by speaking as often as House rules permitted. Person's hostility only intensified with time, as he soon denounced George Washington as "a damned rascal, and traitor to his country, for putting his hand to such an infamous paper as the new Constitution."[2]

Some North Carolina Federalist leaders were optimistic. Archibald Maclaine, for example, observed in early 1788 that three states had ratified, nine more undoubtedly would ratify, and refractory holdouts would be forced to join once the new government commenced; his information gave him little or no doubt that North Carolina would ratify. Others, however, were less sanguine. William R. Davie saw nothing but "the dissemination of anti-federal principles" in Halifax, noting that communications from Virginia had strengthened the Antifederalists; the deference North Carolinians customarily gave to political opinion in that state bode ill in this instance, he thought, rendering ratification quite doubtful.

William Hooper and Hugh Williamson were equally pessimistic and prophetic. In April 1788, Hooper thought papers Iredell had sent him would convert many "political infidels" to the "salvation" the Convention offered, but he feared the infidels would yet prevail. By June, Williamson assumed North Carolina would follow Virginia's lead, but he confessed to a lack of sanguinity. In July, John Swann, Samuel Johnston's son-in-law and a member of Congress, informed Iredell that the Constitution was "ably supported by gentlemen of great literary merit" but that the opposition would not yield an inch. The capital was in "painful suspence for Carolina," he said, and he would be "most sensibly mortified" if it rejected, however unavailing that might be.[3]

His initial pessimism notwithstanding, Davie labored mightily with Iredell in the literary aspect of the ratification effort. By May 1788, he had completed twenty-five pages of "our little collection on...the Federal Government." He informed Iredell of striking what he had written on a religious test, presumably for elected officials, but noted that Iredell might wish to reinsert it. He had left the judiciary article for Iredell, who knew all the objections to it, and had omitted other "popular objections" which should be answered if space limitations permitted. Finally, in deference "to the author of Marcus [Iredell] and others for the liberties...taken with them," the pamphlet was to acknowledge its lack of originality.[4]

The state's Federalist leaders communicated throughout this period on progress of the ratification effort in other states. Davie congratulated Iredell when Maryland ratified and expressed hope that South Carolina and Virginia would do likewise before the Hillsborough convention met. Maclaine gave Iredell "the pleasing intelligence" when South Carolina ratified despite efforts "in the back-country to poison the minds of the people." Williamson informed Iredell when Virginia confederated, noting that North Carolina in opposition could "only expect countenance from Rhode Island or New York," neither of which he hoped the state would emulate. Virginia's decision, according to Davie, greatly "altered the tone" of the Antifederalists and reduced Willie Jones to pressing for rejection "in order to give weight to the proposed amendments."[5]

Federalist leaders also shared information on the debates in other states and relevant philosophical musings. Iredell sent Davie a copy of the Pennsylvania debates as well as "the second balance of the *Federalist*." The latter Davie had requested, believing the need for it greater in Halifax than in Edenton. Maclaine had written Iredell earlier that he expected the *Federalist* in volume form soon and thought the author "judicious and ingenious . . . , though not well calculated for the common people." Charles Johnson of Chowan, soon to be vice-president of the ratification convention, also received the *Federalist* from Iredell and found it "elegantly written." Johnson was surprised, though, that the author would take such pains to state the obvious: that union would enhance the power and commercial advantages of the states. But for the exertion endured to refute them, he could scarcely imagine the Antifederalists' arguments gaining credence.[6]

If sheer force of argument had prevailed, ratification might have been expected. So far as the records reveal, the literary effort of the Antifederalists did not begin to rival that of the Federalists. Indeed, evidence of any Antifederalist activity is sparse. Little written by their leader, Willie Jones, has survived. Only two Antifederalist newspapers, and only one issue of each, have survived for the period between the Philadelphia and Hillsborough conventions.

Having the advantage from the outset may explain this apparent lethargy on the part of ratification opponents. Their numbers included war heroes such as Joseph Graham, William Lenoir, Joseph McDowell, Thomas Person, and Griffith Rutherford; political leaders such as Timothy Bloodworth, Willie Jones, and Samuel Spencer; and religious leaders such as Elisha Battle, David Caldwell, and William Lancaster. Lesser officials, too, swelled their ranks; Archibald Maclaine lamented that in New Hanover County, every official except the county court clerk was decidedly antifederal. The opposition posed thus was considerable, and while short on domestic literary endeavors, the Antifederalists found aid in foreign materials. Bloodworth, Jones, and Person received from New York both antifederal materials and encouragement to remain "steadfast in opposition."[7]

Several months before the Convention that proposed the equivalent federal document, Iredell had written that the state Constitution was a law of the state, albeit the fundamental law. The proffered federal Constitution was also potentially a law, albeit again fundamental in character; and the struggle over its ratification was, in its essence, a debate about the nature of law. The Antifederalists equated law with politics and rough equity. They viewed it as reflecting communal custom, the attitudes of a discrete locale and moment. Minimizing commands from a remote parliament was thus for them a prized objective. By contrast, the Federalists valued certainty and stability over rough equity and justice, and they viewed law as a means to control politics. Influenced by Blackstonian thought, they saw law as a science, with governing axioms and concepts; and they sought, via the Constitution, to thwart the prospect of its conforming altogether to prevailing, contemporary, community sentiment.[8]

On July 21, 1788, the North Carolina ratification convention in Hillsborough became the focal point of this debate, and the proceedings there "resonated with those historical differences." Delegates gathered at the Presbyterian Church unanimously elected Iredell's brother-in-law, Samuel Johnston, then governor, as president of the ratification convention. The convention then appointed Iredell to a select committee to prepare and propose rules and regulations for its governance. The body approved all but one of the committee's recommendations, many of which were undoubtedly the product of Iredell's work. A day later the committee on privileges and elections, on which Iredell also served, recommended that the election from Dobbs County, which had been characterized by riots and violence, be voided and that its members vacate their seats.

With these formalities settled, the delegates broached the serious business of the convention. The proceedings commenced with a reading of the state Constitution and Declaration of Rights, the Articles of Confederation, the resolution of Congress recommending a convention to revise the Articles, and the act of the General Assembly appointing delegates to the federal Convention. Official accounts of the ratifications by Massachusetts and South Carolina were laid before the convention and filed for the members' perusal.[9]

Upon a motion for clause-by-clause discussion — the process followed in each state that had not ratified unanimously — Willie Jones countermoved that the question on the Constitution itself be "immediately put." Surely, he contended, in light of the extended debate and ample opportunity for consideration, every member was prepared to vote; both prudence and frugality recommended instant action. Thomas Person, saddened by any man yet troubled over a question so long considered, seconded Jones' motion.

This furnished Iredell his initial occasion to establish himself as "outstanding in debate" and the "acknowledged leader for ratification." Proclaiming surprise, he objected at length to deciding "without the least deliberation" perhaps the greatest question ever presented to such an assemblage. Even trivial statutes of short duration were properly subjected to debate, he argued; surely the body would not decide "without a moment's consideration" so great and important a question as this. The proposal was the product of extensive deliberation, sanctioned by men of probity and understanding and ratified by ten of the states. Such a document, he urged, should be neither adopted nor rejected overhastily.

Reacting to Jones' frugality motif, Iredell conceded that additional expense from an already diminished public treasury was unappealing. If such was ever necessary, however, it was on this question, which involved "the safety or ruin of our country."

Answering Person's lament over delegates who might have failed to prejudge the question, Iredell took the opposite tack: He would regret being predetermined either way. While confessing to a favorable predisposition, he dubiously denied having resolved to vote for ratification "at all events." He had come for information, he declared solemnly, and to judge only after full discussion whether the Constitution merited his support. He would vote independently and change his opinion if convinced it was wrong. He invited those confident in their opposition to articulate their reasoning. "[P]erhaps we may all concur in it," he speculated, doubting that any delegates were so obstinate or tenacious in their views as to be altogether unamenable to sound reasons for a contrary position. Many delegates, he said, were lawmakers who frequently changed their minds on legislative subjects; that being so, this more-complex and consequential matter required "the most ample discussion." The laudable example other states had set with clause-by-clause discussion could be more readily justified to constituents than "a decision without a moment's consideration."

This initial skirmish went to Iredell and the Federalists. Jones deferentially conceded that if gentlemen differed with him, he would yield. Frugality considerations, he acknowledged, did not rival the magnitude of the subject at hand.[10]

It appears largely taken for granted the following day that there should be discussion. Davie urged debating "with decency and moderation," like a deliberative body, not a military enterprise. The body then resolved itself into a committee of the whole, with Antifederalist Elisha Battle in the chair. David Caldwell, another leading Antifederalist, drew battle lines for the debate at the outset by proposing that the convention commence deliberation with comparison of the Constitution to the fundamental principles of every free government, ratifying when they corresponded and otherwise not.

Caldwell's first principle, that a government is a compact between rulers and ruled, drew Iredell's immediate disapprobation. A compact could be annulled only by mutual consent, he argued; thus, on compact principles, people could "new-model" their government only if rulers became oppressive. The American government, he thought, was grounded on nobler principles. The people founded it, and those in power were their servants. The people thus could reorder it whenever they chose for purposes of their own welfare, not merely because of oppression. Governmental officers had no veto if the people chose change, so the compact theory could never obtain where the people were the font of power.

The convention defeated Caldwell's recommended principles for debate, awarding Iredell another triumph in this the second of the convention's prefatory skirmishes. This left the mode of proceeding unresolved, however. Governor Johnston thus proposed section-by-section discussion, which was opposed because of time constraints. Following "some altercation," Iredell again urged thorough consideration. While rightly claiming that few members had considered the matter more thoroughly than he, he nevertheless professed a lack of confidence in his position. Conversation among men of understanding was always instructive, he argued; and while others might without deliberation arrogate to themselves infallibility, he would never do so. No gentleman would deny the fallibility of human judgment, and he readily assigned that characteristic to his. From Iredell's perspective, this fallibility, the seriousness of the subject, and the awful consequences of an erroneous decision rendered deliberation essential. The greatest men had sanctioned the proffered document, and ten states had adopted it. It thus deserved a "fair trial...paragraph by paragraph"; if it would promote happiness, the decision should then be in its favor.[11]

Iredell was more than vindicated, as the convention voted by a considerable majority for clause-by-clause consideration. He was prepared for any objections that might be offered in this process, being familiar with arguments on both sides offered throughout the country. Davie and Spaight, having been delegates to the federal Convention, were ready to assist but apparently deferred to Iredell's superior scholarship, learning, and ability. Maclaine, too, was equipped for articulate advocacy but lacking in appropriate temperament.

Their antagonists were led by Elisha Battle, Timothy Bloodworth, David

Caldwell, Willie Jones, William Lenoir, Joseph McDowell, Griffith Rutherford, and Thomas Person. Among those voting with these opponents, but not debating, was an obscure delegate named Richard Nixon (no known relation to the future president of the same name).[12]

The decision to debate did not render the Antifederalists articulate; rather, the discussion was heavily weighted toward the Federalists, as their antagonists often simply sat in silence. Indeed, the Federalists betimes were raising objections themselves and then answering them, prompting a protest from William Shepperd, an Antifederalist delegate. "[I]t was very uncommon for a man to make objections and answer them himself," Shepperd observed, and "it would take an immense time to mention every objection which had been mentioned in the country." Maclaine responded that he would answer not only objections made in the convention but also those passed by silently but decried "out of doors" or "in the country." Iredell, too, thought it proper to answer objections made "out of doors" but diffidently concealed in the convention.[13]

The Antifederalists did not wade far into the Constitution before discovering objections. The opening phrase of the preamble, "We the People," drew their initial fire on the ground that the framers had represented state legislatures, not the people at large. When Davie's learned but protracted response failed to satisfy, Iredell replied succinctly that the phrase did not refer to the framers but to the style of the Constitution when ratified.

Next, Iredell defended the powers of the president to sign bills and make treaties. The Antifederalists protested that all legislative power was not vested in the Congress. Iredell denied that the president possessed powers legislative in nature; his power to object, he argued, could lead only to reconsideration and thereby to an enhanced prospect of sound enactments. When Lenoir responded that the treaty-making power was legislative, Iredell replied that every authorized act of government was law. Lenoir's penchant for legislative purity was not satisfied, however, and Iredell persisted, doggedly reiterating that a treaty is the law of the land because the Constitution grants the power to make it.[14]

When Antifederalist Joseph Taylor objected to the provision giving the House of Representatives sole power of impeachment, Iredell justified the clause on grounds of both accountability and deterrence. Every officer should be accountable for his behavior, he contended, and the terror of looming punishment might well deter misconduct. Following disputation over whether the provision applied to state officials, Iredell defended the power as applicable to federal offices only. Speaking eloquently on the concept of dual sovereignty, a refrain to which he would return often, he noted the binary loyalty the new arrangement would impose: to the Union in defined cases, but otherwise to the state. To disqualify him from an office he held under North Carolina law, he asserted, would violate the Constitution, for it applied only to officers of the United States. Answering a charge that even holders of petty offices could be punished only before Congress, often requiring considerable travel and expense, Iredell replied that such officers could still be tried by a common-law court in the state.[15]

The following day Stephen Cabarrus, a Federalist delegate, questioned the length of senators' terms. Before answering, Iredell applauded bicameralism as giving the people "double security." The minority, he argued, is often right. Proper measures would generally receive joint approval, but the presence of another house to oppose or amend improper ones was advantageous. Representatives would promote the interests of the individual states, while equal representation of the states in the Senate would advance the interests of the Union at large. "The people," he said, "will be represented in one house, the state legislatures in the other."

Longer terms did not cede disproportionate power to the Senate, Iredell declared confidently. Larger numbers, immediate representation of the people, and express powers such as origination of money bills gave the House "great weight." There was "additional security" in the election of senators by state legislatures, for respectable men with proven devotion to the national interest would be chosen. While the terms were long, they were not life estates transmissible to descendants. Faithful adherence to duty was probable, but some permanence in station was needed to promote it.

Unlike the House, Iredell continued, the Senate "should not be at the mercy of every popular clamor." Consistency and stability in the law benefited the public; short terms countered these values and deprived the people of valuable experience. Because the business of a senator required knowledge and information greater than that quickly attainable, six-year terms were entirely suitable.

Iredell appended, self-effacingly: "Had my abilities been greater, I should have answered the objection better." His defense apparently sufficed, however, for the provision engendered no further debate.[16]

The right of Congress to alter prescriptions of state legislatures establishing the time, places, and manner of congressional elections provoked extended debate. Opponents demanded that this power remain with the states. Even Samuel Johnston, while professing himself a "great admirer" of the Constitution, found this provision perplexing, and even Iredell was amenable to an amendment limiting its use to situations in which states failed to or could not act. Iredell vigorously denied, however, that the provision empowered Congress to extend the time for elections to any number of years, thereby expanding terms. The provision that representatives must be chosen every second year rendered that construction absurd, he argued, and an absurd construction was to be avoided when a rational one so permitted.

The Antifederalists were not persuaded. Bloodworth responded caustically that the provision so endangered the "democratic branch" that no argument for it would satisfy him. Iredell had "amused... with learned discussions" and condescended to proposed amendments, Bloodworth said, but he devoutly hoped North Carolina would not "swallow" the Constitution until this provision was amended. William Goudy was convinced the clause would lead to aristocracy and tyranny. Caldwell thought Congress could continue its members in office for twenty years or even for life. Though the debate consumed the remainder of the day, Iredell argued the issue no further, and his adversaries were never mollified.[17]

Iredell next rose concerning the section allowing members of the House and Senate to impose secrecy on parts of their journals. The provision was essential to conceal wartime operations, he contended; otherwise, the enemy could discover plans and defeat them. This reasoning applied equally to negotiations with foreign powers.[18]

The provisions for presidential veto and its override evoked a philosophical discourse on the benefits of the separation of powers. This division was essential to the preservation of liberty, Iredell urged, for each power required a defense against encroachment by others. Placing power in one man to negate measures passed by two houses — one representing the people, the other the states — would be dangerous. But the proposed veto allowed the executive branch to defend itself without becoming a part of the legislature. It was a happy medium, Iredell argued, between an absolute negative and no control whatever. It would protect the executive from "ill designs" in the legislature and preclude enactment of many "injurious" laws.[19]

Probably because of the scarcity of hard money in North Carolina, the Antifederalists fought at length the clause empowering Congress to lay and collect taxes, duties, imposts, and excises. Iredell left the Federalist side of this issue to Samuel Johnston, Whitmell Hill, and John Steele. He rose only when Joseph McDowell reintroduced the notion that Congress might continue the terms of its members by interfering with the mode of elections. Moaning that he "thought... this was sufficiently explained yesterday," Iredell repeated the lesson: The terms of office were explicitly fixed and unaffected by Congress' power to control the time and manner of elections.[20]

The provision empowering Congress to raise and support armies elicited an Iredell exposition of such passion that he apologized for the warmth of his expression. Community safety was the primary object of all governments, he stated, and assuring it thus was the duty of all constitutionalists. While the power was subject to abuse, so was all power. The sole question thus was, is the power necessary? If so, the risk of abuse had to be tolerated. Restraint and suppression of internal commotions and foreign hostilities were essential in all countries, he continued, so all governments had the power to raise armies. The only real debate was over its necessity in peacetime, and even then, protection from the machinations of other countries was required. Congress' inability to appropriate money for this purpose for more than two years provided a substantial check on potential abuse, rendering tyranny improbable.[21]

In discussing the clause granting the slave trade a twenty-year continuance, Iredell reprised his opposition to the evil but again defended the proposal on grounds of practical necessity. Immediate termination, if practical, would please him, he said, for the trade was "utterly inconsistent with the rights of humanity" and produced "great cruelties." Abolition would gladden "every generous mind, and every friend of human nature," but the urgent yen for it was wishful thinking. The Convention's majority had wanted it, but South Carolina and Georgia had refused. To reject the Constitution on that account not only would not remedy the evil, it would empower the states to continue it forever. Better a termination twenty years hence than not at all; better to "set an example of humanity . . . , though at a distant period."[22]

Noting past objections and obviously anticipating others, Iredell expounded at length on the office and powers of the president. The office, he observed, would require ability and experience, and he (oversanguinely) expected it always to fall "upon a man of experienced abilities and fidelity." Speaking to the position's express powers, he argued that command of the military ought to rest in the person who most clearly possessed the general confidence of the people. Allowing the president to require written opinions from department heads was, he thought, a good substitute for a council. The reasons for a council in England were inapposite in America, he posited, for there the King could do no wrong and could only be removed extralegally, while under the proposed Constitution, the president was answerable for his misdeeds. The King thus needed advisors responsible for their counsel, while the president did not. "We," he surmised, "are much happier." Still, Iredell offered, the president needed some advice, and the executive officers were as good a source as any. The solemnity of a written memorial would be a check on them, and ultimately the president would get the credit or the blame since his judgment alone would determine whether he followed or rejected the advice.[23]

Addressing the president's power to pardon, Iredell conceded the propriety of equal justice under law, especially in a republican form of government where the law is superior to all individuals and where no person is superior to another under the law. Still, he urged, peculiar circumstances may entitle an offender to mercy, and inflexible adherence to the law thus may cause injustice. Such power might also be necessary to prevent a civil war by forgiving penitent nascent insurrectionists, he argued, or to provide absolution for American spies in wartime. The power thus should reside somewhere, and where better than in a man "possessing the highest confidence of the people"? Cases of impeachment, however, were wisely exempted, for otherwise, "this great check upon high officers of state would lose much of its influence." A perfect system being beyond reach, he concluded, the test should be, not immaculacy, but whether a better arrangement was obtainable.[24]

It now became painfully evident that Iredell's eloquence was not harvesting converts. Robert Miller, an Antifederalist delegate, avowed that while Iredell's explanation had obviated some of his objections, he still could not approve. The president could too easily abuse such extensive powers, he believed; thus, Congress should control the movements of the army.

This rebuff silenced Iredell temporarily as others defended the president's power, with the concurrence of two-thirds of the Senate, to make treaties. Eventually Iredell, too, spoke. This power, he thought, should vest in a body with equal representation from the states, since the sovereignty of the states could be implicated in foreign negotiations. So vested, it was "not likely to be attended with the evils which some gentlemen apprehend."

In closing his defense of this clause, Iredell waxed philosophical, applauding the provisions for amending the Constitution and exhorting to vigilance in the safeguarding of liberty. Only the people could ultimately secure liberty, he warned; their power that created the government could also destroy it if necessary to preserve liberty, but the amendment provisions offered a less-drastic remedy perhaps previously unknown.[25]

Again, Antifederalist skepticism lingered. Judge Samuel Spencer, while deferentially terming Iredell "the worthy gentleman last up," nevertheless challenged his premises. The powers, he thought, were too expansive and untrammeled. While at least not hereditary, aristocracy nevertheless loomed. The expansive powers were destructive of rights and privileges, he concluded, and this "ought to be strictly guarded against."

Iredell, who never held his former judicial colleague in high regard, rejoined rather acerbically. The insinuation that the proposed government would spawn an aristocracy was "uncandidly calculated to alarm and catch prejudices." There was no life tenure, Iredell argued, and all authority would flow directly or indirectly from the people. Because officials would have no power independent of the people, Spencer's foreboding was unfounded.[26]

Iredell's retort silenced Spencer but briefly. He soon reoccupied the floor to assail the judicial article, believing the powers granted the federal judiciary would prove oppressive and expensive and leave the state judiciaries largely unemployed.[27]

CHAPTER 7

Acknowledged Leader for Ratification: The Real Objection

THE FOREGOING REMONSTRANCES WERE MERE PRELUDES TO A PERORATION ON THE REAL FOCUS OF ANTIFEDERALIST OBJECTION TO THE CONSTITUTION: THE ABSENCE OF A BILL OF RIGHTS. "THERE IS NO DECLARATION OF RIGHTS," SPENCER now decried, "to secure to every member of the society those unalienable rights which ought not to be given up to any government." Such was necessary to check men in power, he asserted, to set a boundary between the powers of the government and the rights of the people. Oppression develops by degrees, Spencer continued, and if express bounds were prescribed, the people would note and stem it sooner. If of no other service, he concluded, a bill of rights "would at least satisfy the minds of the people."[1]

Iredell sat silently as Johnston, Maclaine, and Spaight responded to this and related Antifederalist concerns. Ultimately, however, he could remain mute no longer. His hope that others would fully answer was unfulfilled. Important points were yet unmentioned, and it was his duty to speak if he could enlighten.[2]

The Constitution, he stated, neither expressly granted nor prohibited trial by jury in civil cases. Congressmen might themselves need such a trial; therefore, they would hardly dare to deny it. While its removal was one of the causes the Declaration assigned for independence, that deprivation was by a foreign legislature which might continue it forever. This Constitution had not removed it but had simply left it to "our own" legislature.

Absence of a bill of rights, too, deprived of nothing. The concept originated in England, Iredell declared, which had no written constitution and

65

where governmental authority was rooted in the remotest antiquity. A "fixed and certain" constitution there, clearly delineating bounds of authority, would have rendered a bill of rights useless. One would be equally unavailing in this Constitution, which expressly declared the power granted and left all other with the people.

Posing the analogue of a power of attorney, Iredell noted the incongruity in such an instrument directing that the attorney not exercise more power than expressly granted. No attorney authorized to sell the maker's lands in one county, he surmised, would sell those in another and consider the action vindicated because the power failed expressly to provide otherwise. A bill of rights, he averred, would be equally incongruous and dangerous. Maximal ingenuity could not enumerate all the individual rights not relinquished; upon invasion of an omitted right, the government could plead the bill of rights as clear proof the people did not intend to retain powers not expressly granted. A bill of rights thus would be "a snare rather than a protection," Iredell concluded, and "not only unnecessary, but...absurd and dangerous."[3]

Following intervening desultory debate, Iredell, cognizant of their import, augmented his points. The Philadelphia Convention, he said, could not agree on a single mode for trial by jury in civil cases because methods differed in the several states. By omitting the subject altogether, it left any problem in the mode established by Congress readily remediable legislatively. Iredell then reprised his argument that enumerating rights would imply that those omitted could be impaired with impunity. Specify some, he concluded, and he could name others not mentioned.[4]

The Antifederalists remained unconvinced. Spencer reiterated that it was impossible to guard too carefully "essential rights and liberties which ought never to be given up." "There is no express negative," he said, "no fence against their being trampled upon." Matthew Locke was shocked "to hear gentlemen of such great abilities [Iredell] speak such language." The right to trial by jury was clearly insecure, and no ingenuity or subtlety of argumentation could satisfy him otherwise. Liberty came too dearly, and the people were too perceptive of its value, to surrender it hastily.

Surely by now Iredell discerned that he could not satisfy this objection. Indeed, he must have recognized that while other concerns were relatively trivial, the omission of a bill of rights, and particularly a guarantee of trial by jury in civil cases, would prove lethal to the initial ratification effort in North Carolina. He doggedly persevered nevertheless. If by not being provided for, trial by jury was expressly provided against, he would be the Constitution's fiercest opponent. Such a construction, though, he considered "absurd and unnatural," and it was foolish to surmise that a majority of representatives would act counter to their own interest by oppressing the people in this manner.[5]

Iredell next commented extensively on the provision for amendments. It was unique, he said, because past draftsmen had arrogantly thought themselves infallible, while the present framers showed greater diffidence. This Constitution thus could be altered as regularly, though admittedly not as easily, as a statute. When Antifederalist Andrew Bass observed that the introduction of amendments depended altogether on Congress, Iredell countered that Congress had no choice when two-thirds of the states called for a convention. Iredell's discourse generated no further comment, indicating general agreement with the amendment provision.[6]

When the Supremacy Clause was read, Iredell apparently anticipated opposition, for he rose instantly to defend it. It did not, as supposed, grant too much power, he asserted, but provided only for execution of powers already given. To him, this explanation was "the plainest in the world" and should have been "entirely satisfactory."

Timothy Bloodworth disagreed, believing the clause would essentially annihilate the state governments. Iredell rejoined that Congress would execute the powers granted by laws made for that purpose, and the question under the clause would always be whether Congress had exceeded its authority. If not, it must be obeyed; otherwise, not. State constitutions would yield only to powers expressly granted to the federal government.

Bloodworth remained unreconciled. The clause, he thought, would destroy every competing state law, specifically the legal tender laws. It needed borders, defining and limiting its extent. Otherwise, the more-populous northern states would always outvote their southern counterparts. The Constitution thus could destroy the state's currency and prohibit the emission of paper money.

Iredell was equally persevering. While the Constitution proscribed the future emission of paper money, he argued, it did not interfere with that in circulation. Abuse of power, being possible in any government, was not a valid basis of objection. The people would resist it, he surmised, and it was simply a risk that must be taken.

With this, Iredell withdrew from the Supremacy Clause debate. Samuel Johnston then expressed surprise at the opposition. The Constitution and laws enacted pursuant to it were inevitably supreme, he argued; otherwise, one state could repeal laws of the Union, and the whole Constitution "would be a piece of blank paper." Johnston's ineluctable logic failed to persuade, however, and the Supremacy Clause debate ended only upon adjournment for the day.[7]

The next day's proceedings commenced with a reading of the clause prohibiting religious tests for federal officeholders. Henry Abbot, an ordained Baptist minister, noted the concern of some that the Constitution would end the worship of God according to conscience. "The worthy member from Edenton [Iredell]," he said, had defended treaties as the supreme law of the land. Some, however, feared a treaty making Roman Catholicism the official religion, thereby eliminating freedom to worship as dictated by conscience. To many, he continued, the exclusion of religious tests was "dangerous and impolitic," for "pagans, deists, and Mahometans [Muslims]" might obtain offices; indeed, all lawmakers could be pagans.

This demurrer surprised the "worthy member from Edenton." The provision, he urged, was designed to prevent the most-pernicious evils, the mischief of religious persecutions. Religious tests, he said, had perpetrated "the utmost cruelties." But America had shown humanity that unorthodox religious views did not make one "a bad member of society." Rather than being "dangerous and impolitic," the clause was the strongest proof of an intent to secure religious liberty. None would be more horrified than he by the slightest impairment of religious liberties, but the power to make treaties could not include a right to establish a foreign religion.

To the concern that the people might choose representatives having "no religion at all," Iredell responded with a query: Was it possible to exclude any set of men without removing freedom for all? He considered the perceived danger chimerical, for he could not conceive of the people entrusting their rights to the faithless, or even to those of materially different beliefs. Felicity would be served, he said, if religion could "take its own course, and maintain itself by the excellence of its own doctrines." The Divine Author had never sought support from "worldly authority," and the faith had made "greater progress for itself, than when supported by the greatest authority upon earth."

Iredell ridiculed the more-extreme papistic arguments rather mercilessly. He had encountered a pamphlet, he reported, positing the threat of the pope being elected president. Reading the qualifications for the presidency might have quieted the author's fears, Iredell suggested. The president had to be a native and a fourteen-year resident of the United States; the pope had to come from the college of cardinals. It would be most unusual, Iredell urged, for a native and fourteen-year resident of America to go to Europe, enter Romish orders, become a cardinal, be selected pope, "and at length be so much in the confidence of his own country as to be elected President." Surrendering the papacy for the presidency would be equally extraordinary. It thus would be "equally rational and judicious," he concluded, to preclude a European king from the presidency as to foreclose the pope therefrom.[8]

With this derision, Iredell ended his discourse, hopeful that Abbot was satisfied. Abbot, however, still wondered how oaths would be administered with religious tests not required. Iredell apologized, attributing his failure to answer this inquiry to his inability to take notes. He proceeded with a history lesson on the forms of oaths, concluding that the only essential inquiry was whether the oath-taker believed in a Supreme Being and a future state of rewards and punishments. If so, he said, the oath should be one that most binds his conscience; if not, no oath should be considered reliable "since there are many cases where the terror of punishment in this world for perjury could not be dreaded." Abbot, who had threatened to vote against the Constitution if his objections were well founded, must have been satisfied, for he ultimately supported ratification.[9]

Iredell's response to Abbot was his final convention utterance on discrete provisions of the Constitution. Soon thereafter, Samuel Johnston moved that the convention, having fully deliberated, proceed both to ratify and to recommend amendments. William Lenoir immediately rose to commence Antifederalist opposition. The Philadelphia delegates, he said, exceeded their powers, and the Constitution endangered liberties. The proposed government had aristocratical and monarchical features. He could see neither the end of the powers granted nor the reasons for granting them. Rather than securing sovereignty for the states, he opined, the Constitution would "melt them down into one solid empire." The powers given Congress were alarming. Tyranny came naturally to humanity, making it essential to secure rights and liberties. The Constitution thus should not be adopted without amendments. With proper amendments, he was "perhaps ... as ready to accede to it as any man."

Richard Dobbs Spaight, speaking as a framer, responded. He and his fellow delegates went to Philadelphia with full power to amend the extant system, he proclaimed. Lenoir's view that the Constitution would enslave rather than liberate was astonishing. Spaight had had nothing in view but his country's liberty and happiness, and he believed other delegates were equally sincere and patriotic. Adopting amendments before ratifying was unworkable, he posited, because without ratification the state would be like a foreign power.

Joseph McDowell rejoined for the opposition, focusing anew on the Antifederalists' real objection: the omission of a bill of rights. He favored a strong federal government but would never agree to one "that tends to the destruction of the liberty of the people."

William Lancaster also disputed the excellence attributed to the Constitution, preferring amendments before ratification. How could one know, he queried, that proposed amendments would be approved afterward? The safer course was to make them a condition of ratification.

Willie Jones then observed that he had attended the debates with patience. One party had claimed perfection for the Constitution; the other, imperfection. He thought the latter. The alleged dangers of nonadoption, to Jones, were "merely ideal and fanciful." He thus moved the previous question, intending, if the motion carried, to call for amendments to precede ratification.[10]

Jones' motion ended Iredell's brief quiescence. Iredell wanted debate on Johnston's motion to ratify; both Johnston's stature and the magnitude of the subject demanded it. Johnston, too, pleaded for discussion, disdaining "manoeuvres and contrivance" and wishing for full and fair argumentation.

Jones was obstinate, however. Gentlemen's arguments had been listened to attentively, he said, without alteration of opinion. Further disputation thus was useless.

But Iredell was equally intractable. The consequence of carrying the previous question would be North Carolina's exclusion from the Union. There was no right of conditional ratification. If excluded from the Union, there was no assurance of future joinder, Iredell argued, and "the impossibility of existing out of the Union must be obvious to every thinking man."[11]

Tension escalated, as Thomas Person observed that the Federalists had dominated the debate and would merely do so again. Davie accused Person of "ungenerous insinuations" and of agitating his countrymen against the Constitution "out of doors." Gentlemen, he said acerbically, should "act openly and aboveboard," and contrary conduct on such an occasion was "extremely despicable."[12]

Jones again spoke briefly, followed by a clamoring for the question. Iredell restored order by asserting that gentlemen had no right to preclude a member from speaking to the motion. He then noted, somewhat apologetically, his own extensive participation in the debates, attributing it to the reticence of others equally capable. He now wished, nevertheless, to address the Constitution as a whole. The tendered charter he thought safe; no objection raised had persuaded him otherwise. While he could agree with insubstantial amendments, he could not accept the general objection that the proposed powers were subject to abuse. That was true of all power, so if that was the objection, no powers could be given. Tyranny and anarchy posed equal threats to liberty. The happy medium between the two was "the true government to protect the people," and the proposed Constitution was "well calculated to guard against both these extremes."

The difference between amending before and after adoption, he asserted, was great. It was unlikely that ten states had agreed to a bad constitution. If North Carolina failed to adopt, it would be out of the Union. This prospect was reminiscent of the early-Revolution period when Britain exempted New York and North Carolina from a general prohibitory act, trying to divide the northern and middle states and "break the heart" of the southern. Had the spared states been snared in this manner, Iredell stated, independence would have become unlikely.

Tempers flared briefly upon this assertion, as Person accused Iredell of reflecting on the Constitution's opponents "as if they were friendly to the British interest." Iredell resented the interruption, called Person disorderly, and emphatically denied any such intention. Even his devotion to the Constitution could not prompt him to "procure its success by one unworthy action or one ungenerous word," he assured Person.

Returning to his argument, Iredell conceded that the convention should proceed as if no state had ratified but urged consideration of the state's "peculiar situation." "We cannot exist by ourselves," he declared. The state could join others in supporting amendments, but amendments would take time. Meanwhile, North Carolina would be denied participation in decisions binding on it. Congress would enact laws implementing powers the Constitution granted. If the state ratified, its representatives would be involved; if not, its interests would suffer, and subsequent accommodation of them was improbable. Adoption while proposing amendments was thus the safer course, and confidence in ultimate approval of amendments protecting essential liberties was in order. The argument failed to persuade, as Jones' motion for the previous question carried 183 to 84.[13]

The following day the convention debated Jones' motion calling for amendments prior to adoption. Johnston thought this contrary to the intention of the people, who had elected them to determine the ratification issue. He also invoked pragmatism. The present Congress lacked authority to receive amendments. If the state failed to ratify, it would have no representatives to propose amendments in the new one. It could only appoint ambassadors to the United States to present its views on that country's Constitution. Ratifying states could propose amendments and have weight, while North Carolina, a foreign power, could not even vote on them. Any subsequent admission to the Union could be on unequal and disadvantageous terms. Meanwhile, laws injurious to the state could be enacted, and the state would lose its share of duties and imposts.

Johnston's parade of horrors left Jones unshaken. The convention, he said, was not required to ratify "at all events"; it had an equal right to reject. The objection "we shall be out of the Union" left him unruffled; "So I wish to be," he replied. The state could, he thought, join the Union at leisure and share the impost upon entry. Those anxious for federal office could postpone their ambition without alarm. When a convention of the states was called, he believed, North Carolina would receive the call. Finally, Jones invoked Jefferson's wish, expressed to Madison, that nine states would ratify but four reject, thereby assuring amendments.[14]

Jones' insinuation that hunger for federal offices motivated the Federalists rankled. Johnston vehemently denied any such purpose. Jones defended his allusion as warranted by the ill motives assigned to the Constitution's opponents but denied that he had implicated Johnston, whom he held in the highest regard.

Spencer then rose to support Jones' proposal. Prudence, he thought, dictated that amendments precede ratification. Businessmen entering a partnership agreement would not sign first, planning to correct errors later. Similar sagacity was infinitely more necessary in the matter at hand, which affected large numbers of people and millions yet unborn. Brief exclusion from the Union was less dangerous than unconditional ratification; amendments were expected, and North Carolina would then be ready to ratify.[15]

Spencer's remarks set the stage for Iredell's final oration of the convention. To him, this was "a very awful moment," on which "the peace and happiness of our country for ages" depended. The convention thus should consider the consequences and "determine with the utmost caution and deliberation."

The objection that ratification would interfere with their oaths of allegiance to the state was unfounded, he contended, for no oath required sacrificing the country's safety. He had not considered his oath to Great Britain binding when that country attempted to establish tyranny in America. The safety of the people was the supreme law and the object of all government.

The notion that the state could join the Union at any time was equally without foundation, he asserted. There was simply no right to join after rejection; admission would then be by the grace of the confederated states and on their terms. While amendments were proper, the question was whether the state could remain unaffiliated pending their approval. The only safe, prosperous place was within the Union. The dangers of separation were unfathomable, and the necessity of union sufficiently certain that he would surrender much to obtain it.

Failure to ratify would lead to loss of benefits that would accrue to the confederated states: flourishing trade, commodities rising in value, the distress from war gradually removed. North Carolina's share of imposts from all the states would remain in the federal treasury. "[W]e ought to consider," he pleaded, "whether ten states can do longer without one, or one without ten."

Iredell considered amendments probable. Three states had ratified unanimously, he said, but there was considerable opposition in the others. Under these circumstances, he viewed disapproval of amendments designed to satisfy the objections as unlikely. North Carolina could add weight on the side of the amendments, and by failing to ratify, would injure the states wanting them. A moment's separation could become permanent, and gentlemen should pause before contributing to "so awful an event."

Iredell shared Johnston's disdain for the insinuation that the Federalists simply hankered for national offices. He hoped no one thought him "so wicked" as to sacrifice the interest of his country for private gain. Unaware that he would receive perhaps the choicest of federal appointments, he denied that the imputation applied to him; he doubted that it fit others. He had sacrificed one of the Crown's best offices to oppose Great Britain; the richest office in America, he claimed, could not have tempted him to do otherwise. Patriotism alone motivated most delegates, he thought, and he hoped others would be "equally liberal."[16]

Only desultory discussion followed Iredell's final peroration. Jones observed that he assigned unworthy motives to no one. Bloodworth vowed that he had listened attentively, and with maximal objectivity, but had not changed his mind. Temporary exclusion from the Union was trifling, in his view, when "put in competition with our liberties." The surest method to obtain amendments was to withhold consent. Davie noted that four states had recommended amendments; if New York, Rhode Island, and North Carolina were added, there would be a majority favoring, and other states might be compelled to join them. Spencer's partnership analogue "compar[ed] small things to great" but was accurate in one respect: North Carolina was like a "beggarly bankrupt" offering to enter a wealthy partnership on its own terms. Only a decision now to ratify gave it that right, he asserted: "Adoption places us in the Union — rejection extinguishes the *right* forever."[17]

Jones' motion for amendments now passed by a large majority, and the report of the committee of the whole was tabled until the following morning. While resigned to certain defeat, Iredell was not quite through. When the convention reconvened, he ruefully acknowledged that debate had ended and that further contention against an unyielding majority was futile. He had one more tactic to pursue, however. He and his friends, he said, wanted their sentiments recorded; he therefore wished "the yeas and nays" entered in the Journal for the benefit of both constituents and world opinion. This, he presumed, was preferable to a protest which would enhance partisan animosity among the people, something he had tried to avoid. He therefore moved for postponement of the committee's report in order to consider his motion to ratify the Constitution.

The motion was improper, unprecedented, and contemptible of majority opinion, McDowell and others countered. "[B]y no means," Iredell replied; its sole purpose was to show minority opinion and avoid a protest. Another had recommended this method to him, and it conformed to a frequent practice in Congress reflected in its journals.

Jones and Spencer sided with McDowell; Maclaine and Spaight supported Iredell. Davie regretted that gentlemen did not deal fairly and liberally with one another; the motion, he said, was "perfectly parliamentary" and "the usual practice in Congress." The convention, he thought, could not rid itself of it without a vote.

After heated discussion, Iredell agreed to withdraw his motion in order to allow the committee's resolution to be first entered on the Journal. The committee's resolution was then read and entered. It called for a declaration of rights securing liberties and for amendments to "ambiguous and exceptionable" parts of the Constitution, prior to ratification by North Carolina. A Declaration of Rights and twenty-six proposed amendments followed the resolution.

Spencer, seconded by McDowell, moved for concurrence in the committee report. Iredell then moved for postponement to consider his resolution that the Constitution be considered. Altercation and confusion followed, but Iredell ultimately achieved a peaceful solution by offering to move his resolution as an amendment. This satisfied the Antifederalists. Iredell then moved to strike all words except "Resolved, That" and to substitute language noting the wish for amendments subsequent to ratification, but ratifying without them. A series of proposed amendments followed.[18]

Iredell's motion failed by a vote of 184 to 84, one different from the vote by which Jones' motion for the previous question had carried earlier. Person's motion to concur with the report of the committee of the whole then carried by the same vote; those who voted against Iredell's amendment voted for the committee report, and those who favored the amendment voted against it.[19]

Analysis by counties further illuminates the magnitude of the Federalist defeat. Delegates from twenty-five counties voted unanimously against ratification, while delegates from only seven voted unanimously in favor. Those from six additional counties voted solidly in the negative, with one or two abstentions, while those from four additional counties voted solidly to ratify, with one to three abstentions. Thus, delegates from thirty-one counties cast every vote against the Constitution, while delegates from only eleven cast every vote for it. Iredell's region, the northeast, was the only multicounty area that was consistently Federalist.[20]

A final task occupied Iredell during the convention's closing days. New Bern had for some time been recognized as North Carolina's capital, but the Assembly had continued to meet in various towns. State leaders now acknowledged the need for a more-centrally located capital, thus avoiding the necessity of moving public papers from town to town. Because of intense rivalry among advocates of different boroughs, however, the Assembly deadlocked and delegated the issue to the convention. The convention appointed a committee for the purpose, composed of Iredell, Jones, and Maclaine. The precise locale was left to the Assembly, provided it was within ten miles of the place the convention designated.

Iredell nominated "Mr. Isaac Hunter's, in Wake County," notwithstanding that close friends and political allies favored or lived in other sites under consideration (Smithfield, Tarborough, Fayetteville, New Bern, Hillsborough, and the fork of the Deep and Haw Rivers). Maclaine, for example, joined most Cape Fear area residents in favoring Fayetteville. Hillsborough had some claim upon Iredell's allegiance because William Hooper lived there, and Iredell had once seriously considered moving there for health reasons.

While proponents of other sites fought vigorously, Iredell's choice prevailed, and a committee was appointed to select and purchase suitable land. Dissenters were allowed to record their protest in the Journal, and 119 did so, registering a preference for Fayetteville. In 1792 Joel Lane deeded one thousand acres in Wake County to the state, and the cornerstone of the first state capitol building was then laid.[21]

CHAPTER 8

Acknowledged Leader for Ratification: Fatal Disunion Remedied

ROM A PERSONAL STANDPOINT, IREDELL MADE FRIENDS AND BENE-
FITTED GREATLY FROM HIS STELLAR, ALBEIT UNSUCCESSFUL, PER-
FORMANCE AT HILLSBOROUGH. SAMUEL JOHNSTON SOON WROTE
HIM FROM THE ASSEMBLY SESSION AT FAYETTEVILLE, "THERE
is no bill completed except for the division of Rowan County." This lone mea-
sure had import for Iredell, for the new county would bear his name.

The honor delighted him. Few things had surprised or pleased him more,
he told John Steele, the Salisbury representative primarily responsible for the
designation. Polite as always, Iredell implored Steele to convey his gratitude
to others involved in the choice. "My opportunities of rendering any public
service have been very few," he wrote, "but no man's heart is more warmly
disposed to the public interest than mine."[1]

Iredell's near relations shared his pleasure over this unexpected recognition. In England, his brother Arthur "laughed immoderately" at the notion of
an "Iredellshire" and sought an account of that "respectable district" to
which he felt "nearly allied." It was, he said, flattering testimony of high regard for a brother who had given "an 'eclat'" to the family name, and he took
considerable pride in his kinship to one whose eloquence was exceeded only
by his abiding rectitude.[2]

Further encomiums followed in the convention's wake. John Steele avowed
that no one had done more for the common cause. Pierce Butler thought
North Carolina fortunate to have Iredell promoting its welfare; honor and
happiness would follow, he suggested, if the state would only adhere to his
friend's opinions. Hugh Williamson called Iredell one of the best men and

best lawyers in America, who had acquired national recognition for his dialectical prowess at Hillsborough. "The North Carolina debates are considerably read in this place," he wrote from New York, "especially by Congress members, some of whom, who formerly had little knowledge of the citizens of North Carolina, have lately been very minute in their inquiries concerning Mr. Iredell."[3]

Iredell barely paused to savor this acclaim. Even in his efflux of gratitude over the christening of Iredell County, he did not cease to promote the Constitution. His note of thanks to Steele concluded by touting support for the proposed charter as both the surest proof of devotion to the public interest and the sole lifeline from the swamp of anarchy.[4]

Iredell could hardly have escaped relentless devotion to the ratification task. The convention outcome had vindicated Willie Jones, who had seen no need to keep men from their work when the result was preordained. With a single insignificant exception, the votes after the thirteen-day odyssey had been precisely as they would have been before. As Jones observed near the convention's end, gentlemen's arguments had been listened to attentively, but no one had changed his opinion. Or, as Timothy Bloodworth stated more expressively, "Many words have been spoken, and long time taken up; but with me they have gone in at one ear, and out at the other."[5]

At Hillsborough the Antifederalists made the point "that compacts specified rights." The point had historical significance for North Carolinians, whose state Constitution specified a train of rights unusual in length, combining the liberties prescribed in most other state constitutions. All constitutions should so commence, the Antifederalists had urged. "[I]t is necessary that it should be expressly declared in the Constitution," Spencer told the delegates, "and not left to mere construction and opinion." McDowell was more succinct: "I wish to see everything fixed," he said.[6]

For making this point, the Antifederalists deserve much credit for the ultimate adoption of the Bill of Rights. Momentarily, however, their rigidity placed North Carolina in a maligned, precarious, and impotent position, and left the acknowledged leader for ratification distraught. "We are...for the present out of the Union," Iredell wrote Hannah, "and God knows when we shall join to it again." Maclaine thought there would be another convention because "[t]he people...cannot bear the idea of living out of the Union."[7]

New York had ratified while the Hillsborough convention met, leaving only North Carolina and Rhode Island unaligned. Public discourse quite naturally linked the two recalcitrant states, much to the chagrin of North Carolina Federalists. Their allies nationally reacted to the state's rejection of the Constitution with disappointment, shock, and scorn. Madison told Jefferson the state had been expected to fall "into the general stream," and its failure to do so was disappointing. James Jordon, Jr., a Virginia Federalist, wrote Madison, "[G]ood God what can they promise themselves!" Jeremiah Hill, a New England politician, wondered if other states would shun North Carolina for "whoring after Strange Gods." In Massachusetts, North Carolinians were called outlaws and convicts who had been driven from the more-civilized parts of the world. "[E]xtreme astonishment" was the reaction in New York, as some pronounced the state "of little importance to the Union." Hugh Williamson attempted damage control there by publishing an apology in a New York newspaper.[8]

Earlier, Williamson had suffered a foretaste of the alienation that would flow from the refusal to ratify. While the Hillsborough convention met, he notified Iredell that North Carolina's congressional delegation had declined invitations to a dinner to celebrate confederation by ten of the states. It would have been disrespectful, they thought, to bless in their official capacities an event the state had not yet approved.

Exclusion from commemorative social occasions was the most trivial of rejection's consequences, however. More significantly, North Carolina was now a foreign or independent state. It could have no part in selecting the first president, no role in devising the constitutional amendments on which the convention majority had insisted, and no participation if a general constitutional convention were called. Formative national laws would be enacted without its voice and would not apply to it; the Judiciary Act of 1789, for instance, would, until North Carolina ratified, cease to operate at its borders. The state could not aid in securing a more southern, and thus more advantageous, location for the initial seat of the Congress (New York City). Hugh Williamson thought the legislative benefit thus ceded to the "eastern" (northern) members considerable, for they could now "attend with too much ease." Had North Carolina been in the Union, he told Iredell, its representatives could have tipped the scales in favor of a more-southern position. There was a purely pragmatic aspect of exclusion from the new government as well: Williamson could not write as often in the future because of loss of the franking privilege.[9]

North Carolina, Williamson lamented, had "thrown herself out of the Union." Hooper feared the state would "become a by-word among the nations." Iredell wondered just what would become of it, as he foresaw possible anarchy attended with irremediable evil.[10]

Other Federalist leaders clung to a more-roseate view. As noted, Maclaine thought public discontent would prompt another convention. John Swann soon wrote from New York that the state's conduct was now viewed "in a much less censorious light." The convention's resolutions, he said, were "too evincive of a federal disposition at least not to have had considerable influence in changing the public opinion."[11]

Hope this basal "federal disposition" generated, combined with his keen perception of the state's plight while out of the Union, pinned Iredell to the ratification effort. He had barely greeted Hannah upon his return from Hillsborough when he once again applied his considerable talent as a political essayist to the cause of the new government.

Addressing himself to "Friends and Fellow Citizens," Iredell invoked their "most serious attention" to their "awful and affecting" condition. Separation from their wartime companions weakened the common cause and aided shared enemies, he pleaded. Except for its portion of the common debt, which it was unable to pay, the state was now independent of all nations and of other states. The worthies who convened in Philadelphia to remedy problems under the Articles had proposed uniting for a common object, being governed by common counsels; if the Constitution they proposed had defects, it was still superior to the old system in its provision for amendments. Other countries, he stated, could secure change only through revolution or civil war. The proposed system was infinitely preferable, wisely guarding against the extremes of amendments secured either too easily or with too much difficulty.

The amendments provision, Iredell persisted, had facilitated ratification in several states. They, too, were not perfectly satisfied, but unlike North Carolina, they had perceived the dangers of disunion and consented to work for amendments following adoption. "This," Iredell urged, "was the language of patriotism, prudence and affection," and would result in enactment of those amendments essential to security and prosperity.

North Carolina's failure to follow their example sorely vexed him. Were the delegates to Philadelphia and eleven state conventions really so indifferent to the principles of liberty as to consent to a system endangering them? he queried caustically; did the spark of freedom actually dwell only in a majority in North Carolina and Rhode Island, and minorities elsewhere? Surely, he thought, the notion that North Carolina and Rhode Island constituted the only bulwarks of liberty was mistaken. To the contrary, both reason and respectable authorities favored the Constitution.

In world affairs, he continued, the state was situated precariously. It was unknown in Europe, without alliances, and unaided in the event of attack. This was humiliating and dangerous, a path to misery and ruin.

The convention majority may not have considered its action a rejection, Iredell noted, but other states undoubtedly did. Hopefully, upon early action by another gathering, the state would be admitted to the Union on equal terms. If not, a great opportunity would be lost, the first system of laws more injurious to the southern states than otherwise, and supporters of amendments deprived of assistance.

While bad, the situation was not desperate. One assemblage could repair the mischief of another; thoughtful citizens thus should petition the legislature for a new convention. The people's "native good sense," he perceived, was "beginning to break a cloud of prejudice"; there were "many symptoms of a change" which offered "the greatest hopes." He therefore concluded with a cautiously optimistic plea and prayer for union: "God grant that this fatal disunion...may last a very short time longer," he beseeched, while exhorting North Carolinians to embrace their sister states and imploring those states to receive North Carolina with forbearance "as if we had never strayed!"[12]

In September 1788, the *State Gazette of North Carolina* and the *Norfolk and Portsmouth Journal* published this essay. John Swann soon wrote from the national capital to thank Iredell for sending him a copy. The publication, he said, merited "a cool, liberal, and dispassionate reading," and he hoped the good sense of the majority would do it justice.[13]

This essay was not Iredell's only contribution to the literature of the post-Hillsborough ratification effort. While addressing the convention, he had known he was speaking for the record, for he and Davie had hired a reporter to register the debates. In June 1789, they published the debates at their own expense, with Davie chafing somewhat under the burden. It had "disagreeably" fallen on them, he told Iredell, and they had to "trust...the saints" for a "reward *hereafter*." No man, Davie said, would suspect Iredell of profit. While Archibald Maclaine offered to assist, there is no evidence that Iredell and Davie accepted his tender.[14]

Hodge and Wills, printers at Edenton, published the debates, and the *State Gazette of North Carolina* advertised sale of the publication over a period of months. It was widely read, and Iredell's role attracted attention. As noted, the debates were perused in New York, especially by members of Congress, some of whom inquired about Iredell. Iredell's brother Arthur read the script often and was forcibly struck by his sibling's ability; he loaned the debates to their kinsman, Lord Macartney, who made "encomiastic remarks" about Iredell's part. Maclaine used the publication to further the ratification effort and regretted that his supply was inadequate. The work aided Federalist election victories in the back country in 1789.[15]

All patriotism, though, even an Iredell's, has limits. Notwithstanding the importance of the forthcoming General Assembly to the ratification effort, Iredell withstood importunings to become a candidate, citing the press of his law business. Bleak prospects for a new convention may have influenced him as well, for Samuel Johnston had told him the outlook was doubtful. The Assembly nominated Iredell as a delegate to a second federal convention to consider the amendments proposed by North Carolina and other states, but Iredell again refused, almost certainly for the same personal and professional reasons. Finally, during this interim between conventions, he also declined reelection as a commissioner for the Town of Edenton, a post he had held for a number of years.

The voters imposed an additional constraint. When Iredell sought election to the second ratification convention, he was defeated. John Mare, an articulate Federalist merchant, represented Edenton in his stead.[16]

Declinations and defeat notwithstanding, Iredell remained an energetic presence in the ratification effort. Among other endeavors, he joined fellow Federalists in circulating petitions requesting a second convention; Iredell worked the northeast, Maclaine the southeast, and Davie the west. Improving prospects spurred their persistence. Shortly post-Hillsborough, Hooper informed Iredell of Federalist successes in western county elections, and Maclaine soon notified him of a town meeting in Wilmington with only one dissent to a call for a new convention.[17]

The Antifederalists were by no means quiescent, however. In the immediate aftermath of Hillsborough, Willie Jones and Thomas Person urged opposition for another five or six years at least. Jones raised the specter of the federal judicial power and the ruinous consequences if people were required to pay their debts instantly. Religious as well as political forces weighed in against the Constitution, as Lemuel Burkitt, a Baptist minister, preached sermons opposing a strong federal government that would enslave the people. Samuel Johnston perceived a diminution in legislators' expectations for the Federalist cause, especially in the Senate, where many proponents of the Constitution were absent.[18]

Accordingly, the Federalists continued to cultivate fresh support. Maclaine apprised Iredell of a secret meeting at which Federalists had mustered a small majority. Antipathy between the competing forces persisted without abatement, however, as Maclaine expressed distrust of, and equally low esteem for, both Jones and Person. Jones' pride, he said, governed every other consideration, and he would sacrifice anything rather than the cause he had "so scandalously patronized."[19]

Samuel Johnston viewed the ratification schedule presciently. In November 1788, he foresaw no convention until the time of the Assembly session the next fall. By a close vote, the new Assembly indeed set an election in August 1789 for a second ratification convention to convene the following November.[20]

Meanwhile, Federalist hopes were buoyed. In January 1789, Hugh

Williamson shared with Iredell his pleasure that the Constitution would again be before the citizens of North Carolina. Iredell's own confidence was rising. In January 1789, he told an Edenton attorney he was confident the Constitution would be adopted "in November next." In February, Archibald Maclaine opined that a great majority would adopt the new government the next fall. In July, Iredell wrote Pierce Butler that the "obstinacy" would not last beyond November, "especially should capital amendment be proposed." In October, he informed Hannah that prospects from the back country as to the Constitution were excellent.[21]

Madison's announcement in the House of Representatives that he would offer amendments, made partly to encourage North Carolina to join the Union, helped to lower the Antifederalists' sails. In June 1789, Davie informed Iredell that "the Anties" in Halifax, while touting the prophecies that Congress would never consider amendments, had been "confounded...exceedingly" by news of Madison's move. Davie soon conveyed to Madison himself the considerable skepticism that had prevailed in North Carolina and the satisfaction and pleasure his notice had provided the state's Federalists. Pierce Butler, however, was less than sanguine about the genuineness of Madison's commitment; Madison would perhaps offer a few "milk-and-water" proposals, Butler opined, but he was "not hearty in the cause of amendments." Tristrim Lowther, a New York City merchant who had married Hannah Iredell's niece, also informed Iredell that the general opinion was one of doubt that amendments would be offered.[22]

The prospect of a convention without Iredell disappointed his Federalist compatriots. Fellow Edentonian Hugh Williamson had declared his availability for both the Assembly and the convention but would offer from other counties, and only for the convention, if Iredell could represent Edenton. Archibald Maclaine had fervently hoped Iredell could so order his law practice as to attend the convention, for it desperately needed men who could "prevent the majority from running into absurdity." John Steele deplored Iredell's anticipated absence, for there was no one else "from whom we might expect so much at the ensuing struggle."[23]

Iredell's absence from the forthcoming convention did not connote his withdrawal from the ratification effort or from national affairs generally. Shortly before the convention, he was still providing allies with pro-ratification propaganda for use in the back country. Earlier, John Swann had informed him from New York that Congress had prepared to give the new government effect. With its advent, correspondents enlightened Iredell regarding pending legislation and solicited his views. Tristrim Lowther sent him a copy of the proposed Judiciary Act of 1789 "principally drawn up by a Mr.

Ellsworth of Connecticut," with whom Iredell would later serve on the United States Supreme Court. South Carolina Senator Pierce Butler forwarded several pending bills and requested Iredell's opinion on those dealing with the judiciary, tonnage, and imposts.[24]

These informal exchanges between political leaders were not the only contacts between the now independent or foreign state and the new-sprung national government. In May 1789, the governor and Council of State sent President Washington a formal address of congratulation. As president of the Council, Iredell signed it, and its language evinces his style. While the state was not yet part of the Union, the script recited, it anticipated being so shortly. Meanwhile, it had common interests with, and affection for, other states, and waited only for alleviation of apprehensions many of its citizens harbored regarding liberties for which all states had fought and suffered. The state, the address concluded, wished and deserved to be warmly attached with others to "the true interest, prosperity, and glory of America," notwithstanding minor differences as to the means of promoting these concerns. Washington promptly responded, statesmanlike: "A difference of opinion on political points is not to be imputed to freemen as a fault." The decision facing the new delegates would, he said, determine the future political relationship between North Carolina and the states already aligned; it thus was momentous in its consequences, and he invoked divine benediction and guidance for those who would make it.[25]

This cordial exchange implied that both the state and national governments anticipated North Carolina's approaching ratification. Federalist confidence was not unbounded, however, and lingering Antifederalist sentiment and activity still rankled. Two months before the second convention, Archibald Maclaine fumed to Iredell that Anson County had again elected "[t]hat fool, Spencer." Maclaine anxiously awaited news of whether Willie Jones, the Antifederalists' leader at Hillsborough, would again be a delegate. (Jones ultimately did not seek election, probably because he foresaw the Antifederalists' impending defeat.) On a more-positive note, Maclaine thought many "well-meaning members who [were] ashamed of being led by the nose last year" would now "prove very restive." John Steele, though, still thought a struggle loomed; except for Iredell's own district, he told his Edenton ally, the state remained "much divided." Immediately prior to the convention, Samuel Johnston perceived that while supporters of the Constitution expected to prevail by a large majority, "violent and virulent" opposition persisted. Davie, like Steele, had residual doubts; on the convention's opening day, he told Iredell that while the Constitution's friends said there was no doubt, he was not so confident.[26]

Davie's lingering fears proved unfounded. Five days later, after the Antifederalist minority again sought to postpone ratification pending adoption of amendments, the convention voted 195 to 77 to ratify. The turnabout was dramatic. Only fifteen and one-half months earlier, delegates at Hillsborough had refused approval by a margin almost as large. Except in dispersed areas, the state's political sands had shifted, leaving the Federalists clearly in control. Considerably relieved, Davie thought the substantial majority for ratification would not only satisfy friends of the new government, but also give weight to its operation in the state.[27]

Several factors influenced the reversal. Washington's administration was operating the new government in an orderly and effective manner, inspiring confidence at home and respect abroad. Returning economic prosperity, in which North Carolina shared, enhanced the prestige of the new government and confirmed Federalist arguments that the new Constitution offered enhanced benefaction for property, commerce, manufacturing, and both public and private credit. Because the state traded through the ports of Virginia and South Carolina, its economic lifelines were now at the mercy of the new national government; Antifederalist farmers knew that a foreign nation now controlled the interests of both agriculture and commerce. The state was sensitive to the unsavory reputation for radicalism and paper money of Rhode Island, its lone companion in holdout status. It recognized, too, that it was incapable of defending itself militarily against Indians or foreign powers. Madison's proposal and Congress' passage of amendments also aided the Federalist cause. Finally, the educational efforts by Federalist newspapers and leaders, particularly Iredell and Davie, clearly had an impact.[28]

Iredell received warm accolades as a principal architect of the Federalist triumph. From the convention, William Dawson congratulated him on "the happy decision of the important question which has so long and so violently agitated the State." Governor Samuel Johnston and Senate Speaker Charles Johnson wrote similarly. No one had the change in sentiment more at heart or contributed more to produce it, Johnson said; it was a "glorious event," which must have given Iredell "the most singular satisfaction." Archibald Maclaine congratulated Iredell "on the happy change in our situation." Richard Dobbs Spaight thanked him for the "agreeable information" that North Carolina had at length ratified. "[W]isdom has at last presided in our councils," he said, "and enabled the Convention to break through that cloud of ignorance and villainy which has so long obscured our political horizon."[29]

On December 1, 1789, the Federalists celebrated at Edenton. At sunrise a flagstaff in the center of town flew the Union flag, and vessels in the harbor displayed the colors. A salute of twelve twenty-four pounders was fired at noon, and at a dinner in the tavern, twelve toasts were drunk. In the evening the courthouse cupola was illuminated, and from the flagstaff twelve lighted lanterns, representing the twelve adopting states, hung beside a dark one imaging Rhode Island. There was a large bonfire. "Pleasure, joy and satisfaction sat on every countenance," the staunchly Federalist newspaper at Edenton reported, "and the day concluded with that harmony and concord which federal principles always must command."[30]

Surely James Iredell derived the utmost satisfaction from ultimate success in the ratification effort. Shortly before the Edenton celebration, he apprised Hannah that he was at ease about public affairs. "My heart," he now could say, "is . . . as light as a feather." He simultaneously admitted, however, that despair and apprehension had gripped him so thoroughly and so long that he found it difficult to relax. With reunion accomplished and celebrated, perhaps the now-buoyant defender of the Constitution, the acknowledged leader for ratification, could unwind a bit.[31]

III

The Jurist

It doth appear you are a worthy judge;
You know the law, your exposition
Hath been most sound; I charge you by the law,
Whereof you are a well-deserving pillar....

—William Shakespeare
(The Merchant of Venice)

CHAPTER 9

A High and Important Office

I REDELL'S RESPITE WOULD BE BRIEF. EVEN BEFORE RATIFICATION, HIS ACQUAINTANCES SPECULATED ABOUT HIS FUTURE. PIERCE BUTLER WANTED HIS LONGTIME FRIEND IN THE UNITED STATES SENATE; THE "SOUTHERN INTEREST," HE SAID, CALLED FOR MEN LIKE IREDELL TO represent it, to "do it justice." Hugh Williamson, though, conveyed another senator's inquiry as to whether Iredell would accept a federal judgeship, even if it meant moving, since North Carolina was not yet in the Union. Williamson also recommended Iredell to President Washington for a federal judgeship before North Carolina joined the Union. Following ratification, Archibald Maclaine inquired of Iredell's availability for the federal district judgeship for North Carolina; he thought financial considerations might dictate Iredell's practicing in the federal courts instead. "We have a great lack of men to fill law departments," Maclaine lamented. Iredell himself thought he would be the federal judge for North Carolina (and Governor Alexander Martin recommended him for it, apparently unaware of Iredell's appointment to the Supreme Court a few days before), though he disavowed even "the least solicitation" for it.[1]

Unlike Iredell, Samuel Spencer, his former colleague on the state bench, immodestly viewed himself as Supreme Court material, the political obstacles from his virulent antifederalism notwithstanding. Dissatisfied by the General Assembly's withholding of a judicial salary increase, Spencer, in Samuel Johnston's words, was willing to offer his services to the United States and would "condescend" to serve on the Supreme Court or the District Court. Johnston thought neither William Cushing nor John Rutledge would accept a Supreme Court appointment; and Spencer, Johnston said, did not doubt his equality in ability or reputation with either of them. Spencer had asked

William R. Davie to recommend him, and Johnston expected a similar request. Whatever the endorsements obtained, it was not to be; Spencer's former compatriot, James Iredell, would don the federal robe instead.[2]

President Washington was ambitious for the federal judiciary of the infant American republic. Its initial arrangement, he told Edmund Randolph, was "essential to the happiness of [the] country, and to the stability of its political system." Consequently, he told James Madison, he sought "the first characters of the Union" for his inceptive judicial appointments.[3]

Iredell had followed the progress of the federal Judiciary Act of 1789, pursuant to which these appointments would be made; as noted, Tristrim Lowther had sent him drafts of the bill "drawn up by a Mr. Ellsworth from Connecticut." Within two days of the bill's enactment, the president appointed, and the Senate promptly confirmed, six justices for the original Supreme Court. The chief justice, John Jay, had been chief justice of New York. Three of the associates—John Blair, John Rutledge, and James Wilson—had been delegates to the Constitutional Convention in Philadelphia. William Cushing, a noted Massachusetts jurist who had presided over the Massachusetts ratification convention, and Robert Hanson Harrison, a prominent Maryland judge and Washington's comrade-in-arms in the Revolution, completed the roster.[4]

Years later Felix Frankfurter would ask, "Who were these Justices who came on the Supreme Court without any 'judicial service,' without even the judicial experience of an Iredell, who at the age of twenty-six sat on the Superior Court of his state... only long enough—six months—to resign." The captious appraisal the question implies is at least somewhat unfair. While the judicial experience of Washington's initial appointees was indeed limited, all had been substantial lawyers, legal scholars, and/or political leaders in their respective states. As the president had wished, all brought distinguished biographies to the inaugural Court.[5]

Washington's search was not over, however, for five days after his confirmation, Harrison declined the appointment. He had been designated chancellor of Maryland, and he preferred that position. Further, his health was fragile, the circuit travel requirements were unsatisfactory, and Supreme Court service would interfere with his private affairs. Harrison died on April 2, 1790, just before the Court held its first session; his tenure thus would have been quite transient in any event.[6]

The vacuum thus created was momentary, for the president soon named another "first character," James Iredell of North Carolina. Thirty-eight years old when appointed, Iredell remains one of the youngest persons ever to occupy the high bench. He had come to Washington's attention at least as early as his twenty-fifth year, when Joseph Hewes forwarded to Washington Iredell's letter on his thoughts of returning to England. The letter was not answered, which ultimately quite suited Iredell since he had abandoned such thoughts. It is unlikely that Washington recalled the episode, and there is no evidence suggesting a relationship between the two prior to Iredell's Supreme Court tenure.[7]

Samuel Johnston was a confidant of the president and his administration, however. Shortly after North Carolina ratified the Constitution, Johnston, apparently with both Federalist and Antifederalist support, agreed to fill one of North Carolina's seats in the United States Senate. This service spawned intimate relationships with President Washington and Vice-President Adams. The day before Harrison's letter to Washington citing ill health as a reason for refusing the Supreme Court appointment, Johnston informed Iredell that he had waited unsuccessfully on the president, who was "abroad," but had visited the vice-president at his country abode. Six days before Iredell's appointment, Johnston wrote of dining at the president's with the vice-president, the Supreme Court justices, the attorney general, and the secretary of war. He soon told of dining at the president's with most of the Senate and having coffee with the first lady.[8]

Not surprisingly, then, the initial intimations of Iredell's impending appointment came through Johnston. Johnston first informed his young brother-in-law that the president had "inquired particularly" about him and spoken of him "in a manner that gave me great pleasure." Three days later, the president disclosed the reason for his inquiry, which must have excited Johnston's pupil to the point of exhilaration. The senator had just received a message from the president, he said, inquiring whether Iredell would accept an appointment to the Supreme Court vacancy created by Harrison's withdrawal. Johnston hoped to forward Iredell's commission by the next post.[9]

Johnston noted that some eastern (northern) senators initially opposed Iredell's appointment, preferring someone from their own region. If there was a specific candidate, Johnston did not identify him. In stark contrast to many modern-day confirmation proceedings, Iredell's moved facilely, and the appointment attained ultimate unanimity. Iredell was not generally known among the senators, but his South Carolina friend Pierce Butler posted them on his qualifications. A New Hampshire senator, while expressing confidence in Butler, wanted to hear from the candidate's home-state senators. Benjamin Hawkins, Johnston's colleague from North Carolina, thereupon confirmed Butler's accolades and added some of his own. "[T]he Senate," Johnston said, "were then perfectly satisfied."[10]

A cordial exchange followed between the president and his appointee.

Washington forwarded Iredell's commission, disavowing any need to impress upon him the importance of the judicial system in every government, and particularly this one. The system was a principal pillar upon which the national administration must rest, he said, and he thus had sought judges who would bring dignity and stability to the regime and add luster to the national character. Iredell responded with humble gratitude for his appointment to "the high and important office" of associate justice. He was resolved, he vouched, to apply himself unremittingly to the task and to discharge the duties faithfully to the utmost.[11]

The reasons for Iredell's appointment were many. His limited judicial experience, while pertinent, hardly qualified him for this august station. His "Answers" to Mason had attracted national attention and was almost certainly a factor. The most-significant reason, however, was the profound grasp of constitutional questions Iredell displayed in promoting ratification at Hillsborough. The debates there garnered national attention; Washington perused them and was impressed with the youthful leader's ability. Finally, the president wished to reward North Carolina for joining the Union, and the prize appropriately went to the man who had done the most to accomplish the ratification task. North Carolina was underrepresented in the Federalist administration, and one component of Iredell's appointment was to cement the state to the Union. Washington candidly so acknowledged. He had appointed Iredell for his abilities, legal knowledge, and respectable character, the president affirmed; but it had mattered that he was "of a State of some importance in the Union that ha[d] given *No* character to a federal office."[12]

Iredell's lofty promotion did not terminate Samuel Johnston's didactic relationship with him. The senator was soon advising the new jurist on proper decorum; Iredell need not write the Senate, Johnston counseled, but he should write the president and the two principal Senate sponsors of the nomination, Butler and Hawkins. Butler in particular, Johnston noted, had "acted a very friendly part" in the confirmation process. The judges would ride the circuits in rotation, Johnston observed, with the Southern Circuit initially assigned to Iredell and Rutledge. While uncertain as to proper attire for the circuit bench, he thought Iredell's "Bar-Gown" would suffice as a temporary expedient.[13]

Iredell's friends were ebullient and congratulatory. Judge Samuel Ashe thanked him for informing the state's judges of his appointment. Ashe expressed joy and sadness intermingled. Sensible of the state's loss, he was nevertheless pleased to see an associate elevated to "an office of such dignity and importance," one he would undoubtedly fill with enhanced reputation and complete public satisfaction. "While you sit," Ashe concluded, "every jealousy and fear will subside, and every apprehension of encroachment from the newly erected jurisdiction will cease."

Judge Samuel Spencer, his own hopes for the position now dashed, was equally congratulatory. He had enjoyed Iredell's company on the bench and at the bar, and he regretted the loss. The benefit to the public and to Iredell himself was some solace, however.

Joseph Blount, the clerk at Edenton, also regretted the loss to the bar but applauded the president's choice; the county would not soon forget Iredell's many services, he said, and no one was ever more deserving. While Pierce Butler had wanted his friend in Congress, he rejoiced that the Union would no longer be deprived of Iredell's abilities; moving his family to the North would be both healthier for them and more convenient for Iredell, Butler gratuitously advised. John Swann, like Butler, had hoped Iredell would offer for Congress but now rejoiced that he had not. Archibald Maclaine, who learned of the appointment from a New York newspaper, was pleased that the president had acted spontaneously rather than from Johnston's importunings; unanimity in the confirmation process also gratified him.[14]

Other friends were solicitous of Iredell's welfare. Fayetteville lawyer John Hay offered the new jurist lodging while he was en route to and from South Carolina on circuit duty. Halifax attorney John Haywood, while exceedingly pleased, fretted that fatigue from the job might undermine Iredell's health (it would) but wished him much profit and happiness.[15]

Iredell's friends wrote not only to him but to their other friends as well. Benjamin Hawkins, for example, wrote to William Blount, one of North Carolina's delegates to the Constitutional Convention, to tell him of the appointment.[16]

Family members were somewhat overwhelmed. His brother's elevation made Arthur Iredell "extremely vain." While James had always brought him pride, this was a real triumph. His sibling would justify the choice, Arthur predicted confidently, and his life would influence "the remotest corners" of the vast American continent.[17]

Intimations of impending duties soon intruded on the felicitations. While Chief Justice Jay did not know Iredell, he found his appointment quite satisfactory and was highly congratulatory. The most onerous of the circuit assignments would not wait, however; Iredell would indeed take the Southern Circuit, along with John Rutledge.[18]

Iredell himself shared in this effusive, epistolary humor. His response to Hugh Williamson's inquiry about his interest in a federal judgeship reveals marked judicial ambition. Such a position would be quite agreeable, he told Williamson, if the salary permitted him to devote full time to it; indeed, no employment would better suit him. While removal from the state would be painful, it was not an insuperable objection.[19]

While this mood lingered, Iredell again sought reconciliation with his estranged uncle. His missive offers insights into the duties and compensation of the justices, the organization of the circuits, and Iredell's attitude toward the appointment. The change in his situation, he wrote, had been extraordinary and unexpected, for he had made no solicitation for an appointment to "the high & important office." While the duties would be severe, the station was so honorable and the income so considerable ($3,500 a year) that he had accepted with gratitude. The Court would sit at the capital twice annually. A circuit court would also sit twice annually in each state, with two justices of the Supreme Court and a judge of that state serving, any two of whom would constitute a quorum.

The letter failed to evoke a response. Once again, Iredell's efforts at expiation brought only stony silence from Jamaica.[20]

Iredell was genuinely surprised and diffident during this period. He truly had thought he would at most be the federal district judge for North Carolina, and he had not sought even that. The designation as associate justice was, he said, "beyond my most sanguine hopes." "This high appointment was as much beyond my expectations as I fear it is above my merit," he told his new colleague John Rutledge; the "respectable characters" of his fellow jurists would, however, make him strive to be worthy of the position. He had accepted the important trust "with a becoming diffidence," he told Chief Justice Jay, but he hoped to secure the approbation of his colleagues.[21]

Correspondence was hardly Iredell's sole activity at this juncture. Foremost among his many duties was the closing of his law practice and the settling of personal affairs. Notices in an Edenton newspaper mitigated these tasks. He would be "under the necessity of leaving the state in a short time in order to discharge a public duty," he advertised to his townsmen. Those indebted to him thus should pay, and those to whom he was indebted should render accounts. As his initial departure for the Southern Circuit approached, he informed them further that Samuel Tredwell (the husband of Hannah's niece) and Thomas Iredell (the justice's brother) had his power-of-attorney; all remaining matters should now be settled with them.

William R. Davie, Iredell's closest compeer in the ratification struggle, assumed much of the justice's law practice. Archibald Maclaine had informed Iredell that Davie, believing Iredell would be the district judge, had declared an intent to practice at Edenton and thought he would inherit Iredell's business. Davie later confirmed that Iredell could rely on him in Halifax, Edenton, and New Bern, except in instances where he was previously employed.[22]

The trite expression "life would never be the same" fit. Iredell would continue to devote himself to the law but not to his clients. He would develop close, highly supportive relationships with George Washington, John Adams, and their Federalist administrations. Above all, he would log mile after mile riding the federal circuits.

CHAPTER 10

An Associate of Presidents

Whigh hile Iredell had not known Washington, he had long been the president's unblushing admirer. He paid him perhaps the ultimate compliment by putting his birthday on a par with Hannah's; he could no more forget one, he said, than the other. He shared with Hannah his concern when Washington's horse and carriage were inundated while passing a bridge after their passenger had exited. "What a dreadful misfortune it would have been had he remained in the carriage," Iredell remarked.[1]

Friends and relatives reinforced this attachment, calling Washington's a great name by which those of other leaders would be measured. Samuel Johnston in particular bolstered his pupil's devotion to the president and his administration. Washington's 1791 reception in Halifax, North Carolina (while on his Southern Tour, for which he had sought Iredell's advice as to the best routes), fell below Johnston's wishes, the senator informed Iredell; but the president received proper attention elsewhere. The Washington government, Johnston later told Iredell, had "done more good than any other so circumstanced ever did in the same space of time"; it had substantially reduced the public debt, while simultaneously enhancing commerce, manufacturing, agriculture, and the arts. Finally, as the Washington era neared its end point, Johnston predicted to his student that "every lover of virtue and patriotism" would rejoice over the president's enhanced popularity. "[W]ere his virtues less conspicuous," Johnston concluded, "he would be less envied and ... have fewer enemies."[2]

Iredell's sentiments mirrored Johnston's. "The friends of the government are now universally in great alarm," he told Hannah when passage of an administration-sponsored treaty was in doubt. Commentary cordial to the president personally eased the tension, however. Treaty opponents honored themselves and gladdened all but the most insensible by speaking of the president himself in "uncommonly warm and animated terms," said Iredell. He later sent Washington's Farewell Address to Hannah, noting that it had received the highest admiration and that even the president's political opponents had approved.[3]

Early in the original Supreme Court's tenure, Washington conveyed to the justices his cognizance of the Court's importance. Stability and happiness depended in no small degree on the proper interpretation and execution of the laws, he told his appointees, thus necessitating an independent judiciary "as perfect as possible in its formation." As they commenced their first circuit in an "unexplored field," he invited the judges to communicate with him on this subject as they deemed expedient.[4]

Iredell took the president seriously. Responding explicitly to this invitation, he informed Washington that he considered himself duty-bound to expose difficulties or inconveniences he experienced in implementing the untried system. He then detailed two situations he had encountered while on the Southern Circuit. One concerned the undue haste with which a stay for application for a writ of error expired, thereby allowing an immediate execution while a party yet might ultimately prevail. The other involved a provision allowing a state to interplead, without the original litigants' consent, in a case ultimately involving the state's interest. He would have written sooner, Iredell told the president, had he not thought corrective amendments to the Judiciary Act were forthcoming. Because circuit time was rapidly approaching, however, he could no longer justify delay. Washington forwarded the letter to the appropriate cabinet secretaries for comments; eventually, Congress responded to the first problem by authorizing circuit clerks to issue the writs in question.[5]

Iredell treated the president's epistolary proffer as encompassing both official and purely social communications. Shortly after commencing his duties, he wrote Washington from Alexandria that he was mortified to be so nearby yet unable to visit him. Family illness had detained him in New York, he explained, and he had "business of consequence" to transact in North Carolina before proceeding to Georgia on the Southern Circuit. He was grateful for the civilities and attention the president and first lady had bestowed upon him and Mrs. Iredell, and he ardently wished them happiness.[6]

Social interaction between the Washingtons and the Iredells was commonplace. Hannah resided in the capital from 1790–93 and attended Martha Washington's social functions, once observing that the room was so crowded she "could hardly squeeze through to make her a curtsey." Iredell dined with the president frequently. He spoke with him and the first lady at other times, gave Hannah reports on their health, and conveyed presidential greetings to Hannah and to Mrs. Samuel Johnston. On one occasion he even received travel advice from the highest executive level, choosing one route by Richmond over an alternate because "the President rather discouraged my going the other."[7]

Iredell chronicled the Washington years, reporting not only their melancholy occurrences such as Polly Lear's death (*see supra* Prologue), but also their joyous ones. He gave special heed to the president's birthday parties, which were crowded, highly celebratory events. The final one during the presidential years not only observed a birth anniversary but also commenced a farewell commemoration. It was celebrated, Iredell related, "with every possible mark of attachment, affection, and respect, rendered affecting beyond all expression by its being in some degree a parting scene." The first lady, Iredell observed, was moved to tears, both by the outpouring of public respect and the imminent prospect of continual domestic life. The president, too, experienced "emotions...too powerful to be concealed." He partied until between midnight and 1:00 a.m.; the vice-president stayed until nearly 2:00. "[R]epeated huzzahs," Iredell stated, continued long after both had retired.[8]

In view of Iredell's fastidious memorializing of the capital's celebrations, his hometown's failure to observe similar rites surely disappointed him. In Edenton the day passed unnoticed, Hannah's niece informed him; she presciently forecast that it would always be a distinguished one in America, however.[9]

Iredell served as a conduit for transmittal of information and opinions between North Carolina leaders and the federal administration. William R. Davie, for example, once wrote Alexander Hamilton, secretary of the treasury, that he had asked Iredell to secure Hamilton's opinion on a matter for him. Iredell also was perceived to have influence on federal patronage and appointments. Abraham Hodge, Iredell's printer in Edenton, once sought his assistance in getting a young man appointed as a federal inspector for North Carolina. The youth's northern friends, Hodge said, considered Iredell's "interest with the President" such that his support would leave little doubt of success. When John Rutledge resigned from the Supreme Court in 1791, Georgia District Judge Nathaniel Pendleton solicited Iredell's aid in securing the appointment. A minister sought Iredell's assistance in obtaining a military chaplaincy, and William R. Davie implicitly solicited his support for a district court judgeship for Davie's wife's brother-in-law, John Sitgreaves.[10]

There is no record of Iredell's response to these appeals. Sitgreaves was appointed, Pendleton was not, and the fate of the inspectorship and chaplaincy aspirants is unknown. While Iredell claimed that he refused to solicit advancements for others while on the bench, it appears that he was inconsistent in this respect, or at least that, in the modern vernacular, the administration "checked out" certain appointments with him. In 1793 Tench Coxe, assistant secretary of the treasury, wrote Alexander Hamilton that inquiries had been made of Justice Iredell and the two North Carolina senators concerning the position of commissioners of pilotage. Coxe reported that the three agreed on two candidates, saying they knew no persons in North Carolina more suitable.[11]

Whatever his weight on behalf of others, Iredell was unable to influence, on his own behalf, one of Washington's most-significant appointments. In 1795 John Jay resigned as chief justice, having been elected governor of New York. Alexander Hamilton declined the appointment, and the Senate rejected Washington's nomination of John Rutledge. Patrick Henry then refused the post, as did William Cushing, the eldest justice. Cushing did so, in Iredell's words, "with an extraordinary degree of moderation" for reasons of age and health. "I don't know whether a less exceptionable character can be obtained without passing over [Justice] Wilson," Samuel Johnston wrote Iredell, "which would perhaps be a measure that could not be easily reconciled to strict propriety."

This indeed proved to be Washington's dilemma. He wanted to appoint Iredell, whose ability he admired, but the perceived propriety dictated that he not promote Iredell over Wilson, who was his senior on the Court. Wilson was deeply involved in land-speculation ventures which ultimately proved his ruination, both financially and physically; his designation thus could have been embarrassing. The president resolved the problem by appointing Oliver Ellsworth, drafter of the Judiciary Act, from the practicing bar.

Arthur Iredell had craved the appointment for his sibling, dreaming of seeing him as the foremost figure of the law on the American continent. James apparently suggested to him that Cushing should get the nod, but Arthur was unconvinced. Cushing might be a worthy man, Arthur said, but he would continue to think his brother should be the top magistrate. Accordingly, he was "sensibly mortified" when Ellsworth received the position, for he had concluded that Washington could not justly withhold it from Iredell. Indeed, he thought selecting the chief justice from the practicing bar was "very improper & injudicious" anywhere.

By contrast, Iredell was altogether stoic. The expectations of his friends were too flattering, he said, and bypassing Wilson for him would have been improper. He graciously predicted that Ellsworth, a man of understanding and business, would fill the office with distinction.[12]

Iredell steadfastly promoted and defended the Washington government. None of the departments were idle or sinecures, he told a friend. The secretaries of treasury (Alexander Hamilton), state (Thomas Jefferson), and war

(Henry Knox) had the most-difficult tasks, he said, with Hamilton and Jefferson experiencing infinite trouble but performing with uncommon abilities.[13]

The North Carolina General Assembly's directive to the state's federal senators to oppose any administration-sponsored excise or direct tax drew Iredell's forceful criticism. An instruction to withhold consent except in case of absolute necessity would have been grudgingly acceptable to him, but opposition in all events was abhorrent. Did the state wish the country's safety endangered and its government made a mockery merely to gratify North Carolina's wishes in the face of irresistible necessity? he asked sardonically.[14]

The Assembly apparently read public sentiment more accurately than did Iredell and the Federalist administration, for an excise tax imposed on the production of distilled spirits generated the new government's foremost domestic opposition and difficulties. Hamilton proposed the tax, and Congress levied it in 1791. In doing so, they challenged not only a long history of opposition to internal taxes but also an essential agrarian commodity, a social practice, and a way of life. In Kentucky, Thomas Marshall, the father of future Chief Justice John Marshall, enforced the tax with difficulty; in North Carolina, it was virtually unenforceable.

The tax ultimately resulted in violence in western Pennsylvania when warrants were served on distillers who had not paid it. Further resentment ensued when the violators were required to appear before the federal district court in Philadelphia rather than before local or state courts. Shots were fired, a federal marshal and an inspector were forced to flee, and a mob burned the inspector's house after the mob's leader was killed. Several counties organized for resistance, and the disaffection spread. When Washington dispatched troops, however, the insurrection was quelled, and the power of the new government was amply demonstrated.[15]

In defending the tax, Iredell reverted to his old form as a political essayist. Perhaps in deference to his position on the Supreme Court, he wrote anonymously merely as "A CITIZEN OF PENNSYLVANIA" (where he maintained his residence from 1790–93) addressing himself "TO THE CITIZENS OF THE UNITED STATES." Unpopular excises were lamentable, he acknowledged, but necessary to support the public credit; without them, an even more-objectionable direct tax would be essential. Accordingly, he acquiesced "in the consequences of a necessity I cannot control." Unlike in England, where necessities were taxed, this excise extended only to distilled spirits, hardly "a necessary of life." Finally, procedural safeguards, including the right to trial by jury, he thought ample.[16]

When the letter was published in Philadelphia's *Federal Gazette*, Iredell's family and friends must have perceived his authorship. They clearly knew of his fervid support for the administration's position, for he had given Hannah a particularized account of the rebellion and had forwarded newspaper reports of it to Samuel Johnston. Johnston, a hardliner, fervently hoped "a few examples will be made to discourage such doings in the future." "A little wholesome severity," he thought, would "bring [the violators] to a proper sense of their duty." The ultimate resolution, he opined finally, was highly honorable to the government and should confirm its friends and "overawe" its enemies.[17]

Iredell's friends viewed the administration's success as his personal triumph. Davie congratulated him "on the happy termination of the whiskey business," noting that the affair had worn "an ugly aspect" but that the president's "decision and energy" had prevailed. Iredell, in turn, conveyed felicitations to the commander of the army assembled to quash the revolt. It was a "glorious success," he told Henry ("Light Horse Harry") Lee, father of Robert E. Lee, that would have the happy effect of repressing a spirit of discontent while simultaneously enhancing the government's status with other nations. Lee replied with gratitude, observing that his comrades-in-arms truly merited the applause of their countrymen.[18]

Over a year later, Iredell continued to exult in the government's conquest. In charging the federal grand jury for Pennsylvania, he recalled the events "with emotion and gratitude." A large part of the state was in open insurrection, he said, caused by the seduction and prevarication of "a few designing men." The government, he continued, responded with an appropriate blend of diplomacy and force, fulfilling its duty to suppress rebellion by every constitutional means but only after more-humane efforts had failed. Patriots performed their duties, some despite disagreement with the government's measures. The ultimate resolution had been irenic. "Not a drop of blood was hostilely shed," Iredell noted. Amnesty had been offered and accepted, and mercy had been extended to the only two malefactors convicted. There was in the episode, he concluded didactically, a lesson for governments and people everywhere.[19]

Iredell's innominate letter "TO THE CITIZENS OF THE UNITED STATES" perhaps best expressed the philosophical roots of this animated support for Washington's policies and the measures employed to enforce them. Reverting to his ratification-era utterances, Iredell observed that he had always considered a union of the states essential to their safety and prosperity. Mutual jealousies and unfounded suspicions endangered the Union; he therefore had rejoiced when a government was formed to promote the common interest. He deplored the distortion and calumny to which the Congress was subjected, while observing sagaciously that such "is unfortunately the lot of almost all who are in public stations." The welfare of the Union demanded more, however. The well-being of every state and every individual was inseparably interwoven with that of the Union, he concluded, and the Union's survival demanded a proper degree of confidence in those to whom the government was entrusted.[20]

Iredell the chronicler reemerged in the waning days of the Washington presidency. He recorded the 1796 election of John Adams as president and Thomas Jefferson as vice-president (an election in which Iredell himself received three of North Carolina's electoral votes for president) and rejoiced that the two had seemingly buried their differences. There was no doubt that Jefferson would serve as Adams' vice-president, he recounted; indeed, the two were speaking of each other "with great personal esteem," and Jefferson "did not think the choice could fall on a fitter man" than Adams. Iredell described Adams' final address to the Senate as "a very affecting scene" and again prayed for both unremitting harmony between Adams and Jefferson and "that the violence of party spirit will subside."

It was a time of much celebration and commemoration. Iredell enjoyed a final dinner with the president. Mrs. Washington sent her respects to Hannah. Iredell fondly anticipated Mrs. Washington's last drawing room, though fully cognizant that he would be "much moved." The departing president received "affecting proofs" of the reverence for him throughout the Union, said Iredell. Philadelphia merchants sponsored a dinner in the president's honor, his wishes to the contrary notwithstanding. The president was equally unsuccessful in preventing "the Light Horse" from escorting him out of the city, again contrary to his personal preference to go privately.

Iredell finally recounted Washington's course on Adams' inaugural day. Washington, he said, attended "as a private gentleman" and was the first to greet the new president. The crowds so overwhelmed him, however, that he reached his lodgings with difficulty. He emerged to be accompanied to his own house "with unbounded applause." Both he and Adams received "the warmest shouts of approbation" before Washington and his family departed from the capital.[21]

Routine collaboration between Washington and Iredell apparently terminated with Washington's retirement from the presidency. Correspondents kept Iredell informed regarding the former president's well-being, however. Charles Lee, the United States attorney general, once wrote, for example: "General Washington is well, but not so firm in his health as usual." Iredell attempted to maintain contact but was episodically thwarted by circumstances. A few months before Iredell's death, which preceded Washington's by only a few weeks, he informed Hannah that an extra day in Alexandria would have afforded the opportunity for a visit with Washington. "[P]riority in the stage," however, did not allow him to linger. His commitment to the friendship obviously persisted unabated, for he reported to Hannah with some élan events of interest in the Washington family.[22]

Iredell thought Washington, had he permitted it, would have been re-elected unanimously; he was less than fully confident of John Adams' election, however. He thus was jubilant when the vice-president's succession was assured. "The choice," he said, "could not have fallen on an abler or worthier man." Every party maneuver and even French influence were employed against the vice-president, Iredell related, yet no aspersions were cast on his private or public character despite over two decades in high positions.[23]

Adams' ascension insured that Iredell's intimate relationship with, and animated support for, the national administration remained intact. The Adams-Iredell association predated Adams' presidency. Their prior acquaintance is illustrated by an occasion in the final year of the Washington era; the two sat together in the House of Representatives as Fisher Ames defended the administration's position on the Jay Treaty with Britain. Both Adams and Iredell were quite captivated by the Boston orator's rhetoric. Adams wrote his wife:

> Judge Iredell and I happened to sit together. Our feelings beat in unison. "My God! how great he is," says Iredell, "how great he has been!" "He has been noble!" said I. After some time, Iredell breaks out, "Bless my stars, I never heard any thing so great since I was born." "It is divine," said I; and thus we went on with our interjections, not to say tears, till the end. Tears enough were shed.

By his own account, Iredell viewed the speech as one of Ames' "greatest and most eloquent."[24]

This previous affiliation perhaps accounts (though seniority would also) for Iredell's being chosen, with Justices Cushing and Wilson, to attend Chief Justice Ellsworth as he administered President Adams' oath. Iredell then sat with his Court colleagues in the House of Representatives as Adams presented his inaugural address. Iredell's family members knew intuitively that he would be there. "You...have by this time seen the new President installed in office...if I mistake not," Hannah's niece wrote him. Samuel Johnston rejoiced over the event and requested that Iredell convey his compliments to the new leader. Johnston's delight was tempered, however, by his prescient concern that economic constraints could exclude relatively impecunious aspirants from the office in the future. Congress' refusal to enhance the salaries of the president and vice-president, he lamented, would either deter the unprosperous or open them to indelicate means of acquisition.[25]

Iredell now chronicled Adams' administration as he had Washington's. The inauguration was an "affecting scene," he wrote, and the inaugural address produced the highest satisfaction, even to some who had held uncharitable views of Washington's successor. A perceived amelioration of the tension between Adams and Jefferson drew Iredell's approbation. Before the inauguration he had noted that the two were speaking of each other with great personal esteem and that Jefferson "did not think the choice could fall on a fitter man than...Adams." He now observed every appearance of harmony between them, as they lodged together and appeared to be on very friendly terms. Iredell prayed that such would continue, thereby allaying "that vile party-spirit which does so much injury to our country." Justice William Paterson joined in that entreaty, believing parties rendered the country "the sport of every foreign breeze that blows."[26]

With the appearance (it ultimately would prove illusory) of harmony between the president and vice-president established, Iredell concerned himself with relations between the executive and the Congress, and thus with congressional elections. Correspondents posted him on the election of supporters of the Federalist administration. William R. Davie once noted that elections in Halifax were still in doubt and that New Bern and Washington had elected men favorable to Washington but opposed to Adams. Candidates in western North Carolina, he said, were decidedly pro-administration and thus quite promising. Later, Samuel Johnston wrote that there would be a majority against the anti-Adams candidate in all but two counties in his district; the only hope for that candidate, in Johnston's view, was the prospect of votes so thoroughly divided among the many other candidates.[27]

Federalist prospects in North Carolina improved with the election of 1798. One correspondent briefed Iredell on several contests, concluding that his area's representation in the next Congress could be as favorable to the government as the existing delegation was unfavorable. Iredell's brother Thomas, now living in Edenton (see *infra* Chapter 18), informed him similarly and congratulated him on this agreeable shift in fortune.[28]

Iredell's interest in Federalist electoral success was not confined to his home state. Charles Lee of Virginia, the United States attorney general, noted to him the pleasant change in North Carolina and hoped Virginia would follow suit. He informed Iredell that John Marshall and Bushrod Washington were candidates and that he thought most of Virginia's Federalist aspirants would prevail. Some at least, including Marshall, did, and Samuel Johnston congratulated Iredell on these elections. Earlier, Johnston had lain bare his own bias by observing that a state senator whom he thought would be re-elected was "wonderfully federal."[29]

One writer asserts that "Iredell [and other justices] all openly supported their favorite candidate in the turn-of-the-century elections." Iredell died in October 1799 (see *infra* Chapter 21), well before the election of 1800; insofar as it relates to him, the conclusion thus appears mistaken, unless it refers to activities well in advance of the voting date. The historical record does not disclose such overt electioneering on Iredell's part, but his consistent covert involvement on behalf of Federalist candidates is virtually certain. Indeed, that his brother and brother-in-law would congratulate him on the election of Federalist representatives demonstrates how thoroughly they identified him with the Adams administration. In 1799, the year of Iredell's death, Samuel Johnston even wished that Iredell might preserve his health so he could "enjoy the politics of the place [Philadelphia] and the full triumph of the administrators and friends of our government over the malice of their enemies."[30]

Johnston occasionally fretted to Iredell about Adams' decisions on policies, but his criticism was muted—perhaps because of his own sensitivities, perhaps because he well knew Iredell's. When Adams appointed an officeholder Johnston considered unqualified, Johnston regretted to Iredell that the president had "given cause of umbrage to his friends." He hoped flattery did not leave Adams overconfident and lead him into "some scrape fatal to his own reputation and unfortunate for his country." Johnston soon wrote his pupil again, finding it extraordinary that the president had appointed ministers to meet with the French Republic but acknowledging that Adams probably possessed information unavailable to the public.

Such episodic carping notwithstanding, on one occasion the North Carolina General Assembly's faint praise for the president upset Johnston. Its address should have been more admiring of Adams' abilities and integrity, Johnston opined to Iredell, but sensitivity to the electors who had voted against him, one of whom assisted in preparing the address, had prevented it.[31]

Johnston knew Adams before Iredell did and would send his regards to the president and other Philadelphia acquaintances via Iredell. Iredell's social interaction with Adams, like that with Washington, allowed ample opportunity to convey such salutations. From the commencement of Adams' term until Iredell's demise two-and-one-half years later, the president and the justice were social compeers. Iredell attended the first levee of Adams' presidency and reported a large number in attendance. Later, he spoke to the president at church, after which the president took him home for a family dinner. Later still, Iredell reported that he had "been at no play but that to which the President invited me." Following another presidential levee, Iredell dined with the president and "a small select and very agreeable party."[32]

Iredell's untimely death, even before the Adams' administration terminated oversoon (Iredell, at least, would have thought so), ended the relationship. While it lasted, however, the association appears to have been close.

CHAPTER 11

Overt Partisanship from the Bench

P ERSONAL INTIMACY WITH THE PRESIDENTS AND INTENSE COMMIT-
MENT TO THEIR POLICIES EMANATED IN OVERT POLITICAL ACTIVITY
ON THEIR BEHALF. THE HIGH BENCH WAS NO BARRIER. DURING THE
WASHINGTON AND ADAMS ADMINISTRATIONS, FEDERALIST FEDERAL
judges, including Supreme Court justices on circuit, were viewed as representatives or extensions of the national administration. After the Jeffersonian
takeover in 1801, Federalist judges continued to tout their party's policies
from the bench until the 1805 impeachment trial of Justice Samuel Chase for
just such activities. Indeed, the commonplaceness of overt partisan advocacy
from the bench was argued in Chase's defense. Surely it was lawful, his counsel urged upon the Senate, for "an aged patriot of the Revolution" to warn his
fellow citizens of perceived dangers to their liberty and happiness; that practice had "been sanctioned by the custom of this country from the beginning
of the Revolution to this day." The Chase articles, John Quincy Adams told
his father, contained a virtual impeachment of every Supreme Court justice
since the country's beginning.[1]

It was largely through their contact with the judges sitting on the circuit
courts that the American people became acquainted with the new institution
of the federal judiciary, and it was mainly through the judges' charges to grand
juries that the principles of the new Constitution and the government it established became known to the public. A contemporary newspaper account
is graphically descriptive:

> Among the more vigorous production[s] of the American pen may
> be enumerated the various charges delivered by the judges of the
> United States at the opening of their respective courts. In these use-

ful addresses to the jury, we not only discern sound legal information conveyed in a style at once popular and condensed, but much political and constitutional knowledge.

These charges were the foremost feature of the Supreme Court's manifest involvement in partisan politics during this period. While such embroilment rings harsh in modern ears, it was patriotic in motivation and spurred by perceived coeval needs. As Davie observed to Iredell, a jurist's affability had a "conciliatory effect with respect to the government."[2]

Iredell was the consummate activist in this regard. Reflecting values that ripened after Iredell's time, one commentator has observed, with considerable basis in fact, that "no one was a worse offender against the proprieties of the bench."[3] Certainly, Iredell iteratively employed his charges to promote the government, to defend its policies in specific situations, and to advance patriotism generally.

As he had been in the ratification era, Iredell the jurist was a bellman for the Union. He told grand juries at Annapolis, Philadelphia, and Trenton that the necessity of maintaining a strong and cordial union was universally perceived. While some might have differed as to the means, the end was the object of nationwide solicitude. The "mischiefs of disunion," he said, would cause eternal regret, and the Constitution was formed precisely "[t]o prevent so great a calamity."

While virtually rabid in his federalism, Iredell had an equally passionate commitment to the concept of dual sovereignty and perceived no incongruity between the two. The Union contained two sovereignties, he instructed. The objects of the Constitution were solely the preservation and security of the Union; in no instances did it interfere with the internal regulations of a state in matters that concerned the state only. Citizens owed allegiance to the state where state interests alone were implicated and to the federal government in matters of national concern. "Each of these governments," he said, "deserves our equal confidence and respect":

> Each is calculated to promote, though in different ways, the security of those blessings we have here the happiness to enjoy. Both are restricted within those bounds which the people have thought proper to prescribe, and neither can violate, without violating a most sacred duty, the peculiar province of the other.[4]

While Iredell discerned in this design a "complication of authority" that demanded "greater care and attention than formerly," its greater blessings were more than adequately compensatory. The happiness of the country, he concluded, depended both on preservation of the state governments in their sphere of authority and on a strong union of the whole to advance the common welfare. An energetic national government was essential to effect the latter.[5]

This palpable need for a vigorous national government, in his view, made treason an offense meriting frequent consideration. Because every government had a primal duty of self-preservation, treason was globally viewed as a crime of the highest rank. Its object was total destruction of the government itself, he instructed, and thus of all order, peace, security, and happiness connected with it. Where the government was a good one, then, treason occasioned greater misery, public and private, than any other crime. The framers of the Constitution had taken special care, he said, to guard against previous abuses in the prosecution of this truly villainous offense.[6]

In the foregoing charges, Iredell simply promoted the new form of constitutional government in general terms. He stepped beyond that, however, in viewing as virtually treasonous the failure to support specific policies of the national Federalist administrations. From the bench he vigorously defended Washington's policy of strict neutrality toward other nations, first directing grand jurors of his home state on the duties of detachment. Only self-defense or public obligation, he said, could justify risking American freedom and prosperity in European wars. Until Congress authorized such involvement, citizens thus were bound to maintain a state of peace and neutrality; otherwise, Americans could splinter in their support for warring foreign powers, producing irrational absurdities and mischiefs. To preclude such, the president had proclaimed American neutrality and warned all citizens against contravening his edict. The pronouncement, Iredell declared, was necessary and had been warmly received; it both imposed a duty of obedience on every citizen and enhanced the president's already-lustrous fame.[7]

When Congress responded to "an absurd clamor" over the president's proclamation by enacting specific prohibitions, Iredell read provisions of the act to jurors and urged their compliance. Unexampled freedom and unparalleled justice could otherwise be lost, he exhorted, by a blithe disregard for the danger of foreign influence.[8]

Failure to adhere strictly to Washington's neutrality policy merely bordered on the treasonous; an insurrection against a property tax imposed during the Adams administration appeared to Iredell to attain it. In early 1799 John Fries, an auctioneer, led a company of men in eastern Pennsylvania in freeing arrested evaders of the tax. Iredell viewed the events with alarm, depicting them in some detail to Hannah and noting a consequent "immensity of business" for his court.[9]

Iredell would try some of the insurrectionists, yet was not deterred from outspoken defense of the government's measures and a forecast of anarchy if the offenders went unpunished. Under a government ordained by the people, he charged the federal grand jury for Pennsylvania, citizens must obey the laws their representatives enacted. Despite an envied situation, the government had been accused of the vilest tyranny, and an insurrection had commenced based on misperceived breaches of the Constitution. Public exigencies rendered the land tax unavoidable, he argued, yet the authority of the law was resisted, and the government was treated contemptuously. Not knowing all particulars, he refused to specify the crimes involved. The conduct was treasonous, however, if the intent was to prevent enforcement of a federal statute altogether, and was some lesser crime if the purpose was to preclude its enforcement in a particular instance only.

A paradigmatic testimonial to the Federalist government completed this charge. Notwithstanding the efforts to vilify and undermine it, Iredell declared, it had risen in public esteem and confidence. Gross misrepresentations had been rectified and justice impartially administered. Let this government be destroyed, he warned, and anarchy will ensue; "all lovers of order, decency, truth and justice [will] be trampled under foot."[10]

When the revolt ended, Iredell informed Hannah that the prosecutions would soon commence. He cancelled a scheduled appearance in Annapolis to remain in Philadelphia for the trials, as the court underwent ten-hour workdays. Samuel Johnston thought the cancellation "judicious" on both political and deterrence grounds. Allowing the law to take its course "a little severely," he told Iredell, would show that government was "not to be trifled with" and offer a lesson for demagogues. Iredell and Pennsylvania District Judge Richard Peters charged the Fries petit jury, tenuously, that to resist a law by force with intent to defeat its execution entirely amounted to levying war, which is treason. After deliberating about three hours, the jury returned a guilty verdict, which greatly pleased the Adams administration and its supporters. While the administration had no stronger adherent than James Iredell, he must have had qualms about his role in this largely political conviction. Clearly, he had sympathy for the defendant, for he wrote Hannah that "[n]othing could be more affecting than the circumstances." While he agreed with the verdict, he "could not bear to look on the poor man," who, he was told, "fainted away." He dreaded sentencing a man who had "behaved through the whole of his trial with great modesty and propriety" and "now lies in the deepest distress prostrate on the earth." While it meant that his time had been wasted, the grant of a new trial spared him this task (see *infra* Chapter 16).

When Iredell left the trials, Samuel Johnston thought the change would be "something for the better." "Here you will find nothing but order," he wrote, "and an almost universal acquiescence in the measures of the government." Chief Justice Ellsworth considered it a misfortune that, even after weeks of lengthy workdays, Iredell had to leave much of the business undone. He took great pleasure, however, in reading his colleague's "luminous and pointed charge."[11]

Popular sentiment was not a prerequisite to Iredell's praise for the government's measures. Despite mounting resentment over them in his home state and elsewhere, Iredell rushed to the defense of the Alien and Sedition Acts approved by the Federalist-controlled Congress in 1798 and favored by President Adams. Their nature, he opined from the bench, had been misrepresented. Aliens never had leave to stay in any country at will. Governments could always order deportation for those who threatened public safety, and removing enemy aliens on the eve of war was common. The power to exclude them, he continued, was proper, and because Congress often recessed, the president should share the authority. Finally, an alien who behaved properly, he said, had nothing to fear.[12]

Iredell perceived the major objection to the Sedition Act to be the absence of express constitutional power to pass it and its not being warranted under the "necessary and proper" clause. He had argued that position at Hillsborough, he acknowledged, but he now confessed error. A law with no sanction attached was like "a good moral sermon," he said, and had as little effect on "bad members of society." It was therefore "necessary and proper" (his words) to impose a duty and provide a penalty for noncompliance, and the authority for this act indeed resided in the "necessary and proper" clause. Iredell cited several crimes against the United States in support of this rather tenuous conclusion.

What was necessary and proper at a given time, he continued, was for the legislature to determine. When gross misrepresentation occurs, inciting to insurrections such as that in Pennsylvania, every government, he said, has the power to punish such falsehoods.

Responding to the argument that the Sedition Act violated the First Amendment guarantee of freedom of the press, Iredell invoked the Blackstonian doctrine, now long repudiated, that defined such freedom as "laying no *previous* restraints upon publications, and not in freedom from censure for criminal matter when published." One publishing "improper, mischievous, or illegal" material must take the consequences, he posited, and to punish dangerous or offensive writings, as this act did, was "necessary for the preservation of peace and good order, of government and religion, the only solid foundations of civil liberty."[13]

Iredell's charges went beyond mere exhortation to support Federalist policies on major public issues. They also stressed individual responsibility as essential to the government's success. A highly moralistic approach to the criminal law was characteristic. It was the grand jurors' responsibility to ensure that individual misconduct did not defeat the general objectives of government. Private sentiment, he admonished, must yield to "that of the public constitutionally expressed." Even in a country with all political blessings aspired to, there were bad people without appropriate restraint; thus, the grand jurors had significant responsibilities that bore directly on the success or failure of government.[14]

Sentencing hearings also provided forums for bench lectures on individual morality and responsibility. In sentencing a defendant for manslaughter on the high seas, Iredell described the offense as aggravated and the offender as cruel virtually beyond parallel. The victim, he said, was young, foreign, unskilled in the defendant's language, and altogether innocent; ill health made him "less useful" but did not merit "the repeated, unprovoked, unmanly, and inhuman treatment" which led to his death. In sentencing the offender, Iredell referred to the three goals of the newly established criminal-justice system: punishment (determined, he said, by the degree of guilt), rehabilitation ("time in solitary confinement to reflect...and...endeavor to amend"), and deterrence (the sentence was entered, he said, "for the sake of example").[15]

Finally, Iredell's charges featured general prods toward patriotic appreciation for the extant government. "Liberty without law is anarchy," he preached, and "[l]aw without liberty is oppression." A people's habits, manners, principles, and propensities determined what constituted a proper mix of the two. The most people could hope for, he declared, was to choose their government. The American people had that privilege and now had experience from which to appreciate it.

The Constitution and the Union, he further charged, were products of disinterested efforts and voluntary sacrifices. A glory previously unimagined had resulted. The only object yet to be coveted was that "rashness may not throw away what wisdom has so nobly procured." That wish was attainable if every citizen yielded his interests to those of his state and every state viewed the Union's welfare as superior to its own. For the nation to succeed, Iredell urged, every individual must "perform his share of the common trust, or answer for his neglect of it." The object of prosecutions for offenses against the United States was preservation of a Union, without which the rights of an independent people would be lost. The Union had saved Americans from multiple dangers and rescued them from impending ruin; it was the "cement essential to their existence," and no threats or artifices should be capable of weakening it.[16]

Iredell did not emerge from his on-the-bench political rhetoric altogether unscathed. The Jeffersonian Republicans complained vehemently about what they correctly perceived as attacks on their political party by Iredell and other federal judges. Justice William Paterson, in one of his charges, expressly called the Republicans "the disorganization of our happy country." When other justices, including Iredell, adopted Chief Justice Ellsworth's view (expressed to grand juries in South Carolina) that those opposed to the government's existence or to the efficient exercise of its legitimate powers could and should be indicted for subversive activities, Jeffersonians discerned an attempt to institute a common-law crime to punish vocal critics of Adams' Federalist administration. Jefferson himself wrote to Senator Charles Pinckney:

I consider all the encroachments made on [the Constitution] heretofore as nothing, as mere retail stuff compared with the wholesale doctrine that there is a common law in force in the United States of which and of all the cases within its provisions, their courts have cognizance. It is complete consolidation. Ellsworth and Iredell have openly recognized it. Washington has squinted at it, and I have no doubt it has been decided to cram it down our throats.

While Iredell's charges undoubtedly helped to inculcate national patriotism and further the Federalist cause, clearly they also aided in consolidating the opposition.[17]

In one instance, an Iredell charge precipitated a direct attack on him. Following his charge to the grand jury at Richmond in May 1797, the jury declared a letter signed by Congressman Samuel J. Cabell an evil that disseminated unfounded calumnies against the government; divided the people from it; and enhanced a foreign influence ruinous to the country's peace, happiness, and independence. In response, Cabell assailed the judge, the jury, and the court. Antifederalist leaders threatened vengeance. Jefferson urged James Monroe to bring the matter before the Virginia legislature, but Monroe doubted its jurisdiction. Monroe's doubts notwithstanding, Jefferson was inclined to proceed in some way, either against Iredell or the grandjurymen, before Virginia tribunals.

Iredell was not quiescent when confronted with this Republican onslaught. Responding with a fusillade addressed "TO THE PUBLIC," he noted his unmitigated surprise at this "attack upon my judicial character." He denied even knowing that Cabell had written a circular letter or that he had seen such, admitted seeing letters written by other Virginia Congressmen but disavowed considering them when he prepared his charge, and vigorously defended both the charge's contents and its propriety. The practice of grand juries presenting grievances which could not be the subject of criminal prosecutions was well established, Iredell declared, and it had never occurred to him to suppress it. He recalcitrantly defied Cabell or anyone else to show that in the exercise of his judicial office he had been influenced in the slightest by anyone, and he vowed to remain equally uninfluenced by "this new mode of attack by a member of Congress."

Reflecting contemporary Federalist thinking, Samuel Johnston viewed Cabell's offensive as "illiberal and unprovoked" and Iredell's rejoinder as altogether proper. He suggested, though, that mere silence might have been the better response. It could be more suitable, he stated with ageless sagacity, for a public servant to answer such charges only when constitutionally called before a proper tribunal; otherwise, he squanders time preferably devoted to duty and enlivens disputation better put to rest.[18]

Praise for Iredell's charges was more common than criticism. A Boston newspaper found his charge to the Massachusetts grand jury "elegant," and an Edenton publication carried the charge, noting universal sentiment that Iredell combined "elegance with extensive knowledge and liberality." Virginia Governor Henry Lee took pleasure in publicizing Iredell's sentiments, which Lee said did Iredell honor and promoted "a right understanding" of the country's interests. Following an Iredell charge supporting Washington's neutrality policy, one correspondent thought "the great body of the people" quite satisfied to observe "the animated zeal of a federal judge." The judge's efforts to school the public in the duties of citizenship, he predicted, would produce "good effects." William R. Davie considered an Iredell charge excellent, and President Adams spoke to him "in very flattering terms" about his instructions on the land-tax insurrection and the Alien and Sedition Acts.[19]

Many of Iredell's charges were published in newspapers or pamphlets at the request of the juries instructed. Pennsylvania grand jurors, for example, asked permission to publish his charge on the Fries Rebellion. They had heard it, they said, with great satisfaction, and they thought its publication would correct misinformation and preserve peace. Iredell was delighted to forward the charge if it could be "of some service in correcting erroneous opinions." The country's Constitution and laws afforded "the highest degree of rational liberty," he responded, and attempts to subvert them were astonishing and regrettable.[20]

Iredell's brother Arthur sought copies of his charges, apparently as the only accessible source of his sibling's political views. According to Arthur, Iredell "carefully avoided every political subject" when communicating with him, and he both expected and desired that he continue to do so. Arthur wanted to avoid any impropriety should Iredell's letters be opened, he said, for his brother's public character made his positions carry "the greatest weight." In view of Iredell's overt and steady political partisanship from the bench, Arthur's comment is ironic.[21]

Perceptions of the president's popularity, and a desire to benefit from it, could not have motivated Iredell's partisan advocacy. Washington, in particular, did not enjoy clear acclaim in Iredell's home state. As noted, his 1791 reception in North Carolina was somewhat indifferent: Willie Jones, a prominent Antifederalist but one of Washington's hosts for the occasion, refused to greet him as president but welcomed him as a soldier and a man. Thomas Person, one of the most vehement of North Carolina's Antifederalists, had called the president "a damned rascal." When Congress adopted a laudatory reply to Washington's Farewell Address, four of the state's representatives voted against it as "too adulatory."[22]

The impetus was, instead, Iredell's deep and abiding commitment to preservation and enhancement of the Union he had struggled to establish. Davie perhaps best expressed the contemporary rationale for the conduct. "It will hardly be denied," he said, "that all measures, whether of public or private men, which have a direct tendency to destroy or disturb the peace, good government, and happiness of the community, are strictly within the inquest of a grand jury, and of course, proper objects for a judge's charge." Following Iredell's charge on the Fries Rebellion, Davie wrote him that it was "extremely well written, and the times called for every sentiment it contained."[23]

While such overt partisanship from the bench offends modern sensitivities, Davie was right; in Justice Holmes' now well-known words, "the felt necessities of the time" vindicated the conduct. Iredell's activities in this regard further validate William R. Casto's well-documented thesis that the founders viewed the early federal courts as "national security courts." Preserving and strengthening a fledgling national government, whose spawners were less than fully confident of their offspring's survival and success, was considered the judicial branch's foremost institutional purpose; support for the government, rather than conflict with it, was thus the paradigm. "Under the Federalist presidents," Herbert A. Johnson has aptly noted, "the federal courts . . . considered it their duty to support the political positions of the executive and legislative branches."

Judged by this touchstone, the nation's early jurists, including Iredell, quite naturally rationalized their conduct as not only permissible but desirable. As G. Edward White properly admonishes, "moderns [must] consider the historical context of ethical judgments made by past Supreme Court justices."[24]

CHAPTER 12

Not a Time of Great Decisions

ODERNS MUST ADJUST THEIR THINKING IN ANOTHER RE-
SPECT WHEN CONSIDERING THE LATE-EIGHTEENTH-CENTURY
UNITED STATES SUPREME COURT AND ITS JUSTICES. THE
PRESENT-DAY MIND RECOILS FROM A DEPICTION OF THE
nation's highest court as one with few cases, mostly marginal in significance.
Yet, in describing the Court's onset, such a portrayal is accurate.

When Iredell took his seat at the August 1790 Term, his commission was
read, and he was "qualified according to law." He had sworn and subscribed
to an oath before Justice Rutledge while riding the Southern Circuit in May.
The further qualification appears to have been a separate oath required for
Supreme Court, as opposed to circuit court, service. After Iredell's qualification, the Court had little else to do. It admitted two counsellors, ordered
the clerk to procure a seal for a circuit court, and then adjourned for lack of
business.

This state of relative repose persisted. At the February 1791 Term, the Court
again admitted counsellors and adjourned. At the August 1791 Term, it allowed
one motion, denied another, and adjourned. At the February 1792 Term, it
held a motion under advisement until it was withdrawn; a suit was then discontinued, and the Court adjourned. The Court did not render a reported
opinion until the August 1792 Term, two full years after Iredell qualified.[1]

The workload increased as Iredell's tenure progressed. By mid-decade he
complained of long sessions requiring "unremitted attention" and delaying
his departure from Philadelphia beyond original expectations. Concerned
about still-longer sessions later, he nevertheless fretted over the continuance
of cases. He could "scarcely command an hour" for himself, he moaned, and
could not predict when this oppression would cease.[2]

Such laments notwithstanding, the Court's business throughout Iredell's service remained sufficiently minimal that its members could handle their joint duties by convening in the capital only twice annually, in February and August. Practices and procedures, not a heavy caseload, accounted for Iredell's distress. Lawyers' arguments, for example, were unlimited, in one case lasting eight days. As a consequence, the usual practice of sitting from 10:00 a.m. to 3:00 p.m. was occasionally modified by a 9:00 a.m. starting time in order to "dispatch more in proportion than usual."[3]

The English practice of writing seriatim opinions also enhanced the workload. Though foreshadowed during Ellsworth's tenure, it was not until John Marshall's chief justiceship, which commenced almost a year and a half after Iredell's death, that an opinion for the Court replaced the system under which the justices wrote individually.[4]

Several reasons explain the sparsity of early cases. Any new appellate court encounters start-up delay as causes enter the lower courts, records are developed and composed, and briefs on appeal are prepared and filed. Because the Court's jurisdiction was largely appellate, it was not spared this entry-stage slack time. The meagerness of federal legislation at this juncture, and the Court's lack of original jurisdiction over cases arising under federal law, also contributed to the scarcity of filings.[5]

The Court may have heard cases in which no opinions were written or none survive. A nineteenth-century reporter attempted to collect the early decisions and concluded that before 1800, written opinions were the exception rather than the rule. Alexander Dallas reports that the 1793 yellow-fever epidemic dispersed Philadelphia's population, and he could not "trace that any important cause was agitated" at that August Term. In *Calder v. Bull*, Iredell stated that he had not had an opportunity to reduce his opinion to writing. He made the assertion in an opinion that covers three pages of the official reports, so his meaning is unclear. The statement suggests, however, that the justices did not always reduce their opinions, or the totality of their opinions, to writing.[6]

Whatever the reasons, the upshot is that in almost a decade on the Court, even when seriatim opinions were the order of the day, Iredell wrote in only twelve reported cases in which the Court sat *en banc*. His name appears on statements in two others,[7] both insignificant, and in occasional, equally insignificant footnotes.[8]

This paucity of available materials renders it impossible to derive from the cases any comprehensive Iredellian vision of constitutional law — any coherent, overarching jurisprudential theses; seamlessly consistent theories; or seminal principles of law uniquely attributable to him. With the sole exception of his dissent in *Chisholm v. Georgia*,[9] which still engenders debate among scholars and jurists, his Supreme Court opinions constitute neither the most-important nor the most-interesting aspect of his public life.

Obviously, however, a treatment of Iredell's judicial career would be incomplete without glancing attention to the cases in which he wrote; a sequential synopsis thus follows, postponing *Chisholm* for discrete, more-comprehensive consideration.

Settling a Course of Chancery:
Georgia v. Brailsford I

An American state's post-Revolution efforts to confiscate a British subject's property spawned *Georgia v. Brailsford I*,[10] the first case in which a reported United States Supreme Court opinion survives. Samuel Brailsford, a British citizen, sued on a bond to recover a debt from a Georgia citizen who was the surviving partner in the original-debtor firm. Georgia sought to intervene to establish its title pursuant to a confiscation act. The circuit court, with Iredell sitting, rejected the state's application. Georgia District Judge Nathaniel Pendleton, the court's other member, later sent Iredell a pamphlet containing their decision.[11]

When the case reached the Supreme Court, Iredell entered the first recorded and surviving judicial utterance on the potential for conflict presented by justices of that Court sitting as circuit judges. Noting that he had sat on the circuit in the case, he solemnly pledged nevertheless to render his opinion "on the present motion, detached from every previous consideration of the merits of the cause."[12]

The motion was for an injunction to stay the circuit court proceedings and direct payment of the sums claimed to Georgia's treasurer. Alexander J. Dallas, a Pennsylvania lawyer who would later report the case, represented the state. Edmund Randolph, a Virginia lawyer then serving as United States attorney general, represented the defendants (at the time neither law nor professional ethics barred such government officials from simultaneous private law practice).[13]

Justice Thomas Johnson, who had replaced Rutledge in November 1791, thought an injunction could issue only upon assertion of a probable right that would be lost without the Court's intervention; because Georgia's right to the debt could be enforced at common law, the state had not made a case for the Court's interposition. Cushing agreed that the right, if any, was at law and that the law thus provided an adequate remedy.[14]

Iredell, Blair, Wilson, and Jay held a different view. Writing first among them, Iredell initially denied the circuit court's jurisdiction; when a state is a party, he said, the Supreme Court has exclusive jurisdiction. Justice concerns overrode jurisdictional niceties in his thinking, however. It would be wrong for Georgia's claim to be defeated by a judgment between parties over whom the state had no control in an action in which it was not heard. Because the state's claim was precluded in other courts, high-level sleight of hand was in order. The Supreme Court should treat the matter as if Georgia had filed with it for interpleader and should award the injunction, staying the money in the hands of the United States marshal in order to prevent an irreparable injury and to do justice to Georgia.[15]

Blair, too, thought the injunction proper to preserve the status quo pending a decision on the merits after "full enquiry." Wilson, displaying rare judicial candor, conceded his inability to reach a fully satisfactory conclusion; while in his view Georgia should have sought a writ of error, not an injunction, he was willing to enjoin, thereby holding the funds in place until the Court could satisfy itself as to the right and the remedy. Jay likewise thought the extant posture should persist until the applicable law was determined.[16]

With four justices voting in the affirmative, two in the negative, the injunction was issued, leaving the losing attorney irate. The granting of the injunction, Randolph wrote caustically to James Madison, showed

> that the premier [Jay] aimed at the cultivation of Southern popularity; that the professor [Wilson] knows not an iota of equity; that the North Carolinian [Iredell] repented of the first ebullitions of a warm temper; and that it will take a series of years to settle, with such a mixture of judges, a regular course of chancery.[17]

Georgia v. Brailsford II

The passage of time did not abate Randolph's disdain. When the Court reconvened to hear *Georgia v. Brailsford II*[18] in February 1793, he was back on behalf of the original creditor, moving to dissolve the injunction and dismiss the bill. The Court's majority now joined in Chief Justice Jay's cryptic opinion holding that if Georgia had a right to the debt, the right was to be pursued at common law. If the state had not instituted a common-law action by August Term next, Jay warned, the Court would dissolve the injunction.[19]

In one of the early expressions of dissent in American case law, Iredell disagreed. While philosophically considering dissent unfortunate, he was, he concluded, "bound to decide according to the dictates of my own judgment." Only the Supreme Court, as a court of equity, he wrote, could enable

Georgia to maintain the viability of its claim on the merits. The state had shown color of title and had no remedy at law; only exercise of the Court's equity jurisdiction could ensure that the money would not be paid to another claimant prematurely. He would never have consented to the injunction initially, he said, had he thought the state possessed an adequate legal remedy.[20]

Blair also thought the injunction should be sustained. If the British-subject plaintiff obtained the money and left the country, he would be beyond the jurisdiction of the federal courts, Blair noted, and justice might fail. No other court could secure the presence of all the parties and do complete justice; the bill in equity therefore should be sustained, and a court of law involved only in determining legal title to the debt.[21]

When the suit was initially before the Court, Iredell had suggested that it should be tried there. The Supreme Court had exclusive jurisdiction when a state was a party, he noted; thus, when the parties were all before it, it could "direct a proper issue to be formed and tried at the bar." The Court ultimately followed Iredell's proposition. An "amicable action" was entered to determine entitlement as between Georgia and the original creditors, and the issue was tried before a special jury at the February 1794 Term. Chief Justice Jay charged, in accordance with the unanimous opinion of the judges, that the statute did not vest the debt in the state at the time of its passage, the debt was not subject to confiscation but only to sequestration, and the original owner's right to recover had revived at the peace. Responsive to the charge, the jury returned a verdict for the original owner, and the Court accordingly dissolved the injunction.[22]

Jay also charged that the cause had "been regarded as of great importance; and doubtless it is so."[23] Assessed in the warp and woof of time, the significance greatly diminishes. A routine application of ordinary principles of equity, the case is hardly a constitutional or jurisprudential landmark.

Practice, Procedure, and Prizes: *Bingham v. Cabbot*

In *Bingham v. Cabbot*,[24] an American privateer captured a Danish neutral ship and carried it to Martinique, where the plaintiff in error, Bingham, resided as a public agent of the United States. The governor of Martinique, pursuant to authority granted by the French Constitution, ordered the ship's cargo sold and the net proceeds paid to Bingham for disposition as Congress ordered. The ship's owners sued to recover the proceeds. Justice Cushing tried the case alone in the circuit court of Massachusetts, and the plaintiffs obtained a verdict. The defendants appealed to the Supreme Court, asserting that the case was for admiralty jurisdiction exclusively and raising questions as to the extent of the record.[25]

Only Cushing, Iredell, Paterson, and Wilson sat. Their debate over the question as to the record illustrates the Court's early disarray and lack of settled rules on basic matters of practice and procedure. Cushing asserted that in Massachusetts the declaration and pleadings were entered in a book, and this alone was deemed the record; the papers and depositions were referred to only to ascertain what writ issued and what depositions were taken. Paterson, however, thought all papers transmitted from the circuit court were part of the record. Iredell agreed, Cushing ultimately yielded to that view, and Wilson remained silent. The Court thus resolved a significant practice and procedure question on an *ad hoc* basis, without deciding whether common law or Massachusetts practice governed and, more importantly, without adopting rules to govern such questions in the future.[26]

As to whether the cause was exclusively for admiralty jurisdiction, the plaintiff in error maintained that under the evidence, this was a prize cause; that is, it involved property captured at sea by a privateer, claimed as an enemy's property, and therefore liable to appropriation and condemnation under the laws of war. As such, the cause was for admiralty jurisdiction. Paterson and Wilson agreed. Iredell was not prepared to conclude that the circuit court lacked jurisdiction, nor was Cushing. Although Cushing, Iredell, and Paterson, a clear majority, thought evidentiary errors warranted a new trial, the Court did not award one because it did not believe it could remand to a lower court when it was equally divided over whether that court had jurisdiction.[27]

Several leading treatises ignore the case,[28] thus indicating its relative lack of significance.

State versus National Sovereignty: *Penhallow v. Doane's Administrators*

A case of "great importance" in Iredell's view, *Penhallow v. Doane's Administrators*[29] had roiled through the courts for eighteen years when finally heard in the Supreme Court. It was argued for several days — quite ably by both sides, Iredell thought. Its import lay in its resolution, adversely to the contentions of the states, of an issue of state-versus-national sovereignty.[30]

During the Revolution a vessel owned by a citizen of New Hampshire had captured another vessel. A New Hampshire court ordered the captured vessel and cargo forfeited as lawful prize and the proceeds distributed according to law. The owners of the captured vessel appealed to the Continental Congress, which took jurisdiction through its commissioners of appeal.

With the establishment of the Confederation, all cases regarding captures were referred to the Court of Appeals of the new Congress. That court reversed the state court and ordered the property restored to the owners. Because the state objected, this decree was not enforced. Upon the establishment of the federal courts under the Constitution, however, the district and circuit courts ordered payment of damages and costs to the owners. On appeal, the Supreme Court upheld the jurisdiction of the federal courts to decide the case. Thus, the original state-court decision was reversed eighteen years after its entry.

Unresolved issues of federalism still rankled in the new republic, and the circuit court's assumption of jurisdiction and reversal of state-court decrees thought long-settled produced umbrage. The New Hampshire legislature protested against unwarrantable encroachment by the federal courts, resulting in annihilation of all state powers. The country, it lamented, was reduced "to one domination." A Federalist newspaper was equally critical; the decision, it decried, had ruined gentlemen for supporting their state's laws, negated the sovereignty of New Hampshire, and controverted the state's right to legislate.[31]

Given the opportunity, the Court had indeed taken a nationalistic approach. Paterson first articulated this interpretation, and Iredell followed suit. Iredell's Revolutionary-period essayist style creeps somewhat incongruously into this opinion, as he gratuitously states:

> When acts were passed by the Parliament of Great Britain which were thought unconstitutional and unjust, and when every hope of redress by separate applications appeared desperate, then was conceived the noble idea, which laid the foundation of the present independence and happiness of this country (though independence was not then in contemplation), of forming a common council to consult for the common welfare of the whole, so far as an opposition to the measures of Great Britain was concerned.

All prize cases should belong to the national sovereignty, Iredell concluded when he reached the merits, because they were determined by the law of nations, making a prize court a court of all nations. Congress was the appropriate body to exercise national sovereignty, thus making these cases appropriate for the exercise of federal jurisdiction.[32]

Penhallow, then, placed judicial construction behind the assertion of national sovereignty in the new-sprung federal government. Iredell had championed both independence and union; his joinder in this exposition of the federal idea thus does not surprise.[33]

Expatriation:
Talbot v. Janson

Like *Penhallow*, *Talbot v. Janson*[34] was argued at length — "scandalously long," in Iredell's view, allowing little time for anything else. *Talbot*, like *Penhallow*, involved a question of prize in admiralty. The decision awarded restitution of a prize captured by a French privateer illegally fitted out in American ports, and the Court held that no foreign power had a legal right to issue commissions in this country.[35]

Relative to Iredell, the case is significant only for his discussion *obiter dicta* of an issue the Court considered but did not decide: the right of national expatriation. One of the parties, William Talbot, averred that he was a French citizen and claimed that the prize was his. The evidence showed that he was a native Virginian until naturalized in France. As to his claim, the threshold question was whether he was a French citizen. Whether the common-law doctrine as to allegiance and expatriation was to be regarded in America as a rule of municipal law was, and would remain, a vexing question.

Iredell noted that while his opinion was dicta, he chose to "freely express my sentiments on the subject." The mere fortuity of birthplace, he posited, should not compel ongoing attachment to a locale. Amelioration of social or economic status might dictate relocation, and that was a freedom to which he, and most nations, adhered. But it was not a natural, unalienable right; society might impose counter-duties when the public interest or safety required. While that was a legislative decision, only parliamentary folly would restrain a person whose affections were fixed elsewhere.

Still, the mere taking of an oath to another country and being admitted to citizenship there, as Talbot had done, did not discharge one's obligations to his own country. Voluntary expatriation was inadequate; permission from one's government was obligatory.[36]

The Taxing Power
Hylton v. United States

In 1794, for defense purposes during a war scare, Congress imposed a tax on carriages. The question of its constitutionality was among the objections opponents raised in the House of Representatives: Was the tax a direct one within the meaning of Article I, Section 2, which could not be levied except in proportion to the census?[37]

The Court had informed President Washington that it would not give advisory opinions but would settle only actual, bona fide controversies. *Hylton v. United States*[38] was nevertheless presented and decided on an agreed statement of fictitious facts. Daniel Hylton of Richmond refused to pay the tax, explaining somewhat apologetically that his intent was to ascertain a constitutional point, not to delay the payment of a public duty. Hylton owned but one chariot on which the tax and penalty would have been only $16.00, less than the jurisdictional limits (controversies involving over $2,000) of the circuit courts. Hence, the government's agreed-upon facts included the fiction that Hylton had 125 carriages. To avoid detriment to Hylton, it was agreed that if he was adjudged liable, a payment of $16.00, the actual amount of the duty and penalty, would discharge the debt. The recital of this in the official report suggests that the Court was privy to the subterfuge.[39]

Justice Samuel Chase, who assumed his seat just before the *Hylton* arguments, concluded from practical considerations that the tax was not a direct one within the letter or meaning of the Constitution. If it were, states with equal populations, but great inequality in the number of chariots within their borders, would pay the same.

Paterson also grounded his conclusion on functional application. It would be absurd and inequitable, he said, for the entire tax to fall on a few individuals in a state because they happened to own and possess carriages.

Iredell concurred. The tax, he said, "is agreeable to the Constitution," and "the Constitution itself affords a clear guide to decide the controversy." That document, he continued, contemplated as direct only those taxes which could be apportioned. That this one could not be was so evident that while the question "deserve[d] a serious answer,... it [was] very difficult to give [it] one." The tax, in his view, was clearly not a direct tax "in the sense of the Constitution."[40]

Wilson had sat in the circuit court (ruling the tax constitutional) and thus recused. Ellsworth was not yet sworn, and Cushing was absent because of illness. A three-member Court thus decided one of its more-important early cases—important because the Court upheld the government's power to raise revenue effectively, but more so because it was the first case in which the Court passed upon the constitutionality of an act of Congress.

Only Chase adverted directly to the power of judicial review, and he did so diffidently. While it was unnecessary to determine the Court's review power, he declared, if it had such power he would exercise it only "in a very clear case." Such diffidence notwithstanding, the Court's explicit declaration of the constitutionality of an act implicitly proclaimed its equivalent authority to pronounce acts unconstitutional. "[T]he signpost was up."[41]

Alexander Hamilton argued *Hylton* for the government "with astonishing ability and in a most pleasing manner," according to Iredell. James Madison lacked Iredell's enthusiasm for Hamilton's polemics; Hamilton, Madison told

Thomas Jefferson, had tried "to raise a fog around the subject, & to inculcate a respect in the Court for preceding sanctions, in a doubtful case."[42]

Iredell greatly admired Hamilton ("your favorite," Samuel Johnston called him), presciently believing the *Federalist Papers* would immortalize him. Soon after the *Hylton* arguments, and before release of the opinions, the two dined together. Iredell's account of the rendezvous betrays no sensitivity to conceivable impropriety in dining with counsel for one party to a pending controversy, presumably apart from counsel for the other. (While the government paid counsel for both sides, technically they remained adversaries.)[43]

Again, the modern mentality recoils. Once more, however, the Casto hypothesis — that the proper paradigm for appraising activities of the Court and its members in this period is one of juristic support for the national government[44] — elucidates. Hamilton was a leading Federalist thinker and political figure; until a year before his *Hylton* argument, he had been highly prominent in the Washington cabinet as secretary of the treasury. Iredell's admiration of, support for, and friendship with him thus came quite naturally. Viewed in the context of late-eighteenth-century values and mores, the timing of their dinner ceases to astonish.

Constitutionality of State Laws:
Ware v. Hylton

While *Hylton v. United States* had import as the first case in which the Supreme Court passed on the constitutionality of congressional legislation, *Ware v. Hylton*[45] had similar import as the first in which the Court declared a state law unconstitutional. State confiscation of debts owed to British subjects was the font of the controversy. During the Revolutionary War, Virginia enacted a prototypal statute confiscating debts owed to British subjects and ordering them paid to the state's loan office. Daniel Hylton, apparently the same person as the plaintiff in *Hylton v. United States*, paid a portion of a debt to a British subject into the Virginia loan office. When the creditor sued, Hylton pleaded the payment as a partial defense. In the circuit court, Iredell and District Judge Cyrus Griffin ruled with Hylton; Chief Justice Jay dissented.[46]

Nothing else appearing, payment under the statute unquestionably satisfied the debt to the extent of the outlay. The issue, though, was whether the Supremacy Clause of the federal Constitution, which made treaties entered under the authority of the United States the supreme law of the land, gave the fourth article of the 1783 peace treaty with Britain priority over the Virginia statute. The treaty article provided that creditors on either side were entitled to recover the full value of bona fide debts in sterling money.

Chase wrote first, affirming the principle of judicial review: Judges, state and federal, were bound to declare null and void any state law contrary to the treaty (and thus to the Constitution). The natural import of the treaty gave British creditors a right of recovery, he said, the Virginia statute notwithstanding.

While Chase candidly confessed to possible bias (having represented American debtors in a similar suit) and to deficient draftsmanship (having written hastily amidst court attendance and consideration of other cases), his participating colleagues shared his views. National differences, Paterson wrote, should not affect private bargains; the confidence on which contracts were founded should be preserved inviolate, and the treaty clearly restored these parties to their pre-war status. Wilson believed every nation had long considered the confiscation of debts disreputable. The treaty "extended to debts heretofore contracted"; the words could not be plainer, he said, and the treaty thus clearly trumped the statute. Cushing likewise thought the treaty's meaning obvious and its nullification of the statute clear.[47]

Justices who had sat on circuit did not participate on appeal except when the vote was otherwise equally divided. Iredell accordingly recused. He retained an intense intellectual and emotional investment in the case, however. To him, it was "the great Virginia Cause." The subject had "uncommon magnitude" and had excited "high expectation." The decision's consequences had "impressed [him] with their fullest force," he said, and he thus had approached the case with the utmost conscientiousness. Indeed, he had "trembled," he confessed, lest "an ill informed or precipitate opinion" on his part undermine either the country's interests or an individual's rights.[48]

This residual passion constrained him to speak, his recusal notwithstanding. His brethren thus acquiesced to his reading the views he had expressed on circuit, which were unaltered despite admitted vacillation. In an oft-quoted passage, Iredell stated: "We are too apt, in estimating a law passed at a remote period, to combine in our consideration all the subsequent events which have had an influence upon it, instead of confining ourselves (which we ought to do) to the existing circumstances at the time of its passing."

To him, the pertinent circumstances were that when the confiscation act was passed, the war made British creditors alien enemies whose common-law remedies were suspended. They thus could lose every debt when their debtors proved insolvent during the war, and Virginia was granting them a security, otherwise absent, by authorizing receipt of debts on their behalf.

No one, he vowed, reverenced treaties more than he. This one was especially important because it "gave peace to our country after a war attended with many calamities." The war-period essayist reemerged, as he said of the treaty: "It insured, so far as peace could insure them, the freest forms of government, and the greatest share of individual liberty, of which perhaps the world has seen any example."

Only the repeal of extant state statutes, or the passage of others, however, could give effect to the treaty provision in favor of creditors; this had not occurred. Accordingly, he was not forced to conclude that the treaty extinguished both private and public rights (the debtor's right to pay to the state and the state's right to sequester the payment). Such extinction should not be inferred unless compelled, and it was not. Having once lawfully paid the money, the debtor should be discharged; if there was doubt, the debtor deserved its resolution in his favor.[49]

The stakes in *Ware* were high. Financially, the states and many of their residents owed debts to British creditors. In Virginia such obligations were thought to be upwards of $2,000,000. Further, payments under the statute were generally made with significantly inflated paper currency, not the pounds sterling initially contracted for and called for in the treaty; thus, such payments, if permitted, produced a cut-rate discharge. Politically, public opinion on the confiscated debts impacted Federalist Party fortunes. Edmund Randolph, the attorney general, informed President Washington that the debates on the debts were "kindl[ing] a wide-spreading flame." The debtors, he said, were associated with the Antifederalists under Patrick Henry's ascendant banner.[50]

In the circuit court, Henry, as counsel for the debtors, had impressed Iredell favorably. Iredell, who was "much in his company," found him pleasing in manner and liberal in mind. The experience, he said, gave him further reason to detest partisan prejudice.[51]

Antifederalists did not monopolize debtor representation, however. John Marshall, a Federalist to the core, appeared for debtors in the Supreme Court—his only argument there. Marshall decried those who would impair the sovereignty of Virginia, a position state-rights adherents would later use to attack his own decisions as chief justice.[52]

Iredell was effusive in his comments on the *Ware* arguments on circuit. The ability employed was unexcelled, he said, and he would recall the disputations "with pleasure and respect." They had assuaged his fatigue, warmed his heart, and informed his understanding. Of the arguments, the debtor's had the greater appeal, however; the subsequent unanimous opposition of his colleagues left his original opinion unaltered.[53]

In *Ware*, as in *Chisholm*, ardent Federalist sentiments did not preclude Iredell's siding with the states in a conflict between the two sovereignties. Indeed, as in *Chisholm* (see *infra* Chapter 13), they may have prompted it.

Plain Fraud:
Fenemore v. United States

"[P]lain fraud," as Justice Chase termed it, was the mundane subject matter in *Fenemore v. United States*.[54] The federal government sued to recover money Thomas Fenemore allegedly had obtained from it by fraud and deceit. Exhibiting vouchers in support of his claim, Fenemore had successfully represented to the commissioner for settling continental accounts that the government owed him a large sum of money. The account was found not to be a just debt, even in part; upon a jury verdict for the government, the circuit court for New Jersey ordered the money repaid.

Fenemore's counsel evidently conceded that their client's conduct violated "every principle of conscience and equity," but argued legal defenses nevertheless. Their stance failed to impress. To Chase, "[t]he transaction [was] rank from the beginning to the end," and the verdict for the government was correct in every respect. Iredell agreed, trusting that "no man will ever be able to defend himself in an *American* court of justice upon the ground of his own turpitude." To Cushing, the cause was "susceptible of little doubt." Ellsworth concurred. Paterson, having sat on the circuit court, recused.[55]

The case is of little magnitude, sufficiently insignificant that leading commentators on the Supreme Court in the early republic ignore it.[56]

Ex Post Facto, Natural Law:
Calder v. Bull

Unlike *Fenemore*, *Calder v. Bull*[57] has import: first, for its holding that the Constitution's prohibition against *ex post facto* laws applies only to criminal statutes, not civil; and second, for the classic debate between Justices Chase and Iredell, in dicta, over whether natural law is a valid reference point for judicial review of legislative enactments.

At issue was the Connecticut legislature's action setting aside a Hartford probate-court decree that disapproved and refused to record a will. The propounders apparently failed timely to perfect an appeal, and the legislature granted a new hearing. The probate court then approved the will and ordered it recorded. The superior court and the state Supreme Court sustained the action.

On appeal to the United States Supreme Court, the losing parties argued that the legislature's grant of a new hearing was an *ex post facto* law, prohibited by the federal Constitution and thus void. The Court denied them relief, ruling that civil matters were not within the meaning and intent of the term *"ex post facto*" as used in the Constitution. Only Chase, Paterson, and Iredell wrote (Cushing appended two purportless sentences), and their reasoning was harmonious: The clause simply applied to penal statutes only.[58]

For Iredell, this was a volte-face. In the first North Carolina ratification convention, Antifederalists had argued that the clause restraining the states from issuing paper money would operate to discredit state paper currency then in circulation. Iredell, determined to quash every concern that might defeat ratification, had rejoined that the *ex post facto* clause would protect such tender already in circulation; he thus clearly opined that the clause applied in a civil context.[59]

Three years before *Calder*, Paterson, while on circuit, likewise asserted that the clause pertained to retrospective statutes, both civil and criminal. In *Calder*, however, he said it "unquestionably refers to crimes, and nothing else." Perhaps attempting to explicate his capriciousness, Paterson noted in *Calder* that he had "had an ardent desire to have extended the provision in the Constitution to retrospective laws in general." Iredell, by contrast, simply overlooked or ignored his inconsistency.[60]

Calder's relative renown among the early cases is not attributable primarily to its holding the *ex post facto* clause inapplicable to civil cases but to the Chase-Iredell debate over whether natural law is a valid reference point for judicial review of legislative enactments. The temporal context of the dialectic is important. In late-eighteenth-century America, virtually the entire legal community subscribed to natural-law theory. Lawyers viewed law as superhuman in origin. It thus was a mystical body of permanent truths, and judges were not lawmakers but lawfinders, who simply declared the preexisting law and made it intelligible. Policy considerations were thus viewed as impertinent to the adjudication process.[61]

In *Calder*, Chase wrote at considerably greater length than his colleagues, going well beyond the *ex post facto* clause or other specific provisions of the Constitution to consider whether, under natural-law theory, a government could deprive a citizen of a property right.[62] He reasoned essentially as follows.

State legislatures are not omnipotent, even when express state constitutional, or fundamental, law is lacking. The purposes of the Preamble to the Constitution, and the reasons people enter into society, determine the social compact. The exercise of legislative power is limited by its very nature and ends; certain vital principles of free republican governments preclude flagrant abuse of legislative power, even absent express constitutional limitations. "An ACT of the legislature (for I cannot call it a law) contrary to the great first principles of the social compact cannot be considered a rightful exercise of legislative authority," Chase wrote. To entrust a legislature with plenary powers to act arbitrarily and unfairly, he said, counters "all reason and justice"; the people thus cannot be presumed to have authorized such powers, "and the general principles of law and reason forbid them." Legislators may establish rules for future cases: "[T]hey may command what is right, and prohibit what is wrong." They cannot, however, change innocence into guilt (here he slips, apparently unconsciously, into criminal *ex post facto* analysis) or violate the rights of private contracts or private property. To permit such, solely on account of the absence of express restraints, "would...be a political heresy, altogether inadmissible in our free republican governments," Chase concluded.

The Blackstonian influence on Chase's opinion is evident. Chase refuses to call a statute a law if it is contrary to the principles of the social compact. Blackstone had said, similarly, that an absurd or unjust decision was not "bad law"; rather, it was "not law" at all. Chase's aphorism that the legislature "may command what is right, and prohibit what is wrong" is pirated almost verbatim from the *Commentaries*. Municipal law, Blackstone had there said, is properly defined as a rule of civil conduct "commanding what is right, and prohibiting what is wrong." While Chase found no deprivation of a property right in *Calder* because none had vested under the court's decree, he was carefully preserving an option to resort to Blackstonian natural-law theory in future cases if necessary to reach the result he desired.[63]

Though generally an uncritical Washington partisan, Iredell's mentor, Samuel Johnston, had joined other inner-circle Federalists in mild mystification over the President's appointment of Chase to the Court. "I have no personal acquaintance with Mr. Chase," Johnston wrote Iredell upon the appointment, "but am not impressed with a very favorable opinion of his moral character, whatever his professional abilities may be."[64] There is irony, then, in Chase's championing natural law or justice, which is deeply rooted in notions of morality, while Iredell, Johnston's pupil, resisted it. Rejection of natural law or justice as a valid reference point for judicial review was, however, the gravamen of Iredell's opinion.

Apart from constitutional constraints, Iredell maintained, the legislature had plenary power. "[S]peculative jurists" had held that legislative acts counter to natural justice must be void, but he could not imagine that a court possessed the power to declare them so. The framers had defined legislative power with precision in order to confine its exercise to settled boundaries. Acts beyond those borders were unquestionably void, but courts were powerless to pronounce void, based on a mere juristic deduction that they were contrary to some amorphous principle of natural justice, acts that otherwise fell in bounds.

A passion for certainty was the linchpin of Iredell's argument. Natural-jus-

tice notions, he said, were "regulated by no fixed standards." Intellectual ability and utmost purity of spirit notwithstanding, people could differ on the subject. A court could say only that its view diverged from that of the legislature,
which had an equal right to an opinion, on abstract principles of natural justice.[65]

The Chase-Iredell natural-law debate has reverberated through two centuries of American constitutional law — "a running battle that never has sim-
mered down completely."[66] In *Fletcher v. Peck* (1810), John Marshall followed
the Chase philosophy, noting that "there are certain great principles of justice,
whose authority is universally acknowledged, that ought not to be entirely dis-
regarded." Indeed, Marshall commonly took the Chase approach, grounding
decisions on abstract "first principles of American civilization." Concurring
in *Fletcher*, Justice William Johnson invoked reasoning similar to Marshall's,
grounding his position "on a general principle, on the reason and nature of
things: a principle which will impose laws even on the deity."[67] In *Terrett v.
Taylor* (1815), Justice Joseph Story vindicated his position, in part, as "standing upon the principles of natural justice [and] the fundamental laws of every
free government." And in *Loan Association v. Topeka* (1874), Justice Samuel
Miller invalidated a tax on grounds of amorphous "limitations on . . . power
which grow out of the essential nature of all free governments, . . . [i]mplied
reservations of individual rights, without which the social compact could not
exist, and which are respected by all governments entitled to the name."[68]

Renunciation of such reasoning has also been common, however. In *Satterlee v. Matthewson* (1829), Justice Bushrod Washington reflected the Iredell
stance: The Court simply had no authority to strike a statute unless it was repugnant to the Constitution. In dissenting from Justice Miller's opinion in
Loan Association, Justice Nathan Clifford also echoed Iredell's *Calder* opinion.
"Errors of indiscretion which the legislature may commit in the exercise of the
power it possesses cannot be corrected by the courts," Clifford wrote, "[be-
cause] the courts cannot adjudge an act of the legislature void unless it is in violation of the Federal or State constitution." Absent express constitutional limits, Clifford concluded, the legislative power is "practically absolute, whether
the law operates according to natural justice or not in any particular case." The
"vague ground" that an act opposed some "general latent spirit" would not
suffice; indeed, it would "convert the government into a judicial despotism."[69]

Long after the Chase and Iredell pens were stilled, Justice Hugo Black,
joined by Justice William O. Douglas, described Iredell's opinion in *Calder* as
"an early and prescient exposé of the inconsistency of the natural law formula
with our constitutional form of government." "[T]o pass upon the constitutionality of statutes by looking to the particular standards enunciated in the Bill
of Rights and other parts of the Constitution is one thing," wrote Black, but

"to invalidate statutes because of application of 'natural law' deemed to be above and undefined by the Constitution is another." Later still, Justice John Paul Stevens, too, mirrored the Iredell viewpoint: "Nothing in the Federal Constitution authorizes or obligates this Court to frustrate [the state policy in question]," he wrote. And, as recently as 1991, the Judiciary Committee of the United States Senate grappled with the question as it considered President Bush's nomination of Clarence Thomas to the Supreme Court.[70]

Iredell thus was one of the initial protagonists in a dialectic that continues. Scholars generally consider his view the prevalent one for nearly a century, but Chase's ultimately triumphant, though styled as "substantive due process." One writes, descriptively and aptly:

> In practice, . . . some of the Court's more recent decisions under such rubrics as "substantive due process" raise the question whether it is paying lip service to Iredell for the sake of appearances while effectively following Chase — a course of action that arguably compounds usurpation with deception.[71]

Limits on Appellate Jurisdiction:
Wilson v. Daniel

By statute, a civil action could not be removed from the circuit court to the Supreme Court unless the matter in dispute exceeded the sum or value of $2,000. In *Wilson v. Daniel*,[72] the original suit sought a recovery with a value of $200,000, but the jury verdict provided for discharge of the debt upon the payment of $1,800 and the costs. The issue was whether the original amount in suit or the sum necessary to discharge the judgment determined the jurisdictional question.

Chase, Paterson, and Cushing said the former; Wilson, the latter. Iredell recused, having presided on circuit. Upon reargument, Ellsworth, who had been absent before, sided with the majority. Iredell now wrote in dissent, noting that he would abstain if the merits were implicated; because they were not, and because the question was important, he perceived a duty to express his view. The statutory purpose, he said, was to shield the Court from insignificant matters. Congress thus intended that the amount contested on the writ of error control.[73]

This would be Iredell's final dissent. Over time the Court silently, in practice, made the sum in dispute on the writ of error determinative. Thirty-two years after *Wilson*, John Marshall wrote for a unanimous court formally adopting that view and in effect overruling *Wilson*. Iredell's position thus ultimately was vindicated.[74]

Title by Compact:
Sims Lessee v. Irvine

Sims Lessee v. Irvine[75] was an action to settle title to land. The Court, with only Ellsworth writing, determined that Sims had a complete equitable title that was rendered a complete legal title by a compact between Virginia and Pennsylvania. The right, having become an established legal one, remained such notwithstanding the establishment of the new federal government.

Iredell, who was approaching his demise, was too ill to attend. The reporter subsequently secured his notes, however, and published them with the report of the case. Both Ellsworth and Iredell observed that Iredell concurred in the result but for reasons somewhat different from those in the chief justice's opinion for the Court. Because of the cryptic nature of Ellsworth's opinion (one page), the divergence in reasoning is not readily apparent. Further, Iredell's notes offer no particular insights into his philosophy or jurisprudence.[76]

Sims lacks abiding significance and is often ignored altogether in the scholarly commentaries.[77]

"IT WAS NOT A TIME OF GIANT JUSTICES OR OF GREAT DECISIONS," A PRESENT-day scholar concludes. The linkage between these perceived dearths is palpable: Only great cases, astutely decided and articulately reasoned, make giant justices. Even that scholar, however, concludes that the Court in its early years was setting an enduring pattern for future constitutional adjudication.[78] Further, others are now seriously challenging the conventional wisdom that the Court acquired significance only with John Marshall's chief justiceship and his opinion in *Marbury v. Madison*.[79]

Whatever the ultimate verdict on the historical stature of the foregoing early cases, James Iredell was an energetic and consequential presence in their resolution and in the articulation of supportive reasoning. In *Penhallow*, he openly avowed an approach to opinion writing that characterized all his work: "I will endeavor to state my own principles on the subject with so much clearness," he wrote, "that whether my opinion be right or wrong, it may at least be understood what the opinion really is." This zeal for clarity aided the scholar who thought it not a time of "giant Justices" in concluding that, among them, Iredell was one of the two most impressive.[80]

But the most-significant case of that first decade, for Iredell and the Court, the one that alone provides continual and plenteous fodder for scholarly and juristic debate, yet awaits our attention.

James Iredell

From painting by M.L.H. Williams. Courtesy of Divison of Archives and History, N.C. Department of Cultural Resources.

Hannah Johnston Iredell

Wife of Justice James Iredell. Courtesy of Division of Archives and History, N.C. Department of Cultural Resources.

Governor Samuel Johnston

Iredell's law teacher and brother-in-law. Courtesy of Division of Archives and History, N.C. Department of Cultural Resources.

Governor William R. Davie

Iredell's compatriot in the ratification effort. From N.C. Portrait Index, original at University of North Carolina. Courtesy of Division of Archives and History, N.C. Department of Cultural Resources.

Chowan County Courthouse, Edenton, N.C.

Iredell practiced law at this courthouse, which is still in use. Courtesy of North Carolina Collection, University of North Carolina at Chapel Hill Library.

St. Paul's Church, Edenton, N.C.

Courtesy of North Carolina Collection, University of North Carolina at Chapel Hill Library.

Iredell's Fee Book

Courtesy of Southern Historical Collection, University of North Carolina at Chapel Hill Library.

Opposite: **Title Page of Iredell's Revisal**

Courtesy of North Carolina Collection, University of North Carolina at Chapel Hill Library.

L A W S

OF THE

S T A T E

OF

NORTH-CAROLINA.

PUBLISHED, ACCORDING TO ACT OF ASSEMBLY,

BY JAMES IREDELL,

NOW ONE OF THE ASSOCIATE JUSTICES OF THE SUPREME COURT OF THE UNITED STATES.

E D E N T O N:
PRINTED BY H O D G E & W I L L S,
PRINTERS TO THE STATE OF NORTH-CAROLINA.
M,DCC,XCI.

A N S W E R S

T O

MR. MASON's OBJECTIONS

T O   T H E

NEW CONSTITUTION

Recommended by the late CONVENTION at PHILADELPHIA:

BY M A R C U S.

To which is added,

AN A D D R E S S

To the F R E E M E N of N O R T H - C A R O L I N A.

BY P U B L I C O L A.

I OBJECTION.

" THERE is no declaration of rights, and the laws of the general government being paramount to the laws and conftitutions of the feveral ft tes, the declarations of rights in the feparate ftates are no fecurity Nor are the people fecured even in the enjoyment of the benefit of the common law, which ftands here upon no other foundation than its having been adopted by the refpective acts forming the conftitutions of the feveral ftates."

ANSWER.

1. As to the want of a declaration of rights. The introduction of thefe in England, from which the idea was originally taken, was in confequence of ufurpations of the crown, contrary, as was conceived, to the principles of their government. But there no original conftitution is to be found, and the only meaning of a declaration of rights in that country is, that in certain particulars fpecified, the crown had no authority to act. Could this have been neceffary had there been a conftitution in being by which it could have been clearly difcerned whether the crown had fuch authority or not ? Had the people, by a folemn inftrument, delegated particular powers to the crown at the formation of their government, furely the crown which in that cafe could claim order that inftrument only, could not have contended for more power than was conveyed by it. So it is in regard to the new conftitution here : The future government which may be formed under that authority certainly cannot act beyond the warrant of that authority. As well might they attempt to impofe a King upon America, as go one ftep in any other refpect beyond the terms of their inftitution. The queftion then only is, whether

more power will be vefted in the future government than is neceffary for the general purpofes of the union. This may occafion a ground of difpute,—but after exprefsly defining the powers that are to be exercifed, to fay that they fhall all exercife no other powers (either by a general or particular enumeration) would feem to me both nugatory and ridiculous. As well might a Judge when he condemns a man to be hanged, give ftrong injunctions to the Sheriff that he fhould not be beheaded.*

2. As to the common law, it is difficult to know what is meant by that part of the objection. So far as the people are now entitled to the benefit of the common law, they certainly will have a right to enjoy it under the new conftitution 'till altered by the general legiflature, which even in this point has fome cardinal limits affigned to it. What are moft acts of Affembly but a deviation in fome degree from the principles of the common law ? The people are exprefsly fecured (contrary to Mr. Mafon's wifhes) againft ex poft facto laws; fo that the tenure of any property at any time held under the principles of the common law, cannot be altered by any future act of the general legiflature. The principles of the common law, as they now apply, muft furely always hereafter apply, except in thofe particulars in which exprefs authority is given by this

* It appears to be a very juft remark of Mr. Wilson's, in his celebrated fpeech, that a bill of rights would have been dangerous, as implying that without fuch a refervation the Congrefs would have had authority in the cafes enumerated, fo that if any had been omitted (and who is acute enough to recite all the facts & individual rights not relinquifhed by its new conftitutant ?) they might have been confidered at the mercy of the general legiflature.

Iredell's "Answers" to Mason's Objections

THE

JOURNAL,

OF THE

CONVENTION

OF

NORTH-CAROLINA.

At a Convention begun and held at Hillsborough, on the twenty-first day of July, in the year of our Lord one thousand seven hundred and eighty-eight, and of the Independence of the United States of America the thirteenth, in pursuance of a resolution of the last General Assembly, for the purposes of deliberating and determining on the proposed plan of Federal Government, and for fixing the unalterable seat of government of this state.

Journal of the First Ratification Convention, Hillsborough, 1788

Courtesy of North Carolina Collection, University of North Carolina at Chapel Hill Library.

145

State of North-Carolina.

IN CONVENTION, AUGUST 1, 1788.

Resolved, That a Declaration of Rights, asserting and securing from incroachment the great Principles of civil and religious Liberty, and the unalienable Rights of the People, together with Amendments to the most ambiguous and exceptionable Parts of the said Constitution of Government, ought to be laid before Congress, and the Convention of the States that shall or may be called for the Purpose of Amending the said Constitution, for their consideration, previous to the Ratification of the Constitution aforesaid, on the part of the State of North Carolina.

DECLARATION OF RIGHTS.

1st. That there are certain natural rights of which men, when they form a social compact, cannot deprive or divest their posterity, among which are the enjoyment of life, and liberty, with the means of acquiring, possessing and protecting property, and pursuing and obtaining happiness and safety.

2d. That all power is naturally vested in, and consequently derived from the people; that magistrates therefore are their trustees, and agents, and at all times amenable to them.

3d. That Government ought to be instituted for the common benefit, protection and security of the people; and that the doctrine of non-resistance against arbitrary power and oppression is absurd, slavish, and destructive to the good and happiness of mankind.

4th. That no man or set of men are entitled to exclusive or separate public emoluments or privileges from the community, but in consideration of public services; which not being descendible, neither ought the offices of magistrate, legislator or judge, or any other public office to be hereditary.

5th. That the legislative, executive and judiciary powers of government should be separate and distinct, and that the members of the two first may be restrained from oppression by feeling and participating the public burthens, they should at fixed periods be reduced to a private station, return into the mass of the people, and the vacancies be supplied by certain and regular elections; in which all or any part of the former members to be eligible or ineligible, as the rules of the Constitution of Government, and the laws shall direct.

6th. That elections of Representatives in the legislature ought to be free and frequent, and all men having sufficient evidence of permanent common interest with, and attachment to the community, ought to have the right of suffrage: and no aid, charge, tax or fee can be set, rated, or levied upon the people without their own consent, or that of their representatives, so elected, nor can they be bound by any law, to which they have no, in like manner assented for the public good.

7th. That all power of suspending laws, or the execution of laws by any authority without the consent of the representatives, of the people in the Legislature, is injurious to their rights, and ought not to be exercised.

8th. That in all capital and criminal prosecutions, a man hath a right to demand the cause and nature of his accusation, to be confronted with the accusers and witnesses, to call for evidence and be allowed counsel in his favor, and to a fair and speedy trial by an impartial jury of his vicinage, without whose unanimous consent he cannot be found guilty (except in the government of the land and naval forces) nor can he be compelled to give evidence against himself.

9th. That no freeman ought to be taken, imprisoned, or disseized of his freehold, liberties, privileges or franchises, or outlawed or exiled, or in any manner destroyed or deprived of his life, liberty, or property but by the law of the land.

10th. That every freeman restrained of his liberty is entitled to a remedy to enquire into the lawfulness thereof, and to remove the same, if unlawful, and that such remedy ought not to be denied nor delayed.

11th. That in controversies respecting property, and in suits between man and man, the ancient trial by jury is one of the greatest securities to the rights of the people, and ought to remain sacred and inviolable.

12th. That every freeman ought to find a certain remedy by recourse to the laws for all injuries and wrongs he may receive in his person, property, or character. He ought to obtain right and justice freely without sale, completely and without denial, promptly and without delay, and that all establishments, or regulations contravening these rights, are oppressive and unjust.

13th. That excessive bail ought not to be required, nor excessive fines imposed, nor cruel and unusual punishments inflicted.

14. That every freeman has a right to be secure from all unreasonable searches, and seizures of his person, his papers, and property: all warrants therefore to search suspected places, or seize any freeman, his papers or property, without information upon oath (or affirmation of a person religiously scrupulous of taking an oath) of legal and sufficient cause, are grievous and oppressive, and all general warrants to search suspected places, or to apprehend any suspected person without specially naming or describing the place or person, are dangerous and ought not to be granted.

15th. That the people have a right peaceably to assemble together to consult for the common good, or to instruct their representatives; and that every freeman has a right to petition, or apply to the Legislature for redress of grievances.

16th. That the people have a right to freedom of speech, and of writing and publishing their sentiments; that the freedom of the press is one of the greatest bulwarks of Liberty, and ought not to be violated.

17th. That the people have a right to keep and bear arms; that a well regulated militia composed of the body of the people, trained to arms, is the proper, natural and safe defence of a free state. That standing armies in time of peace are dangerous to Liberty, and therefore ought to be avoided, as far as the circumstances and protection of the community will admit; and that in all cases, the military should be under strict subordination to, and governed by the civil power.

18th. That no soldier in time of peace ought to be quartered in any house without the consent of the owner, and in time of war in such manner only as the Laws direct.

19th. That any person religiously scrupulous of bearing arms ought to be exempted upon payment of an equivalent to employ another to bear arms in his stead.

20. That religion, or the duty which we owe to our Creator, and the manner of discharging it, can be directed only by reason and conviction, not by force or violence, and therefore all men have an equal, natural and unalienable right to the free exercise of religion according to the dictates of conscience, and that no particular religious sect or society ought to be favoured or established by law in preference to others.

Amendments to the Constitution.

I. THAT each state in the union shall, respectively, retain every power, jurisdiction and right, which is not by this constitution delegated to the Congress of the United States, or to the departments of the Federal Government.

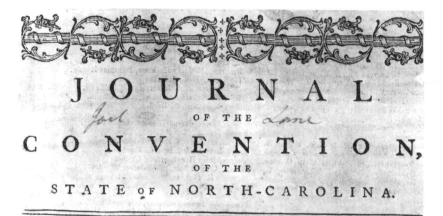

JOURNAL

O F T H E

CONVENTION,

O F T H E

STATE OF NORTH-CAROLINA.

At a CONVENTION begun and held at *Fayetteville*, on the Third *Monday* of *November*, One Thoufand Seven Hundred and Eighty-Nine, agreeable to the Refolutions of the laft General Affembly, bearing Date the Seventeenth of *November*, One Thoufand Seven Hundred and Eighty-Eight.

Journal of the Second Ratification Convention, Fayetteville, 1789

Courtesy of North Carolina Collection, University of North Carolina at Chapel Hill Library.

Opposite: **Hillsborough Convention's Call for a Declaration of Rights Prior to Ratification**

Courtesy of North Carolina Collection, University of North Carolina at Chapel Hill Library.

Ratification Resolution, 1789

The first (above) and last (opposite) pages. Courtesy of Division of Archives and History, N.C. Department of Cultural Resources.

This constitution, and the laws of the United States which shall be made in pursuance thereof; and all treaties made, or which shall shall be made, under the authority of the United States, shall be the Supreme law of the land; and the judges in every State shall be bound thereby, any thing in the constitution or laws of any State to the contrary notwithstanding.

The Senators and Representatives before mentioned, and the members of the several State Legislatures, and all executive and judicial officers, both of the United States and of the several States, shall be bound by oath or affirmation, to support this constitution; but no religious test shall ever be required as a qualification to any office or public trust under the United States

Article 7

The ratification of the conventions of nine States, shall be sufficient for the establishment of this constitution between the States so ratifying the same.

Resolved that this Convention in behalf of the freemen, citizens and inhabitants of the State of North Carolina, do adopt and ratify the said constitution and form of government.

Done in Convention this 21 day of November 1789.

Sam Johnston President of the Convention

James Taylor } Secretaries

149

TO THE PUBLIC.

HAVING feen with great furprize in fome of the public newfpapers an attack upon my judicial chaiacter, figned with the name of Mr. *Cabell*, a Member of Congrefs, I think it proper to take fome notice of it, on account of a miftake in point of fact which he feems to have committed. From the tenor of his obfervations, any one would conclude that I wrote the charge he condemns with a view to draw forth a cenfure upon him or fome other Members of Congrefs who had written circular letters to their conftituents. The truth is, I never knew that Mr. *Cabell* had written any circular letter at all, until I heard the prefentment read in Court, nor have I feen the letter alluded to to this hour. I had indeed feen printed letters of one or two other Members of Congrefs from the fame ftate, but had them not in my thoughts when I prepared that charge, which I wrote deliberately in Philadelphia, in order to be delivered in Maryland and Virginia. The fame charge was delivered fubftantially in both ftates, and without a view to any particular perfon. With regard to the fentiments of that charge, I am ready on all proper occafions to vindicate every word of it, as well as the propriety of delivering fuch a charge on fuch an occafion. In the mean time, I have a right to expect, that if the charge be cenfured, it fhall be cenfured for what it really contains, and not tor what exifts merely in the imagination of the Cenfurer. I have no hefitation in faying, that if it has the tendency Mr. *Cabell* afcribes to it, it does, in my opinion, deferve a feverer cenfure than any he has beftowed upon it.

The conduct of the Court after the prefentment has incurred Mr. *Cabell's* cenfure. It is difficult to fay what can efcape it if the conduct of the Court on that occafion cannot. They knew not fuch a prefentment was in contemplation. It was brought into Court the fame day that the charge was delivered, and without any adjournment having taken place, and agreeably to the ufual practice, I prefume, in Virginia, (though different from that in fome other ftates) was read by the Clerk without even being feen by the Court. None of the circular letters which were the object of the prefentment was produced to the Court, nor in poffeffion of the Judges. The Jury were afked if they had any bufinefs to require their attention longer, of if they wifhed to ftay to confider of any. They anfwer-

ed in the negative. The Attorney for the United States was afked if he wifhed them to be detained longer. He declared he knew of no occafion for it. They were then difcharged. Were the Court to catechife the Jury for their cenfure of a publication which they themfelves had never feen? or to direct a profecution upon a publication without knowing the contents of it? Ought they in any inftance indeed to direct a profecution in the prefence of the Attorney, within whofe particular department it lies, and when no occafion calls for their immediate interpofition? Were they to interfere unneceffarily, they might juftly be charged with becoming parties to a profecution, and incapacitating themfelves from the impartial conduct of Judges afterwards. Whatever might be the intention of the Jury, which was compofed of very refpectable men, it has been a frequent practice in fome of the fouthern ftates for Grand Juries to prefent what they confidered as grievances though they could not be the foundation of a criminal profecution in the Court. I have known fuch prefentments containing very heavy charges againft the government itfelf. It never occurred to me to be proper to fupprefs a practice which I found eftablifhed, whether the exercife of it was agreeable to my private fentiments or not; and I incline to think, had the Grand Jury at *Richmond*, inftead of prefenting thofe circular letters, prefented any obnoxious act of the government, and the Court by an exertion of power arbitrarily fupprefled the prefentment, it would have been the fubject of a very virulent—and poffibly a very juft—invective, by fome of thofe perfons who have no fcruple in condemning the Court for not interfering with this.

With regard to the illiberal epithets Mr. *Cabell* has beftowed, not only on me, but on the other judges of the Supreme Court, I leave him in full poffeffion of all the credit he can derive from the ufe of them. I defy him or any man to fhew, that in the exercife of my judicial character, I have been ever influenced in the flighteft degree by any man, either in or out of office, and I affure him I fhall be as little influenced by this new mode of attack by a Member of Congrefs as I can be by any other.

JA. IREDELL.

Edenton, North-Carolina,
June 21ft, 1797.

Iredell's Response to Samuel Cabell's Charges

Library, Hayes Plantation, Edenton

Courtesy of North Carolina Collection, University of North Carolina at Chapel Hill Library.

151

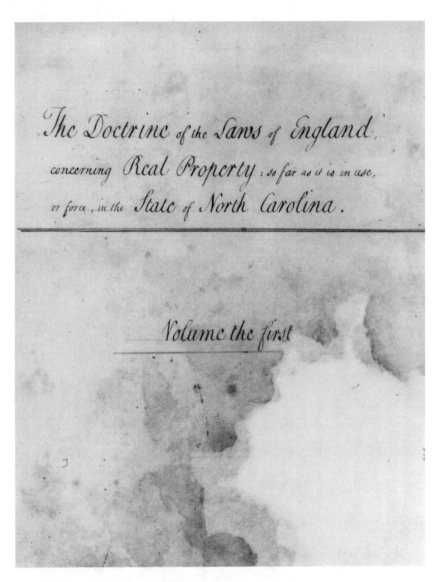

Title Page of Iredell's Treatise on Real Property

Courtesy of Southern Historical Collection, University of North Carolina at Chapel Hill Library.

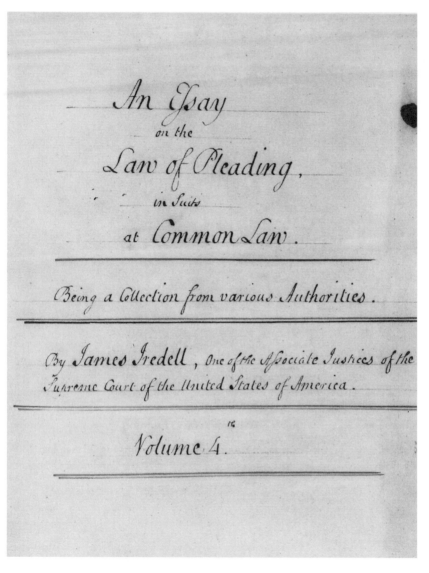

Title Page of Iredell's Treatise on Pleading

Courtesy of Southern Historical Collection, University of North Carolina at Chapel Hill Library.

Justice Wilson's Grave, Edenton

Photographed on the occasion of the removal of his remains to Philadelphia, 1906. Courtesy of North Carolina Collection, University of North Carolina at Chapel Hill Library.

Iredell House, Edenton

1905 photograph courtesy of Historic Edenton.

Iredell Grave, Hayes Plantation, Edenton

Courtesy of Historic Edenton.

CHAPTER 13

Sovereign Power Dragged Before a Court: Chisholm v. Georgia

I T WAS NOT RATIONAL, JOHN MARSHALL HAD POSITED DURING THE RAT-IFICATION DEBATES, "TO SUPPOSE THAT THE SOVEREIGN POWER SHOULD BE DRAGGED BEFORE A COURT."[1] BEFORE THE SUPREME COURT WAS HALF A DECADE OLD, HOWEVER, WHAT MARSHALL HAD viewed as irrational happened, over James Iredell's solitary protest.

In *Georgia v. Brailsford*[2] the state of Georgia had sought to inject itself into a suit. In *Chisholm v. Georgia*,[3] contrastingly, it fought tenaciously to remove itself from one. Edmund Randolph in argument — and Blair, Jay, and Wilson in judicial opinions — noted the transparent incongruity; while quite satisfied with its right to sue citizens of other states, Jay trenchantly observed, Georgia was malcontent when on the receiving end. Charles Evans Hughes remarked similarly almost a century and a half later: Georgia, he said, had "availed herself of the original jurisdiction of the Supreme Court to bring suit, but denied that she could be made a defendant against her will at the suit of an individual."[4]

The adjudicative facts in *Chisholm* were uncomplicated. Robert Farquhar had delivered goods to the state of Georgia for Revolutionary War use, for which Georgia had not paid. Farquhar's executor, Alexander Chisholm, sued to recover the debt. Both Farquhar and Chisholm were citizens of South Carolina.[5]

The Judiciary Act of 1789 gave the federal circuit court jurisdiction over the case. Sitting on the circuit court, Iredell nevertheless dismissed on a technicality for want of jurisdiction. Because the action of debt could lie only for a fixed sum, assumpsit had evolved to give a contracting party redress for promises performed for unspecified sums. The section of the 1789 Process

Act that described the actions available in the federal courts, however, did not mention assumpsit, the writ pursuant to which Chisholm had brought the action. Iredell therefore dismissed, avoiding the more-significant question the Court would encounter when it sat *en banc*: Whether it had jurisdiction to hear and determine a suit by a citizen of one state against another state.[6]

Lingering concern over whether the states had relinquished all their sovereignties gave import to the question. Contemporary newspapers published a letter from Philadelphia voicing this misgiving: If such suits would lie, the writer warned, the states would "have relinquished all their sovereignties, and have become mere corporations upon the establishment of the national government; for a sovereign state can never be sued or coerced by the authority of another government."

The import was enhanced by the states' fears that if Chisholm prevailed, a deluge of actions would follow by refugee Loyalists seeking recovery of debts forfeited by acts of attainder and similarly directed legislation. Various provisions of the 1783 peace treaty lent authenticity to these apprehensions. The potential liability for unpaid pre-Revolutionary British debts was considerable. Twenty-eight years after *Chisholm*, John Marshall aptly described the problem: "[A]t the adoption of the Constitution," he wrote, "all the States were greatly indebted; and the apprehension that these debts might be prosecuted in the federal courts formed a very serious objection to that instrument."[7]

The preratification period heard some alarms. George Mason worried over the absence of any limitation on the federal judiciary and specifically failed to see the propriety of federal jurisdiction over suits between a state and citizens of another state. A draft of a judiciary article found among Mason's papers omitted jurisdiction over such causes. Mason's fellow Virginian, Richard Henry Lee, had likewise opposed the notion that states could be sued by individuals.

Iredell heard similar objections in North Carolina. Archibald Maclaine, a Federalist writing pseudonymously as an Antifederalist, noted that the chief objection to the proposed Constitution was that it would require payment of debts to British subjects (apparently, though not clearly, referring to both state and individual debts). Willie Jones had promoted the Antifederalist cause, William R. Davie told Iredell, by "haranguing the people on the terrors of the [federal] judicial power, and the certainty of their ruin if they are *obliged now* to pay their debts." Samuel Spencer raised objections similar to Mason's, believing the federal courts would operate oppressively; he wanted them uninvolved in all areas of state judicial competence and in "such controversies as must carry the people a great way from home." James Galloway, another Antifederalist delegate, had expressed concern at Hillsborough that the Constitution might compel the state to redeem its public securities at their nominal value, citing the obligation-of-contracts clause.

Leaders of great stature had countered these concerns, however. In the Virginia convention James Madison confronted Mason's disquietude. The objection, he opined, was "perhaps without reason," it not being within the power of individuals to call a state into court. The jurisdiction clause, Madison argued, could only operate to allow a state to bring a citizen before a federal court; citizens had a right to be heard, and if a state condescended to be a party, the court could "take cognizance of it."

When Patrick Henry disagreed, arguing that justice permitted no discrimination between plaintiff and defendant in such controversies, John Marshall defended Madison's position. The intent of the jurisdiction clause, he said, was to enable states to recover claims from individuals residing in other states. Individuals could present claims against states to the legislatures of those states, but without the federal courts, a state could not recover a claim from a citizen of another state. Henry's fairness argument thus was meritless, Marshall argued.

Alexander Hamilton joined Marshall in viewing the state-debt apprehensions as baseless. The Constitution, he said, contemplated state retention of all sovereignty not expressly delegated to the United States. It was inherent in the nature of sovereignty to be unsuable apart from consent; absent a surrender of this immunity in the plan of the convention, it remained with the states. The subject thus had been actively debated when the Constitution was adopted, but the disclaimers of the most-eminent advocates among the Federalists had largely quelled fears of the existence of such federal power and removed them as a barrier to ratification.[8]

The impressive array of leaders who inveighed against the existence of such a federal power did not deter Edmund Randolph from arguing vigorously to the contrary. Randolph had no consistent party affiliation and drew disapprobation from public figures as disparate as Thomas Jefferson and Alexander Hamilton. Jefferson complained of Randolph's "cameleon" quality, "having no color of his own, and reflecting that nearest him," while Hamilton told Washington he had never had confidence in Randolph. In this instance, though, Randolph adhered rigidly to the Federalist position in what has been called "one of his most outstanding exploits." The four judges who concurred with his position all used reasons contained in, or suggested by, Randolph's argument.[9]

The Court asked Randolph to address four questions: (1) Could Georgia, as one of the states now united, be a party-defendant at the suit of a private citizen, even though the citizen and his testator were citizens of South Carolina? (2) If so, did an action in assumpsit lie against the state? (3) Was service on Georgia's governor and attorney general competent service? (4) By what process should the state's appearance be enforced? Randolph responded:

(1) The Constitution gave the Supreme Court jurisdiction over controversies between a state and citizens of other states. This subjected a state to suit in the Court by a private citizen of another state; otherwise, various evils on the part of the states were beyond rectification.

To submit to the "Supreme Judiciary" was not a degradation of sovereignty. In speaking of cases "where a State shall be a party," the Judiciary Act made no distinction between a state as plaintiff and as defendant. The objection that the law prescribed no execution against a state was likewise untenable; the Supreme Court possessed execution authority, either under the Judiciary Act or as a necessary incident of its jurisdiction. The letter and the spirit of the Constitution, combined with the arguments made, dictated the conclusion that a state could be sued by a citizen of another state.

(2) Assumpsit would indeed lie against a state. A state is capable of making a promise and, being an assemblage of moral persons, is itself a moral person. Without that assumption, treaties and other compacts between governmental entities would fail.

(3) Service on the governor and the attorney general was "competent service." While the summons did not specify a recipient, the governor was bound by his oath to defend the state and had sued on the state's behalf in *Brailsford*. He thus was the appropriate object of service. While adding the attorney general was "supererogation," it satisfied the dictates of etiquette by giving notice to the state officer who would defend the suit.

(4) The proper mode of process to compel an appearance was a matter of indifference.

The prostration of states' rights was not his object, Randolph averred. The residual powers of the people and the state legislatures were such, he concluded, that the states "need not fear an assault from bold ambition, or any approaches of covered stratagem."[10]

Silence greeted Randolph's argument, for Georgia was unrepresented. Any appearance would have set a precedent "replete with danger to the Republic," Governor Edward Telfair told the Georgia legislature, and "would have involved th[e] state in complicated difficulties abstracted from the infractions it would have made on her retained sovereignty." Randolph, fretting over the "appearance of precipitancy" and desiring adequate time for the state to deliberate, successfully moved to postpone consideration until the next term. Georgia again refused to appear or to have counsel argue, however.

Alexander Dallas and Jared Ingersoll protested the exercise of jurisdiction but, honoring "positive instructions," declined to argue the question. The Court, cognizant of the case's importance and desirous of any possible enlightenment, invited any member of the bar to state the opposing case. There were no takers, however.[11]

The absence of counterargument, combined with the force of Randolph's advocacy, apparently had an effect, for four of the five sitting justices (Justice Thomas Johnson had recently resigned, and Justice William Paterson had not yet been appointed to replace him) sided with Randolph. Blair, writing first among the majority, looked only to the Constitution. It expressly extended the judicial authority of the United States to controversies between a state and citizens of another state, he said, and like Randolph, he had no doubt that the intent was to encompass cases where a state was a defendant as well as those where it was a plaintiff. The Constitution also gave the Supreme Court original jurisdiction where a state is a party, a status as pertinent to defendants as to plaintiffs; to deny jurisdiction thus would be to refuse cognizance of a case where a state was indeed a party. Finally, service on the governor as chief executive and on the attorney general as the state's lawyer was quite appropriate.[12]

Cushing joined Blair in relying solely on these provisions. The "letter of the Constitution" governed. The clauses subjecting a state to jurisdiction in controversies between two or more states, or between a state and a foreign state, answered the argument that making a state a defendant was not intended because of its adverse effect on state sovereignty — a state must necessarily be a defendant in such suits. Equal-justice concerns also favored this interpretation, for the rights of individuals were as treasured as those of the states. Assumpsit would lie, and service on the governor and the attorney general was proper.[13]

Wilson shared Cushing's equal-justice concerns. His ratification-era utterances foreshadowed his *Chisholm* opinion. In the Pennsylvania convention, Wilson had touted impartiality as the Constitution's foremost feature, stating specifically: "When a citizen has a controversy with another state, there ought to be a tribunal where both parties may stand on a just and equal footing."

Wilson's law lectures had been equally adumbrative of his position. When sued, he instructed, a state or nation should be subject to the judicial powers. The principle was "dignified because it is just." Individuals were bound by human laws, and states were nothing more than aggregations of individuals. Being suable degraded neither a man nor a state.

Wilson commenced his opinion with a nationalistic flavor. The question presented was "no less *radical* than this — 'do the people of the *United States* form a NATION?'" General jurisprudence, laws and practices of particular states and kingdoms, and the Constitution itself would provide the affirmative answer.

The state, Wilson said philosophically, was but an "artificial person," indeed, "the inferior contrivance of man." Like the men who compose it, it should "do justice and fulfill engagements." If one free man could bind himself by law, an aggregate of free men could also, and the dignity of all collectively was equally unimpaired.

"[G]eneral principles of right" precluded sovereign states, as well as individuals, from averting justice. Kings had been subjected to judicial proceedings, and states deserved no better. "[T]he poorest peasant is a man as well as the *King* himself," Frederick the Great of Prussia had observed, so "all men ought to obtain justice, since in the estimation of justice, all men are *equal,* whether the Prince complain of a peasant, or a peasant complain of the Prince." Frederick had, Wilson observed laudatorily, "disdained to mount upon the artificial stilts of sovereignty." The laws and practices of other states and kingdoms likewise offered nothing against, and much to favor, the court's jurisdiction over Georgia.

Finally, the Constitution itself dictated that "legitimate result." The people could, in that instrument, vest in the Court jurisdiction over the states in such suits, and the "[f]air and conclusive deduction" was that they had. Among the Constitution's declared objectives were establishing justice and ensuring domestic tranquillity; among its express prohibitions was denial of the capacity to impair the obligation of contracts, including a state's own. If a state could impair the obligation of its own contracts with impunity, both justice and domestic tranquillity would be negated.

The texture of the Constitution evinced national purposes. The powers established were nationwide in scope. Exemption claims ran counter to "our very existence as a nation." Accordingly, Georgia was amenable to the Supreme Court's jurisdiction. The document itself confirmed this deduction by expressly conferring power over controversies between two states, meaning one state had to be a defendant. It also expressly extended power to controversies between a state and citizens of another state, language which could not have described "with more precise accuracy" the *Chisholm* controversy. The "combined inference" was "that the action lies."[14]

Like Wilson's, Jay's prior experience and commentary augured his position in *Chisholm.* His firsthand acquaintance with the ineffectual nature of the Confederation rendered him an ultra-Federalist, highly supportive of a strong national government. As the Confederation's secretary for foreign affairs, he saw himself as having little power amid great needs. His Confederation-period correspondence thus deplored disunity and the absence of a national spirit, and it urged strengthening of both a national spirit and the powers of a central government. In exhorting the people of New York to ratify the Constitution, he emphasized foreign affairs and the need for further powers to make effectual the exercise of those granted. So intense was Jay's nationalism that the New York Senate had refused to confirm the House's selection of him as a delegate to the Constitutional Convention because of his "well-known ultra-federal opinions."

Jay's contributions to *The Federalist* had conveyed these opinions to the nation and still more pellucidly forecast his stance in *Chisholm*. American prosperity, he had written, depended on the country's people "continuing firmly united." The country was one and should not be split into jealous and alien sovereignties. Its people had instituted, preserved, and perpetuated a federal government because of a "strong sense of the value and blessings of Union."

National unity and a strong national government were essential to the conduct of foreign relations and the maintenance of peace. Providing for their safety, Jay had written, was first among the objects of a wise and free people, and "a cordial Union under an efficient national Government... affords them the best security that can be devised against *hostilities* from abroad." A single national government could better promote peace than thirteen separate states or three or four distinct confederacies, and questions regarding treaties and the laws of nations were better committed to the courts of one national government. There would be fewer causes for war and greater power to settle such issues amicably.

Randolph undoubtedly considered Jay's perspective when he argued that the issues of state suability by foreign citizens and by citizens of another state were interrelated. "To be consistent," he contended in a polemic probably pitched to the chief justice,

> the opponents of my principles must say that a State may not be sued by a foreigner. — What? Shall the tranquillity of our country be at the mercy of every State? Or, if it be allowed that a State may be sued by a foreigner, why, in the scale of reason, may not the measure be the same when the citizen of another State is the complainant?[15]

Jay thus reached the jurisdictional issue "scarcely disposed to take a narrow or circumscribed view of the judicial power of the Federal government, or an enlarged view of the sovereign claims and immunities of the States."[16] His opinion focused initially on the nature of state sovereignty. While thirteen sovereignties had emerged from the Revolution, they had continued to consider themselves one people and to manage their national concerns accordingly. Collectively, they had established the Constitution, acting "as sovereigns of the whole country." They had willed that state governments be bound by the federal Constitution and that state constitutions be made to conform to it.

The European idea of the prince as sovereign and the people as subjects, with the prince unamenable to judicial control or constraint, was repugnant to the relative egalitarianism of the American experiment. At the Revolution, sovereignty had devolved on the people, who were now "sovereigns without subjects" and whose governors were their agents. The unlimited sovereignty held by the princes of Europe was unknown.

Given this limited nature of state sovereignty, was it compatible with suability? The suit would not be by a subject or an inferior, Jay posited, because there were none. Corporations and cities could be sued, so why not a state? One state could sue another in the Supreme Court without degradation. Why, then, was it incompatible that all the people of a state should be sued by one citizen of another, the process and the consequences being the same?

Further, a state could sue a single citizen; indeed, Georgia was doing so in *Brailsford*. A one-way rule, he stated, "is said to be a bad one." "[T]he citizens of Georgia," he wrote disparagingly, "are content with a right of suing citizens of other states; but are not content that citizens of other states should have a right to sue them."

Perhaps, however, by joining the national compact, Georgia had consented to suits by citizens of other states. Prior to the Constitution, there was no national appellate jurisdiction, Jay said, apparently overlooking the special Court of Appeals Congress established in 1780 to determine the disposition of prizes captured at sea and other cases arising under international relations. Grace alone determined suability, a sure prescription for animosities and hostilities. Both justice and policy thus dictated "a common tribunal for the termination of controversies."

The Constitution was designed in part to establish justice. It expressly provided that the judicial power of the United States extended to controversies between two or more states and between a state and citizens of another state. If a state was suing citizens of another state, trial in a national court was necessary to alleviate concerns of partiality. Likewise, where some citizens of one state had demands against the collective citizenry of another, it would be improper for the latter to be the judges of the justice due them.

How, then, should the clause extending the federal judicial power "to controversies between a state and citizens of another state" be interpreted? While in Georgia's view it reached only controversies in which a state was a plaintiff,

Jay thought "[t]he ordinary rules for construction" presaged a different result. The power was remedial; its purpose, to settle controversies. It thus should be construed liberally to reach controversies in which a state was either a plaintiff or a defendant, unless the plain language required otherwise.

The words, however, were unambiguous. They simply would not have been chosen had the framers intended their application to extend only to controversies in which a state might be a plaintiff. The Constitution contained no intimation of such intention. When citizens make demands upon a state which the state resists, it is irrefutable that there is a controversy between them, and "[i]f it is a controversy between them, then it clearly falls not only within the spirit, but the very words of the Constitution."

The clause giving the Supreme Court original jurisdiction in cases "in which a State shall be a party" contained the same idea. The framers could easily enough have said "party-plaintiff" if that was their intent. In common usage, however, "party" applied to both plaintiffs and defendants and thus could not be limited in this case to only one of them.

Jay closed with policy considerations. Holding Georgia in the suit was wise because it was honest and useful: honest as doing justice without respect of persons, useful as offering justice to the most obscure and friendless. Where the people are sovereigns, he concluded, governments and citizens cannot be degraded by appearing together in their own courts to have their controversies determined.

While Jay thus clearly thought the action would lie, he was not insensitive to the politically explosive implications of his position—those springing from public concerns about the problem of state debts. He was, he noted,

> far from being prepared to say that an individual may sue a state on bills of credit issued before the Constitution was established and which were issued and received on the faith of the state, and at a time when no ideas or expectations of judicial interposition were entertained or contemplated.[17]

The majority opinions, then, may be summarized as follows. Sovereignty in America pertained not to princes, but to the people collectively. Sovereignty was not incompatible with compulsory suability because princes had been liable to such suits. Because the individual sovereign or citizen might be sued by another individual, logically an aggregation of individual sovereigns organized into a state might also be. The states were clearly subjected to the Supreme Court's jurisdiction at the suit of other states; therefore, such suability did not violate sovereignty.

The only reason that perhaps prevented a sovereign prince and the United

States from being sued in their own courts — the fact that the executive power necessary to enforce the court's judgment was held by the prince or the government — was inapplicable when a state was sued in the courts of the United States. Even if states once had sovereign immunity, the Constitution — by its declared objectives of justice, interstate harmony, and protection for individual human rights — had divested them of it. Its express language and its failure to exclude suits by individuals against states attested the same result, as did the practical necessity of enforcing both the powers the Constitution gave the federal government and the constraints it imposed on the states.[18]

Notwithstanding his virtually rabid federalism — indeed, as discussed *infra*, perhaps in part because of it — Iredell stood alone in dissenting from these views. Like Wilson's and Jay's, his prior commentary and experience imparted a degree of predictability to his position. In answering Mason's objections to the Constitution, he had posited that state judiciaries were left uncontrolled as to affairs relating only to the particular state. Congress was to keep its hands off of "the mere internal concerns of a state." The federal courts were to have jurisdiction only where the Union was in some way concerned.

In the ratification convention, Iredell had argued similarly. Under the proposed Constitution, the sovereignty and interests of the states were fully protected. Two governments would henceforth command allegiance: that of the Union in defined cases and that of the affected state government in all others.

His charges echoed this theme. There were two governments to which Americans owed obedience, he had told grand jurors: that of the United States in all instances in which authority had been relinquished to it and that of the state governments in all others. Neither could properly violate the peculiar province of the other.[19]

As noted, other Federalist thinkers shared Iredell's perspective that federal jurisdiction was limited to cases implicating federal concerns. Hamilton had said that the Constitution left much sovereign power exclusively with the states, which retained all rights not expressly delegated to the United States. More explicitly anticipating Iredell's position in *Chisholm*, Hamilton had stated: "It is inherent in the nature of sovereignty not to be amenable to the suit of an individual without its consent." All immunity not expressly surrendered thus remained with the states, and only "the obligations of good faith" constrained the states to pay their debts. Madison too thought the federal-jurisdiction clause operated only to allow states to bring suits against citizens, thus preventing citizen unrest with state courts by providing a neutral forum for such claims. Finally, Marshall viewed the intent as only to enable states to recover claims against citizens of other states. "I see a difficulty in making a state defendant," he said, "which does not prevent its being plaintiff."[20]

Iredell's dissent reflected these views. He eschewed equivocation, being "decidedly of [the] opinion that no such action as this... can legally be maintained." The action was in assumpsit, which would lie against a state only by virtue of the Constitution and a congressional enactment conformable to it. Legislative authority, within constitutional bounds, was essential and was lacking, and the power was not one necessarily incidental to the federal courts as such. When the Constitution was adopted and the Judiciary Act passed, neither federal nor state legislation authorized a compulsory suit against a state for the recovery of money. Accordingly, only state common law when the country was settled could authorize such suits, and it did not. Rather, it followed the common law of England in allowing them as a matter of grace only, not on compulsion. The legislature alone could dispense such benefactions, the executive being impotent to expend state funds without direct constitutional or statutory authorization.

One other common-law concept conceivably applied, Iredell continued: that concerning corporations. If a state could be considered a mere subordinate corporation, legislation would still be needed to allow the exercise of federal judicial authority against it, and there was none. The situation was not analogous to that in England, where a corporation was a mere creature of the Crown or the Parliament. State governments, instead, predated the federal and were not its offspring. Rather than the one being the creator of the other, the two governments sprang from the same authority: "The voluntary and deliberate choice of the people."

The analogy was wanting in other respects. Corporate acts were subject to revision by judicial or other authority; states, by contrast, were exempt from federal or other external authority except where the Constitution expressly gave power to the federal government. A corporation was altogether dependent on the government that sired it, while state governments were independent of the federal except in defined particulars.

The judicial article, then, was not self-executing. Congress had enacted no new law to implement the provision in question but "referred us to the old." The old provided no recourse, either by precedent or analogy, that would authorize this suit. The consequence, Iredell concluded, "clearly is that the suit... cannot be maintained."[21]

Iredell was not finished, however. He had largely ignored Randolph's arguments, he subjoined, because they did not affect his. It was not necessary to decide whether the Constitution authorized the suit because even had it done so, an implementing statute would be necessary, and there was none. Championing judicial restraint, he urged that "no judge should rashly commit himself upon important questions which it is unnecessary for him to decide."

Promptly ignoring his own counsel, and recognizing that his utterances might be "in some measure extra-judicial," Iredell then answered the constitutional question. He strongly opposed any construction that would allow a compulsory suit against a state for the recovery of money. Only "express words, or an insurmountable implication," could warrant so drastic a course, and once again, neither was present. Policy considerations could elucidate only in doubtful cases; here, doubt did not plague him, and he "therefore [had] nothing to do with policy." Again trespassing on his professed commitment to restraint, he acknowledged his policy-based differences with Randolph. He prayed for the good that Randolph predicted if Randolph's position prevailed, but he feared the evils with which he thought it pregnant.

Iredell's notes further elucidate his opinion. Neither express words nor fair implication, he wrote, authorized a suit by an individual against a state. The reference to controversies between a state and citizens of another state was surely satisfied by suits by a state against an individual. To apply the provision where the state is a defendant would be inconsistent with its sovereign character and thus ought not to occur by implication. The positions of Randolph, Cushing, and Jay — that the Constitutional Convention could have expressly excluded such suits but did not — failed to bolster their argument. If there was a case where the Convention should have spoken explicitly but did not, this was it. Sovereignties simply should not be "brought to a Bar of Justice" as readily as individuals without express authorization: "We must show our voucher for the exercise of so high an authority."[22]

Commendation has been the regnant response in scholarly assessment of Iredell's dissent. George van Santvoord applauded the minority jurist's "great force of reasoning, and admirable precision and clearness of illustration"; "lucid, logical, compact, [and] comprehensive," he says of the opinion, comparing it favorably to Jay's and viewing it "as a mere legal argument...to be far superior." Hampton Carson also thought the legal analysis "far superior in closeness of reasoning to Wilson's or Jay's" and praised Iredell for "confin[ing] himself strictly to the question before the Court." J.G. de R. Hamilton appraises similarly: "a splendid legal argument," he writes, "closely reasoned, and confined to the question before the court, whether an action of assumpsit could lie against a state." "[F]or clear and lucid reasoning, cold logic, strong argument and high statesmanship," another evaluates, Iredell's opinion was "far superior to that of any of his colleagues." It "far surpassed those of his associates as a legal analysis of the problem presented," writes still another.[23]

Subsequent Supreme Court justices have been equally laudatory. Samuel Miller considered Iredell's opinion "very learned." Joseph Bradley viewed it as "able" and more attuned "to former experience and usage" than the others. In "an exhaustive examination of the old law," said Bradley, Iredell amply demonstrated that the suability of a state without its consent was "a thing unknown to the law"—the position previously advanced by Hamilton, Madison, Marshall, and Mason. Given the reaction to *Chisholm*, the ensuing adoption of the Eleventh Amendment, history, and reason, Bradley and his Court preferred the Iredellian view.[24] Finally, in June 1999 a bare majority of the Court, frequently citing Iredell's dissent, viewed it as according with the original understanding of the Constitution and considered the majority decision "discredited,"[25] thus, as the dissenting opinion observed, rendering the Eleventh Amendment superfluous.[26]

Does Iredell's opinion merit these plaudits, or is it instead, as a present-day scholar writes, "perverse" in its reasoning and "deeply flawed"?[27] In actuality, both perspectives exaggerate. It bears remembering that the Court was writing on a clean slate for a new nation whose constitutional jurisprudence then knew neither paths nor fences. Whether the judicial article was self-executing was undetermined. The provision in question was by no means altogether free of ambiguity. As Justice Souter (joined by Justices Ginsberg and Breyer) noted only recently, the majority interpretation was reasonable but not compelled.[28] In context, neither the majority nor the minority positions were philosophically implausible or legally indefensible and unprincipled. Certainly the language of the Constitution permitted the majority view, Jay's opinion in particular being ably reasoned and thoroughly principled.

What, then, of the assertion that in *Chisholm* Iredell proved himself a liberal constructionist, and the seemingly contradictory claim that there he "adopted a style of constitutional reasoning that anticipated Robert Bork's" and "laid the foundation for future claims of judicial restraint in language that any originalist might well adopt"? While perhaps paradoxically so, there is some merit to both positions. Iredell clearly used language heartwarming to modern-day originalists. It was the duty of Congress to legislate as necessary to effectuate the Constitution, he wrote, while "[i]t is *ours* only to *judge*." "There is no part of the Constitution that I know of," he continued,

> that authorizes this Court to take up any business where they left it, and in order that the powers given in the Constitution may be in full activity, supply their omission by making *new laws* for *new cases*; or, which I take to be [the] same thing, applying *old principles* to *new cases* materially different from those to which they were applied before.

Equally clearly, however, Iredell drew on history, context, and intent, while his colleagues tended to consider only the black letter of the Constitution. Implications from the Constitution's historical origins could, in his perception, have import surpassing that of its precise words. A power could be exercised, Iredell maintained, not only when present in clear, black-letter form, but also "[i]f *upon a fair construction* of the Constitution" it existed. The competing claims demonstrate the unwisdom of attempting to mold ancient thoughts into modern constructs.[29]

Further, to claim that Iredell's *Chisholm* dissent spawned the Eleventh Amendment would overstate. Perhaps, as Justice Stevens recently averred, it "provided the blueprint" for the amendment, but given the state of public opinion (discussed *infra*), the amendment would undoubtedly have passed even had the Court in *Chisholm* been unanimous in the contrary view.[30]

To consider Iredell's dissent the womb of the states' rights doctrine is at least equally hyperbolic. While he firmly supported divided sovereignty, to depict him as an extreme proponent of states' rights is inaccurate, for he held strongly nationalistic beliefs and inclinations.[31]

Why, then, did Iredell assume the lonely role of the solitary juristic defender of the state's position in *Chisholm?* While necessarily speculative, the answer probably lies in his familiarity with the Federalist thought of his time and with contemporary public opinion.

Iredell was almost certainly familiar with the public utterances of leading Federalist thinkers such as Hamilton, Madison, Marshall, and Mason, all of whom had denied the viability of such a suit. More significantly, he was "a canny Federalist" whose circuit travels, especially in the South, exposed him to the strength of residual antinational sentiments. Such tendencies were particularly robust in his home state of North Carolina. He could hardly have forgotten that one of the conditions to ratification opponents of the Constitution had insisted upon at Hillsborough was a redraft of the judicial-power clause to eliminate federal jurisdiction over controversies between a state and citizens of another state. Judge Samuel Ashe's words upon Iredell's appointment to the Court perhaps reverberated in his mind: "While you sit, every jealousy and fear will subside; and every apprehension of encroachment from the newly erected jurisdiction will cease." The hold such concerns had on his fellow citizens, on whose abiding support the still-shaky national experiment depended, could not have escaped the man.[32]

John Orth's thesis that "determinedly Federalist" devotion to the Union motivated Iredell's dissent[33] thus has a ring of plausibility. Iredell's role in the ratification process inevitably sensitized him to lingering concerns that the new federal government would virtually annihilate the states. A perception that the states' residual sovereignty was indeed defunct would have threatened a still-shaky Union; public confidence in the continuing vitality of the states was essential to the security of "government," to the survival of the young national structure whose life still hung by a somewhat-fragile thread. For Iredell to have positioned himself so as to avert this perceived danger would not have been out of character for him or extraordinary and unprincipled when judged by the values of his time. Indeed, the posture fits William Casto's paradigm of the Court in that period as a "national security court."[34] This interpretation leaves unresolved, however, the conundrum as to why Iredell stood alone among colleagues equally fervid in their commitment to the survival and success of the Union.

Reaction to *Chisholm* in the court of contemporary public opinion lends credence to this view. While recently questioned,[35] the conventional wisdom has been that the decision shocked the country. Clearly, rebellion characterized the states' response. The legislatures of Connecticut, Massachusetts, and Virginia instructed their senators and representatives to secure adoption of a constitutional amendment preventing suits by an individual against a state. The South as a whole received Iredell's dissent warmly. Georgia's reaction was the most extreme. It futilely viewed Iredell's opinion as that of the Court, and its House of Representatives approved a bill imposing the death penalty on anyone who levied or attempted execution from the United States Supreme Court in *Chisholm* or any other case for recovery of a debt owed by the state. The measure failed only by virtue of defeat in the Georgia Senate. In Iredell's home state of North Carolina, Federalist leaders, and apparently the informed populace in general, shared his views. Davie excoriated the other judges' opinions, and Johnston informed Iredell that his opinion was "universally applauded."[36]

Years later, John Marshall wrote that "[t]he alarm [over the majority view] was general." Federalists and Antifederalists were united in their distress, and Jeffersonians viewed Iredell's as the true interpretation of the Constitution. The belief that the drafters had not intended the *Chisholm* result was widespread. With avoidance of responsibility for state debts as the primary moving force, adoption of the Eleventh Amendment soon restored equanimity by ensconcing the doctrine of state sovereignty and immunity into the Constitution.[37]

The persisting debate about who was "right" in *Chisholm*, and the correct rationale underlying Iredell's dissent,[38] thus is largely academic. The significant practical reality is that the Eleventh Amendment incorporated into the Constitution the outcome Iredell alone would have reached. The amendment adopted his concepts of divided or residual sovereignty and enshrined them into American constitutional law. Over two centuries later, they remain there, shielded from the whims of Congress — which even Iredell might have allowed to erode them.[39]

CHAPTER 14

The Life of a Post Boy

SONG POPULARIZED BY THE BEATLES MOST APTLY DESCRIBES IREDELL'S LIFE AS A UNITED STATES SUPREME COURT JUSTICE IN THE LATE EIGHTEENTH CENTURY. IN THE MOST-ARRANT SENSE, HE HAD "A TICKET TO RIDE." THE BUSINESS REQUIRED "perpetual itineration," according to Justice Cushing, and Cushing's wife saw the judges as "traveling machines [with] no abiding place." Iredell would, in his brother's words, "lead...the life of a post boy," traveling as much as 1,900 miles in covering a single circuit. While some travel was by waterborne vehicles, he would spend a substantial portion of the remainder of his life on horseback or in horse-drawn conveyances.[1]

Article III of the newly adopted Constitution vested the judicial power of the United States in a supreme court and such inferior courts as Congress might establish. The first bill introduced in the United States Senate became the Federal Judiciary Act of 1789, which constituted the Supreme Court and established the inferior federal courts. Oliver Ellsworth of Connecticut, later the third chief justice, was a member of the committee appointed to organize the judicial system and was the principal draftsman of the bill. A scant three weeks after appointment of the committee, Ellsworth was outlining a proposed system. Public interest in this and other matters before that first Congress was keen. Congressman Alexander White of Virginia wrote to James Madison conveying his surprise at the knowledge he found among landlords and people at country inns regarding the congressional debates and proceedings.[2]

Tristrim Lowther, Hannah Iredell's niece's husband, sent Iredell the proposed bill, predicting "considerable alterations" before it passed both houses. Lowther augured accurately, for the final bill differed substantially from both Ellsworth's initial outline and earlier drafts. The provisions for the circuit courts, in practical effect, were intact, however. While they would hear appeals from the district courts in some instances, their chief function was to sit twice annually in each state as the primary federal trial courts for the nonadmiralty cases the Constitution did not confine to the Supreme Court and that were most likely to be troublesome and important. These included cases based on diversity jurisdiction, cases removed from state courts, and cases presenting important federal criminal and civil issues brought by the United States. Two of the six Supreme Court justices, together with the district judge resident in the state or district where the court sat, composed the circuit court. Each Supreme Court justice thus was required twice annually to travel through one of the three circuits.[3]

Ellsworth had explained the rationale for the circuit courts as follows. One federal judge per state appeared unavoidable. Circuit courts would cost little more, provide system and uniformity, settle many cases at the state level that would otherwise go to the Supreme Court, and provide for a higher grade of offenses. Otherwise, many cases would go to the Supreme Court, placing the states in a subordinate position, subjecting their decisions to frequent reversals, and hurting their feelings. It would be infinitely preferable to give the parties to cases of considerable magnitude a choice of courts in which to seek their remedy.

While Ellsworth's rationale possessed surface soundness, the fact that Congress had economized by establishing courts without judges created problems. Staffing these courts with Supreme Court justices led to an inexorable conflict of interest in that one or two of the justices sitting on a case in the Supreme Court would also have sat in the circuit court. This problem was at least recognized in the congressional debates on the Judiciary Act. In the Senate there were two attempts to amend the bill to preclude a justice who had heard a case in the circuit court from sitting on it in the Supreme Court. While initially successful, these efforts ultimately failed.[4]

The conflict-of-interest problem notwithstanding, considerations of economy, quality control, politics, and uniformity of federal law supported the arrangement. By averting salary payments to a separate set of judges for the circuit courts, the government conserved its meager resources. By assigning the circuit courts to its jurists of highest rank, it assured advocates of a strong federal judiciary that the most-important judges would sit in the trials of cases most likely to cause difficulty, especially those in diversity jurisdiction valued between $500 and $2,000 in which appeals were not allowed. By placing its "highly articulated judiciary" at "the very doorsteps of the people in all of the states," it assured that, through the judges' charges to grand juries as well as their general presence and influence, the message of what many in the hinterlands still considered an alien government would be carried to the populace with "dignity, power, and capability." William Paterson of New Jersey would later serve on the Supreme Court and join Iredell in chafing under the arrangement; in Senate debate, however, he defended it. With circuit courts so constituted, he argued, "you carry law to their homes, courts to their doors—[you] meet every citizen in his own state." The circuit judges, then, "would act as 'republican schoolmasters.'" Finally, circuit riding by the highest judges would enhance the Federalist objective of uniformity of federal law.[5]

While later praised as "probably the most important and the most satisfactory act ever passed by Congress" and while it designed a federal judicial system that would survive without substantial change for a century, the Act had instant critics. Even adherents of the new Constitution disapproved its intricacy, cost, and jurisdictional potency. John Dickinson of Pennsylvania—lawyer, philosopher, and mentor to Justice Wilson—denounced the Act as the most inscrutable he had ever read. William R. Davie told Iredell it was thoroughly defective, so much so as to "disgrace the composition of the meanest legislature of the states." The new chief justice, John Jay, thought that the system was fraught with difficulties and that the judges would often "find themselves embarrassed." Even a leading Congressman, Fisher Ames, saw the Act as experimental and was confident that "a short experience will make manifest the proper alterations." James Monroe told James Madison the bill would exceed all others in the difficulties occasioned and expose the power of the government, or lack thereof, to discharge its functions. Madison himself viewed the Act as "pregnant with difficulties" and "peculiarly complicated and embarrassing"—as "defective both in its general structure, and many of its particular regulations." He hoped the system would quickly be reconsidered "under the auspices of the judges who alone will be able perhaps to set it to rights."[6]

Madison got his wish, in part, for the judges were in the vanguard of the reform efforts. From their perspective, the circuit-riding requirement was the most-serious problem. Two circuit treks and two full Court sessions annually left time for family, personal business, and legal studies at a premium. The circuit task was arduous. It would have been difficult enough for the young and well; it was even more so for some of the justices who were aged or infirm. Travel in the Eastern and Middle Circuits, while strenuous, was ameliorated by being limited from court city to relatively nearby court city, with reasonable accommodations usually available. The Southern Circuit, contrastingly, involved rough, sparsely populated, often unknown terrain, with lodgment undependable and frequently unpleasant.

On his first tour of the Southern Circuit, Iredell observed that he "scarcely thought there had been so much barren land in all America as I have passed through." After a year of Southern travels, he called the duty of his office "very severe & expensive." Chief Justice Jay acknowledged that while the circuits "press hard upon us all," Iredell's share of the task had been "more than in due proportion." Being the most severely affected, then, Iredell was the judges' leader in their reform efforts.[7]

The first proposals for change came, not from the judges, but from Attorney General Edmund Randolph. In August 1790 the House of Representatives asked Randolph to draft needed reforms in the judicial system. In his response, Randolph recommended that the justices no longer ride circuit. Congressman Roger Sherman expressed the prevailing counterview, however, when he commented that "the Superiour Judges can acquire a knowledge of the rights of the people of these States much better by riding the circuit than by staying at home and reading British and other foreign laws." Randolph's proposal, which was never considered, drew Iredell's avid interest. Samuel Johnston, then in the Senate, wrote Iredell at one point that the House had not given up on judicial reform and that he was doing "everything in my power" to promote it.[8]

Contemporaneously with the House's request to Randolph, the Supreme Court justices — with Jay, Cushing, Wilson, Blair, and Iredell present — determined that in the future the justices would be assigned permanently in pairs to one circuit. Iredell had proposed that the circuits be rotated among the justices or, if that was undesirable, at least that any permanent circuit-duty assignments be accomplished by lot. He alone voted against permanent assignments, however, and the vote favoring them surprised and upset him. Rutledge had been absent because of illness, and Blair had voted for permanent assignments under a misconception. Had Rutledge been present and Blair fully informed, the Court probably would have divided equally on the question.[9]

Earlier, the Court had allocated the circuits according to the home states of the justices because, according to Jay, the judges could most appropriately pass on the applications of lawyers in their home districts. With permanent assignments, the most difficult and arduous of the circuits, the Southern, would be Iredell's continuous fate. "[A]lmost frenzied in his desire to avoid that duty again," Iredell was not quiescent in facing this perceived wrong; he wrote to Jay, Cushing, and Wilson, detailing his complaints regarding both the process and the substance of the decision.

He had not been notified that the circuit-rotation question would be voted on, and the vote had "distressing consequences" for him. A matter as significant as a permanent establishment of circuit duties should require notice to the judges; with proper notice, Rutledge might have been present and the judges evenly divided.

The law did not provide for a "fixed duty," nor had the president, who initially appointed only one judge (Rutledge) from the Southern Circuit, contemplated it. (Harrison, whom Iredell replaced, had lived in the Middle Circuit.) So unequal a scheme should not be set in stone based on the reasons for its temporary establishment; a more-equitable allocation of duties should instead be devised.

Iredell could recall only one argument against rotation: Resolution of matters taken under advisement might be delayed if the judges did not return to the same circuit. When weighed with opposing considerations, this did not alter his thinking. No judge, he said, could conscientiously both constantly ride the Southern Circuit and adequately perform his other duties. The judge's health would be endangered, and accidents might prevent his attendance at the courts. He had himself ridden 1,900 miles on his last circuit, and the round trip from Philadelphia covered 1,800 miles. It was improbable that any judge could travel that distance twice annually and be punctual in all his court attendance.

Circuits constantly fixed would render this problem irremediable. The difficulty from judges taking cases under advisement and departing for different circuits, by contrast, was remediable. In most cases the prior judges could transmit their notes on arguments and authorities to succeeding judges, thereby rendering them equally equipped for decision. The original judges, having only heard but not decided the case, should not be disqualified on appeal. While admittedly not as desirable as having the same judges throughout, the lone inconvenience from a change of judges did not justify the enhanced duties and expense that permanent assignments imposed on two of the judges (presumably himself and Rutledge).

Further, compelling reasons of example and policy favored rotation. Some countries not only permitted but required it. Two states, North Carolina and Virginia, required it. In England a judge could not hold court where he was born or where he resided — "a prudent jealousy," in Blackstone's view.

Finally, Iredell pleaded a personal conflict of interest. As the executor of an estate, he was a party defendant in an action pending in the circuit court of North Carolina. If only two judges (he and Rutledge) could hear the case, and one of the two failed to attend, the object of a writ of certiorari Wilson, Blair, and Rutledge had issued would be defeated and the state court empowered to decide the case (because the extant law required two federal judges to decide a case).

His situation, then, was "a very hard one." When he had accepted the position, he had expected rotation. He thus had moved his family to the capital so he could perform his duties more faithfully than he could "in so remote a situation." Despite scarcely bearable private inconvenience and distress, he had submitted to the Court's decision in New York. But for him or "any man" to constantly perform the same tour of duty was impracticable. Duty compelled him to "state the case as it really is," lest the public interest should suffer from his undertaking more than he could realistically perform. The Court thus would not be his last stop in seeking to change the practice. His purpose was admittedly partly selfish — "so as to leave me at least a practicable share of duty." The public interest was also implicated, however — "and [to leave] the public unexposed to the danger of suffering by their business being unavoidably undone."[10]

Jay responded cordially. He had no objection to reconsideration and none to change if the decision appeared erroneous, but he doubted that the "[i]nconveniences" could be remedied except legislatively. Iredell's status as a defendant in one case made it "disagreeably circumstanced," Jay acknowledged, but he and Cushing had reserved points of some importance on the Eastern Circuit that they expected to decide in the spring. Wilson or Blair, perhaps, could attend that court in Iredell's stead. (Blair in fact did so.)

Cushing likewise replied sympathetically. The Southern Circuit indeed appeared "tedious," he wrote, though the Northern (Eastern) was "not without its troubles — its green woods, rocks, & mountains." While he would endeavor to do his duty as the majority determined it, rotation-induced delays in resolving reserved matters concerned him. A constant shifting of judges would produce inevitable delay, notwithstanding case notes transmitted from judge to judge.

Polite collegial responses failed to pacify Iredell's friends. One was astonished that feelings of generosity did not combine with more-weighty considerations to induce a reduction in the "excessive duty with which [Iredell had] been so unequally overburthened." The other justices, he said, had preferred "their own ease and convenience" to "every generous feeling, principle of justice, or regard to public duty." Their conduct was "little, unjust, ungenerous, and unpatriotic," and it "lessen[ed] their character in [his] estimation."

Iredell, however, apparently found the missives somewhat appeasing, for he agreed to ride the Southern Circuit again in the fall of 1791. The agreement was part of an understanding with the president that enabled him to fill the vacancy John Rutledge's resignation had created. Washington appointed Thomas Johnson of Maryland, but only after obtaining a commitment from the justices that Johnson would not be assigned the succeeding Southern tour. He assured Johnson that he expected changes from the next session of Congress, perhaps including the termination of circuit riding. Iredell conceded to Johnson that he went on the Southern Circuit this time "in some measure voluntarily." He was willing to perform this Southern tour alone so the courts might be held. Several courts scheduled for the circuit in 1790 and the spring of 1791 had been cancelled because of illnesses afflicting the justices. Iredell shared the view of many Federalists that the credibility of the new national government with the populace depended in part upon the efficient functioning of the federal courts.[11]

Iredell's mollification was short-lived, however. In January 1792 he informed Jay that he could "no longer undertake voluntarily so very unequal a proportion of duty" and that he presumed he would not be expected to make the Southern trek again soon. He again cited private hardship, public danger from "the performance of an impracticable duty," and the particular circumstance of causes in which he was a party that were pending in the circuit.

When the Court convened for its February 1792 Term, it conferred, at Iredell's request, to consider circuit duty. Two justices were absent — Jay because of the precarious health of his pregnant wife, and Johnson because of his own ill health. Wilson and Cushing remained steadfast in their opposition to rotation. Iredell thus was forced to hold the courts of the Southern Circuit yet again. Gloomy, he once more wrote to his chief justice, this time of "our ineffectual conference about the circuits." He reiterated that he could "no longer agree to be placed on the unequal and distressing footing [?] upon which [he had] so long been." He trusted, however, that no one would be more zealous in the discharge of duty "so far as it is practicable."

Jay must have had some empathy with his beleaguered colleague, for at about this time he agreed to oppose Governor George Clinton of New York, largely in hopes of getting relief from the burdens of circuit riding and long absences from home. Still, he had insurmountable philosophical objections to rotation of the circuits. Only Congress, he responded to Iredell, could remove the difficulties. He regretted the congressional delay, for "the expediency of a revision appears to be generally acknowledged." Justice Johnson, who would attend the Southern Circuit that fall, obtained a similar response to a missive to Jay. Reserved rulings would be frequent in the future, and the Court majority thus thought rotation "inadmissible"; the burden was unequal, however, Jay conceded, and Congress should free the system "from that and several other inconveniences."[12]

Iredell, meanwhile, continued to grouse. He told Justice Johnson that the ineffectual conference on the circuit assignments had been called at his request. The Court's original decision, he said, had precluded rotation upon a vote of only three of the justices. This "doomed" him and Rutledge to the Southern Circuit only. A tinge of sarcasm then entered his assertions; in consequence of that vote, he said, Jay and Cushing "considered themselves proprietors of the Eastern Circuit," Wilson "kept possession" of the Middle, and Blair likewise "became entitled" to the Middle. It was an arbitrary decision ("I can call it nothing else"), the consequence of which was that he had gone on the Southern Circuit three times out of four and on the last circuit had ridden at least one thousand more miles than any other justice. He intended to go again "rather than the circuit should be unattended," but he found the situation "distressing...in the greatest degree."

Johnson clearly empathized. "[Y]ou have enough to complain of," he responded. Indeed, Johnson was contemplating resignation from the Court because of the circuit duty. It was "far from certain," he told Iredell, that he would be "much concerned in the adjustment of circuits," for he would not long continue in the office if he saw that he could not perform the duties. "I cannot bring myself to submit to a burthensome inequality," he wrote. Moreover, Johnson did not expect any relief from Congress. He had requested legislation allowing the circuit judges to "adjourn cases of difficulty into the Supreme Court" for a judgment to be returned to the circuit court for execution, but he did "not think that or either of several other hints [would] gain attention."[13]

Like Johnson, Iredell did not merely complain. He suggested to his colleagues that they each agree to surrender $500.00 per year of their salary— one-seventh of an associate justice's salary, one-eighth of the chief justice's, and probably the approximate amount of the justices' out-of-pocket expenses in riding circuit—if circuit travel were terminated. Any such reduction had to be voluntary on the part of the judges because the Constitution prohibited Congress from diminishing their salary during their tenure in office.

Wilson, Blair, and Johnson immediately consented. Jay wrote Iredell that he would agree if the judges were "relieved entirely from the circuits." Cushing initially balked, prompting Iredell to say, caustically: "I confess I was astonished at Mr. Cushing's hesitating and can only account for it by his finding travelling in the midst of his N[ew] E[ngland] friends much cheaper than any of the rest of us do." Later, after learning Jay's views, Cushing capitulated. "I have no wish to be singular," he wrote Iredell. He approved on Jay's terms— complete relief from the circuits—but anticipated difficulty in securing congressional approval, given that the $3,000 the justices would relinquish would not pay the salaries of the additional judges such action would require.

There is no evidence that Iredell's proposal to reduce salaries in exchange for elimination of circuit duty was ever presented to Congress. Samuel Johnston may well have dissuaded him from pursuing it on account of the difficulties Cushing foresaw. Johnston did secure Iredell a modicum of relief, however, by sponsoring a Senate bill, which Iredell drafted, to alter the times of holding some of the circuit courts. The bill went to committee with the additional instruction to establish a circuit rotation so as to best apportion the burden and not impede the discharge of the duties of the office. As enacted, the bill provided for rotation of circuit assignments. No justice, without his consent, would have to ride the same circuit twice consecutively unless the public service and the vote of four justices required it, nor would a justice be reassigned to a circuit already attended until every other member of the Court had attended it. A delighted Iredell was nearing the end of his third tour of the Southern Circuit when he learned of this salutary development. In the fall he would travel the Eastern Circuit for the first time; Justice Wilson would join him.[14]

Iredell's friends and relatives shared his joy over this amelioration in his situation. William R. Davie congratulated him on Congress' "interposition… against the tyranny and injustice of your brothers of the bench"; Davie regretted, however, that Iredell now would not see his southern friends more than once every two years. John Haywood was "well pleased" that the fatigue of attending the most-distant courts would now be shared by the judges in rotation. Iredell's brother Arthur rejoiced over the more-equitable apportionment of duties, finding it "strange that one judge should be able to evade his duty at the expense of another's pains."[15]

The limited relief rotation provided, which mainly benefited Iredell, did not end the judges' reform efforts. While the rotation question had divided them, they were united in their desire to eliminate circuit riding altogether. It was, Justice Wilson told Justice Johnson, "one part of the judiciary system in which a change is…indispensably necessary." Wilson was not sanguine about the prospects for change, however, finding "no reason to hope that this or any other alteration of moment will soon take place." Lower-court judges also recognized the problem. "The fatigue of so long a journey twice a year is more than the strength of any man can bear," District Judge Nathaniel Pendleton of Georgia wrote Iredell. Pendleton, like Wilson, was not sanguine about the prospects for change, however.[16]

Elimination of the circuit duty was not altogether lacking in congressional support. In February 1792 Congressman William Loughton Smith of South Carolina wrote Edward Rutledge that circuit riding should be abolished entirely. Perhaps spurred by such support, the justices unanimously agreed at their August 1792 session to seek termination of their circuit-riding duties. The fact that all of them would now have to ride the difficult Southern Circuit also undoubtedly influenced their action. Further, Congress had recently burdened them with a new duty while on circuit, that of determining the validity of pension claims of invalid veterans of the Revolutionary War.

Thus prompted, with Iredell as their draftsman, the justices joined in a letter to President Washington transmitting a petition to the Congress. They conveyed their melancholy plight plaintively and explicitly:

> We really, Sir, find the burthens laid upon us so excessive that we cannot forbear representing them in strong and explicit terms.
>
> On extraordinary occasions we shall always be ready as good citizens to make extraordinary exertions; but while our country enjoys prosperity, and nothing occurs to require or justify such severities, we cannot reconcile ourselves to the idea of existing in exile from our families, and of being subjected to a kind of life on which we cannot reflect without experiencing sensations and emotions more easy to conceive than proper for us to express.

The Judiciary Act of 1789 had been considered "a temporary expedient" when enacted, and Congress had since been so occupied with pressing matters that the justices had thought it improper to draw attention to their subject. Now, however, they wanted Congress to know that twenty-seven circuits a year plus two sessions of Court in Philadelphia in the most-severe seasons was "too burthensome" given the size of the country and the small number of judges. To require judges to spend most of their days on the road staying in inns and at a distance from their families was, they said, "a requisition which...should not be made unless in cases of necessity." Some of them lacked the health for the routine, and even the most-robust set of judges could not sustain it for long. Further, public confidence in the impartial administration of justice suffered when the same men corrected in one capacity errors they committed in another. While the justices deferentially declined to suggest specific reforms, they made it unmistakably clear that relief could come only from a complete termination of their circuit duties.[17]

Unfortunately for Iredell, Wilson's early pessimism proved well-founded. While some thought Congress would adopt the portion of Randolph's report keeping the Supreme Court at the capital and putting the district judges on circuit, by December it was evident that Congress would make no substantial change in the system.

Congressional inaction prompted one immediate casualty: Justice Thomas Johnson resigned. As noted, Johnson had adumbrated his early retirement to Iredell before he even took his oath, stating that he would not fill the position long if he could not bring himself to submit to a burdensome inequality. He now wrote President Washington that he had found that the office and the man did not fit. At the age of fifty-nine he could not, he said, spend half of his remaining time away from his family and in situations where "the most moderate desires are disappointed." "My time of life, temper, and other circumstances forbid it," he concluded.

The president, perhaps forgetting that he had assured Johnson upon his appointment that prompt relief from long-distance travel was expected from Congress, mildly chided his appointee. The resignation, he said, conveyed to the public mind "a want of stability in that department," where it was perhaps needed more than in any other. He then appointed Governor William Paterson of New Jersey to Johnson's seat, and Paterson soon set out for the Southern Circuit.

Iredell exulted in Paterson's appointment and particularly in his assignment to the Southern Circuit. While expressing doubt that he was known to Paterson, he told him "no one could more sincerely rejoice" upon hearing of his acceptance of the position. He offered Paterson all possible assistance in making the Southern Circuit agreeable to him, indicating that his four excursions to "that country" gave him great familiarity with it. Cushing also wrote Paterson, conveying a hope for more-auspicious times. "There seems to be a favorable prospect of a radical alteration of the present itinerant system for the better," he wrote, "which may take off the fatigues of travelling & the inconvenience of so much absence from home."[18]

No radical alteration was imminent, but some alteration was. In March 1793 Congress enacted legislation requiring the attendance of one Supreme Court justice, rather than two, at each circuit court. Thus, each justice would have to ride only one circuit annually. The act, Cushing told the newly appointed Paterson, "eases off near half the difficulty." The justices jointly later thanked the Congress for the change, which "afforded them great relief, and enabled them to pass more time at home and in studies made necessary by their official duties."[19]

Problems remained, however. Harry Marchant, the district judge for Rhode Island, expressed continuing apprehension over the circuit system, especially the impropriety of Supreme Court justices sitting with district judges and then hearing appeals from their own decisions. By the end of 1793, Jay was concerned about conflicting decisions within the circuits. "It has happened in more than one instance," he wrote Senator Rufus King, "that questions in the circuit courts decided by one set of judges in the *affirmative* have afterwards...been decided by others in the *negative*—as writs of error do not reach every case, this evil has no remedy." The only solution, he thought, was to "confin[e] the judges to their proper place, viz, the Sup[reme] Court." If this were accomplished, he would consent to a salary reduction in an amount equal to the expenses of attending the circuits.

Three days later, Jay again wrote King, saying:

The federal courts have enemies in all who fear their influence on state objects. [I]t is to be wished that their defects should be corrected quietly — if those defects were all exposed to public view in striking colors, more enemies w[oul]d arise, and the difficulty of mending them increased. When it is considered that the important questions expected to arise in the circuit courts have now been decided in them, I can conceive of no reason for continuing to send the Sup[reme] Court Judges to preside in them, of equal weight with the objections which oppose that measure.[20]

Shortly thereafter the entire Court, except for Iredell, who was absent because of illness, presented Jay's concern to Congress via the president. Different judges deciding similar causes at different times in direct opposition to each other, they submitted, rendered the law unsettled and uncertain and created "apprehensions and diffidence in the public mind." While grateful for the recent alteration that required only one of them to attend a circuit, they questioned whether sessions in the circuits should hinge entirely on the health of one judge. The inconvenience and expense his illness or accident would occasion were obvious. The only solution, it seemed, was Jay's notion of confining the justices to the Court.[21]

Further legislative reform was not forthcoming, however. Accordingly, the justices made a minor adjustment internally. They informally agreed to ease the burden of the justice riding the longest and most difficult of the circuits, the Southern, by each paying him $100.00. An Iredell missive to Wilson reflects the interpersonal delicacy the plan produced. The agreement apparently omitted the time and manner of payment, for Iredell wrote that he was unaware of when the allowance should begin. He considered himself entitled to the money but had been too reticent to make a demand on the other judges at their August Term. A credit against a similar charge upon him was perfectly acceptable, he wrote Wilson, in which case their accounts would be balanced. If that was unacceptable, however, he would gladly pay his debt. Some money clearly changed hands under this arrangement, for the following year Blair referred to Cushing's having "inclos[ed] me a hundred dollars on account of my taking the Southern circuit."[22]

The justices, especially Iredell, continued to both hope and work for legislative reform. The year 1796 brought a new flurry of activity over circuit riding. Iredell saw "some faint hopes" for alteration but was less than sanguine about it. He thought there would be some reforms, he told Hannah, but not the significant ones wished for. There were several plans, he said, some of which would greatly benefit those living near Philadelphia, but none of which would prevent his being absent from home at least six months a year as long as they lived in North Carolina. Ellsworth, by contrast, could contemplate a continuous absence of no more than two months—still, in Ellsworth's view, "quite long enough and a great deal too [?] long."

Intelligence from his brother-in-law, Senator Samuel Johnston, perhaps enhanced Iredell's expectations, for in February 1796 Johnston wrote him that the Senate was considering the judicial system and he hoped it would see the necessity for a separate set of district judges, leaving the Supreme Court justices "to hold that Court only" and reducing their number to one-half as those serving resigned or died. Expense, Johnston said, was the only objection, and it should not govern "so important a business."[23]

Whatever the reason for his relative buoyancy, at about this time Iredell devised his own reform proposal entitled "Alterations Proposed in the Judicial System." He contemplated a division of the country into six federal judicial districts, rather than three, as follows:

1. Georgia, South Carolina
2. North Carolina, Virginia
3. Maryland, Pennsylvania
4. Delaware, New Jersey, New York
5. Connecticut, Vermont
6. Massachusetts, New Hampshire, Rhode Island

The circuit courts would be held once a year, in the spring, by a justice of the Supreme Court and a judge of the district court; the district judge would hold the fall term alone. The plan thus would have diminished considerably both the distances traveled within a circuit and the time devoted to holding its courts. Further, the Supreme Court would convene only once a year, on the first Wednesday in January. Such a plan would indeed have given the beleaguered Iredell approximately six months a year at home.[24]

Once again, however, Iredell's hopes were dashed. By March he was writing Hannah in a much more-dubious vein. After a "great parade," the Judicial Committee had made no report, and he expected "no alterations of moment" following "the fairest prospects." "We are still doomed, I fear, to be wretched drudges," he lamented. Even in earlier, more sanguine days, he had confided to her:

> It is impossible I can lead this life much longer, and I see no prospect of any material change. To lead a life of perpetual traveling, and almost continual absence from home, is a very severe lot to be doomed

to in the decline of life, after incessant attention to business the preceding part of it.[25]

The setbacks and despair of 1796 did not deter continuing complaints and reform efforts in 1797, however. Their letters suggest that the justices may have drafted the Circuit Court Act of 1797, which revised and streamlined the order of circuit riding in the Eastern, Middle, and Southern Circuits. Chase wrote Iredell in March 1797: "I see in the papers that a law has passed respecting the circuit courts. I hope it was not materially altered." The justices had reasoned that the then-current sequence of riding the Middle Circuit—New Jersey, Pennsylvania, Maryland, Virginia, and Delaware, in that order—was inconvenient to justices who lived in the South because they were required, following their Virginia court, to backtrack to the north again to convene the Delaware court. The interval between the Pennsylvania and Maryland court sessions also was too long. The justices proposed changing the date of the Delaware circuit court from June (after the Virginia court) to April (after the Pennsylvania court). Chase explained the rationale for the proposed change by showing, in rather dramatic fashion, the effect of the existing system on Iredell. Iredell, Chase noted, had to pass through Delaware en route from Philadelphia to hold court in Richmond, then backtrack the same distance to hold the Delaware court, thereby adding 534 unnecessary miles to his already unduly burdensome journey. Unless the public interest somehow required it, Chase concluded, a permanent system should not impose such hardship on any government officer.

Notwithstanding its self-evident logic, Congress rejected the proposed change. The new law was some improvement over the old, Chase told Iredell, but the arrangement of the Middle Circuit remained "certainly objectionable, & very inconvenient to me, and most oppressive on you, without any possible benefit to the public."[26]

In view of this rejection, Iredell's only hope for relief was the cooperation of his colleagues. In this instance, he received it. Paterson agreed to take the Delaware court in his stead. "[W]e should be accommodating to each other," he said, "for in this way we shall facilitate our official duty, and render its burden more supportable."[27]

Despite the frequent disappointments, the justices continued to lobby for a saner arrangement. In August 1797 they wrote President Adams asking that he lay their request before the next session of Congress. Holding the Delaware court June 27th instead of April 27th was inconvenient, they said, causing an unnecessary interval between the Pennsylvania and Maryland courts and needless travel for judges living to the southward—all with no commensurate benefit to the public. To enable the state courts to set their calendars accordingly, the judges courteously informed the governor of Delaware that they intended to offer the proposal. Like others before it, though, this reform effort also failed.

Still, the following year found Chief Justice Ellsworth optimistic about prospects for change. In April 1798 he wrote Cushing that he had left pending in the Senate a bill to relieve the justices from circuit riding and to provide five new districts and two new district judges for the circuit courts. The bill, Ellsworth thought, had "a prospect of...making some progress." If essential to passage, compromise was in order. One senator had agreed that the new districts should be stricken "should they appear to embarrass the bill," while another expected the bill's passage before the session ended.

Ellsworth's sanguinity was misguided. Ten days after he wrote Cushing, the Senate postponed further discussion of the bill. It was never again considered.[28]

Justice Wilson's death in Edenton later that year (*see infra* Chapter 20) further compounded the problem of covering the circuits. Justice Cushing's wife, Hannah, wondered to Abigail Adams "[w]hat will become of the Southern," which had been Wilson's assignment; she hoped Iredell would take North Carolina at least. Iredell, who was not scheduled to sit in the fall of 1798, was not pressed into service, however. A few days after Mrs. Cushing's letter, a young Bushrod Washington, having accepted President Adams' appointment to the Wilson seat, wrote his uncle George from Richmond: "I am just preparing to go upon the Southern Circuit, & shall if possible leave this place tomorrow." The former president replied, expressing regret that Wilson had been unable to postpone his demise and wishing the new justice a pleasant circuit, honorable service, and a safe return. "Of *some* of the judges who have gone that circuit," he observed with classic understatement, "the[re] has been heavy complaints."[29]

Ellsworth's appointment the following year as one of three ministers plenipotentiary to France again compounded the problem of covering the circuits. The appointment left Iredell uncertain whether the chief justice would fulfill his assignment to the Southern Circuit. "Whether he still intends to go to the Southward," Iredell wrote Samuel Johnston, "I have not heard him say." Further noting that six senators had voted not to confirm Ellsworth "on account of his being Chief Justice," Iredell admitted to his own bias in the matter: "I by no means like the practice of taking a man from the exercise of one duty to perform another," he confessed.[30]

Throughout the Court's first decade, then, and thus throughout Iredell's tenure, the goal of abolishing the Court's circuit-riding duties proved elusive. The Judiciary Act of 1801, which temporarily eliminated circuit riding, came too late to benefit Iredell, who died in 1799. That Act was repealed in 1802, primarily because the departing Federalist president, John Adams, filled all the judgeships the Act created, leaving no appointments for the new Republican president, Thomas Jefferson. This was the one act in Adams' life, Jefferson later told Abigail Adams, that he considered "personally unkind" and that gave him "personal displeasure." Almost another ninety years would pass before the Supreme Court justices would cease to be regular riders of the circuits.[31]

Shortly after Iredell's confirmation in 1790, Chief Justice Jay informed him that he and Justice Rutledge would attend the Southern Circuit that spring. That was no surprise; Iredell told both Jay and Rutledge that he had assumed the Southern duty would be his. Samuel Johnston had notified Iredell, advising him that the Southern would be his first circuit and Rutledge his initial traveling companion. Johnston had further indicated that the judges were expected to take the Southern Circuit in rotation—a prediction that, as noted, proved for Iredell frustratingly inaccurate until later legislative intervention. An Edenton newspaper duly noted the departure of the town's favorite son on his first circuit travel: "Yesterday," it stated, "the Hon. James Iredell, Esq., ... of the supreme court of the United States, set out from this town on his way to Columbia, in order to hold the circuit court for the state of South-Carolina." He would ride the Southern Circuit again that fall.[32]

As noted, his first relief from that most arduous of the circuits came in the spring of 1791—at his request because of a possible conflict of interest that could render the circuit court impotent in an important matter. Jay informed Iredell of his pleasure in finding that Blair's agreeing to take the Southern Circuit made possible Iredell's attending the Middle one with Wilson. Iredell's brother Thomas, who was now living in Edenton (see *infra* Chapter 18), also exulted in the news.

The fall of 1791 found Iredell again relegated to the Southern Circuit, this time traveling the back country because of the extreme distance. In the spring of 1792 he again attempted to avoid that circuit, pleading anew the suit in which he was a party, which "was not dismissed as [Justice] Blair expected it would be." It was a matter of national honor, Iredell informed the chief justice, for the federal courts to declare whether the writ issued erroneously or ought to be enforced. The significance was enhanced, Iredell urged, because the North Carolina General Assembly had "thanked the state judges for their conduct in disobeying the writ." The matter "should not go off by an act of defiance of the state court," he asserted. Unlike his first effort, however, this one failed, and he was again allotted the Southern Circuit.[33]

A respite from the Southern's rigors followed. He rode the Eastern Circuit in the fall of 1792, the Middle in the spring of 1793, and was unassigned that fall.[34]

The relief was transitory, as the Southern was again his lot in the spring of 1794 — the fifth time in nine circuits. That fall, when he was again unassigned, he resisted Wilson's entreaty that he attend the Southern Circuit in his stead. Though ordinarily convivial and accommodating, Iredell stood firm. Few things could be more painful to him than to decline to comply with any request of his, Iredell wrote Wilson, but his reasons were not trivial. It was impossible to say how much his interest was affected or his mind biased by the causes pending in that circuit in which he was a party. If his taking the Southern Circuit further delayed the suit in the North Carolina Court of Equity, some would think he "had used artifices" for that very purpose. Further, he had attended the same circuit five times in four years, "sometimes with inconceivable distress, anxiety, & inconvenience." He had often left when family members were ill, and if he attended the circuit this time, he would have little time with his family in a six-month period. This, he indicated, was unacceptable "when objects so dear to me" were concerned. He refused Wilson only with the greatest reluctance, he claimed, but his declination was firm.[35]

Following this carefully preserved leisure, Iredell rode the entire Eastern Circuit in the spring of 1795. He had been scheduled to begin the term in the Eastern Circuit but return to the Middle to assist Justice Paterson with the trials of participants in the Whiskey Rebellion. Cushing was to complete Iredell's Eastern Circuit, and Wilson was to finish Paterson's courts in the Middle Circuit. Cushing's medical condition apparently forced a change in the arrangements, however, and Iredell passed the term as the only justice holding the courts of the Eastern Circuit. By doing so, he avoided sitting with Paterson in the Whiskey Rebellion trials, which Paterson found a "disagreeable necessity."[36]

In the fall of 1795, Iredell served the Middle Circuit, holding only the courts of the Virginia district from November 23rd through December 12th. He returned to that circuit in the spring of 1796, conducting the courts of all its states except Delaware, which Wilson took in his stead. He found this circuit "the easiest and most convenient," though he could not expect to be at home until mid-June and would have to return to Philadelphia in mid-July.

In the fall of 1796, Iredell was again unassigned. He had been away from home so consistently that his friend John Hay mistakenly believed it was his first relief from the circuits, whereas in fact he had not been assigned in the autumns of 1793 and 1794.

This repose, like that of the fall of 1794, had to be diligently safeguarded. As in 1794, Wilson asked Iredell to sit for him, this time in Virginia. Iredell again politely but firmly refused. This time he pleaded in explication a case heard there the previous November in which he and Cyrus Griffin, the district judge, had differed. The difference had remained the following term, necessitating another continuance. There was no prospect that he and Griffin would ever agree, he said, and further delay for the same reason might cause both injury and discontent.

Personal circumstances also again dictated the response. He had not been at home six weeks in the past seven months. Even at home he could not expect an hour's "unmixed satisfaction" until the "sickly season" was over in early November. To attend this court, at a distance of 160 miles, would disrupt the "only remnant" of family happiness (should the family escape the sickly season) which he could rely on preceding a minimal absence of five or six months. There were economic consequences too, as he would both incur overhead expenses and neglect his "little private property." "I state these circumstances thus particularly," Iredell advised Wilson, "as I am anxious to show you how unwilling I am to decline any request of yours without the strongest reasons to urge me." The reasons must have been compelling indeed, for the Virginia court went unattended.

In the spring of 1797, Iredell had the Middle Circuit, holding all its courts, again except Delaware, which Justice Paterson took for him. That autumn he was again unassigned. He wrote Hannah gleefully from Philadelphia: "I am to go no circuit this fall." The spring of 1798 saw him again traversing the Southern Circuit, and he was unassigned that fall. In the spring of 1799 he rode his last circuit, the Middle, holding all its courts except Maryland, where no court was held, and Delaware, which Paterson covered.[37]

CHAPTER 15

The Character of the Business Done

I HAVE NO INFORMATION AS TO THE CHARACTER OF THE BUSINESS DONE," WRITES AN EARLIER COMMENTATOR ON IREDELL'S CIRCUIT RIDING. THE ACTUAL WORK OF THE CIRCUIT COURTS IN THE LATE EIGHTEENTH CENTURY IS INDEED SOMEWHAT OBSCURE. IN HIS FIRST ANNUAL message to Congress in December 1801, Thomas Jefferson referred to the circuit courts' business. In urging Congress to contemplate the judicial system, especially as to the newly appointed circuit judges, he procured and tendered "an exact statement of all the causes decided since the first establishment of the courts, and of those which were depending when additional courts and judges were brought in to their aid." The accompanying statistical data shows the bulk of the litigation as suits at common law, with a considerably lesser quantity of suits in chancery, criminal prosecutions, and admiralty causes. The suits at common law ranged from a low of four in Maine to a high of 1,719 in the Eastern District of Virginia. While these figures seem disparate to the point of absurdity, they find support in Virginia District Judge Cyrus Griffin's earlier communication to President Adams. The business of his district, Griffin said, was "probably more than [that of] any three courts in the Union." "[T]he Supreme Judges tell me," he continued, "that the business of the Circuit Court for Virginia is considerably more than [that of] all the Union together."[1]

At least a partial explanation is that prewar indebtedness to British merchants was most highly concentrated in Virginia. The great majority of cases filed in the federal circuit court of Virginia during its early years were for the recovery of prewar British debts.[2]

In general, though, Jefferson's statistics were rather immediately challenged by his secretary of state, James Madison. Madison transmitted to the president new schedules with statements of the suits in the circuit courts for Maryland and Kentucky, as well as a certificate from the clerk of the circuit court for West Tennessee regarding the suits in the federal courts of that state. These were intended, Madison said pointedly, to correct the document in the president's message to Congress and to supply an omission to the first-mentioned schedule. Madison further mentioned "some other imperfections of the document referred to in the message."

Modern scholars also find Jefferson's statistics suspect. They were tendentious in nature, one suggests; Jefferson sought to establish "the dispensability of the new Circuit Courts," and "[t]he test chosen...was delusive in the case of courts dealing with litigation frequently of great intricacy and often protracted." Not only was Jefferson's purpose political, but his data came from overworked court clerks whose thoroughness is problematic. In actuality, "the tabulation in no way reflected the nature and extent of judicial burdens." The justices on circuit had to prepare grand jury charges and petit jury instructions as well as familiarize themselves with the details of protracted litigation. Their work was further complicated by the fact that federal common-law practice was conducted in conformity with that of the state where the circuit court sat, forcing the visiting justices to learn several state procedural variants.[3]

Iredell's "business done" on the circuits contains select passages eloquently reflecting his philosophy and approach to the juristic task. He once humbly acknowledged the fallibility of his guild. "The greatest lawyers, even the greatest judges," he wrote, "are liable sometimes to mistakes in opinion." Lord Mansfield, Lord Hardwicke, and other "illustrious characters," he noted, had often changed their opinions. The most able were also the most candid about their capacity for error, he said, and the most determined "to do right under any circumstances whatever." In light of this human propensity to go astray, he concluded, "[t]he law alone ought ever to be, and I trust ever will be, the guide of our decision."

He spoke anew of constitutions as fundamental law and reiterated his firm belief in the power of judicial review. A constitution was "the fundamental law of the state" and "not alterable by its ordinary legislature [as] all other species of laws are." "A constitution is one thing," he concluded, while "particular and repealable laws subsisting under [it] are another."[4]

In his final appearance as a circuit justice in Raleigh, the capital city of his home state, Iredell wrote a lengthy opinion replete with significant philosophical reflections. The case, *Minge v. Gilmour*,[5] involved the constitutionality of a 1784 North Carolina act[6] abolishing the ancient estate in fee tail and conferring fee simple title upon the holders of such estates.

Iredell acknowledged at the outset his debt to the skillful arguments of counsel, "which alone, in a case of so much novelty...and intricacy...could have enabled me to form an opinion so early." The parties had indeed selected from the best legal talent the young state could offer. John Louis Taylor, then age twenty-nine, was lead counsel for the plaintiff. He soon would be a superior-court judge, later chief justice of the Court of Conference, and still later the first chief justice of its successor, the North Carolina Supreme Court. William R. Davie, whom Iredell considered one of the two best lawyers in the state, represented the defendants. Davie had refused President Washington's offer of the district judgeship for North Carolina because of the "paltry" salary; otherwise, he, rather than his wife's brother-in-law John Sitgreaves, would have sat with Iredell on the case. Blake Baker, Jr., the state attorney general since 1794 when he had defeated Taylor for the position, was associated with Davie for the defense.[7]

Apparently in response to Taylor's argument that the impugned act violated the North Carolina Constitution and thus could not control the case, Iredell reiterated his resolute convictions regarding judicial review. If unwarranted by the Constitution, the act was without authority and void, for the superior power must be obeyed. The Constitution, he said, "is a supreme law, paramount to all acts of assembly, and unrepealable by any." While a legislative act inconsistent with a prior act repeals the former, "when the constitution says one thing and an act of assembly another," the former law controls; it is "a supreme law unrepealable and uncontrollable by the authority which enacted the latter."[8]

The concept of judicial review was not novel in North Carolina, the state's judges, at Iredell's urging, having declared a state statute violative of the state Constitution eleven years earlier (*see supra* Chapter 2). What was new, however, was the notion that federal judges sitting in diversity jurisdiction and applying state law were empowered to declare a state statute violative of a state constitution. The recognition that *Marbury v. Madison* was still five years in the future heightens the innovative nature of the opinion. That the court did not declare the challenged statute unconstitutional undoubtedly diminished the contemporary perception of the significance of Iredell's articulate defense there of the principle of judicial review.

Minge has further significance because it foreshadowed the Iredell-Chase debate over natural law in *Calder v. Bull* (*see supra* Chapter 12). Taylor, as counsel for the plaintiff, had argued that the challenged act was void as contrary to natural justice. "[S]ome respectable authorities," Iredell acknowledged, indeed countenanced such a doctrine. Equally respectable ones maintained the contrary, however, thus forcing him to consult his own reason. His own reason dictated that "no court is authorized to say that an act is ab-

solutely void because, in the opinion of the court, it is contrary to natural justice." He again paid obeisance to the doctrine of judicial review; "[i]f an act
be unconstitutional," he wrote, "it is void." But if constitutional, he continued, it is valid, natural-justice concerns notwithstanding. Such considerations
are for the legislature "without control." While the legislature can be held accountable for abuse of its authority, the act is legal, just as a court judgment
within its jurisdiction is legal, "however erroneous the principles may be on
which the court decided."

The amorphous nature of natural law concerned Iredell. He saw the words
"against natural justice" as "very loose terms" on which "very wise and upright members of the legislature and judges might differ in opinion." Where
such differences existed, whose opinion should control, he asked: that of the
enactors or that of a court "to whom no authority, in this respect, necessarily
results"? This was different, he said, from an unconstitutional act, passed
with no authority and therefore one that "the courts must certainly declare . . .
void." If courts were intended to have power to declare legislative acts void as
contrary to natural justice, the Constitution would have said so. By empowering the legislature to act in certain cases, but not others, the Constitution
plainly declared all countenanced acts valid and all uncountenanced ones
void. Any intent to empower courts to strike acts contrary to natural justice,
he concluded, would certainly have been made express.

The foregoing notwithstanding, cases of problematic construction would
necessarily and properly implicate judicial notions of natural justice. All
courts, Iredell said, are bound to give legislative acts the most-reasonable construction and will do it "as consistently with their notions of natural justice (if
there appears any incompatibility) as the words and context will admit." Such
a construction, he stated, most likely reveals "the true design of the legislature." When the plain words admit of only one construction, however, and are
consistent with the Constitution, no court could say the act was void merely
because it was counter to the court's notions of natural justice.

In *Minge* he would not have so declared in any event. Assuming *arguendo*
that this was a proper ground for decision, he thought the act "not contrary
to the principles of natural justice." His denegation of the existence of such a
power could hardly have been clearer, however.[9]

In one respect this aspect of Iredell's *Minge* opinion offends modern juridic
sensitivities. The Supreme Court had heard arguments in *Calder v. Bull* only
four months earlier, and the seriatim opinions in that case had not been filed
when Iredell released his discourse in *Minge*. The notion that Supreme Court
votes and reasoning are sacrosanct state secrets until opinions are filed apparently had not yet evolved, for in *Minge* Iredell not only closely tracked his dis-

cussion in *Calder* but also referred expressly and openly to the positions of the justices in that case. "In a great case *now [pending] in the supreme court of the United States*," he wrote, the judges were debating whether the *ex post facto* clause of the Constitution applied only to criminal laws. "A majority...appeared to be convinced of it," he wrote, unabashedly unveiling the probable result, "but upon the doubt of one the case was not decided."[10]

The contemporary literature fails to emphasize premature disclosure of the decisions and reasoning of the Supreme Court sitting *en banc* as an argument against its justices sitting as the circuit judges. That stance certainly occurs to the present-day juristic mind, however.

One further Iredell pronouncement in *Minge* merits mention as an articulate reflection of his motivating life-force. Clearly, an abiding belief that private interests must yield to the greater public good influenced his entire existence. Here, he enunciated this creed with unpretentious eloquence. "In a state of society properly regulated," he wrote,

> it must frequently happen that private and public interests in some degree interfere with each other. In such cases is it not unavoidable and agreeable to the very principle on which all governments are formed, that the former should yield to the latter? Yet, clear as this principle is, and necessary as in many cases it is that it should be enforced, many, from injudicious notions of liberty, speak of the rights of each individual as if he subsisted in a state of nature unconnected with any other mortal in the universe, and deriving no benefits from a well-constituted society, which are more than an ample compensation for any accidental sacrifice which the public interest may occasionally require of a subordinate private advantage to a superior public good.[11]

The "business done" on circuit provides another source of Iredell's philosophical musings. The 1792 Invalid Pensions Act prompted from his pen what was, in effect, an advisory opinion on the separation of powers. The Act provided governmental financial assistance to veterans injured in the Revolutionary War and their widows and orphans. The duty of determining the merits of such claims was assigned to the circuit courts, which, if they found a claim meritorious, were to determine the amount of the pension commensurate with the extent of the disability. The secretary of war then had to determine, however, whether the claimant had in fact served as an officer, soldier, or seaman during the Revolutionary War. An executive officer thus had power to reverse a factual determination of a circuit court and to deny what that court had found to be an entitlement. That officer's action was reported to Congress, which made the final determination.[12]

Joined by their district court colleagues, all the justices except Johnson demurred to these new duties. Jay, Cushing, and District Judge James Duane wrote the president from the circuit court for New York; Wilson, Blair, and District Judge Richard Peters did the same from the circuit court for Pennsylvania; and Iredell and District Judge John Sitgreaves followed suit from the circuit court for North Carolina. The various remonstrances agreed that the Constitution committed the judicial power to a separate department, that the Pension Act duties were nonjudicial in nature, and that to subject judicial opinions to revision or control by an executive officer and by the legislature was unconstitutional.

The communication from North Carolina is clearly the product of Iredell's pen. It commences with characteristic Iredellian deference, granting the judges' duty "to receive with all possible respect every act of the legislature" and the "painful situation" any demurral from such obligation produced, especially when the action directed is "founded on the purest principles of humanity and justice." The judges must nevertheless act "according to the best dictates of [their] own judgment," he posited; and so acting, they submitted that the legislative, executive, and judicial branches were separate, independent, and constitutionally limited in their respective empowerments. The judges owed "implicit and unreserved obedience" to the Constitution, and the legislature could not authorize courts to exercise any power not in its nature judicial or, even if judicial, "not provided for upon the terms the Constitution requires." The secretary of war's power over the court's action subjected it "to a mode of revision . . . unwarranted by the Constitution." "[W]ith all due deference," he continued his polemic, the Constitution did not permit a court decision to "be liable to a reversion, or even suspension" by the legislature, which had no judicial power except that of impeachment. Therefore, there was no justification for the circuit court's executing the portion of the Act requiring it to examine and report on the invalid cases.

Nevertheless, respect for the legislature and concern for the victims of war prompted inquiry as to whether the judges could perform the duties "personally in the character of commissioners during the session of a court." This, too, was thought a dubious proposition, for "[t]he power appears to be given to the court only, and not to the judges of it."

Iredell then candidly acknowledged the advisory nature of the letter. No application had been made to the court or to the judges individually, causing the judges "some doubts as to the propriety of giving an opinion in a case which has not yet come regularly and judicially before us." Obeisance was duly paid to the general undesirability of such. Extreme caution "in not intimating an opinion in any case extra-judicially" was customarily expedient.

The reason? "[W]e well know how liable the best minds are, notwithstanding their utmost care, to a bias, which may arise from a preconceived opinion, even unguardedly, much more deliberately, given." The judges had, however, considered this "an exception to the general rule, upon every principle of humanity and justice," because those whom Congress thought worthy of relief could suffer from a short delay or be ruined by a long one. Accordingly, if an application was made, they would "most attentively hear it," and if convinced their opinion was wrong, they would "not hesitate to act accordingly."[13]

Congress evidently perceived the wisdom in the judges' position, for it changed the law the following year. District judges, or any three persons whom those judges commissioned, replaced the circuit judges in the administration of the Act, and their function was reduced to collecting evidence and transmitting it to the secretary of war. Over half a century later, Chief Justice Roger Taney expressly lauded Iredell's remonstrance. "[T]he repeal of the act clearly shows that the President and Congress acquiesced in the correctness of the decision, that it was not a judicial power," he wrote.[14]

His philosophical objections notwithstanding, Iredell ultimately accepted performance of the invalid pension task based on the transparent fiction that he was acting as a commissioner, not as a judge. He was, he informed Hannah, "reconciled...to the propriety of doing the invalid business out of court." He did not reach that accommodation facilely, especially since Justice Wilson, whom he greatly respected, "altogether decline[d] it." He rationalized, though, that he could interpret the Act to warrant performance as a commissioner on an individual, rather than a judicial, basis. "[T]here are expressions in the [A]ct," he wrote in an apologetic, "which...lead to a very probable supposition that Congress may have contemplated it as a personal rather than a judicial exercise of power." Possible conflict between the invalid business and his judicial duties still concerned him, but the perceived remoteness of that prospect prompted him to proceed. While acknowledging that he "ought not to do it if it will be in any manner inconsistent with my judicial duty," or if questions arising from the performance could come before him on the Supreme Court or on circuit, he nonetheless reasoned: "I do not think it can." "Therefore," he concluded, "having no reason...to decline the execution of the trust, I readily accept it."[15]

Two cases involving the Invalid Pensions Act did come before the Supreme Court at its February 1794 Term. The Court evaded the constitutional issue but held untenable any construction of the Act authorizing the justices to function thereunder as commissioners rather than as judges. Iredell missed that entire term because of illness and thus did not participate.[16]

CHAPTER 16

Trials Almost Too Much to Bear

I REDELL'S WORK ON THE INVALID PENSION CLAIMS TYPIFIES HIS DUTI-
FUL APPROACH TO HIS TASKS, WHATEVER THEIR NATURE. "THE INVALID
BUSINESS HAS SCARCELY ALLOWED ME ONE MOMENT'S TIME," HE ONCE
WROTE HANNAH, "AND NOW I AM ENGAGED IN IT BY CANDLELIGHT,
though to go at three in the morning." Life on the federal circuits in the early
republic would have been burdensome for anyone; it was especially so for a
man of Iredell's conscientiousness and disposition.

His friend Archibald Maclaine was prescient about the impending hardships. Maclaine "rejoice[d] upon the public account" as well as Iredell's, but
lamented the severity of the duty. He foresaw changes in the system, but not
immediately. Meanwhile, a round trip through three southern states twice annually, he thought, even without the two sessions in the capital, "would be
enough in all conscience." Modern hindsight produces an identical assessment. Circuit toil, writes one recent commentator,

> was an arduous task involving months of travel. As an example, be-
> tween crisscrossing the Carolinas and Georgia, and then traveling
> twice to New York for Court sessions, Justice Iredell spent eleven
> months away from his home the first year. Things did not get much
> better.[1]

The familial effects of a life Iredell described as one "of perpetual traveling,
and almost a continuous absence from home," were indeed harsh. Iredell had
been married almost seventeen years when he commenced his first circuit
tour. For almost twelve and one-half years, he and Hannah were childless. A
daughter, Annie Isabella, was born December 22, 1785; and a son, James,
was born November 2, 1788. Annie thus was almost four and one-half and

James was one and one-half when Iredell commenced his circuit perambulations. A second daughter, Helen Scrimseoure, was born January 19, 1792, just over a year and a half later.

Upon assuming the supreme bench, Iredell moved his residence and family, first to New York and soon thereafter, when the capital moved, to Philadelphia. Neither place proved satisfactory for Hannah and the children; therefore, partly for their "greater satisfaction" and partly to escape the yellow fever and other "scourges" that affected the northern cities, the family returned to Edenton in the fall of 1793. While Iredell's later correspondence indicates he could have had more time at home had the family been located further north, the difference was minuscule, for he would have been away a considerable portion of the time in any event.[2]

The circuit duties imposed continual, and for Iredell almost unbearable, stress on his family life. He had barely left home in May 1790 when he wrote Hannah of feeling unwell, attributing it entirely to "being so violently affected at parting." Her first surviving letter to him was equally melancholy. "Annie was much distressed at parting with you," she wrote, "she told James in a very doleful tone that Papa was gone." James obviously missed the significance of his father's departure, for "he clapt his hands & repeated very gaily, Pa's gone." Annie, contrastingly, sent word to "please...come home soon." Her first conversation was about him: "[P]oor Papa was gone." "There is no danger of her ever forgetting you," Hannah assured him, for "no child can have a more affectionate disposition."

Apprehensive, Hannah used this opening missive to remonstrate with Iredell to think of his children and take care of his health. "[T]o you they must look for everything," she stressed; if he valued their happiness and independence, he would take care of himself. "[Y]ou never had so much occasion for discretion as on this journey," she admonished. She would think nothing of their voyage to New York if he were with them or meeting them there. "I trust," she wrote, however, "that you will return to us safe & well."[3]

Soon Iredell was conveying, not homesickness, but simple disquietude. He was anxious about Hannah and the children. "How hard it is," he told Hannah, "to be so much out of the way of hearing from you." He trusted their passage to New York would be safe and pleasant and that they would meet there "quite well." His spirits lifted somewhat when he reached the extremity of his first journey southward, rejoicing that he soon would "be returning to the northward." He had no regrets when court adjourned and he and Rutledge were "to leave it tomorrow." "I console myself," he wrote Hannah, "with thinking you are now happily [situated] in New York."[4]

The passage of time failed to ease the pain of separation. Almost a year later, Iredell again communicated to Hannah his loneliness, urging that they correspond almost every day. If he could hear frequently and happily of her, the children, and his friends, the delay in returning to them would bother him less. A day later he was apologizing for this letter's having been written "unintelligibly," explaining that he "had a most abominable pen which [he] had no time to mend." "My being in the line of duty reconciles me to an absence which would otherwise be very painful to me," he wrote: "Tell [Annie and James] I think of them constantly, & love no little girl or boy in the world half so well as them."

A few months later, he again verbalized general apprehension. "God knows what I feel in being obliged to leave you in so painful a situation," he wrote Hannah, signing the letter "with inexpressible anxiety, which I every moment feel." A year and a half into the job, leaving home still made him ill. "My health was not very good the day I left you," he wrote Hannah, "owing, I believe, to the great agitation of my mind at the thoughts of parting, and it was still very indifferent the first day after my arrival in Baltimore."[5]

Iredell's absence from home often extended over a period of months. It would probably be six months before he saw their hearth again, he once wrote Hannah; while the Eastern Circuit was otherwise agreeing with him, he was distressed by the painful situation in which it placed him with regard to his family. The last court in Rhode Island would probably end in late June or early July, he informed, so he could not expect to get home until after the full Court's August Term, which probably would be long.

He missed friends as well as family during these extended absences. "My heart will forever be among my friends in N.C., however painfully separated from it," he wrote an Edenton acquaintance. "I have indeed trials to sustain by this separation almost too much for me to bear, but if I can hear of their health & happiness my own pain will be greatly alleviated."

Friends craved his return to them as well. Any doubt about his returning to reside in Edenton was unthinkable, one wrote: "I thought when I left Philadelphia that it was a matter determined on." An alteration in the law to make such possible was her "most ardent prayer."[6]

The fall of 1792 found Iredell again suffering the angst of disuniting following a brief furlough at home. Only God knew what he had suffered in parting from her, he told Hannah: "The thoughts of your being left in a manner quite alone affect me inexpressibly." So copious was his business that he found it difficult to write to her. "I ... have been & still am very much engaged here," he soon wrote from Hartford, so much so that he was writing "in court in the midst of great business." Notwithstanding the impediments to his reciprocating, he wanted desperately to hear from her. "Don't fail plying me with letters," he admonished her a few days later.

By mid-1793 "plying" apparently meant at least weekly. "Don't, my dear Hannah, omit writing at least once a week," he implored. Soon he was accounting to her for his delay in departing Richmond for the summer recess: "[S]ome business...unexpectedly intervened," he explained. Further delay might ensue; Chief Justice Jay, it seemed, was inclined to loiter a bit on the road, so Iredell might not be at home as soon as he would be if alone. "But God knows," he assured his beloved, "I am very impatient to see you."[7]

The year 1795 was particularly difficult in familial respects, so difficult that Hannah appears to have seriously contemplated moving northward to be with Iredell because he would be away so long. In early March he could not expect to be home until September. While repining was useless, he said, the long absence nevertheless robbed him "of all real pleasure in life." Even "the greatest distinction and civilities" in Philadelphia failed to allay the pain of separation from family, and "the dreadful idea of its continuing perhaps six months longer" preyed upon him "very severely." "[T]hough I everywhere receive the greatest civilities, and am constantly almost among agreeable people," he said, "many a sigh directs me toward Carolina." If Hannah came, she would need "a good servant" or "a gentleman" to accompany her, he wrote.

Iredell's options, however, seemed to lie between Scylla and Charybdis. "It is certain," he wrote Hannah, "if we continue to live in Carolina I must either lead a miserable life or resign and go through all the drudgery, & under very mortifying circumstances, which I did before." To avoid either, he would cheerfully submit to any system of frugality. Living in Philadelphia or any large city would be "madness," he thought. A move to a conveniently located small town was thinkable, however. The only regret, though a very severe one, would be the separation from friends, whom they might, however, "hope sometimes to see."[8]

Deaths of children were then the common experience for most families, and while itinerant, Iredell worried constantly about the health and survival of his children. He always dreaded losing a family member, a prospect, he said, "almost too much for me to bear." The Edenton summers posed special concerns of severe childhood diseases. "[T]he dangers of the approaching summer," he told Hannah, when added to the time and distance between them, affected him "very sensibly." In the spring he feared the approaching summer with its climate-induced ailments. The long separation combined with this disquietude to produce a state he also described as "almost too much for me to bear." Later, with the heat of summer in full sway, he again vented his distress over his situation. "It almost distracts me," he wrote. He could disregard it if Hannah and the children were nearby, he avowed; but without them, he said, "it affects me beyond all expression... [and] embitters every enjoyment of life." "I constantly tremble at the danger you and our dear children may be in without my knowing it in a climate I have so much reason to dread," he told Hannah.[9]

Events beyond Iredell's control affected his situation that summer. He was mortified when the Senate adjourned without confirming a chief justice to replace Jay, who had resigned to become governor of New York. Iredell feared this would generate unavoidable circuit duty for him in the fall, both because of business pending on the circuits and the status of the other judges. If he were to be so unfortunate, he said, he would nevertheless go home following the August Court session, even if he could "stay but a fortnight." The state of business was now such, he said, that it would be rare for any judge to be able to stay at home a whole circuit, meaning he "must either resign or we must have in view some residence near Philadelphia."

These events affected Iredell's disposition unpropitiously. While usually congenial toward and eulogistic of others, Iredell was highly critical of Jay for not resigning soon enough to permit a timely appointment to the chief justiceship — this despite the fact that Jay had been "in danger of dying,... and [still did] not look well." Whatever his reasons, Iredell said, they were "unjustifiable." "[F]ew gentlemen," Iredell feared, "would choose to accept [the position] under such circumstances."

By August Iredell's fears of a fall circuit had subsided, and he hoped to rest entirely. He in fact held only the Virginia court that fall and only from November 23 through December 12. Still, his dominant mood that summer was somber, as epitomized in the following lament to Hannah:

> [W]hat a situation is mine to have so much constantly to apprehend, and still to have the prospect of so long an absence! I will endeavor to bear my situation as well as I can, but it is impossible for me, filled with such distressing anxiety as I am, to bear it much longer.[10]

Bear it he did, however, though not without perduring complaint. The difficult year of 1795 passed, but the circuit rider continued to doubt his capacity to endure. In early 1796 he again told Hannah he could not lead this life much longer. "We are still doomed, I fear, to be wretched drudges," he moaned when prospects for legislative reform faded. He remained so busy he had to write Hannah while in court and sometimes "at intervals," and he could not write to James at all. He could "scarcely command an hour" for himself.[11]

Overtures to Hannah about again moving the family to the Philadelphia area were apparently rebuffed, for he now wrote her conveying sorrow that "what I wrote about our residence gave you pain." "[B]ut really," he said, "my situation at present is extremely distressing." He was convinced there would be no material change, and he continued to fret over the summers' effects on the children's health. These apprehensions precluded satisfaction on any other account. "However," he concluded, "I will avoid as much as possible dwelling on ideas which make me miserable whenever they occur to me." Hannah's refusal to move eliminated the prospect of brief, episodic visits at home. If she had been within two hundred miles, he wrote her in the winter of 1797, he "could have spent some short time at home in the vacation between the courts." As it was, however, any such attempt would have been "folly."[12]

Iredell did not suffer the distress of separation alone. Hannah also felt its sting. In the fall of 1790, when she apparently failed to receive his letters over a period of several weeks, she vented the apprehension this produced. Her anxiety was great, she said, and she would be really miserable if she did not hear from him soon. She could not think of the hazards of his journey "without shuddering almost." "[M]y dearest Mr. Iredell," she wrote, "you know not how painful a situation mine altogether is." By the time he returned, she concluded, Annie would be reading "very prettily" and James would "entertain [him] with a great deal of very sensible conversation in good language very well pronounced." "[C]ome, my dear Mr. Iredell," she implored, "& enjoy these pleasures as soon as possible & make us all happy by once more having you with us."[13]

Hannah's failure to receive Iredell's letters illustrates a related problem of his life on the circuits: Communication while he was away from home was simply unreliable. At about the same time, Iredell was writing her: "I have yet been able to learn nothing of Edenton, which I am very anxious to do." Almost a year later, he greatly regretted that it would be so long before he could hope to hear from her again. Lack of knowledge as to the circuit rider's whereabouts often impeded epistolary intercourse. Samuel Johnston once told Hannah he did not write to Iredell because he did not know where to find him.

Iredell attempted to alleviate this problem by giving detailed instructions regarding his itinerary, but postal exchange remained unpredictable. "I am afraid my letters from you will now reach me with great uncertainty," he once wrote Hannah, "though I leave directions for them to follow me." He then listed his expected destinations over the next several weeks and concluded: "I shall always continue very anxious to hear from you, and shall be particularly so now on account of James' indisposition." A few days later he told both

Hannah and Samuel Tredwell, the husband of Hannah's niece, to direct their next letters to him to New York " 'to be kept at the post office till called for.' "

Human error, too, occasionally precluded epistolary contact. Hannah once wrote Iredell at Philadelphia, fully knowing he could be gone by the time the letter arrived. She did so, she said, because she knew his normal anxiety would be intensified as a result of a long letter she had written the week before "not having gone through neglect in the post office." Dundee, their slave, had left the letter with a young man who stayed at the post office, but Iredell's brother Tom had later found the letter lying on the counter. Hannah was considerably upset, knowing "the pain it will occasion you, particularly at this unfavorable season [the summer, with its attendant health concerns]."

Omission of dispatches from home did indeed disturb him. "I am inexpressibly anxious to hear from you," he once wrote Hannah: "Not a line of yours has reached me since you arrived at your brother's." Even so, mere unhandiness could deter the missives she equally coveted from him. Being "in a very inconvenient house," he once wrote her, "I could not command an opportunity to write till this morning."[14]

After seven years of riding the circuits, Iredell said he had "nothing to complain of but absence from my family and friends." He considerably understated his situation, for his itinerant life imposed multitudinal other grievances. Writing from England, his brother Arthur had the more-accurate perspective: "These circuits," he said, "are not very desirable to you." Even that was classic understatement. Gouverneur Morris had the more-graphic description: The president, he said, "in selecting a character for the bench, must seek less the learning of a judge than the agility of a post-boy." By virtue of his circuit riding as a rural lawyer, superior-court judge, and state attorney general, Iredell was perhaps better prepared than his colleagues for this post-boy existence. Large though North Carolina was, however, it was the merest microcosm of the American nation, and travel within the state only minimally readied the judge for a life on the federal circuits.[15]

Travel, by whatever means, was problematic. Stages ran irregularly, detaining Iredell beyond expectations; they broke down, making him late for court. "[T]he vile condition of the stages," as he described it, caused him to miss connecting conveyances and to face great "difficulty in getting along." Sometimes, he simply missed the stage by the barest of time periods and paid dearly for doing so; once, for example, he missed a coach by half an hour and as a consequence had to employ labor to cut ice in two large swamps, causing considerable delay in his journey.[16]

Stage breakdowns forced the wandering jurist to employ his own horses. This, in turn, caused him concern about the need for the horses at home, as well as anxiety about connecting transportation. Horses, like stages, in effect broke down. Iredell had to stop to have them shod, and they delayed him by becoming lame. He could only "hope... Kinchen will be able to travel."[17]

The "execrable" nature of the roads made travel by horse or stage severe. On Iredell's maiden voyage on the Southern Circuit, he wrote Hannah of his extreme disappointment in the road from Charleston to Savannah. This disenchantment with the main arteries of travel proved career-long. His horses had "a pretty severe ride" from Baltimore, he wrote in 1791, "the greatest part of the way being very bad indeed." He was late arriving in Columbia in 1794 "[o]wing to... the worst roads I ever passed." The roads from Philadelphia in 1795 were "so bad" that they delayed his arrival in New York. In 1796 he encountered the worst arteries he had ever known, and "scarcely passable." In 1798 his journey from Fayetteville, North Carolina, to Camden, South Carolina, was "disagreeable,... the roads [being] the worst I ever knew them." "Disagreeable" likewise characterized his journey from Suffolk to Petersburg, Virginia, in 1798, again "owing to the badness of the... road."[18]

Practical, travel-related concerns surfaced immediately upon Iredell's appointment to the Supreme Court. Before he commenced his first circuit, Archibald Maclaine wrote to advise him of a route from Fayetteville, North Carolina, to Columbia, South Carolina, with particular reference to the better roads and better lodging. There were no published road maps in late-eighteenth-century America, and Iredell received letters directing him to various places, as well as maps showing routes and distances. Virtually all, however, appear imprecise and difficult to follow. He surely proceeded much of the time by feeling his way.[19]

Iredell's colleagues shared this experience. Before embarking on a Southern Circuit assignment, Chase once wrote Iredell seeking assistance with travel and lodging. "I fear the journey," he wrote, "and am anxious for information."[20]

The jurists' travel necessarily involved constant movement of their belongings. Iredell, for example, once wrote Hannah from Philadelphia asking that she send his chair and horses to meet him in Suffolk, Virginia, and listing items he was sending home. This perpetual movement of property involved hazards. While Iredell and Wilson served the Eastern Circuit one fall, the stage lost their trunks. They took another stage back to their prior locale, waited two hours, and ultimately found that a boy had picked them up "and very honestly deposited them safe near the city." To make up the lost time, the judges broke the law by traveling in Connecticut on a Sunday, a practice then proscribed by state statute. "[W]e intend to break the sin," Iredell wrote Hannah, "by going to a meeting on our way about 13 miles off."[21]

Climate and weather produced nostalgia, inconvenience, and peril for the itinerant jurist. When in the North, Iredell missed the early springs in North Carolina. "We are just beginning to see something like spring," he wrote Hannah from Philadelphia in late April 1799. When he was in the South, though, the heat was an irritant, sometimes causing him to delay his journey for several days. In the heart of summer, even Philadelphia could produce "near a fortnight" of intensely hot weather.[22]

Sometimes Iredell described the problem generically, referring simply to "bad weather," "very rough weather," or "the most uncomfortable weather I ever knew at the same season." At other times he was more specific, mentioning snow and ice on the road. "There are mountains of ice," he would write, "presenting the most singular spectacle ever remembered." "We crossed the Susquehannah on the ice," he continued, "and it presents . . . one of the most extraordinary sights ever beheld. . . . The river broke up a fortnight ago, and the ice now there came down in large cakes."[23]

The most-common vexation was rain. Indeed, Iredell's correspondence conveys the impression that rain was virtually interminable throughout the United States in the 1790s. His riding in the rain was "unavoidable." He made entire interstate trips in the rain and experienced "violent torrents of rain for several days." He once reported that his chair "kept me as dry as if I had been in a post chaise." At other times, however, he clearly felt the torrents.[24]

Rain, in turn, led to floods, which made rivers unfordable and detained him for want of a canoe. He had to worry about whether the rivers were open. He experienced water running over the foot of his chair. He had to borrow a slave to assist him through a swamp. He instructed Hannah to send Hannibal, one of his own slaves, by a different route if the waters were high.[25]

One particularly harrowing incident illustrates vividly the flooding hazards Iredell experienced as well as his keen sense of duty. He had left Samuel Johnston's house in Williamston, North Carolina, to attend court in Savannah, when he found the Tar River impassable and all other directions blocked. With little hope of advancing, he nevertheless departed, "resolved to make every effort in my power to get on." He had information that all the bridges had been "broken up" but that a gentleman had been repairing two that morning. When he reached the man's house, the man said he suspected the bridges on the Conetoe Swamp had been "broke up." The bridges were indeed gone, but another gentleman loaned him two slaves with whose aid he thought he might get through. The slaves passed through the swamp and assured him he could pass — that while he would have to go through lots of water, none of it was deep.

Iredell had to "plunge through very deep holes where the bridges had been," but he got through the swamp with some difficulty. He was in high spirits, thinking his difficulties over, but his alarm recommenced when he encountered further water deeper than expected. He nevertheless proceeded, having confidence in the information he had received. He soon entered a long swamp, formidable in appearance. He directed Hannibal, his slave, to proceed with caution but to stop if the water became very deep. When Hannibal stopped, Iredell told him to return immediately and soon discovered that "in two minutes he would have been in swimming water."

"I then found myself in a very disagreeable situation," Iredell said:

> It was impossible to return without the two Negroes I had parted with, and I knew of no house near where I could go to, and the night was advancing fast. After going back a little distance I saw a house not very far off...and there fortunately I found a most obliging man and his wife....The river was then higher than it had been known for 20 years, and was then rising. If it fell,...it would be two or three days before the swamps would be passable without swimming, and I saw no possibility of crossing with my chair and horses without great risk and delay, and had every reason to believe it would be impossible for some time to travel in any road beyond Tarborough. I then... found insurmountable obstacles in any [route]....[T]here was not the slightest probability of my getting to Savannah in time, and...I at length with inexpressible reluctance gave up the attempt.

Thus thwarted, Iredell returned to Samuel Johnston's house to wait for the floods to subside. If he could have traveled in any road towards the sound, he told Hannah, he might have spent two or three days with her. His keen sense of duty precluded this, however. "[I]t would never do," he said, "to lose another court by a regard to my own indulgence, whatever command of time I might be supposed to possess."

Iredell apparently was detained at Williamston at least a week, for he wrote Hannah from there a week later, again graphically summarizing the episode:

> Hannibal and myself were very near being drowned, having entered a swamp which we afterwards understood had 40 yards swimming water. I expected to have gone much sooner, but the waters continued high many days longer than was expected.[26]

Unwarranted criticism was a further grievance Iredell could have asserted, for despite these heroic, life-threatening efforts to attend the Savannah court, he was denounced for his nonappearance. The judge failed to attend or to inform the district judge why he could not come, said an Augusta newspaper.

(It was wrong; Iredell in fact had dispatched from Tarborough an explanatory letter to the district judge.) Some of the suitors had attended from foreign countries and distant states, the paper concluded, and were seriously disappointed by Iredell's absence.

A correspondent of Justice Paterson's continued the censuring. The failure was a serious disappointment indeed, he told Iredell's colleague, for the business on both the law and equity dockets had been greater and more important than ever before. Iredell, the correspondent wrote caustically, "must be more in favor with the newspaper scribblers than J. Chase," for he had escaped the censure heaped on Chase for a nonappearance, though his excuse was weaker than Chase's.

Iredell must have learned of some of the criticism and felt it keenly, for two months after the incident he wrote Timothy Pickering, the secretary of state, detailing the reasons for his default. "I made every effort in my power, and was nearly drowned in the attempt," he insisted, "but [was] obliged at length absolutely to desist."[27]

This was not the only unfair criticism Iredell received for defaulting on a court appearance. An earlier letter to a Philadelphia newspaper carped that citizens had come a considerable distance to the Delaware court without pay, yet the judge had failed to appear. "Mr. Iredell," the epistler stated, "certainly can have no proper excuse." Iredell had come as far as Wilmington on the court day, the writer said; had he come that far the day before, he "might readily have got to New-Castle in time, as many gentlemen went from thence on Monday morning." At a previous court, the author groused, Wilson had arrived at three o'clock when the jury had been summoned for ten. The judges received handsome salaries that came from the sweat of citizens' brows, he said, and citizens thus had a right "to call them to account for their malpractices." "[T]o lavish the time and property of the citizens unnecessarily," the complainer concluded, "is what they cannot, nor will not submit to."

This time Iredell had an apologist. Over the initials "J.M.," a subsequent issue of the paper debunked the critique. It was "unfair and uncandid," it said, to dump the disgrace on Iredell, who was "not in the least chargeable with a breach of duty." His Philadelphia court had not ended until late on Saturday, the weather was very bad that day, no stages ran on Sunday, and Iredell might think it improper to travel on that day in any event. On the following day when the stages stopped at Wilmington, Iredell was then delayed by bad weather and roads. Iredell thus had "every necessary apology... for no[t] attending in time." In sum, "Judge Iredell was not to blame."[28]

Poor lodging on circuit was a further grievance Iredell could have noted.

"The accommodations were in some places very bad," he wrote Hannah from an early court, noting particularly "a very rascally house" where he had to endure drinking, gaming, cursing, and swearing all night. Later he reported suffering from having to sleep in a room with five people and "a bed fellow of the wrong sort, which I did not expect." Later still, he had to share a room with Justice Wilson. Richmond was once "so full that for three or four nights [he] was obliged to lodge in a room where there were three other beds."

Despite the oft-impoverished nature of Iredell's accommodations, they were costly. "Living constantly in taverns has been very expensive indeed," he once wrote. On another occasion he doubted he could make purchases Hannah wanted, "as my expenses are unavoidably so great that I am afraid the money I have left will scarcely be sufficient." "My board here for 2 1/2 weeks only," he said, "amounts to 35 dollars." At the time, judges received no expense allowance. Cyrus Griffin, a district judge with whom Iredell sat on the circuit court for Virginia, once complained to President Adams that he spent one-fourth of his small salary on expenses necessarily attendant to the duties of his office.[29]

High overhead was not the sole victimizer of the roving jurist; sporadic criminal activity affected him as well. "I had all the curtains of my chair down," Iredell once wrote Hannah, "and a scoundrel of a Negro going along the road unstrapped my portmanteau from behind the chair, without Peter [one of Iredell's slaves—see *infra* Chapter 19] or myself perceiving it." The pilferer took Peter's great coat and Iredell's shirts and handkerchiefs. "But luckily," Iredell said, "he left my trunk in the road." While he suspected "who the rascal was," Iredell wrote, he was already late for a New Bern court and thus could not linger to pursue the matter.[30]

Occasional petty irritants on the road were less severe and more affecting. Iredell once had to persuade a family with whom he had often lodged that, as with Mark Twain years later, reports of his death had been greatly exaggerated. The household "had heard so circumstantial an account of my death some time ago," he reported, "that they took me for a brother of mine, and it was with some difficulty I could convince them their information was ill founded." The satisfaction the family expressed upon learning of his survival "affected me a good deal," he said.[31]

The severest personal hardships of the circuit life were the purely physical. On at least three occasions, Iredell's circuit travels involved him in accidents. On the first he was injured, he said, on account of his own careless driving. Part of the rein got under his horse's tail, the horse ran away, Iredell's chair struck a tree, he was thrown out, and a wheel ran over his leg. His pain was such that he "stay[ed] very inconveniently at a house on the road." The only injury, however, was a swelling in his ankle which subsided the next day.

Almost four years later, Iredell was "overturned in a very rascally carriage," but not hurt. "That line of stages," he said, "is generally in bad order," and that journey involved "more difficulties, dangers, & disappointments than I have experienced on any other." A subsequent expedition saw him again overturned, with a fellow passenger seriously injured.[32]

Disease, too, was a near neighbor in those days, and Iredell's time in Philadelphia exposed him to its 1793 yellow-fever epidemic. He received medical advice to stay away from the city, and his friend Senator Pierce Butler offered accessible rural lodging to the Iredell family. Even four years later, when back at Edenton, Iredell informed Samuel Johnston of the persistence of the malady. The latest accounts mentioned its "fatal continuance," he wrote, "without any change for the better." There were no accounts of any deaths among their acquaintances, however.[33]

Disease, moreover, evoked uncommon concern in a man for whom fatigue was a constant companion. Iredell's correspondence is replete with accounts of his almost unremitting exhaustion. With regularity, he was "greatly fatigued," "extremely fatigued," "excessively fatigued," "fatigued to death," or "heartily tired." Marathon court days of eleven hours without a break and protracted journeys of twelve hours' duration, commencing at 3:00 a.m., render his abiding weariness readily comprehensible. The entire lifestyle was, as Georgia District Judge Nathaniel Pendleton said of traveling the Southern Circuit, "more than the strength of any man can bear."[34]

Still further grievances were work-related. While at times court schedules were intense, there was also considerable "down time" when Iredell would lament "so little business to do" rather than so much. "Our court ended the second day," he once wrote from New York, "and as the court at New Haven does not begin [for another ten days], I expect to be here a week longer." In such situations, without the intimate friends whom he preferred to the mostagreeable strangers, time "drag[ged]...heavily." At intervals the circuit life was simply idle, and Iredell's time passed "very dully." He grew tired of this forced inertness, notwithstanding that he "experienced a good deal of civility." He would have come home for four or five days, "[b]ut no such agreeable opportunity offered."[35]

Wasted time on circuit, like idle time, bothered Iredell. When he learned that a juror in the Fries trial (see *supra* Chapter 11) had made pretrial statements strongly prejudicial to the defendant, he perceived no option other than to award a new trial. This was contrary to his inclination, especially given the protracted nature of the initial trial (nine days). He had cancelled a Maryland court appearance to finish the first trial. Samuel Johnston, Justices Chase and Paterson, and Maryland District Judge William Paca had concurred in his decision to stay the course in Philadelphia rather than fulfill his assignment in Annapolis.

His temporal investment was not altogether lost, for Bushrod Washington, who presided at the retrial, requested and received Iredell's notes from the first one. They would, Washington thought, aid in "avoid[ing] unnecessary prolixity, . . . prevent[ing] unnecessary discussions, & . . . the better understanding of such [points] as are important." Iredell never knew of Washington's letter acknowledging receipt of the notes, for he died the day it was written.[36]

Retrials were not the sole cause of wasted time on the circuits. A temporal gap required between indictment and trial produced "down time" in moving court dockets. The undeveloped state of communications also spawned substantial lost time. On his first tour of the Southern Circuit, Iredell waited three days at Wilmington and three at New Bern for information as to when the federal courts would be held in North Carolina. He never obtained it and concluded that none were to be held during that circuit. At least he was somewhat forewarned, as Samuel Johnston had kept him posted on the progress of legislation to extend the Judiciary Act to North Carolina and had predicted that no court would be held there during that circuit. Iredell explained to Hannah that "the unaccountable silence" of the members of Congress had placed him in "a most mortifying situation" and delayed his getting to New York. The problem, however, was lack of communication rather than lack of action, for the act had in fact passed almost a month before he wrote.

Iredell was again frustrated when he attempted to hold the circuit court for North Carolina that fall, again causing him considerable wasted time. He went to New Bern and convened the court but had to adjourn it the following day for want of another judge (the law then required two). John Stokes, the district judge, had died the preceding month, and Justice Rutledge was too ill to attend.[37]

The circuit life bred not only lost time but perpetual scheduling uncertainty as well. "It is yet uncertain whether I may leave this place tomorrow, or not until some days hence," a typical Iredell missive states: "It will depend upon a decision today whether or not the trial of a criminal shall be postponed until the next term."[38]

Iredell undoubtedly frequently wished he could recoup the "down time," for at times there were lengthy court sessions with immense business that required "almost unremitted attention." Sometimes the work "oppressed [him] beyond measure." It left him no time to write anyone but Hannah; he could not even answer a letter from Annie because, he said, "my head is entirely taken up with law points, which require all my attention."[39]

Iredell lamented, as every judge must, the time constraints on decision making. "The question upon which I am now to deliver my opinion," he once wrote, "is a question of extreme magnitude, as every one that affects the Constitution must be." He could have wished for more time, he said, "but the nature of the case forbids it."[40]

Iredell's devotion to duty and the "moment" of the business were such that he could not neglect his tasks. He was "resolved, cost what time it will, to finish the business." When duty required him to stay at a court after others departed, he stayed contentedly. "[N]o charge of neglect or delay shall be imputable to me," he vowed. Hannah, he thought, "would rather see me on Wednesday with my mind at ease than on Sunday in the paltry condition of a man who has sacrificed his public duty to his private feelings."[41]

Arrival at home did not necessarily end the business, for Iredell was still sought out when judicial action was desired. A prisoner in the Edenton jail once applied to him for a writ of habeas corpus, seeking discharge under a congressional act relieving persons imprisoned for debt. Iredell determined that the application did not come within the meaning of the law. Had he been doubtful, he said, he could not have given adequate notice of a hearing because he had to return to Philadelphia to attend the Supreme Court.[42]

Some of the circuit-life hardship was attributable to the other judges. Wilson's failure to attend a fall court at Richmond left Iredell with the business of both courts the following spring. Blair's illness gave Iredell the circuit court for Virginia when he would otherwise have been unassigned. Ellsworth's appointment as minister plenipotentiary to France increased the circuit duties of all the other justices. District Judge Richard Peters' absence to take examinations and issue warrants caused Iredell to sit alone for about a week in the trials of the land-tax insurrectionists. District Judge John Sitgreaves' ignorance of the law led him to impose on Iredell for assistance with a standing-to-sue question. As noted, virtually from his deathbed Iredell had to gather and forward to Bushrod Washington his notes on the Fries trial.[43]

The reputation of the federal courts concerned Iredell; whatever the other judges might do, he was determined "to leave no neglect chargeable" to him. Faithful attendance at the courts strengthened the hand of the infant government. Even Rhode Island, the last holdout from the Union, he said, had become "strongly and zealously attached," largely because of satisfaction with the performance of the federal courts.[44]

Absence of the judges all too often required adjournment of court to the next term, however. Bushrod Washington once found it impossible to reach

Charleston in time for court, for example, so he went on to Augusta. While apparently unavoidable, such dereliction brought disgrace to both the courts and the government. Iredell's home state's experience is illustrative. "[A]ccidental interruptions of the federal courts [by absence of the judges] since their institution in this state, and the entire loss of this term, have brought them into some disrepute, both with the suitors and the people," said a North Carolina newspaper in the fall of 1792. "The last term of our federal circuit court was lost by the nonattendance of any of the Associate Justices," William R. Davie added, and "this circumstance gave considerable dissatisfaction, and has brought the courts into some discredit."[45]

Presence, then, was important, but so was preparation. The burdens of Iredell's circuit life were enhanced by his apparent resolve to hold court fully informed. He would even write the secretary of state requesting that copies of new congressional acts be forwarded to him at Edenton through a designated date and thereafter be sent to stops on his circuit itinerary. He apparently wanted the minutest details, even including acts correcting typographical errors. It required enhanced devotion to duty, and time and energy beyond the norm, but Justice Iredell went to the circuits current on the law. Notwithstanding the accuracy of Gouverneur Morris' observation that "the agility of a post boy" was the prime requisite for Supreme Court service, to Iredell "the learning of a judge" remained important.[46]

CHAPTER 17

Great Civilities and Distinction

LIFE ON THE FEDERAL CIRCUITS WAS NOT ALL HARDSHIP; INDEED, AMENITIES ABOUNDED. ON OCCASION IREDELL DESCRIBED THE WEATHER AS "MOST CHARMING" OR "UNIFORMLY DELIGHTFUL." AT TIMES EVEN THE RIDE WAS "VERY AGREEABLE." THE CIRCUIT rider passed through charming or delightful country and saw very pretty towns.[1]

Iredell portrayed the country around New Haven, for example, as "most beautiful" and the vicinal towns as "in charming situations." They had neat and elegant houses, he wrote, laid out like villages and with large surrounding grounds. All towns had at least two elegant churches with handsome steeples, he said, one Episcopalian and one Presbyterian. New Haven, he told Hannah, "seems to be a very large & handsome town." He regretted that he had been unable to see more of it, "which I particularly wished to do as it was the scene of your brother's [Samuel Johnston's] education."[2]

Riding the circuits allowed Iredell to witness and chronicle the development of the early American infrastructure. Countrywide, he said, the improvements were wonderful. The bridge between Boston and Cambridge far exceeded his expectations, and he passed "an excellent and beautiful bridge over the Merrimack River near Newbury Port."[3]

America's major cities materialized under his gaze. New York City was "increasing and beautifying very fast," he observed. The walk in the Battery was, he thought, "one of the finest in the world." Young trees were enhancing the place. The governor's house "appear[ed] to great advantage," there were more elegant houses in Broadway and on the lower end of Broad Street, and several more were under construction. "Property," he said, "is even dearer here than in Philadelphia."[4]

Like its largest city, the nation's nascent capital city unfolded before his attentive eyes. "I had a view this morning as I passed to George Town of the new federal streets, which will quite eclipse Philadelphia," he wrote Hannah in 1791.[5]

Finally, he observed the maturation of the country's oldest institution of higher learning, Harvard University. His driver took an unaccustomed route so he could see it, he reported in 1792, and he had "great reason to be satisfied, for it is a most beautiful place." He was very pleased, he wrote later after viewing a "quarterly exhibition" at Cambridge.[6]

As Iredell wended his way through the cities, towns, and countryside of the evolving nation, he met with the utmost civility, cordiality, and generosity. Even before he commenced his first circuit, Cullen Pollok, an Edenton neighbor, offered him £175 sterling in hard money. The judge would have difficulty procuring coin for a long and expensive journey, Pollok wrote, and the money was at his disposal if needed, to be repaid when convenient. Archibald Maclaine volunteered William Blount as a source of information regarding routes, distances, and stages. John Hay offered lodging whenever Iredell passed near Fayetteville, North Carolina.[7]

The civility and cordiality with which people plied Iredell during his first circuit tour typifies his entire experience. "I experience the utmost politeness and kindness," he wrote Hannah from Fayetteville soon after leaving home. As he proceeded southward, he was grateful in the extreme for Justice Rutledge's kindness to him. Rutledge had engaged their lodgings in Granby, South Carolina, which were "excellent & retired, upon a fine high hill." He had also provided a canoe for a portion of their journey, and his company made Iredell "consider I have pleasure rather than trouble before me." His perception was accurate; he continued to receive "the greatest and kindest civilities" from Rutledge, whom he found "one of the most agreeable men I was ever acquainted with." The Rutledges housed him in Charleston, and Mrs. Rutledge proved "a truly respectable and amiable woman," who received him "in the most obliging manner." The Rutledges were his Charleston tour guides, and he quickly considered them on a par with William and Ann Hooper of Hillsborough, who were among his closest longtime friends.

Rutledge's extended family helped entertain the roving jurist. A son-in-law took Iredell on a boat excursion, and a daughter played the piano for him. Rutledge's son-in-law and Iredell were soon "upon as social a footing as if [they] had been acquainted for years." In sum, Iredell "experienced as much kindness and attention as if [he] had been their own brother."[8]

The wife of Georgia District Judge Nathaniel Pendleton also granted him "very kind civilities." She provided him with complimentary postal services as well, delivering a letter to Hannah in New York soon afterward.[9]

Iredell's new associates went well beyond the judges and their spouses. He "became acquainted with several very agreeable gentlemen of the first characters in the country." They were so attentive to him that despite his pining for home, he grieved upon parting from them. He was received by everyone everywhere "with the utmost distinction & politeness, and by many of the first families in South Carolina with a degree of unaffected kindness which was gratifying indeed." He even had "the honor of several visits, particularly in a high style, from the British consul in his chariot."[10]

Succeeding circuits brought more of the same. In the fall of 1790 Iredell again passed his time in Charleston "in the usual, agreeable manner." While the Rutledges could not offer him a room because Justice Rutledge's mother was there, their "civilities" remained "very great indeed." Iredell stayed at a boarding house but never dined there. Later, he again received "great civilities" in Charleston and was "engaged" for dinner every day. In Augusta he had excellent lodgings and was "excellently & kindly accommodated" in the home of a lawyer whose wife was away.[11]

Again on the Southern Circuit in the spring of 1792, Iredell once more met with "great distinction and kindness." He rejoiced that he "came southward," for otherwise the absence of judges would have disgraced the federal judiciary. Justice Johnson had defaulted in appearance on account of, Iredell thought, "such violent freshes [floods] that it is not unlikely they may have obstructed him." On this journey he and his horses rested at a private home in Augusta, and he received extreme kindness while spending almost a week with John Hay in Fayetteville.[12]

This litany of kindnesses did not reflect mere southern hospitality, for the beneficence continued when the roving jurist ventured northward. He anticipated "very great civilities" in Boston in the fall of 1792 and was not disappointed. "I have met with the most distinguished civilities," he soon informed Hannah, "not only from gentlemen to whom I had letters, but from many others." He was again engaged every day, often receiving more invitations than he could accept. "The society here," he told Hannah, "is in my opinion extremely agreeable."

Writing to his brother Arthur in England, he was even more effusive. "They absolutely made me sick with too great a profusion of good things," he said, "the only circumstance I had occasion to complain of." Truly genuine hospitality, mixed with unmistakable cordiality and kindness, was characteristic. District Judge John Lowell was particularly kind to him, and he warmed to the city increasingly as his stay progressed. The civilities never ceased, and he "was not a little affected in parting from it." He admonished Hannah to be mindful that the families there deserved their "utmost respect and attention," and he listed "families in Boston and vicinity to whom I am under great obligations for civilities."[13]

New York also accorded Iredell "very great civilities," and he passed his time there, too, "in an agreeable manner." The Cornell family, whom he had represented in *Bayard v. Singleton* (see *supra* Chapter 2), was particularly kind to him. He again received numerous dining invitations and anticipated "a good deal of the New York hospitality."

The smaller boroughs of the North likewise accommodated him lavishly. "[G]enteel families" in Windsor, Vermont, for example, rendered him "great civilities."[14]

Such northern gentility notwithstanding, Iredell's reappearances in the South afforded a distinctive hospitableness. Savannah in 1794 saw him "dining out in a genteel society every day"; he ate "almost within sight of the sea, with salt water immediately before..., and a variety of charming trees interspersed." Richmond in 1795 brought "great civilities and distinction." It was "the usual civilities of this agreeable place" in Charleston in 1798, with engagements every day and dinner at his lodgings only once. "The distinction and kindness...exceeded, if possible, what I experienced before," he told Hannah.[15]

"[T]he justices' correspondence suggests...[an] active social life," a present-day scholar writes of the Marshall Court. "John Marshall's letters to his wife...testify to regular attendance at dinners, balls and other social functions," he continues. The Marshall Court was simply following precedent, however, for clearly the justices on circuit were highly sociable beings from the Court's earliest days. The opening of a circuit court occasioned holiday-like festivities:

> In Boston, the opening of one circuit court was celebrated with a procession that included "eight constables with staves," federal and state officials, "Barristers, Counsellors, other Gentlemen of the Bar," and "Citizens, two and two." At the courthouse the ritual of court day familiar in Anglo-American legal traditions continued: The justices would be seated, order called, venires returned, and the grand and petit juries impanelled and sworn.

While sporadically the circuit rider's time passed "rather dully," at other times there was a surfeit of social activity. "Such a succession of frolickings as some people have in this city is really disgusting," Iredell once wrote Hannah from Philadelphia.[16]

Iredell was clearly the gregarious type, the consummate *bonhomme*, and the social aspects of the circuit life appealed to him. Even his oft-neglected and complaining spouse recognized that, in this respect, his course of life was advantageous. She once wrote his sister-in-law in England that while the distance to Philadelphia was great and Iredell's absence would be long, she took consolation from his being "in a healthier climate and where he can at all times have agreeable society."[17]

While Iredell loathed the circuit travel, he delighted in his traveling companions. The old adage of the English coachmen was apposite: "Good companionship makes short miles." On his first trek southward, he expressed delight in having company the whole way from Fayetteville, North Carolina, to near Camden, South Carolina. It clearly pleased him that he anticipated having company again the following day. This made the journey "a thousand times more agreeable than ... expected." On a later expedition, it pleased him greatly that he "had company extremely agreeable the whole way."[18]

Sometimes the other judges were his fellow wayfarers. "Mr. Jay arrived here [Baltimore] the day before yesterday," Iredell once informed Hannah, "and we are to set off in the stage tomorrow together." Such excursions enhanced collegiality, for Iredell could report a few days later that "Mr. Jay improves infinitely upon intimacy." Still further into the journey, he found himself "more and more pleased" with Jay.

Social exchanges between the justices and their colleagues' spouses were also common. While Jay was on circuit, Iredell had tea "very agreeably" with Mrs. Jay and reported that she "looked extremely well." Later, while Jay was minister to England, he again had tea with Mrs. Jay "on a special invitation."

Iredell made friends with his fellow lodgers as well. "[W]e have very agreeable company in the house where I lodge," he would report from the circuits.[19]

Dinners, teas, and parties were the familiar fare of the circuits. During his first swing through the Eastern Circuit, Iredell recounted that Massachusetts Governor John Hancock had insisted on his dining and spending an evening with him. There was "a very numerous and genteel company of ladies and gentlemen, and some of them danced." This excursion found Iredell engaged every day, sometimes with multiple invitations for the same day. He deemed the society "extremely agreeable." John Lowell, the district judge, was particularly kind to him; on future jaunts he spent weekend time with Lowell and drank tea with Elizabeth Cabot, the wife of one of Massachusetts' United States senators.[20]

In Baltimore Iredell "waited on the new French Minister" and "was very much pleased with him." In Philadelphia he dined privately with his longtime friend Senator Pierce Butler and publicly at a dinner honoring Alexander Hamilton and Henry Knox for their public service. In his home state of North

Carolina, he enjoyed the company of Alfred Moore, who would succeed him on the Court; William R. Davie, his fellow lawyer and political ally; and John Williams, one of the state's judges. While Iredell episodically reported a dearth of invitations, a greater number than he had time to accept was more representative.[21]

Over the course of his circuit life, Iredell regularly indulged his penchant for dancing. On an early trip to Charleston, he stepped lightly with Justice Rutledge's daughter-in-law until 2:00 a.m., yet arose at sunrise and was "perfectly well." At a ball in Boston, he "danced down two dances" with "at least 6 beauties" present "and several more that were nearly such." A ball in an elegant room in Windsor, Vermont, provided such agreeable company that he danced with pleasure until 2:30 a.m. and then "left off with regret." In Philadelphia he went to an evening ball at the British Minister's. The wife of the federal marshal also gave a party and dance at which he "shared in the dancing till one o'clock." Philadelphia offered him still other parties, "less crowded than usual and really very agreeable."[22]

The circuit life also humored the justice's affinity for theater and proclivity for dramatic criticism. He found a Richmond production of Shakespeare's "As You Like It" performed "very indifferently" except for one "really... pleasing actress." "Clandestine Marriage" staged in Philadelphia disappointed him, for it was "wretchedly acted." Even the company of Pennsylvania Governor Thomas Mifflin and Justices Blair and Paterson did not alleviate his distress over this thespian ineptitude. While "The Way to Get Married" had some interesting scenes, Iredell found the title absurd. "[T]here is no matrimonial plot in it," he said, "and a clergyman at the end of a moral sermon might as well say, 'Young ladies, this is the way to get married.'"[23]

Perhaps the foremost amenity of Iredell's circuit life was his close association with the prominent men of his time. In Pennsylvania he traveled and dined with Thomas Mifflin, president of the Supreme Executive Council and later the state's first governor. At Annapolis he dined with "the great [Charles] Carroll," United States senator and Maryland state senator. In Baltimore he breakfasted with Luther Martin, the state's attorney general ("the famous Antifederalist," Iredell called him; Martin subsequently became a Federalist convert because of his hatred for Jefferson). At Philadelphia he dined with the British Minister. Near Boston he met Elbridge Gerry, a signer of the Declaration of Independence, member of the Constitutional Convention, and member of the United States House of Representatives. Gerry gave him a letter of introduction to "one of the first gentlemen" in Boston. The gentleman was probably Theophilus Parsons, a prominent Massachusetts lawyer and later

chief justice of the Massachusetts Supreme Judicial Court, for when Iredell
met Parsons a few days later he referred to him as "the first [foremost] lawyer
I have met with in America, and...a remarkably agreeable man."[24]

When Iredell dined with "the Committee and Corporation of the College
[Harvard]" in Cambridge, he particularly enjoyed sitting beside Massachusetts Lieutenant Governor Samuel Adams. "[T]hough an old man," Iredell
wrote Hannah, Adams had "a great deal of fire yet." He was, the jurist said,
"polite and agreeable" and "the very image of the pictures I have seen of
Oliver Cromwell." Three days after this dinner, Iredell autographed and forwarded to Adams one of his charges. The flowery, deferential language of his
cover letter is amusing and revealing:

> Mr. Iredell, thinking himself highly honored with the conversa-
> tions he has had the pleasure of holding with the Lieutenant Gover-
> nor, and being desirous of convincing him that the principle in his
> late charge which the Lieutenant Governor was pleased to notice
> with approbation is a fixed and invariable one in his mind, takes the
> liberty to enclose a former charge that he happened to have by him in
> which the same principle is still more particularly inculcated.
>
> He hopes the Lieutenant Governor will excuse the freedom he
> now takes, and pardon his adding that he shall always reflect with
> satisfaction on the opportunity of so agreeable though short an ac-
> quaintance with a gentleman to whom America owes such important
> obligations, and from whom he himself has derived both instruction
> and pleasure.[25]

While Iredell clearly relished association with the powerful, their loss of influence did not alter his friendship. Even after John Rutledge's rejection for
the chief justiceship and his ensuing bout with insanity, including two suicide
attempts, he remained Iredell's companion of choice on the latter's travels
southward. "I am to dine today with Mr. J. Rutledge, who has invited a number of other gentlemen," Iredell wrote Hannah in 1798. "This week, I am
told," he continued, "is the first time he has broke from his retirement." A
week later he wrote that he had again dined at his lodgings only once, thanks
to Rutledge's conspicuous friendship and affection, made the more remarkable "considering that...Rutledge had lived totally recluse" before Iredell's
arrival.[26]

The conspicuous figures with whom Iredell associated while on circuit included some of the great lawyers of the time. Patrick Henry, for example, appeared before him at Richmond for the circuit-court arguments in *Ware v.
Hylton* (see *supra* Chapter 12). "The great Patrick Henry is to speak today,"

Iredell told Hannah expectantly. "I never was more agreeably disappointed than in my acquaintance with him," he continued. "I have been much in his company, and his manners are very pleasing, and his mind, I am persuaded, highly liberal."

Iredell apparently did not expect to be impressed with Henry's oratory. He had asserted that Henry was no orator, "that he was a mere *ad captandum* speaker." After listening to Henry for three consecutive days, however, Iredell changed his mind. "Gracious God! he is an orator indeed!" Iredell exclaimed. Henry was, Iredell now said, "certainly the first [best] orator I ever heard — speaks with the most ease, the least embarrassment, the greatest variety, and with an illustration of imagery altogether original but perfectly correct." Henry's manner was gentlemanly, Iredell continued, and he was never known "to say anything personally offensive" except when necessary to defend himself. Henry was "a much more solid character and better reasoner than I expected to find him," Iredell opined, and had a reputation as "a man of real benevolence and integrity."

While Henry's arguments left Iredell largely unsatisfied, he considered them of the highest quality. The cause had been spoken to, he said, "with a degree of ability equal to any occasion," and he would always remember the polemics with pleasure and respect. A "splendor of eloquence" was all-surpassing. "Fatigue has given way under its influence," Iredell said, "and the heart has been warmed, while the understanding has been instructed."[27]

John Marshall's argument followed Henry's. This case won Marshall the admiration of the ablest lawyers and carried his reputation beyond the bounds of his home state of Virginia. He was before Iredell on circuit in other cases as well.[28]

Iredell undoubtedly gained personal satisfaction from these associations, and the circuit life affirmed his psyche in other ways as well. The foreman of a South Carolina grand jury wrote to thank him for his charge. The "animated zeal of a federal judge" and "the good effects of his laudable exertions" in explicating the duties of good citizenship, the foreman said, afforded considerable satisfaction to the public. The grand jury at Raleigh, the capital city of Iredell's home state, thanked him both for his charge and for his expeditious administration of the court's business. The latter was especially important because of the season; it was summer, and proper attention to their crops permitted the members to be away only as "absolutely necessary" for the business of the court.[29]

The Spring 1795 Vermont Circuit Court brought news that Dr. Samuel Cutler, an old friend now living in that state (probably a Loyalist whom Iredell had assisted), had named his youngest son, who was about three years old, for Iredell. Iredell was "very much affected." He would have been equally affected if he could have read a highly encomiastic letter Connecticut Congressman Roger Griswold wrote about him. "Judge Iredell is a man of the most amiable manners conceivable," wrote Griswold,

> without a spark of that haughty superiority of manners which too often characterizes the man in office, he never appears without a dignity which is decent & respectable—his conversation is not only instructive but extremely amusing—always possessing a flow of spirits, which animates not merely himself but other[s]. He discovers a candor in opinions & benevolence of heart which commands the attachment of all those with whom he converses—such is the Judge who now sits in this court & who may be considered not only great but good.[30]

The circuit life, then, indeed offered amenities. Nonetheless, Iredell was not just whining about the hardships. They were real; they were severe; over time, they could be devouring. A prolonged and arduous session with "an immensity of business" at Philadelphia, followed by another at Richmond, took a special toll on Iredell during the spring circuit of 1799. After a brief respite at Edenton, the circuit rider commenced his return to Philadelphia for the Supreme Court's August Term. From Richmond, however, he returned home, physically unable to complete the trip. When the Court convened, the huge oaken chair provided for the sixth of its justices was again vacant. Its tenant for the first near decade of the Court's history was too ill to attend.[31]

IV

The Man

The historian will put before us the men and women as they actually lived, so that we shall recognize them for what they were—living beings.

— *Theodore Roosevelt*

CHAPTER 18

The Most-Serious Mortifications

A CASTLE OVERLOOKS THE PICTURESQUE TOWN OF LEWES, EAST SUSSEX COUNTY, ENGLAND, WHERE OUR SUBJECT FIRST SAW THE LIGHT OF DAY. CURRENT DENIZENS OF THE MUNICIPALITY ARE WELL REMINDED OF THE EIGHTEENTH-CENTURY PRESENCE there of Tom Paine, an Iredell compatriot in the American Revolution who came to Lewes in 1768, the year Iredell departed England for the New World, and stayed until 1774. The Bull House, where Paine lived and is believed to have written one of his major treatises, still stands, now housing the administrative headquarters of the Sussex Archaeological Society. The White Hart Hotel, where he explicated his radical theories to the Headstrong Club, also remains, and the club yet meets, though more as a polite lecture and discussion group than as the true debating society it was in Paine's day.

Both the hotel exterior and the castle bowling green, which also sustained Paine's harangues, contain markers commemorating his presence there. A film shown to the town's visitors calls Paine "Lewes's most famous resident," while ignoring Iredell altogether. The guest in Lewes learns that John Harvard, for whom Harvard University was named, married there, as did a Thomas Jefferson ancestor, but he leaves uninformed that James Iredell, a justice of the United States Supreme Court, was born there. Indeed, it appears that no trace of Iredell's ephemeral presence in the little town survives.[1]

While the village of his nativity has forgotten him, Iredell never forgot his roots there. He expressed thoughts of visiting his native land throughout his life but never found the time or the wherewithal. Long separation from the family of origin he left there did not alter his affection for or attention to it, however. Three of its members died while he was attaining prominence across the sea. The brother closest to him in age (Iredell was the oldest),

Francis ("Billy"), died in 1772 at age twenty, cause unknown. His father, Francis Iredell, Sr., suffered a paralytic stroke in 1766 that forced his retirement from the mercantile business; he died from a second stroke in 1773. The next oldest brother, Charles, was killed in action in 1782 or 1783, at about age thirty, while serving as a midshipman in the British Navy against the French in India. Iredell's mother, Margaret, and his two youngest brothers, Arthur and Tom, outlived him, and extended absence did not abate his affection for and aid to them.[2]

His aged and ailing mother became a special object of Iredell's sentiments and attention. The ties temporarily severed in the Revolutionary War years were quickly reestablished in the wake of the peace, and an odyssey commenced that ultimately brought the elder Mrs. Iredell to America. The sad state of the family's finances, which had prompted Iredell's youthful emigration to America, had not ameliorated during the war years. Following the peace, Iredell learned that his mother's support consisted of an annuity provided by her relatives, Lord and Lady Macartney, and some assistance from her wealthy planter brother-in-law, Thomas Iredell. Otherwise, she depended entirely upon the chapter of accidents (chance, the unforeseen course of events).

Iredell thanked her benefactors profusely and mentioned the generosity of each in his letters of gratitude to the others. He conveyed to Catherine Macartney inexpressible emotion for the annuity she and Lord Macartney had afforded. They had, he said, "saved one of the best of women & of mothers from distress." "[W]ith joy and gratitude," he offered his Uncle Thomas his "most fervent thanks." Long ignorance about his mother's sources of support had caused him the deepest affliction about her situation, he said, and he was deeply grateful to these family philanthropists for "their goodness."[3]

A spendthrift son partially accounted for the elder Mrs. Iredell's pecuniary woes. Shortly after the peace, Iredell learned from his brother Arthur that their brother Tom was perpetually applying to her for relief and that her generosity to him often left her in the greatest distress. A year and a half later, Arthur informed Iredell that their mother remained "as obstinate as ever" in her determination to liquidate Tom's debts "before she enjoys the quiet & happiness of Carolina."

Iredell attempted to solve the problems with both simultaneously by inviting both to come and live with him. Tom accepted rather immediately and arrived in Edenton in late August or early September 1784. Their mother's similar voyage was another six years in the offing, however.[4]

From the immediate post-war resumption of Iredell's correspondence with his Anglican clergyman brother Arthur, Arthur expressed a keen desire to have their mother in America. He was dissatisfied with her life and saw "no prospect of happiness for her on this side of the Atlantic." For six years Arthur plied Iredell with missives pushing their mother toward America. "How much I wish my poor mother was of your party & enjoyed the same ease [as you and Tom]!" he wrote in 1785. "My mother's situation," he said in 1786, "is much more distressing to me than my own." "You are not more anxious to receive her than I that she should go," he continued in 1787, "for she leads a terrible life here, & it is not in my power to alleviate her suffering."

In 1788 Mrs. Iredell suffered a "serious attack," from which Arthur feared she would not recover; by 1789 her health was better, and she was "into a better situation." Still, Arthur said, she "continue[d] to live in a way & with people that disagree and impose upon her." She was living at his expense, and he was "strain[ing] every nerve to advance her money." She "might have subsisted *very* reputably" on it, he opined, "but it has not answered the good purpose I wished." His only hope was for her to go to America.

In June 1790, a few weeks before Mrs. Iredell finally set sail, Arthur wrote James plaintively: "Would to God my mother were with you. Her life on this island is, & in spite of [all my] endeavors will continue to be, very [different] from what either of us would desire." In August, a week after she sailed, he elaborated:

> The more I reflect upon this change in my mother's situation, the more I rejoice at it. You cannot, nor can even Tom who saw her in London & the life she then led, have any conception of the benefit she will derive from so great a reverse of fortune. Here she was at the mercy of a set of miscreants. . . . With you, she will have every advantage & experience every consolation that can smooth the declining path of life.[5]

Iredell had been at least as eager to receive his mother as Arthur had been to send her. He again wrote his uncle of his acute desire to have her come and live with him, expressing his readiness to support her and Tom in the future. "I wish now only for my mother & anxiously hope I will not be disappointed," he told Arthur: "My greatest distress is about her present difficulties, & the debts of Tom that are unpaid." "My principal wish now, my dear mother," he wrote to her

> is to have you with me. This I heartily & earnestly wish for, . . . and I am continually disappointed in my prospects of remitting money to England, which I had hoped to have done this winter, but I find it impossible. My heart bleeds to think of your distresses there without

my having it in my power to relieve you, but here I am persuaded I could enable you to live with comfort, and I hope with happiness, for many would be earnest to promote it.[6]

Iredell's Supreme Court appointment appears to have ameliorated his financial situation somewhat (*see infra* Chapter 20), for in its immediate aftermath he told his uncle it would soon enable him to "make my mother's circumstances perfectly easy." Soon thereafter he and Arthur shared equally in the cost of their mother's voyage to America. After a passage of eight weeks, the elder Mrs. Iredell arrived in New York in September 1790, cheerful and hearty, though suffering from a long-standing intestinal problem. Iredell, who had not seen his mother for twenty-two years, had just departed for the fall tour of the Southern Circuit. The weeks-long delay in their reunion his circuit duties occasioned is one of the more-poignant episodes in Iredell's story. The poignancy is enhanced by the fact that his early departure, and perhaps his entire trip, was a waste. The other judges failed to appear in Georgia, preventing a quorum and necessitating a cancellation of that court. Iredell kept the court open five days, but to no avail. The subsequent court in South Carolina likewise appears to have done no appreciable business, and no court was held in North Carolina.[7]

Hannah felt keenly the emotions these circumstances produced. She wished her husband could have seen his mother before he "set off." Iredell also sensed them. Two weeks after his mother's arrival, he remained uncertain as to her whereabouts. He could only hope she had arrived and beg to be "most dutifully and affectionately" remembered to her. "God knows how impatient I am to embrace and welcome her to America," he added a few days later.

Arthur likewise perceived the poignancy in the deferred reunion. "It was particularly unfortunate that you had but the day before left [New York]," he wrote. He exulted in the event itself, however. Their mother, he told Iredell, gave "the best accounts of her arrival at New York and kind reception in your family." His own happiness was inexpressible. "You have," he told Iredell later, "the real luxury of gilding the evening of a mother's days. . . . The more I reflect upon the great change in her affairs, the more thankful I am that it has taken place!"[8]

It soon became evident, however, that Arthur's motives in the matter were not wholly altruistic or the product of undefiled filial devotion. Minor problems with the elder Mrs. Iredell surfaced immediately. She talked too much to suit Hannah. She complained about her rheumatism. She embarrassed Iredell by continuing to request money from his uncle; he should now be able to provide for her "without troubling any of her friends," Iredell told the uncle.

These peccadillos paled into insignificance, however, beside the problem of major consequence: Margaret Iredell suffered from severe, long-standing alcoholism, a fact which Arthur well knew but failed to disclose to Iredell.

The concealment, Iredell told Hannah, was "cruel & deliberate." Iredell upbraided his sibling severely for his perfidy, and Arthur suffered from it. Arthur told their brother Tom that Iredell had given him "a melancholy account of my mother's indulgence in a failing which I had reason to think she would have gotten the better of in his family." "Did she . . . make too free with liquors when you were in England?" Arthur asked with feigned innocence. "It is a most disgraceful habit," he continued piously, "& has given James the utmost unhappiness." James, he hoped, could "induce her to . . . surmount that only bar to her happiness."

Despite Arthur's arrant acquaintance with their mother's "failings," he told Iredell his "pride & . . . *affection*" were shocked when he learned that she "had degraded herself by the meanest of all indulgences!" Iredell, he thought, could "exert an authority over her" in the matter. "[F]rom the purest motives," he had done so while she was in England, though she gave him "no credit" for his "sacrifice." He admonished Iredell to "use every means in your power of rousing my mother into that rectitude of conduct, from which a departure, in her sex, at her time of life, and in a conspicuous family, is as bad as bad can be." Her problem was so severe, he now told Iredell, apparently for the first time, that doctors had advised him that "any excess" would soon lead to her demise.[9]

Iredell's response did not mince words. He chastised Arthur rigorously for foisting upon him, without warning, a situation which had chagrined him greatly. The letter, Arthur said later, "contain[ed] little more than one subject most painful to us both." It was a "great injustice," Arthur pleaded, to "hint" that he had repressed information regarding their mother's problem. He had had only a "suspicion" that their mother "*now & then* exposed herself in that way." "I had *not* the smallest idea that it had grown to a confirmed habit, & might not *easily* be done away in your family," he told James.

The balance of Arthur's letter thoroughly belied these pious protestations, however, for he proceeded to note that their mother had "imbibed her failing" in London "among people in low life." It had shocked him to learn that despite his pecuniary contributions to her, she had been getting money from friends and relatives in Ireland. If her "disgrace" had wounded Iredell's pride, Arthur wrote, "what must mine suffer, whom in this & many other ways she has subjected to the most serious mortifications!" Had she remained in England, he said, revealing perhaps unconsciously his true motives in vigorously advocating her move, he would never have been free of mortification. Sending her to Iredell, he claimed, was the only way he thought it possible to save her. Were he in Iredell's situation, he "should think it my *duty* to exert an authority over her, which surely would put it out of her power to indulge a vice that perhaps is out of the reach of *argument*." "She wants a protector," he concluded, and "upon whom has she so strong a claim as yourself? You can only protect, by putting it out of her power to commit excess."[10]

Arthur's protestations of innocence failed to impress his jurist brother. Iredell appropriately characterized "Arthur's attempts to justify a cruel & deliberate concealment from me" as "ridiculous." While asking Hannah to convey "[m]y love to my mother," he appended pathetically: "My God! what misery her conduct causes me." He was appropriately apologetic to Hannah, who felt the brunt of the problem during his extended absences. "I feel the utmost pain and anxiety when I think of your situation in all respects," he wrote her. He wrote more specifically: "I feel greatly for your situation in respect to my mother, but have great pleasure in finding our good neighbors are so attentive to you."[11]

In late 1791 the elder Mrs. Iredell expressed dissatisfaction with her lot in the New World and resolved to go to her sister in Ireland. Arthur conveyed to Iredell his concern that at one time that would have worked, but no longer. Iredell soon informed Arthur that he was removing their mother "into the country." He vehemently rejected Arthur's suggestions that he could enforce correct behavior in her. The "duty of coercion" Arthur urged upon him was "utterly contrary" to his nature, Iredell wrote. "I can't without distraction almost even speak to her on the subject," Iredell said, "much less act as her gaoler or her spy." Iredell was shocked and outraged at Arthur's suggestion that Iredell had "done [him] a grievous injury." The only possible injury, Iredell said, was his lament over Arthur's concealing "foibles" which Arthur had acknowledged precluded his "living even in the same kingdom in peace with her." It should have been for him to judge whether residence with him would correct these foibles before she came not only to his country, but also "into the bosom of my family." Not a line from Arthur had intimated more than "a tincture of low manners from low company," Iredell continued. This he had been willing to bear for a time, "thinking it might be corrected," but "I should have thought I injured my family in the cruelest manner if I deliberately brought a parent into it that was to disgrace & make them miserable," he said.

Notwithstanding Iredell's considerable anger, writing his brother in this tone was difficult for him. It made him so unhappy that he "lost the last packet [missed the last outgoing mail], and...delayed [mailing the] letter to the last moment."[12]

The youngest brother, Tom, emphatically sided with Iredell, writing him in James Joyceian stream-of-consciousness style:

> I dread ever making any enquiries about my poor deluded mother, I have not even received a letter from her for some time, is there no place near Edenton it might be better for her being at, than where she is, my God what misery does this one event involve us all in, good God how could Arthur act so.

Arthur meanwhile continued to defend himself (unconvincingly) and to urge upon Iredell a "treatment" of coercion. Iredell's letter, he told its author, "affected me more than I can tell you!" They "differ[ed] much," he said, "on the score of our conduct to her." Arthur thought "a certain degree of coercion & severity" necessary, "[l]ost as she has been to a due sense of right & wrong (such is the sad consequence of that baneful vice!)." He had been emptying his pockets for her while she was in London, he said, which he could ill afford. In return, she had kept "low company" and "lavished upon them what was chiefly drained from me." Arthur again feigned ignorance "of the ascendancy the other fatal indulgence had gained over her."[13]

Iredell now proceeded with his plans to remove his mother to the country. "The sooner the better," he said, expressing "great anxiety indeed that it should be accomplished as soon as possible." His duties on the Southern Circuit necessitated leaving the disagreeable business to his wife. From the circuit he wrote Hannah, hoping that "before this time she is in the country." "I constantly lament my misfortune," he continued, "in being obliged to leave her in town." When at length he received word of her removal, his "heart [was] infinitely lighter."

Initially, the move proved less than wholly satisfactory. Approximately six months afterward, Iredell wrote Hannah wondering whether his mother could be "better placed." If she could be better cared for or more satisfied with another family in the country, he would not object to the change. He did not want her back in town, however.[14]

The change was permanent and ultimately proved quite satisfactory. For the remainder of his life, Iredell visited his mother regularly on Sundays when he was in Philadelphia. He consistently found her well.[15] While it is unclear whether the change solved her problem with spirits, Iredell's surviving correspondence contains no further mention of it. Arthur occasionally inquired about her conduct, but if Iredell answered, the responses have not been found.[16]

Iredell and Arthur apparently planned to share their mother's expenses equally. Whether this in fact occurred — indeed, whether Arthur actually paid anything—is unclear. Samuel Johnston found even the plan perturbing. When Arthur inherited their Uncle Thomas' estate, Johnston wrote Iredell that he hoped Arthur would now relieve him "from the expense of supporting the old lady." While convinced that Iredell derived great satisfaction from having it in his power to make her comfortable in her old age, Johnston thought it "hard on your income, too small by far to make you perfectly at ease, if the expenditure was confined to your own family only." After Iredell's death, Johnston himself supported the elder Mrs. Iredell "with an expectation that her son in England who is in affluent circumstances will sometime or other reimburse me"; Hannah's "bill" on Arthur was returned to Johnston's Philadelphia merchants unpaid, however. Johnston made several demands on Arthur for payments rendered on the elder Mrs. Iredell's account, but apparently to no avail. He was still writing about the account after Mrs. Iredell's death.[17]

While Iredell's mother did quite well following her move to the country, in the mid-1790s she began to complain of old age; Arthur found "impressions of it strongly marked in her letter." In one of Iredell's visits shortly before his death, he observed for the first time some failure in her memory. Shortly after Iredell's death, Benjamin Dungan, the elder Mrs. Iredell's caretaker, wrote Hannah that recently she had failed considerably. She could not dress or undress herself, rise from a chair, or write a letter unassisted. A few months later, he wrote again to say that Mrs. Iredell was well but feeble—unable to rise without help or walk without leading—and had given up writing altogether. She died in September 1802.[18]

Unlike with his mother, Iredell at least had some forewarning that the experience with his brother Tom, the youngest of the Iredell clan, might not be altogether trouble-free. Months before Tom's September 1784 arrival in Edenton, Arthur conveyed to Iredell his concerns about their sibling. The military experience, Arthur thought, was always detrimental and had been so with Tom. "He has naturally a liveliness and propension to gaiety which a military life has indulged," Arthur wrote, "& how far he will be able to turn his mind to any serious pursuit, much less to habilitate himself to severe application, may well be made a question."

Tom's manners, too, Arthur said, were somewhat tainted. An experience across the Atlantic, Arthur thought, would be beneficial. Iredell's "eye & authority" would give Tom advantages not found in England. "At present... his...prospects...are [not] so flattering as to encourage his continuance in the Marines, which...is not a very desirable service," Arthur continued: "I shall acquaint him with what you have written, & advise him to accept your invitation." When Tom did accept, Arthur wrote Hannah that she would find him amiable, with a very good (though uncultivated) head and an excellent heart.[19]

Tom, then, came to America with a liveliness and propensity for gaiety, tainted manners, and an uncultivated intellect. He came, too, notwithstanding his mother's efforts on his behalf, with extensive debts. Iredell could not pay them. His income was barely sufficient for his own expenses, he said, and he had old debts to pay, though he was taking care not to contract new ones. While he was undertaking Tom's care for the future, he saw no promise of being able to pay the "heavy debt" Tom had left in England. It was beyond his means as well, Arthur said; he would pay if able, but had no "near" prospect of such. Perhaps, Iredell suggested, their uncle might relieve them of "this embarrassment." It was the only thing, Iredell said, that "in the least abates the great happiness my brother's arrival has afforded me."[20]

Iredell learned of his brother's safe landing from Alexander Diack, a Norfolk merchant, who wrote on September 3, 1784, of taking Tom by the hand and "participat[ing] in the pleasure your worthy family will enjoy at meeting." Iredell was to suit his convenience in reimbursing Diack for the expense he had incurred. Tom's arrival eased Iredell's anxiety but left him with no spare room in his house. While Iredell would have preferred placing Tom in England for his education, Tom was too old for that. Living with Iredell was his only recourse, and Iredell was clearly delighted to have him. He planned to apprentice Tom to himself and train him for the legal profession. "[H]e may do extremely well here," Iredell wrote their uncle, "and he can live with me till he is qualified to act in it." "[I]f he thought he could devote a few years' study to my profession under me," Iredell told their brother Arthur, "with proper application, he might be sure hereafter of a very comfortable and independent settlement."[21]

Tom's early comportment and commitment to his studies exceeded expectations. Iredell soon informed their mother, uncle, and brother Arthur that Tom was well behaved, without "the least propensity to any vice," and quite assiduous in the study of law. He was considerably exceeding Iredell's expectations, especially in "the dry study of my profession." Tom, Iredell said, showed surprising ability and lived "with the strictest regularity &...cheerfulness." Iredell's "uneasiness" was "at an end," and Arthur thus "augur[ed] great things" for Tom.[22]

Good things, not great, were in store for Tom for a time. Early in his brother's American tenure, Iredell sought to divest him of the British military baggage he had brought with him. He wrote North Carolina Governor Richard Caswell in May 1785, requesting affixation of the state seal to an affidavit from Tom. He noted that Tom "had a small office in the British

Marines, but never served out of England, and his circumstances did not admit of his immediately giving it up." He had come to study law under him, Iredell told the governor, with the intent of becoming a resident whenever he could divest himself of this impedimenta from his past. The effort appears to have succeeded, for the 1790 census shows Tom as a citizen of Edenton. Indeed, he is the only Iredell shown, James having moved himself and his family to New York upon his appointment to the United States Supreme Court.[23]

Moreover, Tom served as master and clerk of the Edenton superior court in the 1780s and 1790s, a position he could not have held in the political climate of that period absent a shedding of any suggestion of Loyalist tendencies. He appears to have done quite well with his law studies and to have been, in a good-natured way, quite pleased with himself. Nelly Blair, Hannah's niece, once reported to Iredell that Tom was "standing here praising himself, a subject so barren & worn out that it is impossible for even him to find anything new or entertaining to say on it to help enliven the imagination." Iredell was pleased not only with Tom's behavior and application to studies, but also that Tom's "health, thank God, is also perfectly good."[24]

Unfortunately, the health report would change all too soon. Only six months after his appearance at Edenton, Tom became quite ill at the home of Jean Blair, Hannah's sister. Jean gave him the very best of care — tea and bark three times a day and dressing his shoulders in the morning. She could not have treated him better, she said, had he been her son. The need for care was ongoing, however, for Jean soon wrote Hannah that Iredell's account of his brother's situation concerned her. She offered to stay with Tom if he was still ill "when Mr. Iredell goes up the country." A few days later still, she expressed regret that Tom's shoulder was "only no worse."

Tom's ailment appears to have been a fairly unremitting form of rheumatism. Relatives and friends were concerned to hear of his "being afflicted with such a cruel disease." Samuel Johnston feared that "without more prudence than young men generally possess, he will experience a premature old age." The disease, according to Johnston, continued "obstinate," and the only hope for relief was the return of warm weather. Iredell informed their Uncle Thomas in March 1790: "My poor brother Tom has had the rheumatism with extreme severity almost the whole of this winter. He is now getting better but I greatly fear it is a chronic disease fixed upon him more or less for life."[25]

Iredell was sadly prophetic, for Tom's complaint remained recurrent. In the spring of 1791, Johnston reported to Iredell that Tom looked thin following "a slight touch of the rheumatism" but that he seemed recovered and was attending court regularly. By the next winter, though, Iredell was informing their brother Arthur that Tom's prospects were "not very good, he having thought proper to quit the profession of the law altogether." Over the years, while on their journeys to the North, Iredell and Johnston bought sarsaparilla, opium, and laudanum with which to relieve Tom's pain.

As commonly occurs, health problems adversely affected Tom's life generally. The promise evidenced early in his American stay seems to have disappeared. By 1793 Arthur was "regret[ting] that Tom's life is passing so unprofitably, & with so little hope of improvement." He wished, for Tom, Iredell's "industry & laudable ambition in applying it." He feared Tom would merely continue to lose ground, however. While "many allowances" were to be made for him, Arthur nevertheless feared that Tom was "inactive and unambitious" and wished he was "as industrious & able as his brother."

The situation did not ameliorate. In the year of Iredell's death, Arthur was still writing him in a similar vein, heartily sorry for Tom's situation, which was "far from a comfortable one." "[S]ome exertion on his part," Arthur opined, combined with Iredell's "interest," might secure Tom a "more honorable and lucrative" position. But, Arthur concluded to James, "in one or two of your last letters you have, with great delicacy, alluded to him in a way which I can no longer misconceive." It appears that Tom continued to live largely indisposed and inactive and at least somewhat at Iredell's expense.[26]

Iredell's brother Arthur could have been Dickens' model for Pip in *Great Expectations*, for like Pip, he spent much of his life awaiting a pecuniary expectancy. He undermined Iredell's reputation with their uncle in order to obtain the legacy, yet steadfastly professed his intent, apparently never fulfilled, to use it partially for Iredell's benefit. Soon after they resumed correspondence following the American Revolution, Arthur informed Iredell that their uncle had assured him he was to be his heir. It would be with great joy, Arthur proclaimed with apparently feigned devotion, that he would employ his newfound wealth to restore Iredell to his native country and spend the rest of his life with him. "I have already formed my plan," he said, and he hoped Iredell was ready for "contemplation & retirement" and would not disapprove. He was robbing Iredell of his birthright, he admitted, but he would be very unhappy could he not "frequently anticipate the time when we should be mutually benefited by *my* plantation either on this or the other side of the Atlantic."

Arthur actively discouraged Iredell from corresponding further with their uncle — "that would probably answer no good purpose" — but assured him that if he inherited the property, Iredell's "ease & independence" would be one of his prime objectives. The estate was large, Arthur said, capable of rendering not only him but his entire family "*comfortable* at the least." Until the tide turned, he begged for Iredell's confidence: *"[B]elieve* me to be what I certainly cannot prove myself," he urged.[27]

For a time Arthur depended entirely upon remittances from his uncle, who had granted an annuity of £100 (annually, presumably) for the nephew and his fiancée. The sum was to be doubled when the uncle's debts were paid. Three-fifths of the property was clear, and the uncle was actively removing the remaining encumbrances.

The remittances fell in arrears, however, and Arthur heard "sad accounts" of his uncle's circumstances; the reports dampened his expectations, rendering them "by no means so sanguine as they were." Poor crops in the West Indies meant no remittance from Jamaica. As a result, Arthur, who was "as poor as a rat," fell into debt. While his finances were not flourishing, he remained confident that his uncle would do all he could for him. "[T]o say true," he wrote Iredell, "he is my sheet anchor."[28]

The uncle's death in September 1796 indeed left Iredell disinherited and Arthur the happy recipient of the bulk of their relative's estate. While long anticipated, both the death and the ultimate slight affected Iredell greatly. He was hurt by his uncle's persevering in his mistreatment of him, he told Hannah, and the omission of a legacy for Tom, who "had done nothing to offend him," was cruel.

As he often did, Samuel Johnston offered Iredell perspective on the matter. Having heard that the uncle "had once made a declaration to that purpose," Johnston said, the actual disinheritance was hardly surprising:

> Whenever old men form a resolution founded either on religious or political prejudices, however erroneous or unjust, they have seldom courage or liberality enough to alter it, even though sensible of their error. Had your uncle been forty years younger, I am inclined to think that he would have acted otherwise.

Iredell, ever sensitive to public perceptions, declined social invitations and wore mourning clothes, asking Hannah to do the same "lest it should be thought I slighted his memory as he left me no legacy."[29]

The exchanges between Iredell and Arthur do not cast the Anglican-clergyman brother in a favorable light. Indeed, the conclusion that he was a real cad seems inescapable. His perfidy in sending their alcoholic mother to Iredell's household, without even a hint as to her condition, is well documented. While their uncle probably would have disinherited Iredell for his role in the American Revolution in any event, Arthur does appear to have encouraged it, all the while protesting to Iredell that he disapproved and intended to make partial restitution. Finally, Arthur seldom saw a son he had fathered, apparently out of wedlock ("[i]t was an unfortunate & very awkward affair," he told Iredell), and the boy was being reared under less-than-propitious circumstances.[30]

Notwithstanding these peccadillos, Iredell demonstrated his magnanimity by maintaining a close epistolary relationship with this sibling throughout his life, save only during the Revolutionary War when political events severed the connection. Each craved communication from the other and upbraided the other when it was not forthcoming. "The post is open — & the most secure way of writing," Iredell would tell his brother, continuing: "The packets come regularly, & the communication is certain — only you must pay the English part of the postage, and I the American." The delight from Arthur's letters was inexpressible, Iredell said, as was his anxiety for Arthur's welfare. Arthur, in turn, would convey "mortification and astonishment" when Iredell failed to write, speculating that surely all his letters had not miscarried.[31]

Arthur kept Iredell posted on the status of his clergy career. He had undertaken the curacy at Guildford, he once wrote; it was laborious and time-consuming, he said, "for I write my own sermons." He hoped to move to Sussex, where he could earn more with less work and be in the neighborhood of Malling, to which he was greatly attached. He wrote later of an opportunity at Lewes, his brother's birthplace, the greatest charm of which was that it was "upon the Sussex coast, and within nine miles of South Malling." Later correspondence and surviving local records show Arthur functioning as a cleric in Lewes and its vicinage.

Arthur sought investment advice from his brother, particularly regarding tracts of land in America. "I hear they are sold remarkably cheap," he wrote, "and that a little English cash goes a great way in such bargains." He also sent Iredell political and religious commentary and solicited his observations. He once forwarded Edmund Burke's latest publication, expecting Iredell's "eulogy" rather than his "critique" because of Iredell's "partiality" for the author. He sent Iredell the Bishop of Landoff's *Apology for Christianity* (in reply to Tom Paine) and *The History of Hastings' Trial*, as well as English newspapers.[32]

Arthur professed perturbation when Tom "robb[ed]" him of the honor of being godfather to Annie Isabella, Iredell's first child who survived. He would get even, he said, when he had an Annie Isabella of his own. Further, he said, "a young James will want a godfather, & I *will* be his, upon condition that you will send the young dog over to me for instruction spiritual & moral."

Arthur was indeed James, Jr.'s "uncle & godfather." When Arthur had twin sons of his own, he named them James and Francis, for his brother and his father. Iredell and Hannah were godparents to the nephew named for Iredell. Arthur's fondest wish was that the boy might resemble his jurist uncle "in the bent of his genius (if he shall have any) and in the sedulous application of his talents."[33]

The wish was appropriate, for Arthur clearly idolized his brother. Even before Iredell's Supreme Court appointment, Arthur noted that Iredell's conduct had always brought credit to both Iredell and his family. He was proud to be related to a man "whose eloquence is only exceeded by the unvarying rectitude of his public and private conduct." The judicial appointment, Arthur later told his brother, was "[s]o flattering a testimony to your merits, and so dignified & *substantial* a reward of them." He had always had reason to be proud, he said, but he now found "triumph" in his sibling's success. He had no doubt that Iredell would justify the choice.

Arthur craved information about his brother's work and his politics. "Whatever respects you would have a great charm for me," he wrote. He requested Iredell's charges and other published papers, expressing great pride in him. The materials he received were an honorable testimony to Iredell's "abilities and industry as a judge, the most important character in all governments." That Iredell had gained the respect and affection of all ranks of people did not surprise Arthur; still, he viewed it as "highly flattering to me, who so well know your worth, & most sensibly feel every event in your life."[34]

When Iredell sent Arthur one of his opinions, presumably his dissent in *Chisholm*, Arthur approved his brother's position "on each point of difficulty." He had shared it with "a good lawyer" who also was "decidedly with" Iredell. He wished to be favored often with such matters, wanting "every publication of which you may be the author or the *hero*, [for] there is no one to whom your professional fame is more dear."[35]

From the time they resumed communication following the war until shortly before Iredell's death, the brothers continuously expressed their desire to see one another again. "Would to God I could be blest with a sight of you," Iredell wrote Arthur early in 1784, "but cursed poverty & business confine me to this country so as to deny me so great an indulgence." Arthur, in turn, told Hannah how much he wished they lived "within reach of each other." Was such happiness in store, he wondered, or would "the wide Atlantic" forever sunder them? "I have formed a thousand pleasing schemes," he said, "all of which will not, I trust, be denied us."

Later, Iredell still considered himself "chained to America" and thought the fetter lifelong. "[B]ut I should be unhappy if I thought I never was to meet you in person," he told Arthur. Arthur, too, his wife said, would be miserable if he thought a visit between them unlikely.[36]

Arthur continued to lament the separation, praying that they would meet "on your side of the Atlantic." In 1794 he raised the possibility of visiting

Iredell and even of emigrating to America. That prospect grew serious when Arthur inherited their uncle's Jamaican properties. Arthur considered moving his family to America and spending the hurricane months with Iredell if Iredell would let him travel with him. Iredell rejoiced at the thought. "God knows how happy it would make me to see you all," he told Arthur. He then informed Hannah that Arthur intended to come to America with his wife and children—to be "as near us as he can find a place to approve of and occasionally come to them from Jamaica where his residence I dare say will be chiefly necessary." The matter obviously weighed heavily on Iredell's mind, for he wrote Hannah again the same day, essentially repeating himself. Tom even made plans to go to Philadelphia to meet his brothers if it was inconvenient for Arthur to travel to Edenton.

Neither the visit nor the move materialized, however. Iredell soon wrote Hannah that Arthur had "suffered a great deal in body & mind" on a trip to Jamaica and was about to sail for England, hoping to see them the next year. He did not see them then. Sadly, the reunion for which the brothers hankered never occurred. Arthur continued to perform clerical duties in the South Malling area through the late 1790s, while simultaneously managing his hereditary properties in Jamaica. He died in Jamaica from a "bilious fever" on November 4, 1804, five years after Iredell's demise.[37]

CHAPTER 19

Felicitous Relationships

ELICITOUS RELATIONSHIPS IN HIS OWN FAMILY MORE THAN COM-
PENSATED FOR IREDELL'S DIFFICULTIES WITH HIS FAMILY OF ORI-
GIN. THIS WAS PARTICULARLY TRUE OF HIS MARITAL CONNECTION.
EARLY IN HIS AMERICAN STAY, IREDELL'S THIRD COUSIN AND
closest English friend, Margaret Macartney, urged him to "guard your heart
with watchful caution till you are better able to maintain a wife & family." Another cousin, Henry Eustace McCulloh, whose port collectorship Iredell assumed, also exhorted him to constrain his youthful passions until he could afford to give them sway. "Your time of life," he counseled, "is the hour of
application and reserve."[1]

The impatience of young love would brook no such delay, however.
Iredell's collector duties and family obligations did not deter a fervent
courtship of Hannah Johnston, sister of his law teacher and general mentor,
Samuel Johnston. Every moment apart from her distressed him, he said, and
filled him "with anxiety I can scarce support." He "behaved to[ward] her with
a particularity of attention that...engaged the eyes of the world." "[H]er affections are engaged," he said, "and a thousand agreeable circumstances
which crowd upon my memory convince me I am the happy owner of them."[2]

"[I]n this country," Iredell wrote his father, "a young man without the joys
of a private family leads [a] very dull and...a less improving life." The dull,
unameliorating life was not for James Iredell. After a three-year courtship, he
married Hannah Johnston on July 18, 1773.[3]

Marriage failed to diminish Iredell's ardor. Over four years later, he still
found any absence from Hannah "dreadfully disagreeable." It distracted him
considerably, in fact. "I have been able to apply to nothing," he wrote her of
one such period, "I can't read; I can't write; I do nothing but wish for you."

On the fifteenth anniversary of their union, he continued to revel in his state of blessedness. The day, he said, had united him "to one of the best of wives and most excellent of women." "May God be praised for his goodness in preserving us so long together," he continued, pledging his every hour to making her "as happy as possible."[4]

While most of the surviving evidence indicates that the relationship was close, loving, and devoted on the part of both partners, it was not tension-free. In 1779 Iredell did something that deeply offended Hannah and strained their association over a period of months. From the tenor of Iredell's letters (regrettably, none from Hannah to him during this period survive), it is reasonable to speculate that the conduct involved another woman in some way. The precise nature and extent of any such involvement, however, appears inscrutable.

What is certain is that Hannah was hurt and that her manifestations of the wound, combined with Iredell's own conscience, anguished him greatly. Her mind, he said, was "in so painful a situation," and he, as a consequence, was "greatly distressed." "[I]nadvertently and by extreme imprudence," he had caused her "many painful moments." He was quite penitent and prepared to devote his entire future life to atoning for the past. He deserved neither compassion nor forgiveness, he said, and the latter would have been impossible but for Hannah's "soul above most women." He prayed that he would never cause her such pain again and begged her, "[f]or God's sake, banish me not forever from your confidence and regard."[5]

Banish him she did not. When tensions entered the marriage at other times, they arose largely from Iredell's frequent and prolonged absences, either in the practice of law or the public service. During his lawyering days, Hannah would grow unwell, dull, and lonesome when she saw neither Iredell nor his brother Tom "from breakfast till night." "[B]eing so entirely alone" made her "more sensible of her indisposition." She also had to endure physical injuries to herself and the children in his absence and without his assistance.[6]

Iredell, too, suffered from their separations and could be rather ill-tempered when Hannah failed to write. Knowing when the post left Edenton, yet receiving no letter from her, left him "very much mortified." While he was willing to assume "mistake or trifling accident," it was, he said, "as when a great state is depending," "our fears are naturally alive." "I hope," he admonished, "I shall not suffer the same anxiety from a similar cause again." Crystal-clear language informed her of his impatience to hear from her: "[N]eglect no opportunity to write," he would admonish.

When another two weeks found him still letterless, he considered himself "very unfortunate," he told Hannah, "in not having heard a single word from you since I left home." He was careful, however, to apologize when his return home was delayed: "[Y]ou may be assured that I shall make no unnecessary delay," he would say.[7]

The Supreme Court years only exacerbated the separation angst, for they enhanced both the distances between them and the intervals between reunions. A few months into Iredell's high-court tenure, Hannah, in New York, was anxious. She had not heard from him in some time and would be "very miserable" absent communication rather immediately forthcoming. She could not ponder "the risk you run without shuddering." "[M]y dearest Mr. Iredell," she wrote with formality characteristic of the period, "you know not how painful a situation mine altogether is." She could prepare for their move to Philadelphia "with some satisfaction" if she could hear from him; otherwise, she would "go about it very heavily." Iredell responded from Edenton that he was unhappy to find her so perplexed. "Would to God I had been able to prevent it!" he said: "I am not able to tell when I can set off, but I shall as soon as possible."[8]

Mail remained extremely important to both spouses. Hannah's missives gave Iredell "great satisfaction," yet he complained about their brevity. He chided her to commence writing before post-day, as he did. He took care to let her know where he would be and when to write. "You see," he would say after detailing his schedule, "I name the post days as a matter of course."

Absence of mail pained them both. Hannah could not enjoy her brother's country estate because of "the difficulty of getting Mr. Iredell's letters." Iredell, in turn, suffered "very great pain" when, though an Edenton mail arrived, he received nothing from her. His anxiety increased when she was ill. "No letter from Edenton this week" rendered him "extremely uneasy...and most anxiously wish[ing] to hear."[9]

In 1799, the year of Iredell's death, Hannah, too, experienced health problems that distressed Iredell greatly. He mentioned her being bled and begged her to "be as careful as possible, and suffer no symptom to pass unobserved." She suffered "three fits of the ague and fever" as well as breast pain, and he longed to know when the pain was gone. An early recurrence of the ague and fever "distresse[d] [him] not a little." Soon he was again "much affected" to learn of her two-day headache and that their daughter Annie had been ill as well. When she was "not perfectly well," he was "much distressed." "[T]ake the utmost possible care," he once exhorted, "and take early morning exercise. It is almost the only kind that is valuable at this season."[10]

Iredell and Hannah epitomized the aphorism that "opposites attract." As his circuit life revealed, Iredell was the consummate *bonhomme*, who clearly liked people and thrived on social situations. Hannah, by contrast, was reticent and retiring. By her own admission, she was "never...intended to move out of the circle of my own family" and "almost as helpless as a child amongst strangers."

This introspective nature made her life in the new nation's capital miserable. She reported to Iredell early in her New York stay that Secretary of War Henry Knox looked forward to Iredell's assuming residence there, several women had had tea with her, and Chief Justice Jay's wife had visited her. But where would she get "the spirits" to pay these "social debts," she moaned, without him there to accompany her? Writing to him and attending to her children, not socializing in the nation's capital, would be her "most pleasing amusement" in his absence.

Hannah steadfastly resisted Iredell's importunings toward the social scene. Notwithstanding his injunctions, she "paid very few visits." She could have gone anywhere with him, she said, but lacked "spirits" to visit strangers alone; only in her own family, she thought, could she "give or receive pleasure." "I have made no visits," she would inform him emphatically. He could not make a "fashionable woman" of her, she said, and thus should resettle her in Edenton to attend to her children and visit others only on the rarest of occasions. While "dreadful... for a fine lady," nothing could be more delightful to her than to be "with the company of a few friends whenever they would be pleased to call on me."

Iredell recognized the nature of Hannah's demure disposition. He told her, in describing Elizabeth Pinkney, wife of the American minister to Great Britain: "The only fault imputed to her is the very same to which you are liable, her too great fondness for retirement and an exclusive attachment to domestic life." He nonetheless persisted in urging her toward minimal sociability, coaxing her at least to write certain acquaintances from time to time.[11]

Episodic tensions and differences notwithstanding, the answer to Hannah's question—"Could you wish a more obedient wife, my dear Mr. Iredell?"—was clearly "no." She was indeed, as she was described upon the presentation of her husband's portrait to the North Carolina Supreme Court, "a prudent and faithful administrator of the domestic economies of their household, and a wise and able friend and counsellor to whom he ever brought the full story of his joys and triumphs, his sorrows and reverses." Iredell was, in turn, as characterized at his funeral, "taken in a conjugal and domestic view,... the tender and loving husband." "The charming letters which passed between them," the portrait-presentation address aptly states, "are the highest evidence of their loving devotion to each other, their mutual trust, confidence and respect."

Hannah survived her "tender and loving husband" by almost twenty-seven years. She died in Edenton on September 13, 1826, and was buried in the Johnston cemetery there.[12]

The Iredells' first child, a boy named Thomas, was born October 1, 1784. Iredell evidently shared news of the expectancy with his friends very early in the gestation period. Almost eight months before the infant's appearance, William Hooper sent the prospective father his congratulations "upon the happy addition to your family." "May it be the forerunner and harbinger of many such causes of rejoicing," he said.[13]

Fortunately, other such "causes of rejoicing" would materialize, for this one soon turned to profound grief when the child died two days after its birth. Hannah, too, was in danger for a time, but she recovered. The loss affected Iredell appreciably. According to Hannah's cousin Penelope Dawson, it left "a settled melancholy in his countenance, which he in vain endeavors to dispel." "Good heaven," she lamented, "why was his hope[] so raised to be blasted again in a moment."[14]

Melancholy letters to relatives and friends aided the momentary father in processing his grief. He trusted in the goodness of God, he told Hannah, that "though we were denied the blessing of his society in this world, we may be blest with it in another, and a better." Writing her from Halifax, North Carolina, he noted "the most shocking mortality among the children here ever known." The Halifax experience was a vivid reminder of their recent loss, which was "melancholy," "dreadful," "ever present to my memory." Composure eluded him. "A momentary gleam of cheerfulness," he said, "is succeeded by the most bitter recollection." He cherished the two days but knew they were "too little regarded at the time." "[W]hat happiness this shocking incident has deprived us of," he bewailed.

Iredell informed his mother that his hope of presenting her with a grandson had been "dreadfully dashed." He reported the "melancholy misfortune" to his Uncle Thomas: "As this was our only child after a marriage of so many years," he said, "it was certainly a most unhappy event." The boy was "an only child, so long & so anxiously wished for," he told his friend Nathaniel Dukinfield.[15]

The joy of other children soon quelled the nightmarish anguish Iredell suffered from the loss of his firstborn. Disregarding a miscarriage Hannah experienced in the summer of 1794,[16] the black angel of death that then hovered so menacingly near all children did not darken Iredell's doorway again in his lifetime.

On December 22, 1785, Annie Isabella Iredell first graced her parents' household. She was named for Hannah's deceased sisters, one of whom, Isabella, had died suddenly in 1766, a few days before her impending wedding to Joseph Hewes, later a signer of the Declaration of Independence. With better reason than before, William Hooper again sent felicitations to his friend "upon the happy addition." Nelly Blair, Hannah's niece, soon told the oft-absent father what a spirited youngster he had. Annie was "the property of the whole family," Nelly wrote, "in high spirits at play," walking "about as stout as anybody," and saying "yes & no & two or three other words quite plain." When Annie was almost three and a half, Nelly, a spirited youth herself, told Iredell his daughter was "as full of health & spirits as you could wish her to be." She would, Nelly predicted, "be quoted as the standard of wildness as often by the careful mothers of the present age as I was by those of the last." Nelly "scarcely [knew] how to live without her."[17]

Iredell, too, ever mindful that death tarried near, wondered how he would live without Annie. She had increased both their happiness and their anxiety, he told Hannah. He thought of her constantly "with a kind of trepidation that almost makes me miserable." "God knows she is almost every moment in my thoughts," he said, "and I eagerly anticipate the time . . . when she can both know and love me."

Always important, the mail had enhanced significance now. Because of Iredell's excessive tenderness and anxiety for Annie, Hannah was not to "miss another post." Peter, Iredell's longtime personal servant (*see infra*), frequented the post office, as the absent father sought news of the "little angel." His love for her was "unutterable," and he longed to see her.[18] Missing Annie's first birthday because of his work mortified Iredell. He worried about her cutting teeth and weaning. He thought of her constantly with both anxiety and affection. He was consistently impatient to see her and feared mortification "if she does not receive me with visible joy on my return." Following her brother's birth, he wanted her to be good for his sake as well as her own. When she was ill, he was ecstatic upon learning of her recovery. When she learned to write, he thrived on her "charming" letters and hoped she would favor him with them frequently. "You know not how happy your letters make me," he told her. He could not resist showing them to his friends. He welcomed reports that she was "so attentive to [her] lessons" and constantly regretted his frequent absence from her.[19]

On November 2, 1788, when Annie was not quite three, a brother named James further enlarged the Iredell household. Anticipation of his arrival prompted heightened frugality. Nelly Blair declined to write to her Uncle Iredell because the prospect of a large family to provide for made it "worthwhile to be more careful." The money he would have spent for her letter (both sender and recipient then paid postage), invested at interest, would suffice to equip his son for travel when he was ready for the practice of law. And a son it must be, Nelly insisted — "no saucy girl to rival my darling Annie." Nelly was prophetic; a son it was, and he would make the law his profession.[20]

Again, Iredell's friends rejoiced with him. Davie found the event "the most agreeable and interesting that could have happened." Nothing could have given Samuel Johnston more satisfaction, and Johnston was impatient to see this "fine boy."[21]

James proved to be a fine boy indeed. He cut his teeth easily, spoke plainly, and grew rapidly. By the time he was three, travelers from Philadelphia to Edenton dwelt "with rapture on the perfections of Master James." "[H]e promised to be a sturdy, bold-faced fellow when he went away [to Philadelphia]," Nelly Blair (now Tredwell) told her Aunt Iredell, "but I did not think he would be so superior as they say he is to children in common."[22]

James grew "very fond of his book" when he went to school. His position at the head of his class delighted his doting father, who reported himself "very near telling it to several." "Tell the dear little fellow it has made me very happy," Iredell instructed Hannah, "and I hope he will keep his place."[23]

Iredell exulted as his son's letter writing improved, solicited correspondence from him "either in French or English," and reveled in learning that a book he had sent pleased the boy and that he was "so fond of reading in it." He thought of him often and eagerly anticipated hearing him "read very well upon my return."[24]

Iredell's "heart glow[ed]" when Samuel Johnston called ten-year-old James "the finest boy [I] ever knew at his age." Johnston's son James took a keen interest in his younger cousin and noted Iredell's pride. He, too, found pleasure in hearing that James was a fine boy, who loved books. "I hope, my dear cousin, you will continue to behave yourself as well, and to make as rapid progress in your education," he admonished, "[f]or you cannot think of the pleasure it gives your affectionate father to hear every person speak so highly of you."[25]

The last child arrived almost two years after Iredell's Supreme Court appointment. Helen Scrimseoure Iredell, named for Hannah's mother, was born January 19, 1792. Shortly before the event, an anticipant Iredell informed his brother Arthur that "[i]n less than a fortnight Mrs. Iredell will have a child." Shortly afterward, his brother Tom congratulated him "on the interesting and happy event of Mrs. Iredell's safe delivery." Samuel Johnston soon found Helen "really a very fine child for one of her age." She was "very quiet," according to Hannah, and grew very fast. By the time she was five, Johnston viewed her as "very flighty and agreeable."[26]

Needless to say, Iredell adored this child as well. As with Annie, he thought of her when he had to be away on her birthdays. He bought her a hat and a doll, promised sugar plums and another doll, and committed to "a very pretty book" when she could read—indeed, promised not to forget her whenever he had money to spare. He thought of her often, hoped she sometimes thought of him, worried that she would not know him because of his long and frequent absences, and wished she would send him "a few of her strokes" written as well as she could.[27]

As his family grew, Iredell and others began to refer to his children in multiples or collectively. The itinerant father would send his "tenderest love to Annie, & a warm kiss to my dear James" and would instruct Hannah to tell them that "no father ever more doted on his children than I do on mine." Once Helen arrived, he spoke similarly of all three. "Kiss my dear children most tenderly for me," he would say, adding: "Tell Annie & James I love them beyond measure. I could send such a message with great truth to Helen if she would understand it."[28]

Iredell bragged to relatives about Annie and James. He had "every reason to be satisfied with the promising qualities" of the children, he told his uncle, excusing his partiality as "justified by the universal opinion of my friends." He could scarcely dare "to wish them other than they are." After Helen's arrival, they were "[a]ll most promising children, and equal to my fondest wishes." "I could not desire finer children than heaven has blessed me with," he claimed.[29]

Letters from the tykes gave him great pleasure, and when they failed to write, he complained. "Why will not Annie write me a single line?" he would moan; "[o]ne line to tell me she loves me would give me great pleasure." "Does my little Helen ever speak of me?" he would inquire. He wanted them to mention him when they awoke and to remember him during his absences. He reveled when Hannah reassured him that the children talked of him often. He craved hearing their conversations, which he preferred to that of "the finest ladies" in Philadelphia. Above all, he longed "most impatiently" to see them, hoping they would think of him in the meantime. "It gives me great pain to be absent so long from you all," he once told Annie, "but as I am doing my duty I must endeavor to be contented, and I hope in the meantime that you and your dear brother and sister will do everything your Mamma tells you; and improve as much as you can."[30]

The children indeed improved, though largely in his absence. Annie would be able to read "very prettily" when he returned, Hannah informed Iredell during his second tour of the Southern Circuit, and James would entertain him "with a great deal of very sensible conversation in good language very well pronounced." From Richmond, Iredell later urged Samuel Johnston to "tell Helen I have very favorable accounts of James, & that he can now read." "I had a very pretty letter from Annie," he continued with obvious pride, "entirely of her own dictating and spelling and without a single fault."

Later still, he was confident Annie would say her lessons properly, and he hoped James would also.[31]

The wayfaring father was afar when his children commenced school. His brother Tom let him know that "Medcaff" (probably John Metcalf) would open his school; it was propitious for Annie and James, Tom felt, that the school was located so conveniently near the Iredells' home. Absence and busyness did not cause the adoring father to lose sight of this important event. "I don't forget this is James's school-day," he wrote Hannah: "How my heart accompanies him in this, which I may consider in a manner his first essay! I entertain the greatest hopes of his and my dear Annie's improvement—and hope our dear little Helen will now begin to take a start too."

Iredell soon rejoiced upon learning that "James goes so cheerfully to school and...Annie learns so quickly." He hoped their academic performance would stimulate Helen. He paid the teacher "for the quarter's schooling of Master James Iredell" and offered to pay for his instruction to Annie. His tutelage of Annie was "small trouble," the teacher indicated, and he would accept at most, as "a very liberal consideration," the amount Iredell had paid him for teaching James. Anything he could do to be "serviceable" to Iredell he would do with "the greatest pleasure." French lessons from the Marquis de Clugny were also part of the Iredell progenies' educational fare.[32]

Iredell was constantly concerned about his children's health. Both Annie and James were seriously ill in the summer of 1789. "[M]y poor children have been lately at the point of death," Iredell told Henry McCulloh, "and the youngest (a very fine boy about 8 months old) is still extremely ill." Two weeks later, the situation was much improved. "[W]e dreaded at one time the loss of both of them together," Iredell wrote Pierce Butler, but "[t]hank God they are now pretty well recovered, & our fears for this time are over."

It was only "for this time," however, for Iredell continued to be anxious about his youngsters, especially their exposure to the then-characteristic summer epidemics. He was at a loss as to what to advise Hannah regarding the summer. He depended on her determination and "the good providence of God," he said, but he dreaded "another experiment at Edenton." Soon he was telling Annie of his lowered spirits upon hearing of her brother's illness.

By contrast, his letters were replete with expressions of gratitude when the children were well. "Thank God that you and my dear children were so well," he could say to Hannah the following winter. He continued to think of them with considerable anxiety, however.[33]

Perhaps prompted by his keen sense of their susceptibility to disease and death, Iredell lavished his tots with gifts. He wanted Hannah to post him on "the wants and wishes of the dear children." He would send Annie a locket,

James a drum, and Helen a book. There was calico and other materials to make clothes for the children. There was an umbrella for Annie, a copy of *Robinson Crusoe* for James, and a picture for Helen. "I can never go about anything with greater alacrity than obliging my dear children when they are good," he would say as he listed for Hannah the items he was sending.[34]

Like most men immersed in both private and public affairs, Iredell was not always the model father. In the immediate aftermath of his state's ratification of the federal Constitution, Hannah scolded him for his neglect of parental duties. He was not displeased, he responded, at her "endeavor to awake me to a proper sense of attention to the interest of our dear lovely children, whose future situation I know ought to be the invariable object of my thoughts." "I hope I shall have discretion enough to correct a fault I know I am liable to," he continued, "& my mind being now easy about public affairs, I think instead of my attention being relaxed it will be greatly increased towards my private ones."

Notwithstanding occasional shortcomings as a father largely because of preoccupation with public responsibilities, Iredell clearly doted on his children and cared for them well. Without question, Bishop Pettigrew's funeral oration depicting him as "the kind and indulgent father" is apt.[35]

Iredell's fondest wish was that his children would become "useful," "valuable," "respectable" members of society.[36] As to the daughters, it was not to be—at least not for long.

Illness attacked Annie "often and severely" as early as her teenage years. She died in 1816 at age thirty following a long illness involving "extreme" suffering, which she bore "with the meekness of a saint." "Never did the grave receive a lovelier victim," recorded a memorialist (almost certainly her brother).

Annie was remembered for a first-rate intellect, literary attainments, mild and amiable virtues, sweetness of temper, and soft and engaging manners. She was, says her grave marker in the Johnston cemetery at Edenton, "[a] daughter in all things worthy of her parents."

To the surviving parent, her mother, she had indeed been "the comfort,...pride,...joy,...staff and hope of her age." Hannah never fully ceased to grieve over Annie's untimely death. At her own death almost eleven years later, a small gold heart marked "A.I.I." was found fastened to her arm by a black ribbon.[37]

Helen, too, brought continuous grief to her elderly mother. At a youthful age she "lost her mind" and entered a hospital for the insane in Cambridge, Massachusetts. Her situation troubled Hannah's declining years greatly. She was "never well," Hannah wrote Helen, and seeing Helen well would "do

[her] more good than anything." "I beg of you, my beloved child," she would write, "to get well that you may return to me. I would go to see you if I were not too weak & infirm."[38]

Helen, appropriately, hoped to return to Hannah in good health. "I should like to return [to] you sometime or other if I should," she wrote Hannah. She addressed this letter to "Mrs. James Ireton" and signed it "H.S. Ireton." Ireton was apparently the original spelling of the name prior to the Restoration in England and was changed to escape the fury of the Royalists at a collateral kinsman, Henry Ireton, who was Oliver Cromwell's son-in-law. Whether Helen was aware of this is unknown. Her physician wrote to her brother, though, that "[t]he error in her name is among those I first noticed in her." He could not tell James of any "very striking change" in her condition, "excepting a diminished motion of the mouth, as though talking with someone."[39]

Helen never recovered. She remained institutionalized at Cambridge until her death in 1869 at age seventy-seven. Hannah bequeathed half of her estate to her son James and her nephew James Johnston to hold as trustees for Helen's support and maintenance. Johnston at some point, perhaps at James, Jr.'s death in 1853, became solely responsible for her support and expenses. The Iredell house in Edenton and some slaves were placed in his possession to assist with Helen's support. At Johnston's death, he provided by will that $250.00 be paid semiannually for her upkeep at the asylum in Cambridge.[40]

James alone fulfilled Iredell's aspirations for his offspring, but he did so illustriously. Samuel Johnston perceived his potential early, considering him one of the more-promising children in America and "the most promising boy of his age" he had known.[41] Following Iredell's death, Johnston sponsored James' education at Edenton Academy and Princeton. At Princeton, James roomed with Thomas Ruffin, later the longtime chief justice of the North Carolina Supreme Court, whom Roscoe Pound would consider one of the ten foremost judges in American history. The friendship Ruffin and the young Iredell forged in their college days was lifelong.[42]

Upon entering Princeton, James displayed an apparently inherited capacity for letter writing, proving himself a prolific and talented correspondent. He signed his name "Ja. Iredell," just as his father had. Like his father, he studied law, and he was admitted to the North Carolina Bar in 1809. Unlike his father, he experienced active military duty, serving as captain of a company of North Carolina volunteers who defended Norfolk, Virginia, in the War of 1812. The following year he was the solicitor of the First Circuit Court.

James followed in his father's footsteps by serving as a trustee of the University of North Carolina and a judge of the superior court. In 1815 he was

appointed a brigadier general of the North Carolina militia. He represented
Edenton in the North Carolina General Assembly in 1813 and from 1816–28.
He was speaker from 1817–27, succeeding his roommate and friend, Thomas
Ruffin. He was elected governor of North Carolina in 1827 and in 1828 was
appointed to complete the unexpired term of Nathaniel Macon in the United
States Senate. After completing Macon's term, he did not seek reelection,
choosing instead to practice law in Raleigh.

In 1836–37 James served as a commissioner to revise the laws of North
Carolina. He prepared a digest of North Carolina reported cases, which was
published in Raleigh in three volumes between 1839 and 1846. He was the
reporter for the North Carolina Supreme Court from 1840–52. Finally, he
was a pioneer of formal legal education in North Carolina; with William Horn
Battle, he opened a law school in Raleigh in 1841 which soon evolved into
the School of Law at the University of North Carolina.[43]

When James was three, Hannah wrote Nelly Blair Tredwell that he would
make "a smart husband bye and bye" for Nelly's daughter Betsey. Betsey died
the following year, but in 1815 James married Nelly's second daughter,
Frances. Their marriage produced eleven children. While there are no known
descendants with the Iredell name now living in North Carolina, there are
several living progeny from this marriage.[44]

James died April 13, 1853, at age sixty-four, while visiting his cousin,
Samuel Iredell Johnston, who was then living in the Iredell homeplace in
Edenton. He was the victim of erysipelas, a staphylococcal infection of the
skin now curable with penicillin but then generally fatal. He was buried with
his parents and older sister in the Johnston cemetery at Edenton.

James was, a contemporary opined, a "venerable man and star of mind,"
"a distinguished gentleman and distinguished in every department of mind to
which he applied himself," a "gentleman of accomplishments and capacious
mind [with] few equals [and] superiors . . . none." Justice Iredell would have
been proud if he could have known of his son's contemporary's reference to
James as "an eminent son [of] an eminent father." Junior fully effected Senior's aspiration that he be a useful, valuable, respectable member of society,
"add[ing] to the fame and dignity of a name rendered illustrious by the public service of his father."[45]

The Edenton house that served as a homeplace for Justice Iredell and his
family was built about 1759 by John Wilkins. In 1773 it was sold to Joseph
Whedbee, a silversmith, who in turn sold it to Iredell in 1778. During their
absence from it from 1790–93, the entire Iredell family longed to be back. "I
often, very often wish myself in Carolina," Hannah told Iredell early in their
New York stay. "My little Annie & James talk of nothing half so often as their

cousin Nelly & Carolina," Hannah wrote Nelly Blair from Philadelphia a few months later, "& there is no place in the world...that their mother would prefer to it." When the time came to return, Iredell himself rejoiced in the prospect of going "to Carolina."[46]

At the time of Iredell's death, the house was "very much out of repair," and the family was living in a structure that belonged to William Pollok while theirs underwent renovation. Iredell devised the cherished homeplace to Hannah, who occupied it until her death in 1826. Recent dendrochronology reports and architectural analysis suggest that Hannah was not satisfied with mere renovations, for the east section of the present house is believed to have been constructed with timbers felled after the growing season of 1800, and the west section with timbers felled after the growing season of 1827. Iredell, who died in 1799, thus could have lived only on the present homesite, not in the extant homeplace.[47]

Like the family, the house has its own story. After Hannah's demise, it remained in James' possession, and apparently rental proceeds from it were used, at least in part, for Helen's support. For a number of years it served as a rectory for St. Paul's Episcopal Church.

Following the deaths of James (1853) and Helen (1869), the house was sold in about 1870 and remained in private ownership until 1949. In December 1948 it was to be sold again and perhaps demolished. The newly organized Edenton Tea Party Chapter of the National Society, Daughters of the American Revolution came to the rescue, however. The Chapter assumed a $15,000 indebtedness on the property and offered to convey it to the state of North Carolina, upon the state's assumption of the indebtedness, for the purpose of permanently preserving it as an important historical site. The 1951 North Carolina General Assembly appropriated $15,000 to satisfy the indebtedness and empowered the Department of Conservation and Development to contract with the James Iredell Association for the restoring, furnishing, and operating of the structure as a public museum. The edifice, the legislation appropriately recognized, "is one of the most important historic structures in North Carolina." The state continued to contribute to the maintenance of the property, while the association assumed responsibility for restoration and furnishing. The house still stands and is operated as a historic site by the state in cooperation with the association.[48]

The story of the Iredell house provides one exception to its owner's customary accommodating and felicitous relationships with extended kin. Iredell's cousin Henry E. McCulloh once begged Iredell to take McCulloh's son George into his home and under his care. "Get him perfected in writing & accounts," McCulloh pleaded, "& use him in your business & breed him up to the law." McCulloh would pay whatever Iredell thought appropriate for board, lodging, and other expenses in an effort to save the boy "from being lost [and from] a life of idleness."

Iredell declined. His family was too large and his house too small, he said. Besides, while he would "with the greatest pleasure" render George any service in his power, the boy could obtain no serviceable education in Edenton. McCulloh was undeterred. "[H]is being in your home is of no great consequence," McCulloh replied, "if he is near and under your eye."

Concerns other than purely spatial appear to have prompted Iredell's refusal. Earlier, in an uncharacteristically bitter letter, he had upbraided McCulloh for being impossible to satisfy, for his mistreatment of Iredell's family of origin, and for foisting his son upon Iredell for financial support when Iredell "had scarcely enough to purchase myself bread." Iredell also had refused to be McCulloh's "general agent," stating: "My heart wishes you no ill, but...it is incapable of disguise, or pretending to an attachment which I do not feel."[49]

This acerbic denunciation and rejection were altogether atypical, for otherwise Iredell was virtually as accommodating and caring to his extended kin as he was to his immediate family. Spatial concerns were cast aside, for example, when George Blair, Hannah's nephew, brought his new bride to the Iredell household shortly before Iredell's death. Iredell had counseled the youth to get married, had taken him to one of President Adams' levees, and had helped him secure a lieutenancy in the United States Navy. It was his suggestion that the newlyweds should reside with him "for the present."[50]

Among his extended kin, Hannah's niece Nelly Blair Tredwell was a special object of Iredell's affection. His letters reflect a distinctive concern for her, as he constantly gives her courting advice, reproof, and affirmation. Nelly, a spirited youth, endearingly called him "Uncle Iredell." In view of "his attention & kindness to me, to all of us," she told Hannah, there was no one whom she held in greater regard.

Nelly reproached Iredell when he failed to write her while he was away. She was "sometimes very unreasonable," he rejoined: "You think that in the middle of a busy court, and by snatching opportunities, I ought to write you long letters, which from the very nature of the thing is impossible." He was truly "affectionately" hers, however, "whether I do or do not write." She had his "tenderest attachment" regardless, he told Hannah. In Nelly's view, though, he had "spoilt" her, and "the least mark of indifference or disregard" from him gave her "more pain than it is possible for me to express."[51]

When Nelly, with "Uncle Iredell" as her chaperone, stayed out late dancing, her mother scolded her severely, noting her "propensity...to dissipation

& often to trifling." Her mother, Uncle Iredell had told her, "hopes you will take a good deal of pains to bring your volatility, at least sometimes, down to a reasonable standard."[52]

His knowledge of her volatility notwithstanding, Iredell unhesitatingly offered himself and Hannah as surrogate parents to Nelly and her sister when their mother died. "[C]onsider me," he said, "as one of your sincerest commiserators, one of your tenderest friends, whose whole life will be employed, as opportunity shall be afforded, in rendering yours as easy and comfortable as possible." Nelly, however, was momentarily inconsolable. "How kindly have you tried, my dear uncle, to reconcile me to myself," she told him, "but it is impossible."[53]

When a lawyer, he was uneasy if he could not see her before departing on his trips. When he rode the circuits as a Supreme Court justice, she awaited his return impatiently. "[W]hen he is gone," she said, "I...feel lost indeed, for the prospect of seeing him has been my constant comfort in all my dejected fits." When his return was overdue, she passed her time "looking out most anxiously."[54]

It was his lot to write her in-laws informing them poignantly of the death of her child. He was concerned when she was again expectant. He declined the "great honor" of her wish that he name her child, but he admitted to Hannah that he would like for it to be "Hannah Iredell" or perhaps "Annie Johnston" for Hannah's late sister—"a person and a name," he said, "I never can think of without inexpressible emotion—an emotion too painful to dwell upon." "But," he concluded, "say nothing to Mrs. Tredwell of this."

On a more-frivolous level, he was the runner for her endeavors at chance. She had a ticket "in the Canal Lottery No. Two," she would write the distinguished but ever-avuncular jurist: Would he be "so good...as to call at Mr. Blackburn's Office and enquire the fate of N. 27867."[55]

The Iredell-Johnston extended family situation merits special mention. For a considerable period preceding her death, Samuel Johnston's wife was quite ill and mostly bedridden. During this time, Hannah aided in educating the Johnston daughters. She was, Johnston said, "more than a mother to them"; he hoped the relationship would be "a means of cementing a lasting friendship between all [their] children."

Iredell likewise generously assisted the Johnston clan. When young Samuel expressed the desire to study medicine, his father enlisted Uncle Iredell to seek out apprenticeships in the Philadelphia area.[56] James, though, was clearly Iredell's favorite among the Johnstons. He bought books for the lad, and the lad's father requested more—specifically, Addison's *Cato*. While at Princeton, James passed extended periods with Iredell in Philadelphia. By day Iredell arranged for James to sit beside the clerk and observe the trials over which Iredell presided, and by night they were theater buffs. They often passed Sundays together, and Iredell observed James grow and improve beyond his expectations. The bond between them was such that James, who was "much affected" by his uncle's kindness, would rush into Iredell's arms upon greeting him. He was, Iredell told Hannah, "indeed a most engaging young man."[57]

When the nascent scholar failed to write home faithfully, his itinerant-jurist uncle checked on his well-being. Shortly before his own death, the affectionate uncle had the nephew's portrait painted. The deep devotion and extensive attention evoked a keen expression of gratitude from the youth's father shortly before the uncle's death. "With respect to [James]," Samuel Johnston wrote Iredell,

> permit me to use the words of the great Cicero, in his letter to Brutus.... "As to my son, if his merit be really as great as you write, I rejoice at it, as much as I ought to do; or if you make it greater than it is, because you love him, even that also gives me an incredible joy, to find that he is beloved by you."[58]

Hannah's cousin Penelope Dawson also came within Iredell's special outreach to extended family. Penelope considered herself "much obliged to Mr. Iredell for all his goodness" and once asked Hannah to thank him "for his obliging favor." When he surprised her with a visit, she told Hannah she was "unwilling to lose any of his company" and was confident Hannah would understand. Iredell, in turn, found Penelope "in point of excellence of understanding, goodness of heart, and a most polite, attractive behavior,... generally allowed to be above all kind of competition."[59]

Iredell had another set of relationships, apparently close, that so far as the surviving record reveals can also be characterized as felicitous — but only in epochal context. He shared with Washington, Jefferson, and other leaders of his time[60] participation in the haunting moral contradiction of abhorrence to slavery in principle, combined with the personal ownership of slaves. When the 1777 North Carolina General Assembly ordered the seizure and resale at public auction of Black freedmen, Iredell joined his friend William Hooper in defending the freedom of more than forty former slaves the Quakers had emancipated in northeastern North Carolina.[61] As a revolutionary-period political essayist, he eloquently attacked the concept of human slavery. Liberty, he said, was "the right of every human creature," and no rule "totally destructive of this universal right" could be just. Had God intended one set of men to be slaves to others, he wrote, "he would surely have distinguished them with some mark suited to the abject character." While Iredell was addressing the political slavery of the American colonies to Great Britain, the application of the thoughts expressed to individual human bondage could hardly have escaped him. Finally, while practical necessity dictated that in advocating ratification of the Constitution Iredell defend the clause allowing continuance of the slave trade, he could not have articulated his opposition to the institution of human slavery more clearly. Its complete abolition, he said, would be "pleasing to every generous mind, and every friend of human nature." "[T]hough at a distant period," he stated, the provision for eventual abolition of the slave trade would "set an example of humanity."[62]

These humane actions and pronouncements notwithstanding, in 1786 Iredell owned fourteen slaves. Throughout his adult life, he used slaves extensively in his work and in personal and family matters. While he clearly manumitted some, he still owned others at his death, as did Hannah at hers twenty-seven years later.[63] As a lawyer, he handled the sale of slaves for clients.[64]

One slave in particular is an integral part of the Iredell saga. Peter was Iredell's traveling companion for over twenty years. Their devotion to one another is conspicuous. Iredell reported to Hannah on Peter's health almost as often as on his own. He cared for Peter virtually as he would have a child. He exercised every precaution for Peter's health and would not make him travel unless convinced it could be done "with perfect safety." He often asked Hannah to tell Peter's "wife," Sarah, that Peter was well. In turn, Peter attended Iredell in illness "with the greatest tenderness and care."[65]

After years on the North Carolina circuits with his lawyer master, Peter also accompanied Iredell in his travels on the national judicial circuits through the spring tour of 1793. The slaveholder showed the same care and concern for his faithful valet there that he had on the state circuits. When Peter was unwell, Iredell teasingly told Hannah he "got a doctor & a judge to him (guess if one or two men) & he is now quite well again." He teased Sarah, too, directing Hannah to tell her, "Peter is perfectly well, but so great a favorite I can't always answer for his fidelity."[66]

The slave fully shared the hardships of the master's itinerant lifestyle. When Iredell traveled with Justice and Mrs. Wilson, Peter had to ride on a separate stage with the baggage. Peter was "out of the way" when Iredell departed on one journey, and the oblivious master did not miss his accustomed companion until later. As a consequence, the loyal servant walked the whole distance. The episode fatigued Peter and mortified Iredell, but according to Iredell, "there was no help for it."[67]

Peter had not only his master's confidence, but that of the master's family as well. Nelly Blair, for example, was not "the least afraid" to have Peter dispatched to bring her to visit her Aunt and Uncle Iredell. Iredell, she said, should not think of coming himself. Peter was to bring her flowers.[68]

When the Iredells moved in 1790, from Edenton to New York and soon afterward to Philadelphia, they took their servants with them. The family returned to Edenton in the fall of 1793, however, leaving Peter behind along with two other slaves, Edy and Dundee. It is evident that Iredell manumitted these three. Peter made his living thereafter by cutting wood, but he continued to attend Iredell when the former master was in the capital. Iredell paid Peter more for assisting him during these brief periods than Peter received from his other work during the remainder of the year. On one trip Iredell sent Peter to check on Hannah's nephew, James Johnston, who was at a nearby school. In 1798 Iredell reported that Peter had escaped the yellow fever and was attending him. Iredell concerned himself with the welfare of Edy and Dundee on these return trips to Philadelphia as well.[69]

Another slave, Hannibal, accompanied Iredell on some of his travels. Iredell cared for him as well, promising him his old great coat on one occasion and buying him a "coarse blanket" when he was coatless on another. He would not send Hannibal out into a hard rain, and he took care of this servant's expenses. He would report to Hannah that Hannibal was well and had behaved "with great propriety." He "answers every purpose I could wish for," Iredell said.[70]

At times hired servants rather than slaves assisted the wandering jurist. One named Andrew "behave[d] extremely well," Iredell said. David, a young mulatto set free under his master's will in Maryland, also "behaved remarkably well" and "prove[d] a most excellent servant." He was "as useful," Iredell said, "as Peter ever was in his best days." Iredell paid David four dollars a month, "comparatively low according to the rate of wages in Philadelphia," Iredell thought.[71]

Early in Iredell's American stay, his uncle Thomas enlisted his aid in selling a runaway slave. He requested remission of the proceeds in herring and in red-oak staves suitable for making sugar hogsheads.[72]

At his death Thomas Iredell owned other slaves, some of whom he apparently had acquired subsequent to execution of the will in which he disinherited Iredell in favor of Iredell's brother Arthur. Arthur initially informed Iredell that under Jamaican law, these slaves would be Iredell's as their uncle's legal heir. A subsequent opinion from Sir William Scott, with which Iredell tended to agree, brought Iredell's title into question. In a rare display of graciousness and generosity, Arthur nevertheless wanted these slaves indeed to be Iredell's. While Iredell indicated he would not have accepted them as a gift, he was willing to resolve the disputed legal point by taking them. Apparently because of pragmatic considerations regarding transportation of this human property, Arthur placed a value of £1,180 on the slaves, with which Iredell was "perfectly satisfied." While problems in their uncle's estate delayed payment, Iredell ultimately executed a bill of sale transferring title to the slaves to Arthur in consideration of £1,180 in Jamaican money.[73]

As to the slaves Iredell did own, substantial evidence supports the claim that he was a "humane master."[74] Nothing in the surviving historical record in any way impugns it.

CHAPTER 20

Friends, Finances, Faith, Fun, Foibles

I REDELL WAS MORE THAN A DEVOTED SON, TOLERANT AND MAGNANI-
MOUS BROTHER, KIND AND INDULGENT FATHER, CARING RELATIVE, AND
HUMANE MASTER. HE WAS A GOOD AND BENEFICENT FRIEND TO MANY
AS WELL. "[S]INCERE AND TRANSPARENT, EASY AND FAMILIAR," APTLY
characterizes him as a friend.[1]

He could refuse aid to a friend pursuing a public office, indicating that
since his elevation to the bench, he had deemed it improper to solicit ad-
vancement for others. Requests for such aid came nevertheless, and his response was not consistently negative. Shortly before his death, an acquaintance sought his assistance in obtaining a naval office. When Davie was
appointed envoy to France, Virginia's federal District Judge Cyrus Griffin solicited Iredell's help in securing a position attending Davie for Griffin's son,
who had spent time in Paris and had aptitude with the French language.
Iredell clearly attempted to assist, for Davie indicated he would have been
pleased to have "render[ed] an acceptable service to a gentleman of your esteem" had the position not already been filled.[2]

Iredell also honored appeals for character references. He once wrote
Alexander Hamilton, then secretary of the treasury, verifying his acquaintance
with two men and avowing his confidence that neither they nor their agents
would have indulged in fraudulent conduct. "So far as I could be personally
concerned in any transaction with them myself," he averred, "I would rely
with confidence upon their integrity."[3]

Friends' petitions for advice and assistance in legal matters were commonplace, even after Iredell became a Supreme Court justice. One posed questions about acceptable specie for satisfaction of debts in state courts and
whether the practice in federal courts was identical. Iredell's exalted status did

not deter this petitioner from demanding an urgent turnaround; "an answer in the course of tomorrow" would suffice, he indicated. John Sitgreaves, the federal district judge for North Carolina, sought Iredell's opinion on jurisdictional matters. Another acquaintance sought his advice "as a friend to the rest of my attornies..., as a favor." Even Samuel Johnston continued to seek his pupil's counsel, acknowledging that Iredell was interested only from "motives of the purest benevolence, with which your actions are on all occasions so pointedly marked."[4]

His friends did appreciate Iredell's beneficence. One wrote to say he would never forget Iredell's generosity, politeness, and "the trouble which my children have given you." Friends inquired after him, too; Pierce Butler, for example, did so constantly. They were honored to assist him. Robert Lenox, a prominent New York merchant, aided Iredell's family in moving from New York to Philadelphia. He was fortunate to be able to serve him, Lenox wrote Iredell, and had no intention of charging for his services; his acquaintance with one he so greatly respected was recompense enough.

Friends were a major consideration in the family's next relocation from Philadelphia back to Edenton. Primarily because of friendships, Iredell anticipated the move "with much pleasure." His friends also eagerly awaited the event, happily anticipating his return to reside among them.[5]

Frequent and prolonged furloughs away from them still occurred, however, and he did not forget them when absent. He regularly implored Hannah to remember him to his friends, listing them by name and conveying concern for their various problems and sufferings. He urged her to stay in touch with them, frequently admonishing her not to "forget to return your visits," and he entertained them when his court schedule permitted.[6]

Certain of Iredell's friendships clearly were special, William R. Davie's among them. Theirs was an easy intimacy, forged initially in the courthouses of North Carolina and strengthened by their joint efforts in the long and difficult struggle to secure ratification of the federal Constitution. Like others, Davie continued to seek Iredell's aid even after Iredell assumed the high bench; for instance, he once asked Iredell to inform him as to the Southern Circuit assignments. Davie also shared his opinions with his highly placed friend. "If your Chief Justice raves on the bench as he does at a town meeting," he once told Iredell, "we shall be highly edified."

When Davie was named envoy to France, a mutual friend informed Iredell of the appointment. It was indeed "highly honorable," Davie in turn told Iredell, but he conveyed apprehension as well as pleasure. The instability of the French government and its "strange, unparalleled character," Davie said, meant that he was casting his reputation "entirely upon *chance*." "[Y]our sensibility will easily anticipate the anxiety I feel under these circumstances," he confided to his longtime compeer.

Perhaps sensing that his demise was imminent, shortly before his death Iredell had a portrait made in Philadelphia and sent copies to Davie and other friends. It was "a fine likeness," Davie responded, "and nothing could have been more acceptable."

Iredell and Davie would have been pleased if they could have known that, in 1836, North Carolina would form a new county, adjacent to the one bearing Iredell's name, and name it for Davie. In life they had stood together in many endeavors, foremost among them the ratification of the Constitution and the founding of the University of North Carolina. In death their principal memorials would now be side by side in perpetuity.[7]

Iredell's friendships with William Hooper and his wife, Ann, were equally special. Early in Iredell's legal career, Hooper, soon to be a signer of the Declaration of Independence, saw himself as "much the gainer in intellectual improvement and amusement" from the association. He knew of no acquaintance he had commenced with greater pleasure, and he pledged to "endeavor earnestly to cultivate and in some measure... to deserve it."

Iredell received more tangible benefits from the affiliation. He was a frequent guest in the Hoopers' home; indeed, they forbade him to stay elsewhere when he was in their vicinity. Their "uniform kindness" was more than he could adequately acknowledge, and his "situation" while with them was "quite agreeable." He considered the family "one of the most excellent... in the whole creation," and the hours passed with it were quite pleasing; indeed, he could not be happier except when with his own family.

Ann Hooper charmed Iredell upon their initial acquaintance. He found her appearance "very ordinary" but her mind "highly cultivated," her sentiments "just and noble," and her natural abilities "very great." She had read widely and spoke "with great correctness and elegance." Her conversation was "extremely interesting, and equal to high subjects," and her knowledge of history was extensive.

Over a year before Hooper's death, Iredell informed Mrs. Hooper of her husband's "indisposition." He did so, she said, "in the tenderest manner"; he was "so cordial, benevolent, and disinterested a friend," who had given "assiduous attention" to Hooper and "tenderness to the whole family." When Hooper died, Iredell shared with the widow his longtime dread of "this melancholy event." His sympathy, he assured her, had been with her constantly, and he now joined in her sorrows. Hooper's demise did not end the friendship between Iredell and the widow; shortly before his own death, Iredell spent a week with Mrs. Hooper while en route to a court in Raleigh.[8]

Iredell was a sensitive individual, who felt the loss of friends keenly. "It is one of the painful circumstances attending the life I lead," he once said, "that I form many agreeable acquaintants whose society is dear to me, and from whom I part with an uncertainty of ever seeing them again." "My disposition is not such," he continued, "that I can feel such a situation with indifference." The accuracy of this self-appraisal is reflected in Iredell's intense suffering when he lost both his friend Archibald Maclaine and his brother-in-law John Johnston within a short period early in his federal-circuit travels. "My God!" he wrote, "how many awful trials of this kind are we doomed to sustain only in the course of a very short life! And what would be human existence but for the hope of a better and happier futurity." "Of all human evils," he told his friend Nathaniel Dukinfield in similar vein, "the loss of friends is the greatest, and would to me be insupportable if I thought this life terminated our existence." That Dukinfield could bear news of his own mother's death "with all the cursed stoicism of a philosopher" appalled Iredell.

From his own grief experiences, Iredell perceived the wisdom in Davie's statement to him that "there is something in the sympathy of a friend which can be gotten from no other source." As a consequence, he was truly kind and sympathetic to those who mourned. "[H]ow greatly I am indebted to your sympathizing friendship," an acquaintance whose wife had died wrote him, "and to that humanity and benevolence which hath led you to take part in my sorrows."[9]

Iredell's kindly, sympathetic friendship found its most-notable expression in the tragic, poignant circumstances surrounding the death of his Supreme Court colleague James Wilson. Early in their joint tenures, Iredell developed a special fondness for his new associate. Wilson was "a very agreeable companion," Iredell told Hannah, noting that their "sentiments in general agree[d] perfectly well." Before submitting his Revisal of North Carolina laws to the governor and the General Assembly, Iredell secured a review from his scholarly compeer. On the second reading Wilson found an error which—"to my credit," Iredell said without explaining how—he had overlooked on the first. By the fall of 1794, when Wilson was completing his first tour of the Southern Circuit, the relationship was such that Iredell implored Wilson to spend time with him and Hannah while southward. "[Visit] this part of the country before you return," he urged, and "accept during your stay here an apartment under our humble roof where, with no elegance, you would meet with a most sincere welcome." News that Wilson's "affability and politeness" had given "great satisfaction to both the bar and the people" no doubt pleased Iredell greatly.[10]

When Iredell made his acquaintance, Wilson was a widower, his first wife having died in 1786. In 1793, at age fifty-one, he married Hannah Gray of

Boston, who was nineteen. The union was the source of jocose gossip. An amused John Quincy Adams wrote his brother:

[T]he wise and learned Judge & Professor Wilson has fallen most lamentably in love with a young lady in this town, under twenty, by the name of Gray. He came, he saw, and was overcome. The gentle Caledon was smitten at meeting with a first sight love — unable to contain his amorous pain, he breathed his sighs about the streets; and even when seated on the bench of justice, he seemed as if teeming with some woeful ballad to his mistress eye brow....

Cupid himself must laugh at his own absurdity in producing such an union; but he must sigh to reflect that without the soft persuasion of a deity who has supplanted him in the breast of modern beauty, he could not have succeeded to render the man ridiculous & the woman contemptible.[11]

Lamentably, the new groom would soon suffer financial reverses that would lead to his ruin and untimely demise. In the 1780s and 1790s Wilson had speculated extensively in undeveloped lands in several states. Like other speculators of the period, by the mid-1790s he began to default on his loans. "Ruin is staring in ye faces of most of ye land speculators," warned Edward Burd of Philadelphia, and "[t]he day of reckoning is at hand,...no prospect of disposing of their lands." For Wilson, Burd's jeremiad proved prophetic. He was soon writing his son for bail money, then telling him to "bring with you all the money that shall be possible." He told his lawyer: "You can have no conception of what importance it is to me to have some funds. Twenty thousand dollars would, I believe, secure everything: Ten thousand would secure a great deal....Without funds much *must* be lost." Funds were not forthcoming, and Wilson soon told his lawyer: "I have been hunted — I may be hunted — like a wild beast: I have suffered much — I may suffer essentially in my health and otherwise." As Wilson approached death, he was so destitute that neither he nor his young wife even had clothes sufficient for circuit travel.[12]

Iredell and his family were pained observers of their friend's decline. "The misfortunes of Judge Wilson throw an unfortunate gloom over his house," Iredell wrote Hannah when the Court convened for its February 1797 Term, "though I have been there two or three times and experienced all their former kindness." When the Court next convened in August, matters had worsened. Iredell had to report Wilson as truant, "in a manner absconding from his creditors." "What a situation!" he lamented: "It is supposed his object is to wait until he can make a more favorable adjustment of his affairs than he could in a state of arrest."

By the Court's next convening in February 1798, Wilson had settled on Iredell's hometown of Edenton as a sanctuary from his creditors. Iredell called on Mrs. Wilson upon his return to Philadelphia, and she cried upon learning that her spouse was not coming. She immediately began to consider returning to Edenton with Iredell, who would be going to the Southern Circuit. She evidently did so, for soon afterward Iredell sent his respects "to the Judge and Mrs. Wilson" at Edenton. He then wrote Hannah from Charleston, grateful for news that Wilson and his wife were well but "still a little uneasy about that writ."[13]

Iredell's return to Philadelphia for the August 1798 Court Term brought him more dire news for Wilson. Wilson's lawyer had absconded, having defrauded some of his most-intimate friends, including Wilson. The frauds were in the $60,000 range. Stating the obvious, Iredell concluded that "this must unavoidably add to Judge Wilson's distresses."

These distresses were already taking their inexorable toll. Samuel Johnston had written Iredell a few days earlier that Wilson had been ill. "What upon earth will become of him and that unfortunate lady who has attached herself to his fortunes," Johnston wondered. Wilson showed no "disposition to resign his office," but surely, Johnston concluded, "if his feelings are not rendered altogether callous by his misfortunes, he will not suffer himself to be disgraced by a conviction or an impeachment." Like Johnston, Thomas Iredell expressed concern to his brother, reporting that Wilson was "by no means well" and that he did not exercise adequately.[14]

Four days after Tom wrote, Wilson's demise obviated impeachment concerns. Iredell had just returned from Philadelphia and found Wilson "speechless." During much of his last illness, Wilson was delirious and refused treatment that "might possibly have restored him." Wilson's "distress of mind owing to his pecuniary difficulties" undoubtedly precipitated the event, Iredell observed.

Some accounts place Wilson's death at Iredell's home; others, at Horniblow's Tavern in Edenton. Horniblow's is the almost certain locale. The day after Wilson's death Iredell invited Mrs. Wilson to come to his house, a needless proposition if she was already there. He later told Wilson's son that the Wilsons had stayed at Horniblow's, and his papers contain an account of James Wilson with John Horniblow dated 1798, the year of Wilson's demise.[15]

Wilson's destitution was so severe that the family could not afford to return him to Philadelphia for interment. The Johnston cemetery at Edenton thus accommodated the remains for over a century. In 1906 they were disinterred and ceremoniously returned to Wilson's home state for reinterment at Christ Church, Philadelphia. A marker in the Johnston cemetery memorializes Wilson's transient presence there.[16]

Wilson's death did not end Iredell's involvement with his affairs. He immediately wrote Secretary of State Timothy Pickering to advise of Wilson's demise and to urge prompt filling of the consequent Court vacancy. Wilson had been assigned to the Southern Circuit, where "business of the utmost consequence" was pending. It was not practical for Iredell himself to supply that circuit, he said, because he had been away from home almost the entire year and would be absent for months again at the beginning of the next. Further, he could not attend the North Carolina courts because the matters in which he was a party were still pending and would not brook further delay. The entreaty was productive, for Bushrod Washington, the former president's favorite nephew, soon filled the vacancy and attended the Southern Circuit that fall. John Marshall had declined the appointment, preferring to remain at the bar.[17]

Iredell also continued to comfort and assist the bereft family and widow. He advised Wilson's son on matters involved in settling the estate. The young widow lived in Iredell's home for several months while recovering from her ordeal and settling her husband's affairs in Edenton. She returned to Philadelphia only when Iredell journeyed there in January 1799 to prepare for the Court's February Term. Three months before his own death the next fall, Iredell was still assisting the family, remaining especially attentive to Mrs. Wilson. He sent her a book, hoping "it may sometimes be the means of recalling to your recollection the person who presented it." He admitted the selfish motive of wishing "to live with some esteem in your memory as long as I possibly can." He visited her regularly when in Philadelphia, and she consistently forwarded her love to Hannah and the Iredell children.[18]

Iredell's contemporaries recognized his benevolence. Having friends like the Iredells in her moment of sorrow, wrote Philadelphia lawyer William Rawles, was "a happy circumstance for Mrs. Wilson, and must be most grateful to her near connections." The widow's troubles would be mitigated by Iredell's kindness, wrote Justice Cushing. "[I]t will be a consolation to the children," wrote Bishop William White, "that in the extremity of Mrs. Wilson's distress, she found a reception under your hospitable roof."

It was indeed a consolation to the children. "We are much indebted to you and Mrs. Iredell," wrote Wilson's son; "we cannot help regarding the attention paid to her as a favor conferred on ourselves." Nor was the benefaction lost on the widow. "Mr. Iredell has been kind beyond everything," she said;

"he has watched by me night and day." "When I reflect on the painful scenes I passed through at Edenton," she told Mrs. Iredell, "I always remember with pleasure the kind, the friendly attention I received there from those [for] whom I have the greatest esteem and affection."[19]

There is a twentieth-century sequel to the Wilson-Iredell story. In the 1930s Burton Alva Konkle, who had led the effort to return Wilson's remains to Philadelphia, notified leaders of the North Carolina Bar of his efforts, through the Pennsylvania Bar Association, to have a portrait of Wilson painted and presented to the Supreme Court of the United States upon the dedication of its new building. The North Carolina Bar, Konkle suggested, should do the same for Iredell, so his portrait would hang by Wilson's "as the two leaders of the two schools of constitutional interpretation."

The Iredell family greeted Konkle's idea with enthusiasm. Mrs. James Iredell IV conveyed their keen interest. "[I]t would be splendid," she wrote Konkle, "if such a thing can be done." The family associated the names of Wilson and Iredell closely, she said, "as they became such staunch friends." Martha S. Iredell tweaked Konkle, however, about his role in the transfer of Wilson's remains from Edenton to Philadelphia. While acknowledging that Wilson probably should be buried in Philadelphia, she observed that "little Edenton" was proud and "would have preferred to have had Wilson's remains to simply remain as placed so many years ago."

Unfortunately, the North Carolina Bar did not share the family's zeal. It was the Depression Era, and Bar leaders responded that funds simply were not available for this purpose. They would "have to forego this pleasure," they indicated. As a consequence, Wilson's portrait hung at the Court for four decades before one of his distinguished friend and compeer appeared. Only in 1976, under the leadership of Chief Justice Warren Burger and in conjunction with the celebration of the nation's bicentennial, was a portrait of Iredell commissioned and presented to the Court. The Wilson and Iredell portraits now hang near one another in the Court's Early Justices Hall.[20]

While Iredell did not suffer Wilson's dire pecuniary fate, he, too, was not a wealthy man. Indeed, the financial struggle that impelled his youthful voyage to America proved inveterate.

Like Wilson, Iredell was a landowner. In 1787 he held 1,500 acres at "Tuckahoe on Trent River in the County of Jones [N.C.]," approximately 300 acres "near the above," 200 acres on "Beaver Creek" in Jones County, 2,130 acres in Onslow County, a 400–acre island "lying in [the] Chowan River," and his house and lot in Edenton. Apparently none of this was income-producing property, however, and throughout his life he lacked ready cash. In 1776 he declined an appointment to the Congress because of his "cursed poverty." While serving as North Carolina's attorney general, he once departed Halifax before Governor Thomas Burke arrived, having been "called home by business of indispensable necessity." He was "always ready to attend [the courts] as my duty requires," Iredell wrote the governor somewhat apologetically, but he could not defray the expense without public money. "I am not ashamed of confessing my poverty," he wrote, "as it has not arisen from any dishonorable cause." "My circumstances have suffered deeply," he continued, "but if I can just bear myself above water, I am content to suffer still."[21]

As a lawyer, Iredell would tell Hannah of his hope to get "money of consequence" but follow with news of "an indifferent court in point of money" and of his expectations being disappointed. At times sums that "would do no great good to any but a very poor man" boosted his spirits a bit. He would send Hannah small sums, wishing he could send more and sorry she was "left so bare." Soon afterward he would forward a "trifle" more, "almost ashamed" to do it and having "scarcely enough left to pay [his own] expenses." Safety concerns could deter his sending "a little" even when he otherwise could. He would fail to pay his taxes and have to ask his brother to do it for him. As his family grew, relatives would cease to write in order to save him the expense of postage.[22]

After the peace, Iredell informed his mother and his brother Arthur that he had contracted extensive debt during the Revolutionary War and that collection of debts owed to him was slow. Post-war inflation also took its toll on his resources. "[M]y difficulties since the peace," he told his mother, "have been much enhanced by a paper currency in this country that has raised the price of everything, & almost totally prevented, except for merchants, the means of remitting money abroad."[23]

Poor business practices intensified Iredell's financial woes. He kept indifferent records of his accounts and failed to secure them properly. Two years after his accession to the high bench, his brother Tom informed him that the North Carolina General Assembly had appropriated a further sum for his Revisal, which Tom would use to settle Iredell's debts. His affairs on the creditor side, however, were hopeless. "You unfortunately having taken so few notes," Tom wrote, "& the perplexed state in which your accounts stand, has put it almost totally out of my power to pursue a course of law, and little otherwise can be done." Tom shared primary responsibility for Iredell's fiscal interests with Samuel Tredwell, Hannah's niece Nelly's husband, when Iredell assumed his judicial tenure. Samuel Johnston had power of attorney to receive Iredell's judicial salary, and mortgagors were authorized to make payments directly to Hannah.[24]

Iredell apparently believed Supreme Court service would ameliorate his monetary plight. He wrote his uncle that the salary of $3,500 per year was "of so much value" that it was a motivating factor in his accepting the appointment. Some of his friends also perceived an advantage. "I hope...you will now be relieved in a great degree from the many embarrassments which surrounded you," wrote one. Another, though, was more realistic: "Considering the trouble & necessary expense attending [the job]," he wrote, "I think you are not too well paid."[25]

The prescience of the latter friend was soon evident. Iredell learned from Samuel Johnston that he would receive his judicial salary quarterly from the date of his commission, but that notwithstanding the utmost frugality, living in New York was very expensive. Hannah, who receives well-deserved credit for managing Iredell's finances wisely and judiciously, soon reinforced Johnston's caveat. "[C]onsidering our expenses on the road," she told her husband, there was "no great stock of money." She had already borrowed from New York merchant Robert Lenox, and she admonished her itinerant spouse sternly about his finances. Both must consider their expenses carefully, she said, if they were to keep his affairs from embarrassment. Even then, payment of debts owed to him or an appropriation for his Revisal would probably be necessary. It was time, she said, for him to "think" and to calculate his necessary expenditures. "[M]y dearest Mr. Iredell," she admonished, "do not think me impertinent in mentioning such things, but join with me in reflecting on them." She soon wrote again that she anticipated being "very much distressed" before his next quarterly salary payment fell due. "[I]t is very expensive living here," she said, and "I am told it is still more so at Philadelphia."[26]

Hannah appears to have gotten Iredell's attention, for thereafter he was at least episodically cognizant that she needed money. The shortness of purse did not abate, however. Iredell soon found himself too impecunious to buy books for his children. The family's return to Carolina was prompted in part, Iredell said, by the fact that it could live cheaper there and by his desire "to save something for my children." While his brother hoped the move would "secure an affluence," making him "much more like Croesus," it was not to be. Iredell continued to insist that Hannah inform him of her monetary needs but to report inability to make desired purchases because his expenses left him with inadequate funds. He thus deferred such purchases despite habitually borrowing against his next paycheck to meet current living expenses. He needed prior notice whenever Hannah planned to spend more than a designated and carefully limited sum.[27]

Congress did little to mitigate this adversity. No judicial pay raise was even proposed in 1797, Iredell told Hannah; while the Senate was "well inclined," it feared that such a proposition might defeat raises for the president and vice-president, which could not be considered again for four years. Iredell consequently, Samuel Johnston indicated, never seemed to have enough money. Shortly after Iredell's death, Johnston informed Arthur Iredell that Iredell "never realized any part of the money he received" as a lawyer or a jurist. "[H]e was guilty of no vicious excesses," Johnston said, "and his wife is remarkable for her frugality and economy, yet at the end of each quarter his purse was empty." Hannah experienced a still-further reduced financial situation in her widowhood.[28]

From his youth Iredell was a passionately committed Anglican. His spiritual interests clearly surpassed mere formal, organized religion. An essay penned in the year he came to America at age seventeen reveals him as deeply and genuinely religious. He was ready to declare the Christian religion "a divine institution" and prayed that he would "never forget the precepts of [God's] religion, or suffer the appearance of an inconsistency in my principles and practice." Imperfection, he said, was the lot of humanity, and sins "heartily and truly repented of" would be forgiven.

At a time when Deism was prominent in Edenton and the established Anglican church was weak throughout the South, especially in North Carolina, Iredell was "not ashamed to think seriously of religion" and hoped "no example [would] ever induce [him] to treat it with indifference." Men laugh at religion, he told his brother Francis, "either because they know nothing of it, or care nothing for it. Men of shallow understandings or bad hearts are those who generally rank themselves in the list of free thinkers." "[F]ree thinkers" were subjects of his special disdain. Iredell heartily condemned "the libertine writings of professed Deists, whose immoral lives made them dread an account hereafter."[29]

Perceptions of slippage in his piety bothered him. When he thought his religious principles and practice had slackened, he wished to "consider them attentively & abide by them firmly." "I fear God, & have no other fear," he said. "[T]here is a God who will one day call us to account," he continued, "and this reflection, *properly entertained*, is a great guard to virtue — *improperly neglected*, we grow less averse to the thoughts, and in time, to the practice of vice." Prompted by these deeply ingrained beliefs, Iredell set aside Blackstone to read sermons, which he then used to lead worship services when the regular director was ill.[30]

This youthful interest and commitment proved lifelong. His strong faith led to financial sacrifice. When Edenton parishioners supplemented Bishop Charles Pettigrew's annual salary from the Society for the Propagation of the Gospel by more than seventy pounds, Iredell subscribed for four pounds, hedging his pledge on his survival and the ability to pay it. His fervent faith also produced intolerance. Shortly before his death, he told Pettigrew "he could not well brook the idea of men who hold principles confessedly inimical to the Christian religion getting into offices and places of high trust and responsibility."[31]

Supreme Court service brought no diminution in Iredell's piety. He remained a regular communicant, whether in the capital or on circuit. When the capital moved to Philadelphia and his family moved with it, Iredell advised Hannah from his assigned circuit to "engage a seat in St. Peter's Church." His Sunday letters while on circuit would say, "I must go to breakfast and then dress for church or meeting."[32]

Iredell's commentary from the circuits frequently contained religious references. An expedition to the Southern Circuit found him traveling and lodging with an itinerant Methodist preacher: "[A] very worthy, good man," Iredell said, "but extremely weak." Iredell noted the minister's salary, sixty-four dollars a year plus expenses "to go constantly about preaching." It pleased him that the clergyman "seem[ed] to be a good government man [a supporter of the national administration]."

Iredell attended a handsome church in Charleston and heard a good sermon, well-delivered. A later visit there brought an excellent sermon from a Tory parson who had been banished and had no regular parish. When Iredell ventured to Baltimore, he heard a favorite preacher there discourse "with his usual excellence." He was mortified when heavy rain prevented his hearing this minister on another occasion.

He was not always so fortunate, however. He encountered a bad preacher in Baltimore, and he and Justice Wilson found "a very dull" one with "not a genteel congregation" in Wallingford, Connecticut. On a visit to Christ Church in Philadelphia, "unfortunately Blackwell preached." "This was additionally mortifying," Iredell indicated, "as Mr. Bond [a favorite] preached at St. Peter's."[33]

Iredell's first tour of the Eastern Circuit convinced him of the enhanced degree of religious tolerance in that region. He perceived "an extraordinary degree of liberality, even on religious subjects." Simultaneously, however, gentlemen were "perhaps more untinged with infidelity or an indifference about religion altogether than any other set of men of condition in any other country." Even the clergy, he noted, "have generous and enlarged minds, mix on a sociable footing with each other, and have as noble sentiments of indulgence to a real difference in religious opinions as can be expected from any men sincerely attached to a religion they cherish."

Indulgence for such differences in opinion, combined with intellectual curiosity, led Iredell and others (including Vice-President Adams, Justice Cushing's wife, and members of both houses of Congress) to attend the Universal Church in Philadelphia to hear Joseph Priestley, a Unitarian minister and theologian. Initially, Priestley met with great favor from Iredell and others. His audience was "as crowded...as could attend." Because Priestley spoke with distinctness, plainness, perspicuity, candor, and good sense, Iredell "heard him the whole time with the highest pleasure and admiration." As Priestley prepared to conclude, Iredell was pained, as if about to part "with a most intimate friend." There was "universal eagerness in the whole congregation to express their admiration to one another."

Soon, however, Iredell was "quite done with Priestley." With Mrs. Cushing and Philadelphia's "most respectable" citizens present, Iredell heard Priestley

> show the necessity of [Christianity] from the great prevalence of vice and debauchery in the heathen world, and give many instances of it in such shocking terms of indecency as not only must have deeply affected every lady of common sensibility present, but excited the highest indignation in every gentleman who knew how to respect the honor and delicacy of the sex.

The explicit sexual references, Iredell opined, had "completely sunk" Priestley in the public estimation, and he would henceforth "speak perhaps to little more than bare walls."

Iredell's dire predictions proved overwrought, for Priestley's audience soon returned. Even "some ladies" went the next Sunday, Iredell reported, "*but not many.*" A few "vindicated" what Priestley had said. "[T]hank God," Iredell said, "they are none of my acquaintances." Priestley had preached, Iredell said, "not only remarkably well, but unexceptionably, since the day I was out of humor with him."[34]

Iredell appreciated not only good preaching, but the contributions of the fine arts to the worship experience. He found a fine organ "extremely agreeable," and "most delightful vocal music" tempted him to "encore." He also thought "fine paintings on religious subjects" were "great helps to devotion, and...very useful in impressing more strongly the great events they are calculated to represent."[35]

As noted, Iredell clung tenaciously to a belief in an afterlife, consoling himself on the loss of friends with "the hope of a better and happier futurity." In light of his religious beliefs and practices, it is not surprising that Bishop Pettigrew would say of him: "In the run of above twenty years, I have often heard high encomiums on the merit of this great and good man; but never, in a single instance, have I heard his character traduced, or his integrity called into question."[36]

A serious religious commitment did not render Iredell a prudish Pecksniff. On the contrary, he was fully capable of displaying a risque sense of humor. The following from a letter to Hannah is illustrative:

> [E]xtreme sanctity has sustained a great blow in this neighborhood lately. A maiden about the age of 30, one of the sect called Quakers, a resident with the prim Mr. Peal, and herself remarkable for the most straitlaced affection, lately offended him with the sight of too big a belly, for which she was indebted to his son and has since been expelled [from] the father's house. They say it is only a repetition of an old disorder of which her conversion never thoroughly cured her....If [Nelly] wants any more particulars, they say the young damsel went to him!

Others shared similar comments with him, no doubt to his pleasure. Samuel Johnston once wrote him, for example, that "[s]ince the commencement of this severe season [temperature below 11° F] several weddings have been consummated in this neighborhood,...and it is thought that if the mercury continues below the freezing point a few days longer, there will be several others."

Iredell appreciated physical beauty in the opposite sex and was quite open about it. He once described a woman to Hannah as "so very handsome that if it was allowable for one woman to have more husbands than one, she would not be long without receiving an application." He later informed Hannah of his attending a dance where "there were at least six beauties...present, and several more that were nearly such."[37]

Dancing was probably Iredell's favorite form of entertainment. "Your uncle dance[s] quite nimbly," a friend once wrote Nelly Blair. "Your sons...are now at a ball," the retiring Hannah would tell the elder Mrs. Iredell. "[T]hey are both fond of dancing," she said, "the eldest full as much so as the youngest, though were you to see the gravity of his countenance when he sits biting his nails over a law book, you would hardly think it possible he could be so delighted with a country dance."

Business did come before pleasure, making a dance an irritant when it interfered with work. "There is a ball tonight," Iredell once wrote Hannah, "to which I shall unwillingly go out of compliment to the invitation, it ill suiting my court business." The addendum "otherwise, I should like it very well" conveyed his usual disposition, however. The fact that he often danced into the wee hours best reflects his typical attitude toward the activity.[38]

Clearly, the theater was another favorite pastime. Like the dances, he sometimes attended it "with great reluctance," again presumably because of the press of business. And he could be quite the critic: "Only one or two performers worth looking at," he would say. One performance left him "disgusted": The actors were "execrable," he said, the place "abominable," and much of the audience unable to see or hear. The climax of this "uncomfortable evening" saw two of the actors fighting behind the lowered curtain and the audience rushing upon the stage "to see the row." The more-usual instance, though, found Iredell delighting in the thespian world and discovering in it an important social and recreational outlet from the rigors of his judicial duties.[39]

A further form of entertainment disturbs the modern mindset. Like his leader George Washington, Iredell was not above attending an occasional cockfight. Nor did he refrain from taking sides. "The grand cock fight is at last ended," he would tell Hannah unapologetically, "N. Carolina victorious by two battles."[40]

Admittedly, there is little evidence of trivia in Iredell's life apart from these episodic dances, plays, and cockfights. It was more typical to find him requesting that Hannah send him his "spectacles and the last six volumes of Gibbon."[41] Sporadic instances of dalliance tend to humanize an otherwise quite-serious persona, however.

Other traits serve to further humanize the iconic image. Swearing, for example, was a serious problem for the man. While Justice Wilson's wife aided in rectifying this problem, Iredell was still subject to occasional relapses. "Tell Mrs. Wilson I frequently remember her admonition about exclamation and swearing, and am sure I have improved by it," he once wrote Hannah, "but the vile roads I had to pass sometimes unavoidably made me transgress." Shortly, he wrote again: "You may tell Mrs. Wilson that I have nearly effected my reformation as to swearing and exclaiming, and if I can do it thoroughly shall owe her unspeakable obligations for the friendly frankness with which she corrected those failings." The practice must have been habitual, for its absence was conspicuous. Justice Rutledge, Iredell once noted, "remarked, with surprise, that I never swore, which seems to be an equal proof of my former sin and present reformation."[42]

The iconic image is further dulled by the fact that the man was avowedly ambitious and covetous of homage. "My ambition has ever directed me," he once told Pierce Butler, "next to the approbation of my own heart, to wish for the esteem of men of sense and virtue." "I thank God I have hitherto been fortunate in that respect," he added, "and I am exceedingly happy that so respected and so valued an approbation as yours is not withheld from me."[43]

Iredell could be forgetful. He once left his razors at home, and his "patience was almost exhausted, making a most scandalous appearance" before Nelly Blair could forward them to him.[44]

He could also be careless or inconsiderate. "[O]ne half of the blots in this letter," Hannah once told Nelly, "are owing to Mr. Iredell's snuffing the candle."[45]

CHAPTER 21

King of Terrors and Terror of Kings

UMAN LIFE HUNG BY A PRECARIOUS THREAD IN LATE-EIGH-
TEENTH-CENTURY AMERICA, AND DEATH, THAT "[D]ARK
MOTHER EVER GLIDING NEAR WITH SOFT FEET,"[1] CAME TO
IREDELL BEFORE HE HAD FULLY BLOOMED. EVEN AT A TENDER
age, he had reflected pensively upon that inevitable eventuality. "Death has
been very busy in his attacks of late—perhaps, in turn, he may pay me a
visit," he wrote at age eighteen, adding fatalistically: "If so, God's will be
done. Let me endeavor to regulate my conduct in such a manner as to have no
gloomy fears at his approach." Over two years later he wrote similarly of the
uncertainty of life, prodding himself to prepare for a danger to which he was
"continually exposed." "May I live today as cautiously as if I was sure of dying
tomorrow," he wrote self-goadingly.[2]

A lifelong proclivity for nettlesome minor illnesses may have prompted
these ruminations. Shortly before age nineteen, Iredell described himself as
"very unwell," so much so that he could not continue his journal. The following year he informed his mother that he had been "more severely [ill] than
I ever was before."[3] As an adult, he frequently endured colds, fevers, intestinal complaints, and stomach disorders. He suffered from rheumatism, an eye
inflammation, and a near-fatal attack of cholera morbus.[4]

At times Iredell described his health problems more generally: an unspecified "disorder," "my health was very bad," "[m]y very ill health prevented my
attending some courts," "my health for some time past has been very bad," or
"I was a little unwell." He once described his physical status as "very critical
and dangerous" for almost a year.[5]

The primitive state of late-eighteenth-century medicine worked against
him. He treated his complaints with bark, bitters, chicken water, cream tar-

279

tar, magnesia, rhubarb, salts, and snake root. An occasional "blooding" was a supposed safeguard to protect his health while traveling. More-curative medicaments were then unknown.[6]

Geography likewise was not in his favor. Edenton was at least widely believed to be "a most extreme unhealthy spot; trying beyond measure to the best constitution." Its swamps and stagnant bay, Pierce Butler told Iredell, were "enough to heed the most pestilential disorders." Iredell did not disagree. "Your observations on the unhealthiness of this town are certainly just," he replied.

A change of abode was Butler's proposed solution to Iredell's recurrent health problems. Iredell again responded agreeably. He, Samuel Johnston, and their families had suffered so severely, he said, that they had seriously considered moving to Hillsborough, "a very healthy town in this state in the back country."[7]

Other friends joined in encouraging the relocation. William Hooper, believing Iredell's severe attacks would render him more susceptible to such disorders, rejoiced that he and Johnston "talk[ed] seriously of coming among us." A Hillsborough friend told Nelly Blair that such a move by the Johnston and Iredell families would "complete [her] happiness." The friend's father was confident Iredell would "have a better chance of health & long life by leaving the low country."[8]

Notwithstanding continued urging from Butler and Hooper, the change never materialized. "[T]here is a difficulty," Iredell told Hannah, "owing to the want of houses, and of convenience, and workmen to build." The water at Hillsborough also had a "laxative" quality that "renewed [his] complaint." Finally, and probably most importantly, there was the tug of Edenton. Family and friends there wanted him to stay. Nelly Blair conveyed their sentiments to her favorite uncle. "[G]ive me leave to ask what success you have had in getting a house at Hillsborough," she wrote Iredell; "none at all — you don't wish for any there — you have got a surfeit of the place — and are surprised how you could ever like it — will I hope be the answer." It was.

Except for the brief venture to New York and Philadelphia, the Iredells continued to cast their lot with Edenton, even though Edenton's malaria generated fever and agues more or less annually — even though, as a friend wrote Iredell, "once in every year at least you run the gauntlet for your lives notwithstanding the utmost regularity and temperance in your manner of living."[9]

Probably the foremost enemy to Iredell's physical well-being, though, was neither the primitive state of medicine nor geographical location, but the man himself. An abiding penchant for unremitting hard work on the part of one so

frailly constituted could hardly have been salutary. There clearly was a dri-
venness about the Iredell persona that militated against robust good health.
His philosophy reflected this. He was critical of "spend[ing] too much
time in an unprofitable, idle manner" and was determined to "have ambition
enough to deserve a good account of myself" and to produce a "habit of industry & application." "Indolence in any is shameful," he wrote in his youth,
"quite inexcusable [and] an effectual bar to improvement." "[N]othing," he
said, "is to be acquired without industry."

His lifestyle also reflected it. He lived under constant pressure and time
constraints, occasionally not even writing to Hannah for lack of time. "I fear
it is my fate to end my life as I set out in it," Samuel Johnston once wrote him,
"without any prospect of rest until I am laid in the resting place appointed for
all mortals." Iredell could have said the same. He was "very quick in his walk
and movements," a man of "gravity" who never did things "by halves."[10]

Almost fourteen years before Iredell's death, a physician friend chided him
about his physical habits, scolding him for "too close application to study,
and want of exercise." Persistence in that course, he warned, would deprive
Iredell of his health and thousands of his friendship. While medicine afforded
temporary relief, only a lifestyle change offered a long-term remedy. "The
doctor," Jean Blair had told Hannah shortly before, "has been very particular
in his inquiries about...[Iredell's] health."[11]

Others who knew the man shared the medic's concerns. William Hooper
was "too well acquainted" with Iredell's study and work habits to imagine that
he would allow adequate time to recover from an illness. Nathaniel Dukinfield
fretted over a bad account of Iredell's health; upon hearing good accounts of
Hannah's and Annie's, he wished Iredell's was as propitious. Arthur Iredell
lectured his older brother on the importance to his children of his survival and
admonished, "What business had you in court with a fever, sir?"[12]

Iredell's spouse and her brother joined Arthur in prodding the jurist about
his responsibility to his family. "I flatter myself that your affection for your
children will be a sufficient inducement for you to take care of yourself," Hannah once told him. As Iredell's final summons neared, Samuel Johnston
echoed her sentiments, entreating Iredell "to avoid, by every means in your
power, the most distant possibility of your taking the infection of that fatal
fever." Iredell's life was more important to the public, and particularly to his
family, Johnston reminded him, "than any temporary omission of your official
duties."[13]

Friends joined family in craving longevity for him. Pierce Butler wished
him many years "to enjoy the honorable station where the unanimous voice of
such of your fellow citizens as had a right to a voice on the occasion [Iredell's

confirmation proceedings] has placed you." He was reverberating Samuel Johnston's sentiments. "I...am very glad to know that you have got your Commission," Johnston had written earlier, "and pray that you may live & keep your health long to enjoy it." Grand jurors in Iredell's court also wished him "a long succession of years, with the blessings of health and prosperity added thereto."[14]

Naturally, Iredell fully shared these aspirations. On his fifteenth wedding anniversary he told Hannah he trusted that his future life would be devoted to making hers as happy as possible and that "God in his mercy [will] grant that the blessed opportunity of doing so may be extended to a very late period." Seven years later he still coveted "many years of happiness in the enjoyment of each other."[15]

On one occasion he actually acted to further that objective. Recognizing that the laboriousness of his profession was adversely affecting his health, he contracted the circuit in which he practiced law. Still, he could not escape exposure to a hot sun which left him "a little unwell for 3 or 4 days." "[U]gly weather" yet affected his health, even when he was "as cautious as possible." Prolonged illnesses thus would continue to delay his production of work long since promised to a client.[16]

Then came the rigors of the federal circuits, where "heat sometimes almost overcame" him and colds were "scarcely possible to avoid travelling in the stages" or from "incessant application at court." The "many kind entertainments," while pleasant, augmented the undermining of his health. Iredell would now report himself "excessively fatigued," "harassed to death with the fatigue of a court," "extremely fatigued," "fatigued to death," or, as death approached, experiencing "extraordinary fatigue."[17]

Illness prevented Iredell's attendance at the New York court on his Fall 1792 Eastern Circuit tour. He missed the February 1794 Term of the full Court for the same reason. Indisposition also precluded his appearance at both the February and August 1799 Terms. Shortly after the August 1799 Term, he proclaimed himself "for a considerable time entirely recovered." It was delusional thinking, however.[18]

Iredell was not alone in being thus affected by the severe and exhausting labors of the circuits. Justice Chase missed circuit duties in the winter of 1799 because of illness, and he feared that fatigue from resumption of duties would "bring on some other of [his] complaints." Justice Paterson almost simultaneously wrote Iredell that his "state of health [was] by no means good." Like Chase, Paterson was "apprehensive that fatigue and hard duty would cause a return" of his problems. "Without health," he had told Iredell earlier, "all other earthly pleasures lose much of their relish."[19]

Washington indeed would have done well, as a modern scholar has noted, "to have inquired into the health and vigor of each candidate [for the Court], for the task which lay ahead was such that its discharge would require *mens sana in corpore sano.*" The assignment of holding the circuit courts was, as Iredell wrote during the Court's efforts to change the system, "too burthensome" and a "painful and improper situation." Without question, it eroded his health and contributed significantly to his early demise. "The fatigue to which you had been exposed during the Circuit was well calculated to produce this consequence," Bushrod Washington said perspicaciously of the affliction which proved to be his colleague's last.[20]

Although Iredell's final summons arrived rather suddenly ("after three days illness [unspecified]" by one account; following "an illness [unspecified] of 37 hours" by another; "after a few days illness [unspecified]" by Samuel Johnston's reckoning), there were ample premonitions. Over the last few months of his life, the man made episodic references to his good health, but health-related complaints were far more common. The increasing emotional strain on him during the trial of John Fries and the Northampton Insurgents is apparent from his May 1799 letters to Hannah. He refused to yield to the physical and emotional fatigue, however. "There is still a great deal to be done," he wrote Hannah from Richmond as he neared the end of his active time on the bench, "and I shall exert myself to the utmost in order to finish."[21]

Several months before Azrael, the dark angel of finality, visited, two Iredell missives to Samuel Johnston evidenced handwriting conspicuously diminished in lucidity. Johnston must have taken note, for he began to prepare Hannah for her impending sorrow. "Mankind are vulnerable in so many ways," he told the sister who had married his student, "that no one can assure himself of being secure from some great misfortune." "[Y]et," he continued, "this is a subject that we should not suffer our minds to dwell too intensely on. A sense of it should prepare us to meet whatever may happen with as much fortitude as our nature is capable of."

Soon Johnston would notice uncharacteristic neglect of common social courtesies on the part of his former pupil. When Iredell failed to respond to his letters with customary promptness, Johnston feared they had miscarried. "Had they come to hand," he told Hannah, "he is too punctual not to have taken notice of them." He was concerned upon learning a few days later that Iredell's being "so much indisposed" had occasioned the delay. "I fear his zeal for the service will induce him to expose himself more than he ought," Johnston concluded. Despite having business in Philadelphia he wanted Iredell to handle, Johnston was relieved when his beloved kinsman chose not to attend the August 1799 Court Term "in the state of health [he was] then in."[22]

Iredell must have known he was failing. The Philadelphia winter had been severe, making, he said, for "abominable walking," and thereby further diminishing his already too-limited physical exercise. A sense that his brush with mortality loomed near may well have impelled his largess in sending his picture to numerous friends during that last excursion to the capital city. When he later postponed the May 1799 court in Richmond to a day certain in June, he carefully hedged a commitment to "certainly be there" when the court reconvened, with the caveat "if I am alive and well." The futility of his June effort to recover his strength at Richmond and proceed to Philadelphia also must have told him something, for he returned home to give assiduous devotion of waning strength to his unfinished legal treatises (*see infra* Chapter 22).[23]

"So near home," Iredell wrote Annie in late May 1799, perhaps perceiving how true, in an ultimate sense, the phrase soon would prove. "How much shall we regret your absence!" Hannah Wilson wrote Iredell in August 1799, undoubtedly imperceptive of how soon the exclamation would characterize an abiding reality.[24]

"Old Time, that greatest and longest-established Spinner of all," ceased to weave for Iredell on October 20, 1799. Death, aptly described by an Iredell correspondent as "that king of terrors and terror of kings," came early in his forty-ninth year. Life in America, his uncle had said long before, seldom extended beyond fifty years. Iredell's demise at age forty-eight provided proof for his relative's postulate.[25]

Concluding tasks, public and private, remained:

On the public side, John Adams soon appointed Alfred Moore—whom Iredell had thought one of his state's ablest attorneys, but whose performance and popularity as a lawyer, and later as a superior court judge, had declined—to replace Iredell on the Supreme Court. John Steele, the state representative who had been instrumental in the naming of Iredell County, was now the comptroller of the federal treasury. Steele recommended Moore to Adams for the seat.[26]

On the private side, there was a bill to be paid for "medicines, attendance, etc.," for the Iredell family from June 15–October 23, 1799. Two of Iredell's children were "dangerously ill" at the time of his death, so it is unclear how much of the invoice was on Iredell's account. Other debits had to be settled as well.[27]

Joseph Anthony, a Philadelphia merchant and Iredell family friend, closed out the jurist's business affairs in the capital city. On November 6, 1799, unaware of Iredell's demise, Anthony wrote to advise that he had forwarded to him some articles that had been left in his care. Soon afterward, then fully informed, he transmitted Iredell's accounts with the Bank of the United States and with himself to Samuel Johnston. He canceled Iredell's subscription to John Fenno's pro-administration paper and forwarded to Johnston a bill for thirty-eight cents due on that account. The landlord's account, Anthony indicated, would follow by the next post. "[T]o say we do not most sincerely condole with his family would not be doing justice to our own feelings," Anthony told Johnston.[28]

A grave marker had to be secured. The family had difficulty settling on language appropriate to memorialize so distinguished a decedent. The words ultimately chosen list his dates of birth, emigration to North Carolina, and death; mention his honorable public service, culminating on the Supreme Court; and commemorate his exemplary character.[29]

Finally, there was a grief process to be endured. "In every friend we lose, we die," Pierce Butler had observed to Iredell. Samuel Johnston had told him, similarly, "The shock which nature receives on parting with a long and much loved friend will not at once give way to reflection, religion or philosophy." The shock of Iredell's departure would pain his family and friends well into the future. They perhaps could have found solace in the words of one of his mourners, the president who had appointed him to the Supreme Court, to Henry Knox upon the death of Knox's son. "He that gave, you know, has a right to take away," said Washington, "his ways are wise, they are inscrutable, and irresistible."[30]

CHAPTER 22

A Parting Assessment

H AD WE BEEN PRIVY TO IREDELL'S DEATHBED REFLECTIONS, WE PROBABLY WOULD HAVE OBSERVED A MAN LARGELY IMPERCEPTIVE OF HOW HEAVILY THE HAND OF HISTORY WOULD REST UPON HIM — A MAN WHO THOUGHT, LIKE HAMLET, THAT AT best "there's hope a great man's memory may outlive his life half a year." We certainly would have seen a man who was quite cognizant of his imperfections. "Nothing is more fallible than human judgment," he had told the Hillsborough ratification convention. "Mine," he acknowledged, "has often proved so." He knew, too, that he had enemies. Long before, William R. Davie had informed him that the compensation Iredell had thought proper for his Revisal was unattainable because Iredell "had enemies where I least expected them." He knew, further, that even his friends could find his stubbornness and tenacity exasperating. Archibald Maclaine had once told him, for example, when unable to lure Iredell to the Maclaine position on a public question, "You would maintain your opinion at the stake."[1]

True, Iredell lay on the precipice of the last great adventure knowing that contemporary opinion of his private character was largely quite favorable. He appeared to Hannah's cousin Penelope Dawson to be "all goodness." His friend John Stokes likewise spoke glowingly of his "goodness." Another found his kindness flattering until she "looked around and found [him] the common friend of humanity." "[M]otives of the purest benevolence," Samuel Johnston had told him, "on all occasions so pointedly marked" his actions. "[T]he goodness of his heart & benevolence of his disposition," said Nelly Blair Tredwell, "will forever engage the friendship & affection of all who know him."[2]

His public character and service also brought him sentiments of honor while he lived. He had raised himself to "respectable eminence," his brother

Arthur had said, while "promot[ing] the happiness of the present & future generations." Arthur had refused to tell him—"lest [he] should be made vain"—what the ship captain who brought their mother to America had said about him.[3]

Hugh Williamson had told Iredell he was "one of the best men, as well as best lawyers in America." "Yes, Iredell," William Hooper had said to him, "you have a conscience that will ever bear you up under the pressure of the most pungent calamity, and a heart like yours all alive to the misfortunes of others can never be wounded without the consolation of universal sympathy." Pierce Butler had let Iredell know he had long considered North Carolina "fortunate in claiming you to aid in her councils and promote her welfare." "I am sure," Butler had said, "if she is sensible of the justness of your opinions, she will be led to true honor and substantial happiness." William Paterson, Iredell's Supreme Court colleague, had informed him that he had many friends in the southern states and had opined that the same was undoubtedly true "wherever you are known." Those whom Iredell had served there, Paterson had advised, were pleased by the thought of his returning. Finally, a minister in Augusta, Georgia, had advised him of the high esteem for him there, wishing him a life of prosperity and "such a close of it as shall place you in the blessed choirs in heaven."[4]

As Iredell joined those choirs in heaven, Bishop Pettigrew portrayed him as "so humane, so sympathetic, so charitable, so humble, and so easy of access." It was astonishing, Pettigrew said, "that one in so many different spheres of elevation could preserve his reputation so fair and unblemished." "[N]o man supported the dignity of office better than he did," Pettigrew claimed. Contemporaneously, Samuel Johnston depicted him to a now-bereft brother as "a tender husband & father, a faithful friend, an able & upright judge and a steady patriot."[5]

Iredell knew of many of these contemporary portrayals. The encomiastic judgments yet to flow from the stream of time probably would have astonished him, however. The personal assessments mirrored those of his age. David Lowry Swain, governor of North Carolina and president of its university, would consider him "able and learned [and] a gentleman of singular purity." Iredell's character would delight a reader of the first published set of his letters and papers. "What a remarkable man he was," the reader would say, noting especially Iredell's "strength of mind & principle coupled with his strong affections and pure habits."[6]

A subsequent editor of his papers would conclude that he was "one of the most thoughtful and magnanimous men of his time." A chronicler of North Carolina history would consider him a "gracious personality, great legal authority, graceful letterwriter, of pronounced literary tastes, with a genius for friendship." "He had the manners and graces of the gentleman in the truest sense of the term," a twentieth-century commentator would say; he was "singularly kind-hearted and thoughtful of the feelings and interests of others" and "universally respected for his ability as a judge and his character as a man."[7]

As a public man, he would be considered "remarkably able"[8] and "one of our great statesmen-jurists,"[9] who "possessed the elements of greatness within him."[10] Julian P. Boyd would regard him as "one of the most admirable but neglected figures of the American Revolution"; Bernard Bailyn, as "one of the most penetrating minds among the federalists."[11] Supreme Court historian Hampton Carson would describe him as "ever bold and outspoken in speech and courageous in conduct" and "the ablest legal reasoner in the State."[12] Another scholar would credit him with as much influence as anyone, possibly more, in maintaining the doctrine of judicial power in the early days of the American republic.[13]

As a jurist, George van Santvoord would consider him "one of the ablest." "As a constitutional lawyer," van Santvoord says, he "had no superior upon the bench. His judicial opinions are marked by great vigor of thought, clearness of argument, and force of expression."[14] Another scholar would say, "this country has seen few men more learned in the law, of more commanding eloquence, or more gentleman-like accomplishments."[15] Iredell's opinions, still another would conclude, were "so strong, clear, and logical . . . that they always compelled attention and respect, even when they failed to persuade. Unquestionably he was the ablest constitutional lawyer upon that bench until the advent of Marshall, and, in all other respects, the equal of Justice Wilson."[16] Henry Groves Connor, an early-twentieth-century North Carolina Supreme Court justice and federal district judge, likewise thought Iredell's opinions on constitutional questions "evince[d] a very high order of judicial statesmanship."[17] Late-twentieth-century scholars would perceive him as "a source of considerable satisfaction" to the president who appointed him[18] and "one of the more influential of the early justices."[19]

The moribund Iredell would not likely have predicted that his judicial career would be of such interest that, long after his death, shreds of his robe would be preserved in his state's Hall of History. The display of the robe at the North Carolina Exposition of 1884 would have pleasantly shocked him. The esteem with which eminent future jurists would view him would also have been a pleasant surprise. John Marshall saw him as "among the considerable men" of his state and "a man of real talent"; Felix Frankfurter, as "one of the really brilliant minds of his period, if not of our entire history." Iredell

was, Frankfurter thought, "in many respects a forerunner of Marshall and especially important in that first decade in the history of the Judicial Branch of
our government, not to speak of his importance in the Revolutionary history
of North Carolina and in the debates over the ratification of the Federal Constitution." The idea of a late-twentieth-century edition of Iredell's papers was
Frankfurter's.[20]

Biographers of his contemporaries were also laudatory. Davie's biographer
would find Iredell "talented, ardent, and sincere."[21] "He was an excellent
lawyer, and a man of fine and amiable character," an Oliver Ellsworth biographer would say,[22] and a profiler of Patrick Henry would describe him as "a
great jurist and one of the strong men of his time."[23]

"[T]he friend of Washington, the compeer of Marshall and Story," a late-
nineteenth-century essayist would say of him, concluding that "few men have
laid [the judicial ermine] aside with more purity and honor."[24] An eminent
late-twentieth-century historian would rank him (with Elbridge Gerry, John
Jay, George Mason, James Monroe, and others) just behind the "giants" of
the formative era of American history.[25]

Subsequent assessment of his epistolary legacy would also have surprised
Iredell. As a youth, he took no special pride in his penmanship. "I just sit
down and carelessly let my thoughts flow from my pen," he told Hannah during their courtship, "without too much anxiety about the expression." This
claimed disregard for style notwithstanding, Iredell would be viewed as his
state's best letter writer, and his letters as the best source of the state's social
and political history, during the late eighteenth century. The missives "were
models," writes one commentator, "and numbering, as he did, among his
correspondents the chiefest men of the day, hand down ... living pictures of
the leading characters and stirring events of his life."[26]

Griffith McRee's publication of many of these communications in the mid-
nineteenth century provided a collection rightly described as "invaluable for
an understanding of social and political affairs in the later eighteenth century,
prized by all investigators of national as well as of state history." Iredell's letters while on the Supreme Court are properly viewed as "illuminat[ing] the
contemporary scene in a decade when [North Carolina] was endeavoring to
compose the factional divisions that threatened to rend the Union."[27]

David Lowry Swain could hardly have been more wrong, however, in concluding that, once published, the manuscripts themselves would "be a matter
of comparatively little importance" or "of small consequence."[28] The publication by McRee, who married one of James, Jr.'s daughters, was indeed a
contribution of monumental proportions to an understanding of the man and
the period. The compilation was by no means complete, however. The

McRee volumes omit significant letters, unduly truncate others, and somewhat distort still others.[29] Without the full panoply of the surviving Iredell communications, works such as this one and the early volumes of the *Documentary History of the Supreme Court of the United States* would have been severely diminished, if not impossible. Editors of the *Documentary History* readily acknowledge their debt. "Without Iredell, the chronicler," they admit, "these volumes would not be possible." Iredell's epistolary legacy contributed significantly to making him those editors' favorite among the early justices and to causing the editor-in-chief actually to grieve when working with documents bearing on his death.[30]

Iredell would have been pleased if he could have known that publication of his epistolary legacy would influence and inspire prominent jurists of the future. Walter Clark, who served on the North Carolina Supreme Court from 1889–1924 and contributed substantially to the progressive development of the law in his time, studied the papers in his youth. Sam J. Ervin, Jr., who served on the North Carolina Supreme Court from 1948–54 and later attained fame as the chair of the United States Senate Watergate Committee, did also.[31]

There are yet other matters the moribund jurist would not have anticipated: the toast, by name, to him and the other original trustees of the University of North Carolina at its centennial celebration in 1889; the presence in the University's Memorial Hall, long after his death, of a stone tablet commemorating his public service; the 1995 erection of a statue on the campus honoring him and the other original trustees.[32] He would not have expected to find the president of the American Bar Association, in an address to the 1920 annual convention, citing his early expressions on judicial review as urging "with the utmost precision and strength... the subsequently familiar doctrine of *Marbury v. Madison*."[33] The 1940 pilgrimage to Edenton by some of his descendants to join local dignitaries in honoring him on the sesquicentennial of his appointment to the Supreme Court[34] would have surprised and delighted him. He would have enjoyed the sentiments his relatives conveyed to Judge Henry Groves Connor following the 1912 publication of Connor's law review article about him; unlike in the late twentieth century, residents of Lewes, England, his birthplace, were then keenly interested in him, and his North Carolina relations held his memory "in reverent regard." "We are indeed proud of him in every respect," an English relation wrote to Connor, "and must ever regret that an unworthy government of our own, for the time being, led to the rupture that ensued."[35]

The Library of Congress' 1950 observance of the bicentennial of his birth would also have gratified Iredell. It came a year early, probably because

McRee's rendering of his tombstone inscription incorrectly shows his birth year as 1750 rather than 1751. Visitors to the Library observed a display of "a remarkable record of a great legal mind," including a notebook in Iredell's hand on cases he heard on circuit in 1793 when John Marshall, among others, argued before him. The document, a Library bulletin states, "reveals this great legal mind striving to establish under the new Constitution the great body of precedents which has become the law as interpreted by the Supreme Court of the United States."[36]

There was a further remembrance on October 20, 1999, as Iredell's hometown of Edenton observed the bicentennial of his death. Denise Iredell, the widow of an Arthur Iredell descendant, came from England to join a past president of the James Iredell Association in laying a wreath on the grave. At a service in St. Paul's Church, the rector read excerpts from Bishop Pettigrew's funeral oration and offered prayers from Iredell's time. The present author gave the principal address. Tours of the Iredell House, with its entrance draped in black gauze, followed a luncheon address on eighteenth-century funeral customs.

Some posthumous assertions, grossly exaggerated or distorted to support a legal or political argument, would likely have appalled Iredell. Two days before his twentieth birthday, he urged his mother, "Be not afraid of the pistols you have sent me." They might be needed for self-defense, he said, though he doubted it, as there was peace; she could rely, he assured her, on his "prudence and self regard for a proper use of them." Over two centuries later, this letter was cited to sustain the polemic that "[b]earing arms for personal protection was an unquestioned right in the minds of the Founding Fathers." It is highly doubtful that the youth about to enter his third decade had anything that comprehensive in mind or that a not-quite-twenty-year-old's reassurance to his mother is legitimately representative of the generic thought of so large and diverse a group as "the Founding Fathers."[37]

The Iredell deathbed vigil would not have found its subject contemplating that over two centuries later, the oldest courthouse still in use in his state would have his name engraved on an interior wall or that when his county constructed a new courthouse in the late twentieth century, its exterior wall would contain a quotation from his legal writings. He would have been surprised if he could have known that over two centuries later, lawyers waiting in the anteroom to argue cases before the North Carolina Supreme Court would observe his portrait, that a law-school fraternity and city streets would bear the Iredell name, that the Young Lawyers Association of the North Carolina county named for him would present a James Iredell award to a senior practitioner viewed as a positive role model for younger attorneys, and that the

James Iredell Institute and Fellows Program would enhance civics education for North Carolina social-studies teachers.[38]

Perhaps Iredell's greatest surprise would have come in the fall of 1987. Almost two centuries after he assumed his seat on the Supreme Court, another nomination to that Court was pending before the United States Senate Judiciary Committee. Once again the attention of the American people was riveted upon the Senate's ornate Caucus Room — the scene of earlier hearings on the sinking of the Titanic, the Army-McCarthy controversy, the Watergate crimes, and the Iran-contra affair; the site of John and Robert Kennedy's declarations of their presidential candidacies; the locale, later, of the Clarence Thomas-Anita Hill imbroglio and Hillary Rodham Clinton's testimony on national health-care reform. Now, it was President Reagan's nomination of Judge Robert Bork that captivated the public interest. As the Cable News Network beamed the proceedings to a waiting nation, a witness invoked Iredell's name and thought in opposition to the nomination.

In responding to the Antifederalists' contention at Hillsborough that the Constitution should not be ratified without a bill of rights, Iredell had posited that if certain rights were specified, the government might later argue that others, not relinquished but not enumerated, were denied. Bork, the witness reasoned, was the embodiment of Iredell's misgivings. "Iredell vividly describes and condemns precisely a perverse originalism like Judge Bork's," the witness testified, "that would anachronistically limit the protection of rights to those enumerate [sic] rights protected in 1787 and 1791." Bork's "interpretive philosophy illustrates...one of the Founders' fears," the witness concluded. "He is Iredell's nightmare, an interpreter who would, in defiance of the Ninth Amendment, anachronistically betray the central premise of our Constitutionalism, the protection on fair terms of all our rights."[39]

Iredell's ratification-period utterances would again be heard in the United States Senate as the Congress considered impeachment of President William Clinton in the autumn of 1998. Senator Robert Byrd of West Virginia quoted Iredell's declaration that the power of impeachment was designed "to bring great offenders to punishment...for crime which it is not easy to describe, but which every one must be convinced is a high crime and misdemeanor against the government." The power arose, Byrd further quoted Iredell, "from acts of great injury to the community, and the objects of it may be such as cannot be easily reached by an ordinary tribunal." In the removal trial, Representative Charles Canady, one of the House managers, also quoted Iredell, referring to Iredell and Alexander Hamilton as having set forth the general principles on impeachment in the ratification debates. Writing in the *Wall Street Journal*, Judge Robert Bork likewise quoted Iredell on impeachment.[40]

The tragedy, of course, is that Iredell's story is incomplete — that because of his untimely demise, we can only speculate about what he might have accomplished if given the number of years allotted to Thomas Jefferson, John Marshall, or even George Washington. Though historians may frown, "alternate" or "counterfactual" history — contemplating the "what ifs" — is gaining in attention and popularity.[41] Applied briefly to Iredell, this approach holds a certain fascination.

At his death, Iredell had completed a treatise on evidence and a lengthy essay on statutory construction. His leisure time in the last three or four years of his life was consumed by work on two major treatises left incomplete: one on common law pleading, and one on the law of real property. The legal expositions in these works are well done and neatly arranged. Major points are summarized in the margins in modern hornbook style. None were published, however; had the author lived a bit longer, they might well have been, and he might well be remembered as the first and foremost of the early American authors of major legal treatises.[42]

More significantly, it is entirely reasonable to speculate that had he lived until then, James Iredell, not John Marshall, would have succeeded Oliver Ellsworth as chief justice. James Wilson, whose seniority to Iredell had been an impediment when Washington had wanted to appoint Iredell earlier, was at rest in the Johnston family cemetery at Edenton. Of the original Court, only Iredell and William Cushing would have remained.

Cushing, while senior to Iredell, was old; so ill that he missed entire Court terms; and, at least in many quarters, quite unpopular. When the office of chief justice had been vacant in 1796, William Plumer of New Hampshire had pronounced Cushing a man "I love and esteem." "[B]ut time, the enemy of man," Plumer added, "has much impaired his mental faculties." Congressman Jeremiah Smith thought him "superannuated & contemptible." John Marshall, then the secretary of state, considered him ill-suited for the chief justiceship. Cushing had declined the position once because of his age and infirm health. It is entirely reasonable to conclude that he would have done so again.[43]

President Adams offered the appointment to John Jay and wrote his son that should Jay refuse, "I shall follow the line of judges most probably and then there will be a vacancy." Adams' wife, Abigail, confirmed that if Jay refused, the appointment would be offered to Cushing, and if he declined, it would go to Paterson, who was next in seniority.[44]

Jay did refuse. Had Iredell lived and Cushing, as expected, declined, following the line of judges would have led the president to Iredell. There would have been no need to turn to Adams' secretary of state, John Marshall, whose appointment, according to one of his biographers, "was not greeted with applause from any quarter."[45] Adams could, and probably would, have appointed the associate justice next in seniority, whose relationship with him and his administration could hardly have been closer, and whose appointment, as in the past, clearly would have been warmly received. Iredell, not Marshall, would then likely have ensconced the principle of judicial review into the fabric of the American experiment. Instead of being obscure, as a North Carolina newspaper described him in 1987,[46] Iredell might hold Marshall's place in the history of American law and constitutional jurisprudence. Marshall would then be regarded as just another leading member of the Virginia Bar with episodic public service.[47]

Iredell's entire history virtually compels the conclusion that, given the greater life span allotted to many of his peers, his achievements would have mounted. But "death, a necessary end, / Will come when it will come."[48] Moreover, incomplete by no means equates with insignificant. It is true that Iredell has relatively rarely been a cynosure of the historian's musings — that twentieth-century appraisers, who ranked all pre-Marshall Court justices as average or below, rated his Supreme Court performance as merely average.[49] It is fair to conclude, nonetheless, as did a previous student of Iredell's life and career, that his character and merits have been too-little known.[50]

It was said of Charles Doe, chief justice of New Hampshire in the late nineteenth century, that " 'he was born into the judgeship of New Hampshire, [and] he there lived and wrought and died.' "[51] To speak similarly of Iredell would perhaps say too much. It would be more accurate to assert that he attained a judgeship of the United States in what ideally should have been midlife and there he died prematurely before he had fully wrought.

To consign him to the dustbin of history on that account would be altogether erroneous, however. At his death his revolutionary-period essays, his defense of judicial review and the Constitution, and his commitment to the residual sovereignty of the states were firmly chiseled into the fabric of the American experiment. The story that proceeds from the impoverished, insecure emigrant of seventeen to the eminent, accomplished statesman-jurist of forty-eight reads like an epic poem.[52] When the cold pen of history records the ablest of the American founders, it spares ink unwisely if James Iredell is not among them.[53] He was nonpareil within his state and among a select group of leaders nationally. Like his colleague and friend James Wilson,[54] he came to America in his youth to seek his own fortune and stayed to contribute significantly to the formation of ours.

Notes

Author's Acknowledgments

1. Stephen B. Oates, *Abraham Lincoln: The Man Behind the Myths* (New York: Harper & Row, 1984), 33.

PROLOGUE
A Very Affecting Death

1. Baker, 261–62; Fitzpatrick, 31:360 (Washington to Knox, September 8, 1791) (death of Knox's son); Ray Brighton, *The Checkered Career of Tobias Lear* (Portsmouth, N.H.: Portsmouth Marine Society, 1985), 49, 80, 91–93, 109, 114–15; Smith, *Patriarch*, xv–xvi, 81; James Iredell to Nelly Tredwell, July 30, 1793, NCAH.

2. McRee, 1:1, 7–9 (ed. essay); Higginbotham, 1:xxxvii (ed. essay), 12 (Henry E. McCulloh to Francis Iredell, March 3, 1768), 80 (Iredell to Margaret Iredell, October 3, 1771), 107 (Iredell to Francis Iredell, Sr., July 20, 1772).

3. Higginbotham, 1:xlix (ed. essay), 94 (Iredell to Hannah Johnston, ca. April 1, 1772), 96 (Iredell to Samuel Johnston, April 7, 1772), 180, 183 (Iredell's Diary, November 11–12, 1772), 459 (Iredell to Hannah Iredell, August 19, 1777).

4. Henderson, 1:567–68, 624; Higginbotham, 1:xlv–xlvi (ed. essay), 241 n.2; Weeks, 198–99.

5. *E.g.*, Higginbotham, 1:8–11, 11 n.1, 36–39 (Iredell's essays on religion), 68 (Iredell to Francis Iredell, Jr., June 15, 1771), 143 (Penelope Dawson to Samuel Johnston, ca. 1773), 173, 177, 203, 208 (Iredell's diary entries).

6. James Iredell to Hannah Iredell, March 11, 1796, NCAH.

7. Hugh T. Lefler, "North Carolina History — A Summary View of What Has Been Done and What Needs to be Done," *North Carolina Historical Review* 38 (1961): 216, 225.

8. Linda Greenhouse, "Focus on Federal Power," *The New York Times*, May 24, 1995, at 1 (commenting on *U.S. Term Limits, Inc. v. Thornton*, 514 U.S. 779(1995)).

CHAPTER 1
That Amusing Study, the Law

1. McRee, 2:105 (Iredell to Archibald Neilson, June 15, 1784); Higginbotham, 1:7 (McCulloh to Iredell, September 11, 1767), 48 (Margaret Macartney to Iredell, April 30, 1770), 65 (same, March 20, 1771).

2. Roscoe Pound, *The Formative Era of American Law* (Boston: Little, Brown and Co., 1938), 81, 127 n.1.

3. Higginbotham, 1:172 (Iredell's Diary, August 23, 1790).

4. Higginbotham, 1:xlix (ed. essay), 56 (ed. note), 153, 155 (Nathaniel Dukinfield to Iredell, May 14, 1773), 160 (same, August 9, 1773), 194 (Iredell's Diary, December 12, 1772); McRee, 1:55 (ed. note). Although an uncritical lover of Blackstone while a student, Iredell later would call the principle of parliamentary sovereignty over the American colonies enunciated in the *Commentaries* "narrow and pedantic." Higginbotham, 1:lxiii (ed. essay), 265 (Iredell's "To the Inhabitants of Great Britain").

5. *Ibid.*, 1:li (ed. essay), 55–56 (ed. note); McRee, 1:74, 102 (ed. notes); Saunders, 7:485 (William Tryon, "A View of the Polity of the Province of North Carolina in the Year 1767").

6. McRee, 1:92–93 (Thomas Iredell to Iredell, August 19, 1771); Maclaine to Iredell, August 29, 1787, Duke.

7. Higginbotham, 1:452 (Iredell to Hannah Iredell, May 2, 1777), 2:3 (same, January 14, 1778), 7 (same, March 12, 1778), 39 (same, July 2, 1778), 147 (same, May 13, 1780), 364 (same, December 2, 1782); McRee, 2:111 (same, October 15, 1784); John C. Fitzpatrick, ed., *The Diaries of George Washington, 1748–1799* (Boston: Houghton Mifflin, 1925), 4:164–66; C. Christopher Crittenden, "Overland Travel and Transportation in North Carolina, 1763–1789," North Carolina Historical Review 8 (1931): 239 (*passim*).

8. Higginbotham, 1:445 (Iredell to Hannah Iredell, April 28, 1777), 2:90 (same, June 14, 1779); Iredell to Helen (Nelly) Blair (Hannah's niece), October 22, 1785, NCAH.

9. Higginbotham, 1:106 (Iredell to Francis Iredell, Sr., July 20, 1772), 2:90 (Iredell to Hannah Iredell, June 14, 1779), 158 (same, May 24, 1780), 196 (same, November 26, 1780); Iredell to Hannah Iredell, October 17, 1786, NCAH.

10. Higginbotham, 2:58 (Iredell to Hannah Iredell, December 12, 1778), 90 (same, June 14, 1779), 112 (same, September 20, 1779), 365 (same, December 2, 1782), 414 (same, May 31, 1783); John Burgwin to Iredell, October 6, 1787, Duke.

11. Higginbotham, 2:157 (Iredell to Hannah Iredell, May 22, 1780), 192 (same, November 16, 1780), 354 (same, October 9, 1782), 402 n.6, 404 (Iredell to Hannah Iredell, May 23, 1783), 448 ("Instructions to Chowan County Representatives"), 451 (ed. note).

12. Higginbotham, 1:143 n.1 (suggesting speech impediment not serious or constant), 193 (Iredell's Diary, December 9, 1772), 2:140–41 (Iredell to Hannah Iredell, April 13, 1780); McRee, 1:76 (Iredell's funeral homily, Rev. Charles Pettigrew); Iredell to Hannah Iredell, May 24, 1786, NCAH.

13. Higginbotham, 2:194 (Iredell to Hannah Iredell, November 18, 1780), 415 (same, June 2, 1783), 424 (Iredell to Arthur Iredell, July 30, 1783), 470 (Iredell to Thomas Iredell, uncle, ca. November 1783); McRee, 2:101 (same, May 28, 1784).

14. Higginbotham, 2:87 (Iredell to Hannah Iredell, June 11, 1779), 113 (same, October 1, 1779), 150 (same, May 18, 1780), 342 (same, May 17, 1782), 424–25 (Iredell to Arthur Iredell, July 30, 1783).

15. McRee, 2:142 (William Hooper to Iredell, August 1, 1786); Waldrup, 98–99, 148; Iredell to W. John Cameron (of Petersburg), September 1, 1787, NCAH.

16. Higginbotham, 1:109 (Iredell to Francis Iredell, Sr., July 20, 1772), 241–42 (Iredell to Governor Josiah Martin [apparently—no name or address shown], July 9, 1774), 2:133 (Iredell to Hannah Iredell, December 8, 1779), 135 n.2, 198–99 (Iredell to Hannah Iredell, December 8, 1780), 346 (Governor Alexander Martin to Iredell, June 24, 1782), 363–64 (Iredell to Hannah Iredell, November 25, 1782); McRee, 2:117–18 (Iredell to Nathaniel Dukinfield, January 7, 1785).

17. Waldrup, 91–93, 119 n.1; Iredell's Fee Book, SHC.

18. Waldrup, 172–73.

19. *Ibid.*, 174–76, 184–86.

20. *Ibid.*, 233.

21. Higginbotham, 1:lxxxv–lxxxvi (ed. essay), 2:74–78 (Iredell's Petition on behalf of Henry Eustace McCulloh), 372–74 (McCulloh to Iredell, February 5, 1783), 380–82 (same, March 17, 1783), 382–85 (same, March 28, 1783), 395–96 (Iredell to McCulloh, ca. May 1, 1783), 467–69 (same, November 28, 1783); McRee, 2:103–04 (Iredell to McCulloh, June 15, 1784), 116–17 (same, January 6, 1785); McCulloh to Iredell, February 20, 1784 and August 1, 1790, Duke. See Isaac S. Harrell, "North Carolina Loyalists," North Carolina Historical Review 3 (1926): 575, 585 (McCulloh "with the exception of the Granville heirs, . . . the heaviest loser under the Revolutionary seizures in the State"); Blackwell P. Robinson, "Willie Jones of Halifax, Part II," North Carolina Historical Review 18 (1941): 133, 143–45.

22. Higginbotham, 2:203–04 (Petition of Margaret Pearson), 204 (ed. note); McRee, 2:252 (Dukinfield to Iredell, February 4, 1789).

23. Iredell to an unnamed client, January 5, 1791, NCAH.

24. John Burgwin to Iredell, March 30, 1786, NCAH; Iredell to Hannah Iredell, April 14, 28, 1797, NCAH; Isabella Mease to Iredell, April 26, 1797, NCAH.

CHAPTER 2

The Fundamental, Unrepealable Law

1. Bernard Schwartz, *A History of the Supreme Court* (New York: Oxford University Press, 1993), 10.

2. Act of Dec. 29, 1785, ch. VII, 1785 N.C. Sess. Laws, reprinted in Iredell, 553–54 (also in Clark, 24:730–31).

3. N.C. Const. of 1776, §§ 14 (Declaration of Rights), 44.

4. Robert O. DeMond, *The Loyalists in North Carolina During the Revolution* (Durham: Duke University Press, 1940), 53–56, 180, 188–89; William S. Price, Jr., " 'Men of Good Estates': Wealth Among North Carolina's Royal Councillors," North Carolina Historical Review 49 (1972): 72, 79, 80 n.5; Waldrup, 258–59.

5. Eva Murphy, "Singleton, Spyers," in Powell, *DNCB*, 5:352–53; Clark, 17:337, 413, 18:114, 121, 174, 189, 340, 397, 420, 450, 459, 20:49, 65, 103 (unsuccessful attempts); Holton, 60–64; Waldrup, 254, 264.

6. Clark, 17:419–21 (Maclaine protest); McRee, 2:51 (Iredell to Hannah Iredell, May 21, 1783), 133 (Iredell to William Hooper, January 29, 1786), 134 (Iredell to James Hogg, January 29, 1786).

7. Waldrup, 285–86 n.4; McRee, 2:93 (Iredell to Pierce Butler, March 14, 1784).

8. McRee, 2:119–20 (Maclaine to Iredell, March 7, 1785), 489 (Iredell's "Memorandum concerning the Granville claim to lands in North Carolina") (emphasis added); Holton, 125–26; Waldrup, 261–69; William R. Davie to Mary Edwards, June 14, 1787, Davie Papers, NCAH; Iredell's Fee Book (entry for November 20, 1787), SHC.

9. *Bayard v. Singleton*, 1 N.C. 5, 10 (1787).

10. Waldrup, 267–68.

11. *Ibid.*, 268–69; Holton, 126–27 n.29.

12. Samuel Johnston to Alexander Scrysmoure, July 11, 1784, Hayes Collection, SHC; unsigned, undated script, almost certainly Johnston's, in Hayes Collection, SHC.

13. Higginbotham, 2:449 (Iredell's "Instructions to Chowan County Representatives").

14. McRee, 2:145–49 (Iredell's "TO THE PUBLIC").

15. *Bayard*, 1 N.C. at 6–7; McRee, 2:148 (Iredell's "TO THE PUBLIC").

16. *Bayard*, 1 N.C. at 8–10.

17. Clark, 20:288, 292; McRee, 2:183 (William R. Davie to Iredell, December 13, 1787), 247 (Samuel Johnston to Iredell, November 20, 1788), 274–75 (same, December 1, 1789); Waldrup, 282.

18. Claims that *Bayard* was the first case to declare a legislative act unconstitutional — e.g., Lefler and Newsome, 243; McRee, 2:145 n.*; Peele, 69; and Powell, 217 — probably exaggerate. One writer posits that the first such case was *Commonwealth v. Caton*, written by Chancellor Wythe for the Supreme Court of Virginia in 1782. Dillon, 3:199. For a compilation of colonial precedents and early state cases showing several such decisions predating *Bayard*, see Haines, *Judicial Supremacy*, 74–77. Nevertheless, a recent work refers to *Bayard* as "the first *reported* state case in which a judicial tribunal held a legislative enactment unconstitutional." Levy, 98 (emphasis added). Clearly, *Bayard* was at least among the first such cases. Because of (1) its temporal proximity to the federal constitutional convention, and (2) the presence of Alfred Moore — one of the attorneys in *Bayard* — on the United States Supreme Court when it decided *Marbury v. Madison*, it is reasonable to attribute greater influence in establishing the doctrine of judicial review to *Bayard* than to the other cases.

19. McRee, 2:169 (Richard Dobbs Spaight to Iredell, August 12, 1787).

20. McRee, 2:173–75 (Iredell to Richard Dobbs Spaight, August 26, 1787). For further commentary on *Bayard v. Singleton* and Iredell's views on judicial review, see the following: Berger, *Government*, 304; Connor, *Rebuilding*, 1:395–96; Burton Craige, *The Federal Convention of 1787: North Carolina in the Great Crisis*

(Richmond: Expert Graphics, 1987), 108–11, 114–15; Dougherty, 31–36; Goebel, 130–31; Haines, *Judicial Supremacy*, 40; Haines, *Role of Supreme Court*, 17–18; Henderson, 1:489–91; Herndon, 125–30; Higginbotham, 1:lxxxix–xc (ed. essay), 2:449 ("Instructions to Chowan County Representatives"), 451 n.1; R. Don Higginbotham, "James Iredell and the Revolutionary Politics of North Carolina," in W. Robert Higgins, ed., *The Revolutionary War in the South: Power, Conflict, and Leadership* (Durham: Duke University Press, 1979), 79, 96; Price, 434–35; Robinson, 165–67; Robert von Moschzisker, *Judicial Review of Legislation* (Washington, D.C.: National Association for Constitutional Government, 1923), 36–38.

21. Waldrup, 281, 298 nn.58, 59.

22. *The Federalist*, Nos. 78 at 524, 80 at 535 (Alexander Hamilton) (J. Cooke ed., 1961).

23. Haines, *Judicial Supremacy*, 54; Dougherty, 32.

24. Casto, 216–17; see also Charles F. Hobson, *The Great Chief Justice: John Marshall and the Rule of Law* (Lawrence: University Press of Kansas, 1996), 63–64.

25. Levy, 98–99.

26. Dougherty, 31, 36; Dillon, 2:249.

27. Friedman and Israel, 277–78.

28. Elliot, 4:179, 194.

29. *Calder v. Bull*, 3 U.S. (3 Dall.) 386, 399 (1798).

30. See *Marbury v. Madison*, 5 U.S. (1 Cranch) 137, 175–79 (1803).

31. *Ibid.*, 176.

32. McRee, 2:146 (Iredell's "TO THE PUBLIC").

33. *Marbury*, 5 U.S. (1 Cranch) at 176.

34. McRee, 2:148 (Iredell's "TO THE PUBLIC").

35. *Marbury*, 5 U.S. (1 Cranch) at 177.

36. McRee, 2:148 (Iredell's "TO THE PUBLIC").

37. *Martin's North-Carolina Gazette* (No. 80), New Bern, July 11, 1787, at 2 (emphasis added).

38. Berger, *Government*, 309. For a recent general treatment of Iredell and judicial review, see William R. Casto, "James Iredell and the American Origins of Judicial Review," Connecticut Law Review 27 (1995): 329 (*passim*).

39. See Higginbotham, 1:449 (ed. note); Waldrup, 150, 383; William H. Hoyt, ed., *The Papers of Archibald D. Murphey* (Raleigh: E.M. Uzzell & Co., 1914), 1:205 (Colonel Ransom Sutherland to Archibald D. Murphey, April 10, 1821) (reference to Iredell as among principal lawyers in North Carolina at that time).

CHAPTER 3

Sufferings in the Public Service

1. N.C., Ordinance to Appoint Certain Commissioners to revive the Statutes and Acts of Assembly heretofore in force and use in North Carolina and to prepare bills for the consideration of the next Assembly (Dec. 21, 1776), reprinted in Clark,

23:987; 1711 N.C. Sess. Laws, ch. 1, sec III, reprinted in Clark, 25:153; Act of Dec. 24, 1777, ch. XXV, 1777 N.C. Sess. Laws, reprinted in Iredell, 345 (also in Clark, 24:36); Act of May 2, 1778, ch. V, 1778 N.C. Sess. Laws, reprinted in Clark, 24:162–63 (also in Iredell, 353–54); *Steelman v. City of New Bern*, 279 N.C. 589, 592, 184 S.E.2d 239, 241 (1971); *Development Co. v. Parmele*, 235 N.C. 689, 694, 71 S.E.2d 474, 478–79 (1952) (receipt of common law); Connor, *History*, 1:418; Higginbotham, 1:lxxviii (ed. essay) (commentary).

2. Higginbotham, 1:423 (Johnston to Iredell, December 7, 1776), 424 n.1. See Lefler and Powell, 219–20, 282; Lefler and Newsome, 206.

3. N.C. Const. of 1776, §§ 13, 21, 23.

4. Clark, 24:iii (ed. note), 36–42, 48–75 (acts establishing courts and court procedures). See Henderson, 1:326; Higginbotham, 1:lxxviii (ed. essay); Allan Nevins, *The American States During and After the Revolution 1775–1789* (New York: Macmillan Co., 1924), 364 (court law "good because Iredell had drafted it").

5. Clark, 11:825 (*North Carolina Gazette*, December 26, 1777); Kemp P. Battle, "An Address on the History of the Supreme Court," 103 N.C. 339, 354 (1889); Higginbotham, 1:469–70 n.1; McRee, 1:368–69 (ed. essay), 2:143 (Archibald Maclaine to Iredell, August 3, 1786).

6. Higginbotham, 1:lxxviii–lxxix (ed. essay), 468–69 (Hooper to Iredell, December 23, 1777), 470 (Maclaine to Iredell, December 25, 1777).

7. Higginbotham, 1:lxxxvii–lxxix (ed. essay), 2:7, 25, 28 (Iredell to Hannah Iredell: March 12, 1778; May 23, 1778; May 28, 1778); McRee, 1:395 (ed. note), 396 (Abner Nash to Iredell, June 16, 1778).

8. Higginbotham, 1:lxxviii–lxxix (ed. essay), 2:32–34 (Iredell to Richard Caswell, June 13, 1778) (see also Iredell to Caswell, December 31, 1778, in Clark, 13:341), 36 (Richard Caswell to Iredell, June 16, 1778); Waldrup, 25.

9. Higginbotham, 1:lxxix (ed. essay), 248 n.2 (McGuire), 2:36–38 (Chowan County criminal presentments in Iredell's hand and bearing his signature), 37 (ed. note), 39 (Iredell to Hannah Iredell, July 2, 1778) (shows him back in practice), 85 (Richard Caswell to Iredell, May 26, 1779), 85 n.2, 127 (permanent commission as attorney general); Cheney, 182, 195 n.49; Iredell to Abner Nash, October 26, 1779, NCAH; Clark, 13:948 (salary); temporary commission, NCAH.

10. Higginbotham, 2:102 (Hooper to Iredell, August 15, 1779), 119 (Nash to Iredell, October 26, 1779), 129 (Iredell to Hannah Iredell, November 25, 1779).

11. *Ibid.*, 82 (Iredell to Hannah Iredell, April 19, 1779), 128 (Iredell to Hannah Iredell, November 25, 1779); Waldrup, 40–43, 72.

12. Act of May 9, 1777, ch. III, 1777 N.C. Sess. Laws, reprinted in Iredell, 284–86 (also in Clark, 24:9–12); Waldrup, 42–47.

13. Wallace Brown, *The Good Americans: The Loyalists in the American Revolution* (New York: William Morrow and Co., 1969), 60, 226–27; Robert M. Calhoon, *The Loyalists in Revolutionary America 1760–1781* (New York: Harcourt Brace Javanovich, 1965), 439–47; William H. Nelson, *The American Tory* (New York: Oxford University Press, 1961), 92; Carole W. Troxler, *The Loyalist Experience in North Carolina* (Raleigh: North Carolina Division of Archives and History, 1976) (passim); Waldrup, 44, 67–68, 73–75.

14. Waldrup, 69–72, 76.

15. Higginbotham, 1:lxxii (ed. essay), 346–47 (Joseph Hewes to Iredell, March 26, 1776), 354–55 (Iredell to Joseph Hewes, April 29, 1776), 2:425 (Iredell to Arthur Iredell, July 30, 1783).

16. Higginbotham, 2:425 (Iredell to Arthur Iredell, July 30, 1783); Clark, 15:671–72 (Iredell to Judge John Williams, December 14, 1781) (also in Clark, 19:891 (same)).

17. Higginbotham, 2:379 (Archibald Maclaine to Iredell, February 21, 1783); Iredell to H.E. McCulloh, June 15, 1784, NCAH; McRee, 2:144 (Archibald Maclaine to Iredell, August 3, 1786); Iredell to Electors of Edenton, August 15, 1788, NCAH; McRee, 2:249–50 (Iredell to William Cumming, January 6, 1789); Waldrup, 366 n.1 (examples of legislators reporting to Iredell and seeking his advice).

18. McRee, 2:125–26 (William Hooper to Iredell, July 6, 1785), 164 (Archibald Maclaine to Iredell, July 11, 1787); Iredell to Richard Dobbs Spaight, August 26, 1787, NCAH; Waldrup, 336.

19. Iredell to Speakers of North Carolina Senate and House, October 16, 1789, NCAH; McRee, 2:277 (ed. note); Iredell to Governor Alexander Martin, November 21, 1791, NCAH. Justice William Paterson of New Jersey also compiled a revisal of his state's laws while serving on the United States Supreme Court. Paterson to Iredell, April 27, 1799, Duke.

20. Clark, 20:491, 500; 21:26, 37, 251, 611; 23:981–82 (N.C. Const. of 1776, § XVI); Cheney, 165.

21. Battle, 1:821, 2:426; Clark, 24:454–55, 25:22; McRee, 2:270 (ed. note), 371 (Iredell to Hannah Iredell, October 21, 1792); R.D.W. Connor, ed., *A Documentary History of the University of North Carolina 1776–1799* (Chapel Hill: University of North Carolina Press, 1953), 1:71–73; Iredell to Trustees of the University, November 16, 1790, NCAH; file marked "James Iredell, Sr. — Miscellaneous Papers, Smith Academy, Edenton — Minutes of Trustees, 1782–1785," NCAH; John Witherspoon to Iredell, January 8, 1787, Duke, and Iredell to Witherspoon, February 19, 1787, Cupola House Papers, SHC. Universal education that drew Iredell's admiration would, at the time, have applied to white males only.

CHAPTER 4

An Open and Eager Part in Rebellion

1. McRee, 1:74 (Thomas Iredell to Iredell, undated; McRee places the letter in 1770); Clark, 11:765–66 (Josiah Martin to Lord George Germain, September 15, 1777); Berger, *Writings*, 184 ("ablest").

2. Higginbotham, 1:lv–lvi (ed. essay).

3. Saunders, 6:1261 (John Ashe, Speaker, to Arthur Dobbs, Governor, October 31, 1764), 7:123, 125 (*North Carolina Gazette*, November 20, 1765), 143–44 (William Tryon to Seymore Conway, December 26, 1765); Maurice Moore, *The Justice and Policy of Taxing The American Colonies in Great-Britain, Considered* (Wilmington, N.C.: Andrew Steuart, 1765) (passim).

4. Saunders, 7:168c–e (text), d (*North Carolina Gazette*, February 26, 1766), 169–73 (William Tryon to Seymore Conway, February 25, 1766), 174 (Jacob Lobb to William Dry, January 14, 1766), 175 (William Dry to Robert Jones, Jr., January 16, 1766, and Jones to Dry, February 3, 1766), 177 (forty citizens to William Dry, February 15, 1766). See generally John Phillip Reid, *Constitutional History of the American Revolution* (Madison: University of Wisconsin Press, abridged ed. 1995), 30; Lawrence Lee, "Days of Defiance: Resistance to the Stamp Act in the Lower Cape Fear," North Carolina Historical Review 43 (1966): 186 (passim).

5. Higginbotham, 1:lxxiv (ed. essay), 107 (Iredell to Francis Iredell, Sr., July 20, 1772), 111 n.2, 231 (Hooper to Iredell, April 26, 1774), 305 (Hewes to Iredell, May 23, 1775), 318 (Hannah Iredell to Arthur Iredell, probably late 1775), 348 (Johnston to Iredell, April 5, 1776); Mary C. Engstrom, "Hooper, William," in Powell, *DNCB*, 3:199–202.

6. Higginbotham, 1:lxiv (ed. essay), 282–83 (Arthur Iredell to Iredell, January 31, 1775), 285–86 (ed. note); Morning Chronicle and London Advertizer, London, January 16, 1775, at 2; genealogical file, Duke (note regarding signature of Jean Blair, Hannah's sister). For an example quoting Arthur's letter, see William P. Cummings and Hugh F. Rankin, *The Fate of a Nation: The American Revolution Through Contemporary Eyes* (London: Phaidon Press, 1975), 28–30.

7. Higginbotham, 1:280 (Thomas Iredell to Iredell, January 8, 1775); McRee, 2:135 (Iredell to Thomas Iredell, February 23, 1786).

8. Higginbotham, 1:400, 410–11 (Iredell's essay on the causes of the American Revolution), 312 (Neilson to Iredell, July 8, 1775), 319–20 (McCulloh to Iredell, October 2, 1775), 323 (Iredell to McCulloh, November 1, 1775), 339 (Hooper to Iredell, January 6, 1776).

9. Saunders, 9:xx–xxvi (ed. essay); Higginbotham, 1:lix–lx (ed. essay); Crow, 14; Pauline Maier, *American Scripture: Making the Declaration of Independence* (New York: Alfred A. Knopf, 1997), 110–11, 145–46.

10. Higginbotham, 1:163–65 (Iredell's "Essay on the Court Law Controversy," September 10, 1773).

11. Higginbotham, 1:230 (Hooper to Iredell, April 26, 1774), 1:lxi–lxii (ed. essay); Saunders, 9:743 (Speaker John Harvey to Governor Josiah Martin, December 9, 1773, on refusal to fund courts), 9:1037–38 (Edenton, Chowan County freeholders), 1043–49 (First Provincial Congress).

12. Higginbotham, 1:lxii–lxiii (ed. essay), 251–67 (Iredell's "To The Inhabitants of Great Britain," September 1774) (also in McRee, 1:205–20). On Blackstone's concept of parliamentary sovereignty, see William Blackstone, *Commentaries* (St. George Tucker ed., 1803, reprinted South Hackensack, N.J.: Rothman Reprints, 1969), 2:160–62 (Parliament has "sovereign and uncontrollable authority" and "can...do everything that is not naturally impossible"; "what the parliament doth, no authority upon earth can undo"). On the influence of this essay on the Third Provincial Congress in North Carolina, see Don Higginbotham, "Decision for Revolution," in Lindley S. Butler and Alan D. Watson, eds., *The North Carolina Experience: An Interpretive and Documentary History* (Chapel Hill: University of North Carolina Press, 1984), 129–30.

13. Higginbotham, 1:lxiv–lxv (ed. essay), 288 (Neilson to Iredell, February 4, 1775), 297 (Arthur Iredell to Iredell, April 25, 1775).

14. *Ibid.*, lxvi (ed. essay), 292 (Iredell to Hannah Iredell, March 31, 1775), 304 ("Subscription for a Post Rider, May 6, 1775); Saunders, 9:1141–42 (Proceedings of the Safety Committee in Chowan County, March 4, 1775).

15. Higginbotham, 1:lxvi, lxxi (ed. essay), 328–38 (Iredell's "Principles"); Henry S. Commager, ed., *Documents of American History* (New York: Appleton-Century-Crofts, 1973), 1:100–02 (Declaration).

16. Higginbotham, 1:lxxii (ed. essay), 346 (Hewes to Iredell, March 26, 1776), 354–55 (Iredell to Hewes, April 29, 1776).

17. Saunders, 9:1141–42 (Proceedings of the Safety Committee in Chowan County, March 4, 1775), 1282–85 (Proceedings of the Safety Committee in Mecklenburg County, May 31, 1775); Crow, 19–20, 24–25, 27; Higginbotham, 1:317 (Johnston to Iredell, September 5, 1775), 349–50 (Johnston to Iredell, April 17, 1776); Johnston to Joseph Hewes, March 3, 1776, Hayes Collection, SHC.

18. Higginbotham, 1:lviii, lxxiii, lxxvi–lxxvii (ed. essay); Don Higginbotham, "James Iredell's Efforts to Preserve the First British Empire," North Carolina Historical Review 49 (1972): 127, 127; McRee, 1:283 (ed. note).

19. Higginbotham, 1:lxxiii (ed. essay), 370–411 (Iredell's essay "Causes of the American Revolution").

20. *Ibid.*, 349 (Johnston to Iredell, April 13, 1776, and ed. note), 367–68 ("A Declaration By The Vestry of St. Paul's Church," Edenton, June 19, 1776) (also commemorated by a tablet presently in the church itself), 369 (Joseph Hewes to Iredell, June 28, 1776), 415 (Iredell to Thomas Jones, July 15, 1776), 415 (Jones to Iredell, July 23, 1776). See Maier, *supra* note 9, at 63, 217 (showing Halifax Resolves as first among state and local declarations of independence); Price, 430; Watson, "States' Rights," 251–52.

21. Act of May 9, 1777, ch. I, secs. XIV, XXI, 1777 N.C. Sess. Laws, reprinted in Clark, 24:3–5; Higginbotham, 1:lxxx (ed. essay), 462 (Iredell's exemption certificate).

22. *Ibid.*, 1:412 (John Johnston to Iredell, July 4, 1776), 414–15 (Iredell to Thomas Jones, July 15, 1776), 415–16 (Jones to Iredell, July 23, 1776), 417 (Jones to Iredell, August 17, 1776), 419 (Jasper Charlton to Iredell, August 24, 1776).

23. *Ibid.*, 1:lxxxii (ed. essay), 420–21 (Iredell's essay "Creed of a Rioter"), 422–23 (ed. note); William Hooper to Joseph Hewes, December 16 (?), 1776, typescript, NCAH; Saunders, 10:401 (Governor Josiah Martin to Lord George Germain, May 17, 1777); Wood, 83; Robert L. Ganyard, "Radicals and Conservatives in Revolutionary North Carolina: A Point at Issue, The October Election, 1776," William and Mary Quarterly 24 (Third Series, 1967): 568 (passim).

24. Higginbotham, 1:427–43 (Iredell's essay "To his Majesty...").

25. Act of Dec. 24, 1777, ch. VI, 1777 N.C. Sess. Laws, reprinted in Iredell, 321–26 (also in Clark, 24:84–89); Higginbotham, 1:454–55 (oath), 2:15 (Edenton grand jury to Iredell, May 1, 1778), 2:16–23 (charge). See Samuel A. Ashe, *History of North Carolina* (Greensboro, N.C.: Chas. L. Van Noppen, 1908; reprint, Spartanburg, S.C.: Reprint Co., 1971), 1:591–92; Helen B. Smith and Elizabeth V. Moore,

"John Mare: A Composite Portrait," North Carolina Historical Review 44 (1967): 18, 34.

26. Higginbotham, 2:45–48 (Iredell's "To the Commissioners of the King of Great Britain for restoring Peace, & c."), 48 (ed. note), 140 (Iredell to Hannah Iredell, April 13, 1780).

27. Ibid., 175, 177 (Iredell to Hannah Iredell, October 8, 1780), 178 n.4, 225–26 (ed. note), 226 (Jean Blair to Hannah Iredell, April 20, 1781), 234 (same, May 3, 1781), 236 (Johnston to Iredell, May 8, 1781), 243 (Alexander Black to Iredell, May 16, 1781), 260 (Johnston to Iredell, June 27, 1781), 284 (Iredell to Hannah Iredell, August 29, 1781).

28. Ibid., 245 (Jean Blair to Hannah Iredell, May 19, 1781), 251 (Jean Blair to Iredell, May 29, 1781), 266 (Jean Blair to Iredell, July 21, 1781), 297 (Archibald Maclaine to Iredell, September 21, 1781), 328 (William Hooper to Iredell, February 17, 1782).

29. Ibid., 291 (Iredell to Hannah Iredell, September 11, 1781), 294–95 (same, September 16, 1781), 295–96 (ed. note), 298 (Jasper Charlton to Iredell, September 21, 1781); Crow, 48. Governor and Mrs. Burke assisted Iredell during a portion of his illness, and the governor was apologetic when "necessary business" called him away. Iredell later reported that the governor had escaped from his captivity by boat and speculated that sentries had been bribed to allow him to pass unchallenged. McRee, 1:541–42 (Iredell to Hannah Iredell, September 11, 1781), 2:8 (same, February 11, 1782); John S. Watterson, III, "The Ordeal of Governor Burke," North Carolina Historical Review 48 (1971): 95, 104, 109–10.

30. Higginbotham, 2:293–94 (Johnston to Hannah Iredell, September 14, 1781), 317 (Butler to Iredell, November 16, 1781), 388 (Iredell to Hannah Iredell, April 10, 1783), 393 (same, April 16, 1783), 397–98 (Butler to Iredell, May 5, 1783), 417–18 (Iredell to Hannah Iredell, June 9, 1783).

31. Ibid., 430–32 (resolutions), 446–51 (instructions); Fitzpatrick, 26:483–96 (Washington's letter). See Higginbotham, 1:lxxxviii–lxxxix (ed. essay); Wood, 189–90 (use of instructions).

32. Higginbotham, 2:337–38 (Arthur Iredell to Iredell, April 30, 1782), 399 n.1, 424–25 (Iredell to Arthur Iredell, July 30, 1783), 428 (Iredell to Thomas Iredell, brother, July 30, 1783); McRee, 2:48 (Arthur Iredell to Iredell, May 30, 1783), 101 (Iredell to Thomas Iredell, uncle, May 28, 1784), 262 (Iredell to Lord MacCartney, July 15, 1789).

33. Higginbotham, 2:428 n.1, 438 (Arthur Iredell to Iredell, August 18, 1783), 458 (same, November 17, 1783), 470–71 (Iredell to Thomas Iredell, uncle, ca. November 1783); McRee, 2:101 (Iredell to Thomas Iredell, uncle, May 28, 1784), 134–37 (same, February 23, 1786); Iredell to Thomas Iredell, uncle, February 11, 1784, NCAH.

34. Higginbotham, 2:423 (Arthur Iredell to Iredell, July 28, 1783), 458–59 (same, November 17, 1783); Arthur Iredell to Iredell: February 18, 1784; January 29, 1786; July 2, 1787, NCAH; Marcus, 3:161 n.4.

35. Iredell to Thomas Iredell, February 11, 1784, NCAH; Higginbotham, 1:251–67 (Iredell's "To the Inhabitants of Great Britain"), 329 (Iredell's "Principles

of an American Whig"), 389 (Iredell's "Causes of the American Revolution"). See Fordham, "Political Ideas," 16; Herndon, 88–89.

CHAPTER 5
Ablest Defender of the Constitution

1. McRee, 2:35–36 (Nash to Iredell, January 18, 1783); C. Vann Woodward, *The Future of the Past* (New York: Oxford University Press, 1989), 133.

2. James G. Exum, Jr., and Gary R. Govert, "North Carolina and the Federal Constitution: A Commitment to Liberty," in A.E. Dick Howard, ed., *The Constitution in the Making: Perspectives of the Original Thirteen States* (Williamsburg: National Center for State Courts, 1993), 183, 187; Alpheus T. Mason, *The States Rights Debate: Antifederalism and the Constitution* (Englewood Cliffs, N.J.: Prentice-Hall, 1964), 11, 27.

3. McRee, 2:484 (Iredell's Charge to the Federal Grand Jury for the District of Virginia, Richmond, May 23, 1796); Henry McG. Wagstaff, *States Rights and Political Parties in North Carolina — 1776–1861* (Baltimore: Johns Hopkins Press, 1906), 14–15; Blackwell P. Robinson, "Willie Jones of Halifax, Part II," North Carolina Historical Review 18 (1941): 133, 146. See Fordham, "Political Ideas," 24.

4. McRee, 2:161 (Davie to Iredell, May 30, 1787 and June 19, 1787), 162 (Spaight to Iredell, July 3, 1787), 163 (Williamson to Iredell, July 8, 1787), 165 (Davie to Iredell, July 17, 1787; Iredell to Davie, July 19, 1787), 167 (Williamson to Iredell, July 22, 1787; Davie to Iredell, August 6, 1787), 168 (Spaight to Iredell, August 12, 1787), 172 (Iredell to Spaight, August 26, 1787); Clinton L. Rossiter, *1787: The Grand Convention* (New York: W.W. Norton & Co., 1987), 127, 150; Robinson, 180, 188–89; Trenholme, 95, 97.

5. McRee, 2:163 (Williamson to Iredell, July 8, 1787), 167 (same, July 22, 1787), 168 (Davie to Iredell, August 6, 1787; Spaight to Iredell, August 12, 1787).

6. *Ibid.*, 179 (ed. note); Trenholme, 100.

7. McRee, 2:104–05 (Iredell to Archibald Neilson, June 15, 1784), 170–71 (ed. note), 171–72 (Stephen Cabarrus to Iredell, August 18, 1787; Iredell to Cabarrus, August 21, 1787); Iredell to Pierce Butler, March 14, 1784, NCAH; Iredell to Whitmell Hill, May 1787, NCAH; Iredell to Stephen Cabarrus, August 18, 1787, NCAH; Iredell to James Cotton, August 20, 1787, NCAH; James Cotton to Iredell, August 20, 1787, NCAH; Trenholme, 100–02.

8. Trenholme, 120; Julian P. Boyd, ed., "A North Carolina Citizen on the Federal Constitution, 1788," North Carolina Historical Review 16 (1939): 36, 36, 53.

9. McRee, 2:180–81 (ed. note), 181–83 (Iredell's "Address to Grand Jury for the District of Edenton"). The Address is also published in Hugh T. Lefler, ed., *North Carolina History Told By Contemporaries* (Chapel Hill: University of North Carolina Press, 1934), 134–36.

10. Robert A. Rutland, ed., *The Papers of James Madison* (Chicago: University of Chicago Press, 1977), 10: 336–37 (Jefferson to Madison, December 20, 1787); Robert A. Rutland, *James Madison: The Founding Father* (New York: Macmillan

Publishing Co., 1987), 21, 23–27, 39, 91, 239; James Madison, *Debates in the Federal Convention of 1787* (James McClellan and M.E. Bradford, eds.) (Richmond: James River Press, 1989), 616–17. For Mason's objections and a brief biographical sketch, see Cecelia M. Kenyon, ed., *The Antifederalists* (Indianapolis: Bobbs-Merrill Co., 1966), 191–95, 236–37.

11. McRee, 2:186–88 (Iredell's "Answers to Mason's Objections") (Evans #45276).

12. *Ibid.*, 188–92.

13. *Ibid.*, 193.

14. *Ibid.*, 194–99.

15. *Ibid.*, 199–202.

16. *Ibid.*, 202–03.

17. *Ibid.*, 204–11. Iredell referred to the *Federalist* for a more complete treatment of the standing army question. He probably was alluding to Hamilton's "No. 8"; of the *Federalist* essays on this question, it alone predates Iredell's answers to Mason. See *The Federalist* No. 8, at 44–48 (Alexander Hamilton) (Jacob E. Cooke, ed., 1961).

18. McRee, 2:212.

19. *Ibid.*, 212–13.

20. *Ibid.*, 213–14; Levy, 151–52.

21. McRee, 2:214–15.

22. *Ibid.*, 186, 219 (ed. notes); McLean to Iredell, February 10, 1788, Duke; Witherspoon to Iredell, April 3, 1788, Duke (published in part in McRee, 2:221–22); *State Gazette of North Carolina*, Edenton, N.C., March 27, 1788, at 3 (advertising "Answers"); Connor, "James Iredell," 235; Lefler, 12; Watson, "States' Rights," 264; Weeks, 249. Forty-nine of the eighty-five *Federalist* essays postdate Iredell's "Answers"; compare McRee, 2:186, 215, with Jacob E. Cooke, ed., *The Federalist* (Middletown, Conn.: Wesleyan University Press, 1961).

CHAPTER 6

Acknowledged Leader for Ratification: Prefatory Skirmishes

1. McRee, 2:183 (Maclaine to Iredell, December 25, 1787), 185 (Hooper to Iredell, December 31, 1787), 215 (Davie to Iredell, January 11, 1788), 220 (Iredell's "To the Freemen of the Town of Edenton").

2. Clark, 20:128–29 (Governor Caswell to the General Assembly, November 21, 1787), 196–97, 369–74, 378–79; McRee, 2:224–25 (Thomas Iredell, brother, to Iredell, May 22, 1788); Trenholme, 104, 107.

3. McRee, 2:216 (Maclaine to Iredell, January 15, 1788), 217–18 (Davie to Iredell, January 22, 1788), 222 (Hooper to Iredell, April 15, 1788), 226 (Williamson to Iredell, June 11, 1788), 229 (Swann to Iredell, July 7, 1788). By convention time, Hooper had acquired a misplaced sanguineness and had "not a tittle of doubt" but that North Carolina would ratify. *Ibid.*, 229 (Hooper to Iredell, July 8, 1788).

4. *Ibid.*, 223–24 (Davie to Iredell, May 1, 1788). It is not known whether the pamphlet was printed, and so far as is known, it does not survive. Trenholme, 124.

5. McRee, 2:224 (Davie to Iredell, May 1, 1788), 225–26 (Maclaine to Iredell, June 4, 1788), 227–28 (Williamson to Iredell, July 7, 1788), 230 (Davie to Iredell, July 9, 1788).

6. *Ibid.*, 218 (Davie to Iredell, January 22, 1788), 219 (Maclaine to Iredell, March 4, 1788), 230 (Davie to Iredell, July 9, 1788), 598–99 (Johnson to Iredell, January 14, 1788); Trenholme, 124–25.

7. McRee, 2:216 (Maclaine to Iredell, January 15, 1788), 231 (Davie to Iredell, July 9, 1788); Michael Lienesch, "North Carolina: Preserving Rights," in Gillespie and Lienesch, 343, 347–48; Trenholme, 129–30. The papers are *Martin's North-Carolina Gazette*, December 19, 1787, and the *Wilmington Centinel and General Advertiser*, June 18, 1788; see Trenholme, 130 n.134.

8. McRee, 2:148 (Iredell's "TO THE PUBLIC" essay); Higginbotham, 1:74 (Iredell to Francis Iredell, Sr., July 31, 1771) (law as science in Blackstone); Pratt, 580–81, 587; Berger, *Government*, 252; G. Edward White, *Patterns of American Legal Thought* (Indianapolis: Bobbs-Merrill Co., 1978), 10, 20, 33, 66.

9. Elliot, 4:1–4; Pratt, 587. For a summary account of the North Carolina ratification convention, see Bernard Schwartz, *The Bill of Rights: A Documentary History* (New York: Chelsea House, 1971), 2:932–77; for biographical sketches of the delegates, see Stephen E. Massengill, *North Carolina Votes on the Constitution: A Roster of Delegates to the State Ratification Conventions of 1788 and 1789* (Raleigh: N.C. Division of Archives and History, 1988).

10. Elliot, 4:4–7; Connor, "James Iredell," 236; Pratt, 587; Trenholme, 147, 166; Watson, "States' Rights," 260–61.

11. Elliot, 4:7–15.

12. *Ibid.*, 4:15, 250 (Nixon); Trenholme, 147–50; David Witherspoon to Iredell, April 3, 1788, Duke (mentions Nixon as antifederalist delegate); Alexander B. Andrews, "Richard Dobbs Spaight," North Carolina Historical Review 1 (1924): 95, 109.

13. Elliot, 4:29–30, 33; Trenholme, 166–67; Alden, 398–99.

14. Elliot, 4:15–23, 26–28.

15. *Ibid.*, 4:32–37.

16. *Ibid.*, 4:37–42.

17. *Ibid.*, 4:50–72. Iredell's admonition on construing statutes so as to avoid absurd results remains a viable maxim. "It is fully established that 'the language of a statute will be interpreted so as [to] avoid an absurd consequence.'" *Taylor v. Crisp*, 286 N.C. 488, 496, 212 S.E.2d 381, 386 (1975) (quoting *State v. Spencer*, 276 N.C. 535, 547, 173 S.E.2d 765, 773 (1970)).

18. Elliot, 4:73.

19. *Ibid.*, 4:74–75.

20. *Ibid.*, 4:75–94; on the scarcity of hard money, see Lefler and Newsome, 103, 146, 276.

21. Elliot, 4:95–99.

22. *Ibid.*, 4:100–01.

23. *Ibid.*, 4:106–10.

24. *Ibid.*, 4:110–14.

25. *Ibid.*, 4:114, 125, 130.
26. *Ibid.*, 4:131–34.
27. *Ibid.*, 4:136–37.

CHAPTER 7

Acknowledged Leader for Ratification: The Real Objection

1. Elliot, 4:137–38.
2. *Ibid.*, 4:139–44.
3. *Ibid.*, 4:144–49.
4. *Ibid.*, 4:165–67.
5. *Ibid.*, 4:168–72.
6. *Ibid.*, 4:176–78.
7. *Ibid.*, 4:178–80, 185–88.
8. *Ibid.*, 4:191–96; Powell, 125 (Abbot).
9. Elliot, 4:196–98, 250 (Abbot's vote for ratification).
10. *Ibid.*, 4:200–16; Watson, "States' Rights," 262 (Spaight).
11. Elliott, 4:216–17.
12. *Ibid.*, 4:217–18.
13. *Ibid.*, 4:218–23.
14. *Ibid.*, 4:223–26; see Julian P. Boyd, ed., *The Papers of Thomas Jefferson* (Princeton: Princeton University Press, 1955), 12:569–70 (Jefferson to Madison, February 6, 1788); Price, 425.
15. Elliot, 4:226–28.
16. *Ibid.*, 4:228–34.
17. *Ibid.*, 4:234–38.
18. *Ibid.*, 4:240–49.
19. *Ibid.*, 4:250–52; Powell, 227.
20. Trenholme, 163–64.
21. Clark, 20:197, 22:26, 28–29, 33; A. Roger Ekirch, *"Poor Carolina": Politics and Society in Colonial North Carolina, 1729–1776* (Chapel Hill: University of North Carolina Press, 1981), 39; Herndon, 168–70; Charles E. Johnson, "History of the Capitol," The North Carolina Booklet (North Carolina Society Daughters of the Revolution, 1905), 5:73–75, 80; Houston G. Jones, *For History's Sake* (Chapel Hill: University of North Carolina Press, 1966), 74; Powell, 146–47.

CHAPTER 8

Acknowledged Leader for Ratification: Fatal Disunion Remedied

1. Johnston to Iredell, November 20, 1788, NCAH (published in part in McRee, 2:246–47); McRee, 2:254 (Iredell to Steele, February 17, 1789). Steele subsequently assured Iredell that his gratitude had been duly conveyed to all who shared in the name proposal. Steele to Iredell, September 26, 1789, Duke.

2. McRee, 2:258 (Arthur Iredell to Iredell, May 30, 1789), 267–68 (same, October 6, 1789).

3. *Ibid.*, 2:248 (Williamson to Iredell, January 5, 1789), 263–64 (Butler to Iredell, August 11, 1789), 265 (Williamson to Iredell, August 12, 1789), 267 (Steele to Iredell, September 26, 1789).

4. *Ibid.*, 2:254 (Iredell to Steele, February 17, 1789).

5. Elliot, 4:4, 143, 217; Gillespie and Lienesch, 349; Powell, 225.

6. Elliot, 4:150, 152; Gillespie and Lienesch, 351, 359.

7. Iredell to Hannah Iredell, August 3, 1788, Duke; McRee, 2:240 (Maclaine to Iredell, September 13, 1788).

8. Gillespie and Lienesch, 343; McRee, 2:241–42 (Williamson to Iredell, September 22, 1788); Robert A. Rutland, *The Ordeal of the Constitution* (Norman: University of Oklahoma Press, 1966), 281 (citing Jeremiah Hill to George Thatcher, August 29, 1788, Thatcher Papers, Boston Public Library); Robert A. Rutland and Charles F. Hobson, eds., *The Papers of James Madison* (Charlottesville: University Press of Virginia, 1977), 11:238 (Madison to Jefferson, August 23, 1788), 246 (Gordon to Madison, August 31, 1788); Trenholme, 192 n.3, 193, 196; *Warren-Adams Letters* (Massachusetts Historical Society, 1925), 2:303 (James Winthrop to Mercy Warren, August 26, 1788).

9. McRee, 2:236 (Williamson to Iredell, July 26, 1788), 241–42 (same, September 22, 1788), 255 (same, March 2, 1789); Powell, 229; Trenholme, 216–17, 226, 230–32.

10. McRee, 2:236 (Williamson to Iredell, August 23, 1788), 238 (Hooper to Iredell, September 2, 1788); Iredell to Pierce Butler, July 25, 1789, NCAH.

11. McRee, 2:240 (Maclaine to Iredell, September 13, 1788), 241 (Swann to Iredell, September 21, 1788).

12. Lefler, 21–38. This essay has not been attributed to Iredell with unequivocal certainty. Lefler believed it to be Iredell's, and the present author is so convinced almost beyond doubt. Iredell's correspondence indicates that by late August 1788, he had prepared and distributed an address to the people of the state on the consequences of failure to ratify. McRee, 2:240 (John Swann to Iredell, September 21, 1788). This essay is dated August 18, 1788. Lefler, 38. As Lefler notes, "[t]he style, nature of the argument, and other evidence [also] point to Iredell's authorship." *Ibid.*, 15–16.

13. *Ibid.*, 16; McRee, 2:240 (Swann to Iredell, September 21, 1788).

14. Davie to Iredell, December 19, 1788, and December 21, 1789, Duke, and January 23, 1789, Emmet Collection, New York Public Library (copy in Davie Papers, SHC); Iredell to Hugh Williamson, January 22, 1789, NCAH; Maclaine to Iredell, February 22, 1789, Duke; Powell, 228.

15. McRee, 2:262 (Maclaine to Iredell, August 11, 1789), 265 (Hugh Williamson to Iredell, August 12, 1789), 269 (Arthur Iredell to Iredell, November 3, 1789), 279 (same, February 2, 1790); Arthur Iredell to Iredell, February 2, 1790, NCAH; John C. Cavanagh, *Decision at Fayetteville: The North Carolina Ratification Convention and General Assembly of 1789* (Raleigh: N.C. Division of Archives and History, 1989), 11; Trenholme, 197. An advertisement of the publication appeared

first in the July 2, 1789, issue of the *State Gazette of North Carolina* and in numerous issues thereafter.

16. McRee, 2:236 (ed. note); Samuel Johnston to Iredell, November 14, 1788, NCAH; Iredell to Hugh Williamson, January 22, 1789, NCAH; Archibald Maclaine to Iredell, September 15, 1789, Duke; Cavanagh, *supra* note 15, at 11; Clark, 21:94–95, 22:39; *State Gazette of North Carolina*, Edenton, N.C., April 2, 1789, at 3.

17. McRee, 2:238 (Hooper to Iredell, September 2, 1788), 243–44 (Maclaine to Iredell, October 27, 1788); Trenholme, 199.

18. McRee, 2:239 (William R. Davie to Iredell, September 8, 1788), 245 (Johnston to Iredell, November 8, 1788); Powell, 225; Watson, "States' Rights," 260.

19. McRee, 2:246 (Maclaine to Iredell, November 17, 1788).

20. *Ibid.*, 2:246 (Johnston to Iredell, November 20, 1788); Clark, 20:v, 22:iii (ed. notes); Act of Nov. 20, 1788, 1788 N.C. Sess. Laws, reprinted in Iredell, 653 (incorrectly shows date as 1789; 1788 is correct—see Francis-Xavier Martin, *The Public Acts of the General Assembly of North Carolina* (New Bern, N.C.: Martin & Ogden, 1804), 1:460); Lefler and Newsome, 269.

21. McRee, 2:248 (Williamson to Iredell, January 5, 1789), 249 (Iredell to William Cumming, January 6, 1789), 254 (Maclaine to Iredell, February 22, 1789); Iredell to Butler, July 25, 1789, NCAH; Iredell to Hannah Iredell, October 22, 1789, NCAH.

22. McRee, 2:258–59 (Lowther to Iredell, May 9, 1789), 260 (Davie to Iredell, June 4, 1789), 265 (Butler to Iredell, August 11, 1789); Davie to Madison, June 10, 1789, Davie Papers, SHC; Price, 438.

23. McRee, 2:248 (Williamson to Iredell, January 5, 1789), 254 (Maclaine to Iredell, February 22, 1789), 267 (Steele to Iredell, September 26, 1789).

24. *Ibid.*, 241 (Swann to Iredell, September 21, 1788), 260 (Lowther to Iredell, July 1, 1789), 265 (Butler to Iredell, August 11, 1789), 266 (John Williams to Iredell, September 11, 1789).

25. *State Gazette of North Carolina*, Edenton, N.C., July 9, 1789, at 2–3; Abbot and Twohig, 3:47–48 (Washington to the Governor and Council of North Carolina, June 19, 1789), 48–49 (ed. note).

26. McRee, 2:266 (Maclaine to Iredell, September 15, 1789), 267 (Steele to Iredell, September 26, 1789), 271 (Johnston to Iredell, November 13, 1789; Davie to Iredell, November 16, 1789); Price, 438.

27. Clark, 22:48–49; William R. Davie to Iredell, November 22, 1789, Duke; William Dawson to Iredell, November 22, 1789, Duke; Samuel Johnston to Iredell, November 23, 1789, Duke (Dawson and Davie stated the vote as 193 to 75; the official record shows it as 195 to 77); Lefler and Newsome, 269; Newsome, 299.

28. Forrest McDonald, *We the People: The Economic Origins of the Constitution* (Chicago: University of Chicago Press, 1958), 113–15, 310–21; Newsome, 296–99; Lefler and Newsome, 269; Price, 438–39; Watson, "States' Rights," 264–65.

29. McRee, 2:272 (Dawson to Iredell, November 22, 1789; Johnston to Iredell, November 23, 1789), 273 (Johnson to Iredell, November 23, 1789; Spaight to Iredell, November 26, 1789); Maclaine to Iredell, November 26, 1789, NCAH.

30. *State Gazette of North Carolina*, Edenton, N.C., December 3, 1789, at 2; Trenholme, 241; Watson, "States' Rights," 265.

31. Iredell to Hannah Iredell, November 26, 1789, NCAH.

CHAPTER 9
A High and Important Office

1. McRee, 2:264 (Butler to Iredell, August 11, 1789), 265 (Williamson to Iredell, August 12, 1789), 275 (Maclaine to Iredell, December 9, 1789); Iredell to Henry McCulloh, March 31, 1790, NCAH; Abbot and Twohig, 4:58 (Williamson to Washington, September 19, 1789), 5:184 (Martin to Washington, February 27, 1790).

2. McRee, 2:274–75 (Johnston to Iredell, December 1, 1789).

3. Jared Sparks, ed., *The Writings of George Washington* (Boston: Russell, Shattuck, and Williams, 1836), 10:26 (Washington to Madison, August 10 (?), 1789), 34 (Washington to Randolph, September 27, 1789).

4. McRee, 2:260 (Lowther to Iredell, July 1, 1789); Richard B. Bernstein and Kym S. Rice, *Are We To Be a Nation? The Making of the Constitution* (Cambridge: Harvard University Press, 1987), 260.

5. Felix Frankfurter, "The Supreme Court in the Mirror of Justices," in Jesse H. Choper, ed., *The Supreme Court And Its Justices* (Chicago: American Bar Association, 1987), 139. For commentary generally agreeing that Washington had appointed worthy individuals, see Bates, 47; Casto, 54–70; Warren, *History*, 44–46.

6. Bernstein and Rice, *supra* note 4, at 260. See also Douglas S. Freeman, *George Washington: A Biography* (New York: Charles Scribner's Sons, 1954), 6:253, 253 n.95; Haines, *Role of Supreme Court*, 1:121; Julius J. Marke, *Vignettes of Legal History* (South Hackensack, N.J.: Fred B. Rothman & Co., 1965), 53; Warren, *History*, 42–43.

7. Higginbotham, 1:346 (Hewes to Iredell, March 26, 1776), 354 (Iredell to Hewes, April 29, 1776).

8. McRee, 2:272 (Johnston to Iredell, November 23, 1789), 278 (same, January 30, 1790), 284 (same, March 4, 1790); Johnston to Iredell, November 29, 1789, NCAH, and February 4, 1790, Duke.

9. McRee, 2:281 (Johnston to Iredell, February 1, 1790); Johnston to Iredell, February 7, 1790, NCAH (McRee's omission of this letter is puzzling; it is one of the more-significant ones in the Iredell papers).

10. Johnston to Iredell, February 11, 1790, NCAH, and March 6, 1790, Duke; McRee, 2:279–80 (ed. note).

11. Fitzpatrick, 31:10–11 (Washington to Iredell, February 13, 1790); McRee, 2:284 (Iredell to Washington, March 3, 1790).

12. Sidney H. Asch, *The Supreme Court and its Great Justices* (New York: Arco Publishing Co., 1971), 18; Ashe, 2:201; Baker, 171; Bates, 46; Carson, 154–55; Friedman and Israel, 127–28; Donald Jackson and Dorothy Twohig, eds., *The Diaries of George Washington* (Charlottesville: University Press of Virginia, 1979), 6:28–29; Lefler, 12; Shnayerson, 65.

13. Johnston to Iredell, March 6 and 18, 1790, Duke; March 21, 1790, NCAH.

14. McRee, 2:280 (Butler to Iredell, February 10, 1790), 287 (Ashe to Iredell, April 10, 1790); Swann to Iredell, March 5, 1790, Duke; Maclaine to Iredell, March 10, 1790, NCAH; Blount to Iredell, March 24, 1790, NCAH; Spencer to Iredell, April 9, 1790, NCAH.

15. Hay to Iredell, March 24, 1790, NCAH; Haywood to Iredell, April 10, 1790, Duke.

16. Alice B. Keith, ed., *The John Gray Blount Papers* (Raleigh: N.C. Department of Archives and History, 1959), 2:15 (Hawkins to Blount, February 11, 1790).

17. Arthur Iredell to Iredell, May 5, 1790, NCAH.

18. Jay to Iredell, March 10, 1790, Duke.

19. Iredell to Williamson, August 29, 1789, NCAH.

20. Iredell to Thomas Iredell, March 8, 1790, NCAH.

21. Iredell to Henry McCulloh, March 31, 1790, NCAH; Iredell to Rutledge, April 9, 1790, Duke; Iredell to Jay, March 3 and April 8, 1790, NCAH.

22. Iredell to Henry McCulloh, March 31, 1790, NCAH; Maclaine to Iredell, March 10, 1790, NCAH; Davie to Iredell, April 20, 1790, Duke; *State Gazette of North Carolina*, Edenton, N.C., April 10, at 4; May 21, at 3; and May 28, at 4, 1790 (notices).

CHAPTER 10

An Associate of Presidents

1. Iredell to Hannah Iredell, February 13 and October 21, 1787, NCAH.

2. McRee, 2:283 (Archibald Neilson to Iredell, February 28, 1790), 307 (Arthur Iredell to Iredell, February 1, 1791), 332 (Johnston to Iredell, May 23, 1791); Arthur Iredell to Iredell, June 3, 1794, NCAH; Johnston to Iredell, May 10, 1792 and March 26, 1796, NCAH; Abbot and Twohig, 7:473 (ed. note), 480–82 (Iredell memorandum regarding routes).

3. McRee, 2:474–75 (Iredell to Hannah Iredell, April 15, 1796), 513 (same, May 25, 1797); Iredell to Hannah Iredell, March 18, 1796, NCAH.

4. Abbot and Twohig, 5:313–14 (Washington to the United States Supreme Court, April 3, 1790).

5. McRee, 2:338–41 (Iredell to Washington, January 23, 1792); Goebel, 546. See Cibes, 128–29.

6. Iredell to Washington, September 20, 1790, Washington Papers, Library of Congress (published in Elizabeth G. McPherson, ed., "Unpublished Letters from North Carolinians to Washington," North Carolina Historical Review 12 (1935): 149, 160–61).

7. McRee, 2:441 (Iredell to Hannah Iredell, March 30, 1795), 460 (same, February 20, 1796), 491 (same, February 9, 1797); Hannah Iredell to Helen (Nelly) Blair Tredwell, November 15, 1791, NCAH; Iredell to Hannah Iredell, September 8, 1791, and July 17, 1795, NCAH. See Baker, 301–02, 339.

8. McRee, 2:440 (Iredell to Hannah Iredell, February 26, 1795), 493 (same, February 24, 1797); Iredell to Hannah Iredell, February 26, 1796, NCAH. See

Baker, 233–34; John W. Tebbel, *George Washington's America* (New York: E.P. Dutton & Co., 1954), 357, 369–70.

9. Helen (Nelly) Blair Tredwell to Iredell, March 4, 1797, NCAH.

10. Harold C. Syrett, ed., *The Papers of Alexander Hamilton* (New York: Columbia University Press, 1965), 9:503 (Davie to Hamilton, November 17, 1791); McRee, 2:336 (Hodge to Iredell, December 1, 1791), 342 (Rev. Adam Boyd to Iredell, February 15, 1792); Davie to Iredell, December 2, 1790, Davie Papers, SHC; Pendleton to Iredell, March 5, 1791, Duke.

11. McRee, 2:426 (ed. note); Syrett, *supra* note 10, at 14:230 (1969) (Coxe to Hamilton, March 22, 1793). See Cibes, 133.

12. McRee, 2:449 (Iredell to Hannah Iredell, July 24, 1795), 460 (same, February 19 and 20, 1796), 462 (Johnston to Iredell, February 27, 1796); Arthur Iredell to Iredell: September 1, 1795; December 1, 1795; and April 5, 1796, NCAH; Iredell to Helen (Nelly) Blair Tredwell, March 25, 1796, NCAH (McRee, 2:465, incorrectly shows this letter going to Hannah). See Henry J. Abraham, *Justices and Presidents: A Political History of Appointments to the Supreme Court* (New York: Oxford University Press, 2nd ed., 1985), 75; Warren, *History*, 124–41.

13. McRee, 2:328 (Iredell to John Hay, April 14, 1791).

14. *Ibid.*, 329.

15. Thomas P. Abernathy, *The South in the New Nation, 1789–1819* (Baton Rouge: Louisiana State University Press, 1961), 217–24; Jeffrey J. Crow, "The Whiskey Rebellion in North Carolina," North Carolina Historical Review 66 (1989): 1, 6–7, 12–13, 28.

16. McRee, 2:307–20 (Iredell's "TO THE CITIZENS...").

17. *Ibid.*, 2:427 (Iredell to Hannah Iredell, August 3, 1794), 428 (Johnston to Iredell, September 10, October 1 and 15, 1794), 430 (same, November 26, 1794), 431 (same, December 10, 1794).

18. *Ibid.*, 2:431 (Davie to Iredell, December 15, 1794), 432 (Iredell to Lee, December 26, 1794), 437 (Lee to Iredell, January 21, 1795).

19. *Ibid.*, 2:469–70 (Iredell's Charge to Grand Jury for the District of Pennsylvania, Philadelphia, April 12, 1796).

20. *Ibid.*, 2:320 (Iredell's "TO THE CITIZENS...").

21. *Ibid.*, 2:491–92 (Iredell to Hannah Iredell, February 9, 1797), 493 (same, February 17, 1797), 494 (same, March 3, 1797), 496 (Iredell to Samuel Tredwell, March 10, 1797); Iredell to Samuel Tredwell, March 3, 1797, NCAH. As to Iredell's electoral votes, see McRee, 2:482 (ed. note); Edward Stanwood, *A History of the Presidency* (Clifton, N.J.: Augustus M. Kelley, 1975) (2 vols., revised ed. by Charles Knowles Bolton), 1:51; H.G. Jones, "Tar Heels Popular in 1796," *The Durham Sun*, Durham, N.C., December 4, 1985, at 8–C.

22. McRee, 2:537 (Lee to Iredell, September 20, 1798); Iredell to Hannah Iredell, January 24, 1799, NCAH (in McRee, 2:543, in part).

23. Iredell to Thomas Iredell (uncle), December 26, 1796, and Iredell to Arthur Iredell (brother), February 11, 1797, James Iredell Association, Inc., Edenton, N.C.

24. Charles Francis Adams, ed., *Letters of John Adams Addressed to his Wife* (Boston: Charles C. Little and James Brown, 1841), 2:226–27 (Adams to Abigail

Adams, April 30, 1796); McRee, 2:475 n.*; Smith, *Adams*, 891–92; Iredell to Hannah Iredell, April 29, 1796, Duke.

25. McRee, 2:494 (ed. note); Baker, 344; *Columbian Centinel*, Boston, Ma., March 15, 1797, at 2; Helen (Nelly) Blair Tredwell to Iredell, March 4, 1797, NCAH; Johnston to Iredell, March 11, 1797, NCAH.

26. McRee, 2:495 (Paterson to Iredell, March 7, 1797), 496 (Iredell to Samuel Tredwell, March 10, 1797); Iredell to Hannah Iredell, February 9, 1797, NCAH.

27. McRee, 2:480 (Davie to Iredell, November 11, 1796); Johnston to Iredell, August 4, 1798, NCAH.

28. Peter Browne to Iredell, August 11, 1798, NCAH; Thomas Iredell to Iredell, August 17, 1798, NCAH.

29. McRee, 2:536 (Lee to Iredell, September 20, 1798); Johnston to Iredell, November 21, 1798 and May 18, 1799, NCAH.

30. Cibes, 137; Johnston to Iredell, February 2, 1799, NCAH.

31. McRee, 2:542 (Johnston to Iredell, December 24, 1798), 550 (same, March 23, 1799); Johnston to Iredell, March 16, 1799, NCAH.

32. McRee, 2:520 (Iredell to Hannah Iredell, February 5, 1798); Iredell to Hannah Iredell, March 29, 1797 and February 28, 1799, NCAH; Johnston to Iredell, July 28, 1798, NCAH.

CHAPTER 11

Overt Partisanship from the Bench

1. *Debates and Proceedings in the Congress of the United States, Eighth Congress, Second Session* (Washington: Gales and Seaton, 1852), 556–58; *Trial of Samuel Chase, An Associate Justice of the Supreme Court of the United States* (Washington: Samuel H. Smith, 1805; reprint, New York: Da Capo Press, 1970), 2:326–28; Worthington C. Ford, ed., *Writings of John Quincy Adams* (New York: Macmillan Company, 1914), 3:116 (John Quincy Adams to John Adams, March 14, 1805). See generally Beveridge, 3:206; George L. Haskins and Herbert A. Johnson, *History of the Supreme Court: Foundations of Power: John Marshall, 1801–15* (New York: Macmillan, 1981), 213–34, 238–45; William H. Rehnquist, *Grand Inquests: The Historic Impeachments of Justice Samuel Chase and President Andrew Johnson* (New York: William Morrow and Co., 1992), 15–134. On the function of Supreme Court justices on circuit as representatives of the new federal government, see R. Kent Newmyer, "Justice Joseph Story on Circuit and a Neglected Phase of American Legal History," American Journal of Legal History 14 (1970): 112, 114–15, 124, 133–35.

2. Jay, 101–03; McRee, 2:431 (Davie to Iredell, December 15, 1794), 435 (ed. essay); Warren, *History*, 58–59 (quoting *Farmer's Weekly Museum*, Walpole, N.H., June 17, 1799), 273–76; White, *AJT*, 8.

3. Claude G. Bowers, Address to North Carolina Bar Association, May 5, 1927, in Henry M. London, ed., *Proceedings of the Twenty-Ninth Annual Session of the North Carolina Bar Association* (Raleigh: Mitchell Printing Co., 1927), 39.

4. File captioned "James Iredell, Sr. — U.S. Circuit Court Papers 1790–1799 —

Addresses to Grand Jury," NCAH (Trenton, April 2, 1793; Philadelphia, April 11, 1793; Annapolis, May 7, 1793). The Annapolis charge is published in McRee, 2:386 (quoted portions at 387).

5. McRee, 2:348 (Iredell's Charge to the Grand Jury for the District of Georgia, Savannah, April 26, 1792). For another Iredell charge on this theme, see *ibid.*, 366 (Charge to the Grand Jury for the District of Massachusetts, Boston, October 12, 1792).

6. *Ibid.*, 468–69 (Iredell's Charge to the Grand Jury for the District of Pennsylvania, Philadelphia, April 12, 1796). For another Iredell charge on this theme, see *ibid.*, 367–68 (Charge to the Grand Jury for the District of Massachusetts, Boston, October 12, 1792).

7. *Ibid.*, 410–14 (Iredell's Charge to the Grand Jury for the District of North Carolina, Raleigh, June 2, 1794).

8. *Ibid.*, 501–02 (Iredell's Charge to the Grand Jury for the District of Pennsylvania, Philadelphia, April 11, 1797).

9. *Ibid.*, 547 (Iredell to Hannah Iredell, March 14, 1799); Iredell to Hannah Iredell, April 11, 1799, NCAH. See also McRee, 2:549 (Justice Samuel Chase to Iredell, March 17, 1799; Robert Lenox to Iredell, March 20, 1799). See generally Smith, *Adams*, 1004, 1006–07, 1010, 1033–34.

10. McRee, 2:551, 568–70 (Iredell's Charge to the Grand Jury for the District of Pennsylvania, Philadelphia, April 11, 1799).

11. Marcus, 3:319–20 (ed. essay), 361 (Iredell to Hannah Iredell, May 11, 1799); McRee, 2:573 (Iredell to Hannah Iredell, April 25, 1799), 576 (Ellsworth to Iredell, June 10, 1799); Iredell to Hannah Iredell, April 18 and May 2, 1799, NCAH; Samuel Johnston to Iredell, May 18 and 25, 1799, NCAH.

12. McRee, 2:553–57 (Iredell's Charge to the Grand Jury for the District of Pennsylvania, Philadelphia, April 11, 1799); Lefler and Newsome, 280–82; Smith, *Adams*, 975–76.

13. McRee, 2:560–66 (Iredell's Charge to the Grand Jury for the District of Pennsylvania, Philadelphia, April 11, 1799).

14. File marked "James Iredell, Sr. — U.S. Circuit Court Papers 1790–1799 — Addresses to Grand Jury," NCAH (Richmond, November 23, 1795).

15. File marked "James Iredell, Sr. — U.S. Circuit Court Papers. 1795 June. Mass. Circuit Court," NCAH ("Address to Joseph Wood in pronouncing sentence upon him," Boston, June 16, 1795).

16. McRee, 2:483–86 (Iredell's Charge to the Grand Jury for the District of Virginia, Richmond, May 23, 1796), 508–09 (same, May 22, 1797).

17. Bates, 80; Felix Frankfurter and James M. Landis, *The Business of the Supreme Court: A Study in the Federal Judicial System* (New York: Macmillan Co., 1928), 20; Haines, *Role of Supreme Court*, 175–77; Higginbotham, 2:24 (ed. note); Warren, *History*, 163–64; Alan F. Westin, "Out-of-Court Commentary by United States Supreme Court Justices, 1790–1962: Of Free Speech and Judicial Lockjaw," Columbia Law Review 62 (1962): 633, 640–41.

18. McRee, 2:510–11 (ed. note), 511–13 (Iredell's "TO THE PUBLIC," June 21, 1797), 515 (Johnston to Iredell, July 5, 1797).

19. *The Independent Chronicle and the Universal Advertiser*, Boston, Ma., October 18, 1792, at 3; *State Gazette of North Carolina*, Edenton, N.C., November 30, 1792, at 1; McRee, 2:426 (Lee to Iredell, July 22, 1794); T.J. Guignard to Iredell, August 22, 1794, Duke; Iredell to Hannah Iredell, April 21, 1797, Duke; Davie to Iredell, June 25, 1797, Duke.

20. McRee, 2:570 (Grand Jury for Pennsylvania, Philadelphia, to Iredell, May 15, 1799), 570-71 (Iredell to Grand Jury for Pennsylvania, Philadelphia, May 15, 1799). See also *ibid.*, 408-09 (similar request from Grand Jury for North Carolina, June 2, 1794); Iredell to Hannah Iredell: October 21, 1791; April 28, 1792 (in McRee, 2:346, in part); October 25, 1792; and May 8, 1798, NCAH (all referring to appreciation for or publication of charges). For an example of a published Iredell charge, see *State Gazette of North Carolina*, Edenton, N.C., November 30, 1792, at 1.

21. McRee, 2:375 (Arthur Iredell to Iredell, December 4, 1792); Arthur Iredell to Iredell, March 31, 1794, NCAH.

22. McRee, 2:224-25 (Thomas Iredell, brother, to Iredell, May 22, 1788); Powell, 231-32, 234; Christopher T. Graebe, "The Federalism of James Iredell in Historical Context," North Carolina Law Review 69 (1990): 251, 262.

23. McRee, 2:514 (Davie to Iredell, June 25, 1797), 577 (same, June 17, 1799).

24. Casto, Chapter 4 (*passim*), 213, 249-53; Herbert A. Johnson, *The Chief Justiceship of John Marshall 1801-1835* (Columbia: University of South Carolina Press, 1997), 68; White, "Working Life," 20.

CHAPTER 12

Not a Time of Great Decisions

1. 2 U.S. (2 Dall.) at 400-02 (reporter's notes); Marcus, 1(#1):182-83, 340-41, 6:1. See Campbell, 3; Warren, *History*, 51.

2. Marcus, 1(#2):754 (Iredell to Hannah Iredell, March 6, 1795), 755 (Iredell to Helen Tredwell, March 7, 1795), 755 n.1 (Iredell to Hannah Iredell, May 7, 1795), 845 (same, March 11, 1796), 854 (same, July 29, 1796), 855 (same, August 5, 1796); McRee, 2:452 (same, August 13, 1795).

3. McRee, 2:477-78 (Iredell to Hannah Iredell, August 3, 1796); Iredell to Hannah Iredell, February 20, 1795, and February 8, 1798, NCAH.

4. Casto, 110-12 (foreshadowing); Goebel, 777; White, *AJT*, 201; White, "Working Life," 42 n.153.

5. Currie, 3; Marcus, 6:3.

6. *Ibid.*, 9 (citing 131 U.S. App. at xvi (1889)), 9 n.29; 2 U.S. (2 Dall.) at 480 (reporter's note); *Calder v. Bull*, 3 U.S. (3 Dall.) 386, 398 (1798) (Iredell, J.).

7. *Huger v. South Carolina*, 3 U.S. (3 Dall.) 339, 341-42 (1797); *Del Col v. Arnold*, 3 U.S. (3 Dall.) 333, 335 (1796).

8. *E.g.*, *Hills v. Ross*, 3 U.S. (3 Dall.) 331, 331 (1796); *Olney v. Arnold*, 3 U.S. (3 Dall.) 308, 318 (1796); *Cotton v. Wallace*, 3 U.S. (3 Dall.) 302, 304 (1796).

9. *Chisholm v. Georgia*, 2 U.S. (2 Dall.) 419, 429 (1793) (Iredell, J., dissenting).

10. *Georgia v. Brailsford*, 2 U.S. (2 Dall.) 402 (1792).

11. Pendleton to Iredell, June 22, 1792, Duke; see Marcus, 6:102 n.

12. *Brailsford*, 2 U.S. (2 Dall.) at 405–06.

13. *Ibid.*, 404–05. See Bates, 57; van Santvoord, 56; Warren, *History*, 103.

14. *Brailsford*, 2 U.S. (2 Dall.) at 405–08.

15. *Ibid.*, 406.

16. *Ibid.*, 407–09.

17. Moncure D. Conway, *Omitted Chapters of History Disclosed in the Life and Papers of Edmund Randolph* (New York: G.P. Putnam's Sons, 1888), 168 (Randolph to Madison, August 12, 1792) (also in Marcus, 6:130). See Bates, 57–58; Warren, *History*, 103–04.

18. *Georgia v. Brailsford*, 2 U.S. (2 Dall.) 415 (1793).

19. *Ibid.*, 418–19.

20. *Ibid.*, 415–17 (Iredell, J., dissenting). See Haines, *Role of Supreme Court*, 123; Percival E. Jackson, *Dissent in the Supreme Court: A Chronology* (Norman: University of Oklahoma Press, 1969), 20.

21. *Brailsford*, 2 U.S. (2 Dall.) at 418 (Blair, J., dissenting).

22. *Ibid.*, 406 (Iredell, J.); *Georgia v. Brailsford*, 3 U.S. (3 Dall.) 1, 1–5 (1794). See Bates, 58; McRee, 2:358–59 (ed. essay); van Santvoord, 57; Warren, *History*, 104.

23. *Brailsford*, 3 U.S. (3 Dall.) at 3.

24. *Bingham v. Cabbot*, 3 U.S. (3 Dall.) 19 (1795).

25. *Ibid.*, 19–32.

26. *Ibid.*, 27 n.*, 32–33, 41–42; *see* Goebel, 677–78, 689.

27. *Bingham*, 3 U.S. (3 Dall.) at 29–33, 39–42.

28. The following, for example, ignore the case altogether: Currie; Haines, *Role of Supreme Court*; Warren, *History*.

29. *Penhallow v. Doane's Administrators*, 3 U.S. (3 Dall.) 54 (1795).

30. *Ibid.*, 89; Iredell to Hannah Iredell, February 20, 1795, NCAH (in McRee, 2:440, in part); Haines, *Role of Supreme Court*, 139; Warren, *History*, 122–23. The Court minutes show the arguments extending over the period from February 6–16, 1795. Marcus, 1(#1):234–38.

31. *Penhallow*, 3 U.S. (3 Dall.) at 54–79; Bates, 61 n.†; Haines, *Role of Supreme Court*, 139; Warren, *History*, 122–23 (citing *New Hampshire Gazette*, May 26, 1795).

32. *Penhallow*, 3 U.S. (3 Dall.) at 90–91; Goebel, 767–68; Haines, *Role of Supreme Court*, 139–40.

33. Carson, 180; Haines, *Role of Supreme Court*, 140–41.

34. *Talbot v. Janson*, 3 U.S. (3 Dall.) 133 (1795).

35. Iredell to Hannah Iredell, August 13, 1795, NCAH (see Marcus, 1(#2):780); Simeon E. Baldwin, *Life and Letters of Simeon Baldwin* (New Haven: Tuttle, Morehouse & Taylor Co., 1919), 410 (Iredell to Simeon Baldwin, August 18, 1795); Warren, *History*, 133–34, 134 n.1.

36. *Talbot*, 3 U.S. (3 Dall.) at 161–64; Goebel, 771, 774; James H. Kettner, *The Development of American Citizenship, 1608–1870* (Chapel Hill: University of North Carolina Press, 1978), 275, 279–81; McRee, 2:451–52 (ed. essay); van Santvoord, 208.

37. Casto, 101; Goebel, 778; van Santvoord, 284.

38. *Hylton v. United States*, 3 U.S. (3 Dall.) 171 (1796).

39. *Hylton*, 3 U.S. (3 Dall.) at 171–72; Goebel, 779; Haines, *Role of Supreme Court*, 147; Warren, *History*, 147.

40. *Hylton*, 3 U.S. (3 Dall.) at 171, 173–75 (Chase); 179 (Paterson); 181–83 (Iredell).

41. *Ibid.*, 175, 183–84; Casto, 104; Currie, 32–33; Friedman and Israel, 192 ("signpost"); Goebel, 778; Levy, 59, 63; Warren, *History*, 146–47.

42. McRee, 2:461–62 (Iredell to Hannah Iredell, February 26, 1796); J.C.A. Stagg, ed., *The Papers of James Madison* (Charlottesville: University Press of Virginia, 1989), 16:247 (Madison to Jefferson, March 6, 1796); Warren, *History*, 149.

43. McRee, 2:462 (Iredell to Hannah Iredell, February 26, 1796); Iredell to Baron de Poellnitz, April 15, 1788, NCAH; Samuel Johnston to Iredell, February 25, 1790, NCAH. Clearly, Iredell was thoroughly cognizant of the impropriety of private discussions about a suit with a party thereto. See Marcus, 6:506–07 (Iredell to Thomas Martin, November 12, 1795).

44. Casto, 247–53.

45. *Ware v. Hylton*, 3 U.S. (3 Dall.) 199 (1796).

46. *Ibid.*, 199–220; Currie, 37–41; Friedman and Israel, 192; Goebel, 749–50.

47. *Ware*, 3 U.S. (3 Dall.) at 220–45 (Chase), 245–56 (Paterson), 281 (Wilson), 281–84 (Cushing); Goebel, 749–52.

48. *Ware*, 3 U.S. (3 Dall.) at 256–57 (and 256 n.*); Marcus, 1(#2):754 (Iredell to Hannah Iredell, February 26, 1795).

49. *Ware*, 3 U.S. (3 Dall.) at 256–80 (and 256 n.*); Currie, 37; Goebel, 751, 753–54. For examples of the "oft-quoted passage," see Berger, *Writings*, 50–51; Berger, *Government*, 8–9.

50. Casto, 99; Friedman and Israel, 192; Warren, *History*, 144.

51. McRee, 2:394–95 (Iredell to Hannah Iredell, May 27, 1793).

52. *Ware*, 3 U.S. (3 Dall.) at 210; Bates, 68–69; Friedman and Israel, 192; Warren, *History*, 145.

53. *Ware*, 3 U.S. (3 Dall.) at 257; McRee, 2:464 (Iredell to Hannah Iredell, March 11, 1796), NCAH.

54. *Fenemore v. United States*, 3 U.S. (3 Dall.) 357 (1797).

55. *Ibid.*, 357–60 (facts), 362 (concession), 363 (Chase), 363–64 (Iredell), 364 (Cushing, Ellsworth, Paterson). Like Paterson, Iredell had heard the case on circuit. Marcus, 2:358–59, 359 n.1. It is unclear why he did not recuse.

56. The following, for example, do not mention the case: Bates; Currie; Carson; Haines, *Role of Supreme Court*; and Warren, *History*. Casto and Goebel refer to it only on points of practice or procedure, not substantively. Casto, 111 n.99; Goebel, 627 n.27, 673 n.33, 790 n.94.

57. *Calder v. Bull*, 3 U.S. (3 Dall.) 386 (1798).

58. *Ibid.*, 386–400.

59. Elliot, 4:180, 185; William W. Crosskey, *Politics and the Constitution in the History of the United States* (Chicago: University of Chicago Press, 1953), 1:337–38.

60. *Vanhorne's Lessee v. Dorrance*, 2 U.S. (2 Dall.) 304, 319–20 (C.C.D. Pa.

1795) (Paterson, J.); *Calder*, 3 U.S. (3 Dall.) at 396–97 (Paterson, J.); Crosskey, *supra* note 59, at 1:341–42, 346.

61. Casto, 2, 34–35, 158, 238; White, *AJT*, 2.

62. See Paul Brest and Sanford Levinson, *Processes of Constitutional Decision-making: Cases and Materials* (Boston: Little, Brown & Co., 1992), 107–08; William B. Lockhart et al., eds., *Constitutional Law: Cases — Comments — Questions* (St. Paul, Mn.: West Publishing Co., 7th ed. 1991), 337–38.

63. *Calder*, 3 U.S. (3 Dall.) at 387–89; William Blackstone, *Commentaries* (St. George Tucker ed. 1803; reprint, New York: Augustus M. Kelley, 1969), 1:43–44 ("right," "wrong"), 70 ("not law").

64. McRee, 2:462 (Johnston to Iredell, February 27, 1796); Warren, *History*, 143–44 (incorrectly attributes the quote to Iredell).

65. *Calder*, 3 U.S. (3 Dall.) at 398–99.

66. Currie, 47–48.

67. *Fletcher v. Peck*, 10 U.S. (6 Cranch) 87, 133 (Marshall), 143 (Johnson) (1810); White, *AJT*, 9 ("first principles").

68. *Terrett v. Taylor*, 13 U.S. (9 Cranch) 43, 52 (1815) (Story); *Loan Association v. Topeka*, 87 U.S. (20 Wall.) 655, 663 (1874) (Miller).

69. *Satterlee v. Matthewson*, 27 U.S. (2 Pet.) 380, 413–14 (1829) (Washington); *Loan Ass'n*, 87 U.S. (20 Wall.) at 668–69 (Clifford, J., dissenting).

70. *Adamson v. California*, 332 U.S. 46, 91, 91 n.18 (1947) (Black, J., dissenting); *Nevada v. Hall*, 440 U.S. 410, 426 (1979) (Stevens); Hearings on the Nomination of Judge Clarence Thomas before the Committee on the Judiciary, United States Senate, One Hundred Second Congress, First Session, Part I (Washington: U.S. Government Printing Office, 1993), 20, 54, 64, 81, 111, 179–80, 202. See generally Currie, 41–49; Lockhart, *supra* note 62, at 337–46.

71. Currie, 48 (quote); Jethro K. Lieberman, *The Enduring Constitution: A Bicentennial Perspective* (St. Paul, Mn.: West Publishing Co., 1987), 263, 282. For further commentary on *Calder*, see the following: Berger, *Government*, 251–52; Edward S. Corwin, *Liberty Against Government: The Rise, Flowering and Decline of a Famous Judicial Concept* (Baton Rouge: Louisiana State University Press, 1948), 66; Currie, 41–49; David P. Currie, *The Constitution of the United States: A Primer for the People* (Chicago: University of Chicago Press, 1988), 52; Louis Fisher, *Constitutional Dialogues: Interpretation as Political Process* (Princeton: Princeton University Press, 1988), 71–72; John V. Orth, "Exporting the Rule of Law," North Carolina Journal of International Law and Commercial Regulation 24 (1998): 71, 74–75; Christopher Wolfe, *The Rise of Modern Judicial Review: From Constitutional Interpretation to Judge-Made Law* (New York: Basic Books, 1986), 108–09, 145–46. On natural law, see generally Charles G. Haines, "The Law of Nature in State and Federal Judicial Decisions," Yale Law Journal 25 (1916): 617 (passim); Russell Hittinger, "Liberalism and the American Natural Law Tradition," Wake Forest Law Review 25 (1990): 429 (passim); Helen K. Michael, "The Role of Natural Law in Early American Constitutionalism: Did the Founders Contemplate Judicial Enforcement of 'Unwritten' Individual Rights," North Carolina Law Review 69 (1991): 421 (passim).

72. *Wilson v. Daniel*, 3 U.S. (3 Dall.) 401 (1798).

73. *Ibid.*, 404–06.

74. *Gordon v. Ogden*, 28 U.S. (*3 Pet.*) *33* (1830); see William G. Brown, *The Life of Oliver Ellsworth* (New York: Macmillan Co., 1905; reprint, New York: Da Capo Press, 1970), 253–54. Regarding *Wilson*, see generally Goebel, 680–81; Haines, *Role of Supreme Court*, 157; McRee, 2:532–33 (ed. note); van Santvoord, 290–91, 291 n†.

75. *Sims v. Irvine, 3* U.S. (*3 Dall.*) 425 (1799).

76. *Ibid.*, 456–57 (Ellsworth), 457 n.*, 457–66 (Iredell).

77. Currie; Carson; Haines, *Role of Supreme Court*; and Warren, *History*, do not mention the case. Casto cites it only as an example of a pre-Marshall opinion for the Court accompanied by a dissenting "opinion." Casto, 111 n.99. McRee (2:543–44 ed. note) gives the case glancing laudatory reference, largely parroting van Santvoord (299), who considered the notes "one of [Iredell's] best and most carefully written opinions." Van Santvoord is technically inaccurate in designating the notes as an "opinion," though they are in opinion style.

78. Currie, 58.

79. E.g., Casto; Scott D. Gerber, ed., *Seriatim: The Supreme Court Before John Marshall* (New York: New York University Press, 1998); Jay; Marcus, *Documentary History* (six volumes to date); Maeva Marcus, ed., *Origins of the Federal Judiciary: Essays on the Judiciary Act of 1789* (New York: Oxford University Press, 1992).

80. *Penhallow, 3* U.S. (*3 Dall.*) at 92; Currie, 57 (the other was Paterson).

CHAPTER 13

Sovereign Power Dragged Before a Court: Chisholm v. Georgia

1. Elliot, 3:555.

2. *Georgia v. Brailsford*, 2 U.S. (*2 Dall.*) 402 (1792) (see Chapter 12).

3. *Chisholm v. Georgia*, 2 U.S. (*2 Dall.*) 419 (1793).

4. *Chisholm*, 2 U.S. (*2 Dall.*) at 473; Charles E. Hughes, *The Supreme Court of the United States: Its Foundation, Methods and Achievements: An Interpretation* (Garden City, N.Y.: Garden City Publishing Co., 1936), 118.

5. Goebel, 726; for a somewhat different account, see Warren, *History*, 93 n.1. The Goebel account is the more common one — see, e.g., Peter C. Hoffer, "Constitutional Silences: Georgia, the Constitution, and the Bill of Rights — A Historical Test of Orginalism," Georgia Journal of Southern Legal History 1 (1991): 21, 29. The official reporter, Alexander Dallas, does not recount the facts, but the salient facts — that the plaintiff was a citizen of South Carolina and the suit was against the State of Georgia — are clear. Doyle Mathis, "Chisholm v. Georgia: Background and Settlement," Journal of American History 54 (1967): 19 (passim), contains factual detail about the case not found elsewhere.

6. Judiciary Act of 1789, ch. 20, 1 Stat. 73; Process Act of 1789, ch. 21, 1 Stat. 93; Hoffer, "Constitutional Silences," *supra* note 5, at 29–30; *Chisholm*, 2 U.S. (*2 Dall.*) at 430 (Iredell, J., dissenting) ("The action is an action of assumpsit"); minutes, notes, opinion, in file marked "Legal Papers 1789–1799," Duke.

7. Goebel, 741–42; Warren, *History*, 92–93; Yarborough, *33*; *Cohens v. Virginia*, 19 U.S. (6 Wheat.) 264, 406 (1821) (Marshall, C.J.).

8. Elliot, 3:523–27, 533, 543, 555–56, 4:136, 190–91; McRee, 2:239 (Davie to Iredell, September 8, 1788); Miller, 380–82; *The Federalist*, No. 32, at 199–200; No. 81, at 548–49 (Alexander Hamilton) (J. Cooke, ed., 1961); Warren, *History*, 91; William A. Fletcher, "A Historical Interpretation of the Eleventh Amendment: A Narrow Construction of an Affirmative Grant of Jurisdiction Rather Than a Prohibition Against Jurisdiction," Stanford Law Review 35 (1983): 1033, 1047–50; Yarborough, 17, 30–32, 41–42, 52–61, 69 n.1; *State Gazette of North Carolina*, Edenton, N.C., March 27, 1788, at 1–2 (Maclaine). For a recent consideration of the founders' views by a current justice of the Supreme Court, see *Seminole Tribe of Florida v. Florida*, 517 U.S. 44, 105–06, 142–44 (1996) (Souter, J., dissenting).

9. Moncure D. Conway, *Omitted Chapters of History Disclosed in the Life and Papers of Edmund Randolph* (New York: G.P. Putnam's Sons, 1888), 190–91 (Jefferson to Judge Tucker, August 11, 1793); Henry C. Lodge, ed., *The Works of Alexander Hamilton* (New York: G.P. Putnam's Sons, 1903), 10:123 (Hamilton to Washington, October 16, 1795); Leonard D. White, *The Federalists: A Study in Administrative History* (New York: The Macmillan Co., 1948), 165; Fordham, "Iredell's Dissent," 158; Yarborough, 98, 100 n.1.

10. *Chisholm*, 2 U.S. (2 Dall.) at 420–29; original summons, *Chisholm* case file, National Archives, Washington, D.C.

11. Herman V. Ames, ed., *State Documents on Federal Relations: The States and the United States* (New York: Da Capo Press, 1970) (reprint: original Philadelphia: Dept. of History, University of Pennsylvania, 1905), 8–9; Bates, 55; Goebel, 726–28; Yarborough, 93–95, 93 n.1; *Chisholm*, 2 U.S. (2 Dall.) at 419.

12. *Chisholm*, 2 U.S. (2 Dall.) at 450–52.

13. *Ibid.*, 466–69.

14. James D. Andrews, ed., *The Works of James Wilson: Being His Public Discourses Upon Jurisprudence and the Political Science, Including Lectures as Professor of Law, 1790–92* (Chicago: Callaghan & Co., 1896), 2:151–53; Elliot, 2:491; Yarborough, 132–34; *Chisholm*, 2 U.S. (2 Dall.) at 453–66. William R. Davie was less than awed by Wilson's opinion; it "is more like an epic poem than a judge's argument," he wrote Iredell, "and we look in vain for legal principles or logical conclusions." McRee, 2:382 (Davie to Iredell, June 12, 1793).

15. Henry P. Johnston, ed., *The Correspondence and Public Papers of John Jay* (New York: G.P. Putnam's Sons, 4 vols., 1890–93), 3:75 (Jay to Egbert Benson, September 12, 1783), 81 (Jay to General Schuyler, September 16, 1783), 85 (Jay to Gouverneur Morris, September 24, 1783), 90–91 (Jay to Alexander Hamilton, September 28, 1783), 172 (Jay to John Adams, October 14, 1785); Frank Monaghan, *John Jay* (New York: Bobbs-Merrill Co., 1935), 268–69; George Pellew, *John Jay* (Boston: Houghton, Mifflin and Co., 1890), 244–50; *The Federalist* No. 2, at 8–10, No. 3, at 13–17 (John Jay) (Jacob E. Cooke, ed., 1961); Yarborough, 151–60; *Chisholm*, 2 U.S. (2 Dall.) at 424.

16. Yarborough, 163.

17. *Chisholm*, 2 U.S. (2 Dall.) at 469–79; Bates, 20–21; Yarborough, 167.

18. Yarborough, 178–79.

19. Elliot, 4:35 (convention); McRee, 2: 193 (Iredell's "Answers"), 348 (Charge to the Grand Jury for the District of Georgia, Savannah, April 26, 1792), 387 (Charge to the Grand Jury for the District of Maryland, Annapolis, May 7, 1793); Yarborough, 194, 232–35, 235 n.1.

20. *The Federalist* No. 9, at 55; No. 32, at 200; No. 81, at 548–49 (Alexander Hamilton) (Jacob E. Cooke, ed., 1961); Elliot, 3:533 (Madison), 555–56 (Marshall). See Miller, 380–82; Fletcher, "Eleventh Amendment," 35 Stan. L. Rev. at 1047–49; *Hans v. Louisiana*, 134 U.S. 1, 12–14 (1889); Yarborough, 233–34, 240–41, 318.

21. *Chisholm*, 2 U.S. (2 Dall.) at 430–49 (Iredell, J., dissenting); see Yarborough, 195.

22. *Chisholm*, 2 U.S. (2 Dall.) at 449–50 (Iredell, J., dissenting); Iredell's *Chisholm* notes, NCAH; Yarborough, 221–23.

23. Van Santvoord, 60–61, 61 n.* (quoted in McRee, 2:380); Carson, 175; Hamilton, *Iredell, James*, in Dumas Malone, ed., *Dictionary of American Biography* (New York: Charles Scribner's Sons, 1932, 1933), 5:493; Davis, 31; Fordham, "Political Ideas," 65.

24. Miller, 380; *Hans v. Louisiana*, 134 U.S. 1, 12–19 (1890) (Bradley, J.).

25. *Alden v. Maine*, 144 L. Ed. 2d 636 (1999); see especially *ibid.* at 661.

26. *Ibid.*, 682.

27. Casto, 192, 197.

28. *Seminole Tribe*, 517 U.S. at 106 (Souter, J., dissenting).

29. Hamilton in Malone, ed., *DAB, supra* note 23, at 5:493 (liberal construction); Fordham, "Iredell's Dissent," 166 ("liberal-constructionist"); Hoffer, *supra* note 5, at 33–34 ("originalist"); *Chisholm*, 2 U.S. (2 Dall.) at 433, 449 (Iredell, J., dissenting). See Henderson, 1:441; G. Edward White, *The Marshall Court and Cultural Change, 1815–35* (New York: Macmillan Co., 1988), 129, 129 n.189.

30. *Seminole Tribe*, 517 U.S. at 76 (Stevens, J., dissenting); see Fordham, "Iredell's Dissent," 165.

31. See Friedman and Israel, 131; Fordham, "Political Ideas," 1; Hamilton in *DAB, supra* note 23, at 5:493; Orth, "The Truth," 260–62; Yarborough, 231, 271–72, 300–01, 325–33.

32. Lefler and Newsome, 273–75; Elliot, 4:246 (proposed amendment #15); McRee, 2:287 (Ashe to Iredell, April 10, 1790); Orth, "The Truth," 266–67; Shnayerson, 70; Yarborough, 180, 184, 186–88, 190–92, 325.

33. Orth, "The Truth," 266–70.

34. Casto, Chapter 4 (passim), 213, 249–53.

35. See *Seminole Tribe*, 517 U.S. at 106 n.5 (Souter, J., dissenting).

36. Fordham, "Iredell's Dissent," 162–63; William D. Guthrie, "The Eleventh Article of Amendment to the Constitution of the United States," Columbia Law Review 8 (1908): 183, 185; Haines, *Role of Supreme Court*, 138; McRee, 2:380–81 (ed. essay), 382–83 (Davie to Iredell, June 12, 1793); Francis N. Thorpe, *A Constitutional History of the American People, 1776–1850* (New York: Harper & Bros., 1898), 1:177–78; Warren, *History*, 96, 100–01; Yarborough, 2–3; Johnston to Iredell, April 10, 1793, NCAH.

37. *Cohens v. Virginia*, 19 U.S. (6 Wheat.) 264, 406 (1821) (Marshall, J.); Fletcher, "Eleventh Amendment," 35 Stan. L. Rev. at 1058–59; Fordham, "Iredell's Dissent," 163; Lefler and Newsome, 274–75; Carl B. Swisher, *American Constitutional Development* (Boston: Houghton Mifflin Co., 1943), 87–88; Thorpe, *supra* note 34, at 1:177–78; Yarborough, 2–3, 333–34.

38. See, e.g., John V. Orth, *The Judicial Power of the United States: The Eleventh Amendment in American History* (New York: Oxford University Press, 1987), 13–14, 22, 42, 69–70, 74–75, 137–38, 149, 159; Orth, "The Truth" (passim).

39. See Orth, "The Truth."

CHAPTER 14

The Life of a Post Boy

1. Marcus, 2:125–26 (Arthur Iredell to Iredell, February 1, 1791) (also in McRee, 2:306), 138 (William Cushing to Iredell, February 13, 1791), 247 (Iredell to Thomas Johnson, March 15, 1792), 250 n.2 (Hannah Cushing to a Cushing relative, January 1792), 3:154 (Samuel Chase to Iredell, March 12, 1797); McRee, 2:290 (Iredell to Hannah Iredell, May 29, 1790).

2. Warren, "New Light," 49, 57, 59–61, 65; Charles F. Hobson and Robert A. Rutland, eds., *The Papers of James Madison* (Charlottesville: University Press of Virginia, 1979), 12:343 (White to Madison, August 17, 1789).

3. Holt, " 'The Federal Courts Have Enemies,' " 305–06; McRee, 2:260 (Lowther to Iredell, July 1, 1789).

4. Warren, "New Light," 76–77, 95.

5. Holt, "To Establish Justice," 1488–89, 1489 n.235; Holt, " 'The Federal Courts Have Enemies,' " 307–08; Marcus and Van Tassell, 31–32.

6. Holt, " 'The Federal Courts Have Enemies,' " 301–04 (location of original manuscript John Jay to Edward Rutledge, November 16, 1789, cited at 305 n.13, is unknown); Holt, "To Establish Justice," 1516–17; Seth Ames, *Works of Fisher Ames* (Indianapolis: Liberty Classics, 2 vols., 1983), 1:717 (Ames to George Richards Minot, September 6, 1789); Maeva Marcus and Natalie Wexler, "The Judiciary Act of 1789: Political Compromise or Constitutional Interpretation" in Maeva Marcus, ed., *Origins of the Federal Judiciary: Essays on the Judiciary Act of 1789* (New York: Oxford University Press, 1992), 13–14; Hobson and Rutland, eds., *supra* note 2, at 12:317 (Madison to Samuel Johnston, July 31, 1789), 331 (Monroe to Madison, August 12, 1789), 402 (Madison to Edmund Pendleton, September 14, 1789); McRee, 2:335 (Davie to Iredell, August 2, 1791); William T. Read, ed., *Life and Correspondence of George Read* (Philadelphia: J.B. Lippincott & Co., 1870), 481–82 (Dickinson to George Read, June 24, 1789); Smith, *Wilson*, 35–36, 203, 226, 248; Charles Warren, *A History of the American Bar* (New York: Howard Fertig, 1966), 241–42.

7. McRee, 2:288 (Iredell to Hannah Iredell, May 10, 1790); Jay to Iredell, March 16, 1791, NCAH: Iredell to Thomas Iredell (uncle), July 6, 1791, NCAH; Holt, " 'The Federal Courts Have Enemies,' " 308–09.

8. Marcus, 2:122 (ed. essay) (citing Roger Sherman to Simeon Baldwin, January 21, 1791, Sherman Papers, Yale University), 231 n.5; McRee, 2:335–36 (Johnston to Iredell, November 13, 1791).

9. McRee, 2:320–22 (ed. essay), 322–25 (Iredell to Jay, Cushing, and Wilson, February 11, 1791); Holt, "'The Federal Courts Have Enemies,'" 311–12.

10. Marcus, 2:131–35 (Iredell to Jay, Cushing, and Wilson, February 11, 1791) (also in McRee, 2:322–25); McRee, 2:320–22 (ed. essay); Holt, "'The Federal Courts Have Enemies,'" 311.

11. Marcus, 2:135 (Jay to Iredell, February 12, 1791), 136 n.2, 137–38 (Cushing to Iredell, February 13, 1791), 138–39 (Charles Johnson to Iredell, February 13, 1791), 154 (Jay to Iredell, March 16, 1791), 246–47 (Iredell to Thomas Johnson, March 15, 1792); Holt, "'The Federal Courts Have Enemies,'" 318–19, 319 n.72; Jared Sparks, ed., *The Writings of George Washington* (Boston: Russell, Shattuck, and Williams, 1836), 10:182 (Washington to Johnson, August 7, 1791).

12. Marcus, 2:235 (ed. essay), 238 (Iredell to Jay, January 17, 1792), 239 (same, February 16, 1792), 243 (Jay to Iredell, March 3, 1792), 244 (Jay to Johnson, March 12, 1792). While disagreeing with Jay over rotation, Iredell did not want to lose him as chief justice. Iredell to Jay, February 16, 1792, Duke.

13. Marcus, 2:246–47 (Iredell to Johnson, March 15, 1792), 251 (Johnson to Iredell, March 31, 1792); Holt, "'The Federal Courts Have Enemies,'" 328.

14. Marcus, 2:235–37 (ed. essay), 239 (Iredell to Jay, February 16, 1792), 247 (Iredell to Thomas Johnson, March 15, 1792), 248 n.6, 249 (Jay to Iredell, March 19, 1792), 250 (Cushing to Iredell, March 26, 1792); Journal of the Senate of the United States (Washington: Gales & Seaton, 1820), 1:412–14; Judiciary Act of 1792, ch. 21, sec. 3, 1 Stat. 253; Holt, "'The Federal Courts Have Enemies,'" 328–30; Goebel, 559.

15. Marcus, 2:278 (Davie to Iredell, May 25, 1792), 281 (Haywood to Iredell, June 18, 1792), 288 (Arthur Iredell to Iredell, July 31, 1792).

16. *Ibid.*, 245 (Wilson to Johnson, March 13, 1792); McRee, 2:344–45 (Pendleton to Iredell, March 19, 1792); Holt, "'The Federal Courts Have Enemies,'" 329.

17. Marcus, 1(#2):732 (Smith to Rutledge, February 13, 1792), 2:235 (ed. essay), 288–89 (Justices of the Supreme Court to George Washington, August 9, 1792), 289–90 (Justices of the Supreme Court to the Congress of the United States, August 9, 1792); Holt, "'The Federal Courts Have Enemies,'" 331–34.

18. Marcus, 2:251 (Johnson to Iredell, March 31, 1792), 344 (Johnson to Washington, January 16, 1793), 1(#1):81 (Washington to Johnson, February 1, 1793), 2:341 (ed. essay), 1(#1):87–93 (letters and documents regarding Paterson appointment), 2:345 (Cushing to Paterson, March 5, 1793), 346 (Iredell to Paterson, March 6, 1793); Holt, "'The Federal Courts Have Enemies,'" 335–36 n.143; David M. O'Brien, *Storm Center: The Supreme Court in American Politics* (New York: W.W. Norton & Co., 1986), 104.

19. Judiciary Act of 1793, ch. 22, sec. 1, 1 Stat. 333–34; Marcus, 2:345 (Cushing to Paterson, March 5, 1793), 345 n.2, 443 (Justices to Congress, February 18, 1794); Holt, "'The Federal Courts Have Enemies,'" 336–37.

20. Marcus, 2:342 (Marchant to Theodore Foster, January 1, 1793), 434 (Jay to King, December 19, 1793), 434–35 (same, December 22, 1793).

21. *Ibid.*, 442 (Iredell to Edmund Randolph, February 13, 1794) (illness), 443–44 (Justices to Congress, February 18, 1794).

22. *Ibid.*, 438 (ed. essay), 498 (Iredell to Wilson, November 24, 1794), 3:61 (Blair to Cushing, June 12, 1795). The *Documentary History* editors found no evidence as to how long the plan operated, Marcus, 2:498 n.4, nor has the present author.

23. Iredell to Hannah Iredell, February 10, 19, 1796, NCAH; Marcus, 3:92 (Samuel Johnston to Iredell, February 27, 1796), 96 (Iredell to Hannah Iredell, March 18, 1796), 98 n.101 (Ellsworth to Abigail Ellsworth, March 20, 1796).

24. Marcus, 3:97–98 (Iredell's "Alterations Proposed in the Judicial System").

25. McRee, 2:464 (Iredell to Hannah Iredell, March 11, 1796), 465 (same, March 31, 1796).

26. Marcus, 3:151 (ed. essay), 153 (Chase to Iredell, March 7, 1797), 155 (same, March 12, 1797), 239–40 (Chase to John Rutledge, Jr., January 12, 1798).

27. McRee, 2:495 (Paterson to Iredell, March 7, 1797).

28. Marcus, 3:151 (ed. essay), 220 (Justices to John Adams, August 15, 1797), 221–22 (Justices to Governor Gunning Bedford, August 15, 1797), 251 (Ellsworth to Cushing, April 15, 1798), 251 n.1.

29. *Ibid.*, 3:296 (Hannah Cushing to Abigail Adams, October 8, 1798), 299 (Bushrod Washington to George Washington, October 19, 1798), 300 (George Washington to Bushrod Washington, October 24, 1798).

30. *Ibid.*, 3:324 (Iredell to Samuel Johnston, February 28, 1799). Apparently Ellsworth did ride the Southern Circuit that spring. *Ibid.*, 3:324 n.1, 493.

31. Beveridge, 3:50–100; Lester J. Cappon, ed., *The Adams-Jefferson Letters: The Complete Correspondence Between Thomas Jefferson and Abigail and John Adams* (Chapel Hill: University of North Carolina Press, 1988; reprint, 1959 original), 270 (Jefferson to Abigail Adams, June 13, 1804); Richard E. Ellis, *The Jeffersonian Crisis: Courts and Politics in the Young Republic* (New York: Oxford University Press, 1971), 15–52; Levy, 78; Marcus, 2:341 n.19, 444 n.4.

32. Marcus, 2:11 (Jay to Iredell, March 10, 1790), 23 (Iredell to Jay, April 8, 1790), 23–24 (Iredell to Rutledge, April 9, 1790); McRee, 2:285 (Johnston to Iredell, March 18, 1790), 536 (circuit assignments); *State Gazette of North Carolina*, Edenton, N.C., May 1, 1790, at 2 (in Marcus, 2:54).

33. Marcus, 2:154 (Jay to Iredell, March 16, 1791), 537–38 (circuit assignments); McRee, 2:325 (circuit assignments), 337–38 (Iredell to Jay, January 17, 1792); Thomas Iredell (brother) to Iredell, March 4, 1791, NCAH; Iredell to Samuel Tredwell, August 17, 1791, NCAH.

34. Marcus, 2:538–39 (circuit assignments).

35. *Ibid.*, 437 (ed. essay), 539–40 (circuit assignments), 477–78 (Iredell to Wilson, August 5, 1794).

36. *Ibid.*, 3:1 (ed. essay), 6 (Paterson to Euphemia Paterson, February 20, 1795), 490–91 (circuit assignments).

37. *Ibid.*, 3:133 (Iredell to Wilson, August 20, 1796), 222 (Iredell to Hannah

Iredell, August 16, 1797), 491–93 (circuit assignments); McRee, 2:464 (Iredell to Hannah Iredell, March 11, 1796); Hay to Iredell, September 8, 1794, Duke.

CHAPTER 15
The Character of the Business Done

1. Nash, 60; James D. Richardson, *A Compilation of the Messages and Papers of the Presidents, 1789–1897* (Washington: Government Printing Office, 1896–99), 1:331; Document No. VIII, Accompanying the President's Communications to Congress of December 8, 1801, *Message and Communication from the President… 8th of December, 1801 With the Accompanying Documents* (Washington: Smith [1801]; Worcester, Mass.: American Antiquarian Society, Early American Imprints, 2nd series, no. 1509, 1964), Readex microprint; Marcus, 1(#2):870 (Griffin to Adams, November 10, 1798).

2. Stanly Elkins and Eric McKitrick, *The Age of Federalism* (New York: Oxford University Press, 1993), 254; Charles F. Hobson, ed., *The Papers of John Marshall* (Chapel Hill: University of North Carolina Press, 1987), 5:259–63 (ed. note); Charles F. Hobson, "The Recovery of British Debts in the Federal Circuit Court of Virginia, 1790 to 1797," Virginia Magazine of History and Biography 92 (1984): 176–200.

3. *American State Papers, Misc.* (Washington: Gales and Seaton, 1834), 1:319–25; Goebel, 569–73, 570 n.84. For further statistical data on the business of the early federal courts, see John P. Frank, "Historical Bases of the Federal Judicial System," Law and Contemporary Problems 13 (1948): 3, 17–18.

4. *United States v. Mundell*, 27 F. Cas. 23, 29–32 (C.C.D. Va. 1795) (No. 15,834).

5. *Minge v. Gilmour*, 17 F. Cas. 440 (C.C.D.N.C. 1798) (No. 9,631). The ensuing discussion of *Minge* has been informed in part by an incomplete, unpublished paper, Martin H. Brinkley, "'Where Justice Must Be Equally Administered': A Portrait of the Federal Courts in North Carolina, 1790–1805" (copy in author's files; used with permission).

6. Act of 1784, ch. 204, sec. 5, 1784 N.C. Sess. Laws, reprinted in Potter's Revisal, 467; see Orth, "Fee Tail" (passim).

7. *Minge*, 17 F. Cas. at 440; Kemp P. Battle, "An Address on the History of the Supreme Court," 103 N.C. 341, 368–69 (1889); Walter Clark, "History of the Supreme Court of North Carolina," 177 N.C. 616, 620–21 (1919); McRee, 2:298 n.* (Davie's declination); Claiborne T. Smith, Jr., "Baker, Blake, Jr.," in Powell, *DNCB*, 1:88–89; Iredell to an unnamed client, January 5, 1791, NCAH (opinion of Davie).

8. *Minge*, 17 F. Cas. at 442.

9. *Ibid.*, 443–44.

10. *Ibid.*, 443 (emphasis added); see Orth, "Fee Tail," 783, 783 nn.61–64.

11. *Minge*, 17 F. Cas. at 445.

12. Invalid Pensions Act of 1792, ch. 11, 1 Stat. 243–45. There are numerous commentaries on the Invalid Pensions Act; see, e.g., Bates, 51–52; Cibes, 176–78; Goebel, 560–65; Haines, *Role of Supreme Court*, 128–30; Jay, 106–11; Marcus,

2:235–36 (ed. essay), 302 n.1; McRee, 2:357–58 (ed. essay); van Santvoord, 54–55; Warren, *History*, 69–83; Maeva Marcus and Robert Tier, *"Hayburn's Case*: A Misinterpretation of Precedent," Wisconsin Law Review 1988, 527 (passim).

13. *Hayburn's Case*, 2 U.S. (2 Dall.) 409 (1792); Goebel, 561. A copy of the letter in Iredell's hand is contained in a file marked "miscellaneous," Iredell Papers, NCAH (in Marcus, 6:284–87; see commentary, *ibid.*, 36–39); see also McRee, 2:357 (letter "drawn by Judge Iredell").

14. Invalid Pensions Act of 1793, ch. 17, 1 Stat. 324–25; *United States v. Ferreira*, 54 U.S. (13 How.) 40, 50 (1852) (Taney, C.J.). See Friedman and Israel, 129; Marcus and Van Tassell, 40 n.26.

15. McRee, 2:361 (Iredell to Hannah Iredell, September 30, 1792) (also in Marcus, 2:301); Iredell's "Reasons for acting as a Commissioner on the Invalid Act [October 1792]," NCAH (in Marcus, 6:288–91); Marcus and Van Tassel, 39, 39 n.24, 40.

16. The cases, *Ex parte Chandler* and *United States v. Yale Todd*, are not reported but are recorded in the minutes and docket of the Supreme Court. *See* Cibes, 199–200; Marcus, 1(#1):222, 226, 494; Marcus and Van Tassell, 40 n.26; Warren, *History*, 79–81, 81–82 nn.1, 2. As to Iredell's absence from the February 1794 Term, see Iredell to John Jay, January 21, 1794, NCAH; Marcus, 2:442 (Iredell to Edmund Randolph, February 13, 1794); McRee, 2:405 (ed. note).

CHAPTER 16

Trials Almost Too Much to Bear

1. McRee, 2:362 (Iredell to Hannah Iredell, October 4, 1792) (also in Marcus, 2:304); Maclaine to Iredell, March 10, 1790, NCAH; Robert J. Wagman, *The Supreme Court: A Citizen's Guide* (New York: Pharos Books, 1993), 41.

2. Marcus, 3:94 (Iredell to Hannah Iredell, March 11, 1796); McRee, 2:292, 306, 398–99 (ed. notes), 399 (Iredell to Helen (Nelly) Blair Tredwell, August 12, 1793); Spence, 62–63 (dates).

3. Iredell to Hannah Iredell, May 2, 1790, and Hannah Iredell to Iredell, May 6, 1790, NCAH.

4. Marcus, 2:65 (Iredell to Hannah Iredell, May 10, 1790); Iredell to Hannah Iredell, May 29, 31, 1790, Duke.

5. Iredell to Hannah Iredell: April 6, 7, 1791, NCAH; September 4, 1791, Duke; September 7, 1791, NCAH (also in Marcus, 2:207).

6. McRee, 2:440 (Iredell to Hannah Iredell, February 26, 1795); Iredell to Mrs. McKenzie, June 19, 1792, and Helen (Nelly) Blair Tredwell to Iredell, January 10, 1793, NCAH.

7. Marcus, 2:295 (Iredell to Hannah Iredell, September 20, 1792); Iredell to Hannah Iredell: October 2, 11, 1792; May 16, June 7, 1793, NCAH.

8. Iredell to Hannah Iredell, March 6, 27, 1795; Iredell to Helen (Nelly) Blair Tredwell, March 7 and May 27, 1795, NCAH.

9. Iredell to Hannah Iredell: March 6, 1795; April 7, 1795 (also in Marcus, 3:23); May 7, 1795; July 2, 1795 (also in Marcus, 3:66), NCAH.

10. Iredell to Hannah Iredell, July 2 (in McRee, 2:447–48, but somewhat altered), 17, and August 13, 1795, NCAH; Marcus, 3:490 (circuit assignments).

11. McRee, 2:464 (Iredell to Hannah Iredell, March 11, 1796), 465 (same, March 31, 1796); Iredell to Hannah Iredell: April 20 and August 3, 1796, NCAH; April 29, 1796, Duke.

12. Iredell to Hannah Iredell, March 11 and April 8, 1796, NCAH (latter in Marcus, 3:105); McRee, 2:492 (Iredell to Hannah Iredell, February 17, 1797) (also in Marcus, 3:152–53) (Marcus has "silly" where McRee has "folly"; "folly" is probably the word used in the original letter in NCAH, though the word is difficult to read).

13. Hannah Iredell to Iredell, November 11, 1790, NCAH.

14. Iredell to Hannah Iredell: September 24, 1790, Duke; September 11, 1791; May 7, 1795; May 27, 1795; January 20, 1797, all NCAH; March 18, 1797, Duke. Samuel Johnston to Hannah Iredell, May 9, 1793, NCAH. Iredell to Samuel Tredwell, May 27, 1795, NCAH. Hannah Iredell to Iredell, August 19, 1797, NCAH.

15. Annals of Congress, 7th Cong., 1st Sess., 38 (Morris); Don Higginbotham, "Iredell, James, Sr.," in Powell, *DNCB*, 3:254; Marcus, 2:366 (Arthur Iredell to Iredell, April 29, 1793); Iredell to Helen (Nelly) Blair Tredwell, March 10, 1797, NCAH.

16. McRee, 2:477 (Iredell to Hannah Iredell, July 29, 1796); Iredell to Hannah Iredell: September 11, 1791; January 21, 1795; January 23, 1797; January 18, 1799, all NCAH; January 31, 1798, Duke. See Nash, 59–60.

17. McRee, 2:298 (Iredell to Hannah Iredell, October 8, 1790); Iredell to Hannah Iredell: October 21, 1791; April 7, 1794; January 23, 1797, all NCAH.

18. McRee, 2:385 (Iredell to Hannah Iredell, May 5, 1793), 442 (same, April 7, 1795); Iredell to Hannah Iredell: May 29, 1790, Duke; September 11, 1791; April 15, 1794; January 29, 1796; January 21, May 1, 1798, all NCAH.

19. Marcus, 3:267–71 (E.M. Bay to Iredell, May 13, 1798, and enclosure with directions); Maclaine to Iredell, March 31, 1790, Duke; E.M. Bay to Iredell, May 18, 1797, Duke; file marked "James Iredell, Sr., U.S. Circuit Court Papers—Routes & Mileages (Southern Circuit)," NCAH.

20. Chase to Iredell, March 15, 1797, Duke; as to the circuit referred to, see Marcus, 3:492.

21. McRee, 2:359 (Iredell to Hannah Iredell, September 23, 1792) (also in Marcus, 2:295–96); Marcus, 2:297 n.2; Iredell to Hannah Iredell, August 8, 1794, NCAH.

22. Marcus, 2:79 (Iredell to Hannah Iredell, June 18, 1790) (also in McRee, 2:291, in part); Iredell to Hannah Iredell: October 2, 1791; July 24, 1795; April 25, 1799, all NCAH.

23. McRee, 2:345 (Iredell to Hannah Iredell, April 8, 1792); Iredell to Hannah Iredell: July 24, 1795, and March 14, 1799, NCAH; January 31 and February 1, 1798, and January 29, 1797, Duke; Iredell to Annie Iredell, April 5, 1798, NCAH.

24. Marcus, 2:204 (Iredell to Hannah Iredell, September 4, 1791); McRee, 2:445 (Iredell to Hannah Iredell, May 27, 1795), 516 (same, August 11, 1797). Iredell to Hannah Iredell: September 16, 1791, Duke; November 28, 1790; September 25, 1791; August 13, 1795; January 22, 1797, all NCAH.

25. McRee, 2:437–38 (Iredell to Hannah Iredell, January 28, 1795); Iredell to

Hannah Iredell: November 15, 1790; August 12, 1796; January 28, 1798; January 22, 1799, all NCAH; Iredell to Samuel Tredwell, January 20, 1796, NCAH.

26. Marcus, 3:245–46 (Iredell to Hannah Iredell, April 10, 1798), 252 (same, April 17, 1798).

27. *Ibid.*, 3:246 (Iredell to Hannah Iredell, April 10, 1798), 257 (*City Gazette*, Augusta, Georgia, May 5, 1798), 278 (Iredell to Pickering, June 16, 1798), 280–81 (John Young Noel to William Paterson, July 20, 1798).

28. *Ibid.*, 2:369–70 ("A Citizen of New-Castle County [Delaware]" to *National Gazette*, May 1, 1793), 375–76 ("J.M." to *National Gazette*, May 10, 1793).

29. *Ibid.*, 1(#2):870 (Griffin to Adams, November 10, 1798), 2:210 (Iredell to Hannah Iredell, September 19, 1791), 212 (same, October 2, 1791), 396 (same, June 7, 1793), 3:27 (same, April 21, 1795), 82 (same, November 27, 1795); McRee, 2:360–61 (same, September 25, 1792).

30. Marcus, 2:229 (Iredell to Hannah Iredell, November 11, 1791).

31. *Ibid.*, 3:255–56 (Iredell to Hannah Iredell, May 1, 1798).

32. McRee, 2:346–47 (Iredell to Hannah Iredell, April 26, 1792); Iredell to Hannah Iredell, January 23, 1795, and February 3, 1796, NCAH.

33. McRee, 2:400 (Dr. B. Duffield to Iredell, September 5, 1793), 400–01 (Butler to Iredell, September 9, 1793); Iredell to Samuel Johnston, October 20, 1797, Hayes Collection, SHC. See Goebel, 553.

34. Marcus, 2:249 (Pendleton to Iredell, March 19, 1792), 358 (Iredell to Hannah Iredell, April 4, 1793), 370 (same, May 3, 1793); McRee, 2:371 (Iredell to Hannah Iredell, October 21, 1792), 394 (same, May 20, 1793), 426 (same, August 3, 1794), 477 (same, July 29, 1796); Iredell to Hannah Iredell, May 5, 1791, Duke, and March 28, 1799, NCAH (in McRee, 2:550, but in somewhat altered form).

35. McRee, 2:386 (Iredell to Hannah Iredell, May 16, 1793), 443 (same, April 15, 1795; see original, Duke, for full text) (also in Marcus, 3:25), 523 (same, May 8, 1798); Iredell to Hannah Iredell, May 16, 1796, and May 12, 1797, Duke.

36. Marcus, 3:319–20 (ed. essay), 354 (Paterson to Iredell, April 27, 1799), 355 (Chase to Iredell, April 28, 1799), 356 (Paca to Iredell, May 3, 1799), 361 (Iredell to Hannah Iredell, May 11, 1799), 365–66 (Johnston to Iredell, May 18, 1799), 366 (Iredell to Hannah Iredell, May 19, 1799) (also in McRee, 2:575), 381 (Washington to Iredell, August 20, 1799), 389 (same, October 20, 1799). See generally Bates, 76; Raymond Walters, Jr., *Alexander James Dallas: Lawyer — Politician — Financier, 1759–1817* (Philadelphia: University of Pennsylvania Press, 1943), 79–82; Francis Wharton, *State Trials of the United States During the Administrations of Washington and Adams* (New York: Burt Franklin, original 1849, reprinted 1970), 458–609 (first trial), 610–48 (second trial).

37. Marcus, 2:80 n.1 (Judiciary Act extended to North Carolina June 4, 1790), 106 (ed. note); McRee, 2:284 (Johnston to Iredell, March 4, 1790), 291 (ed. note); Iredell to Hannah Iredell, July 2, 1790, and April 6, 1791, NCAH; Johnston to Iredell, May 9, 1790, Duke. See Crockette W. Hewlett, *The United States Judges of North Carolina* (New Bern, N.C.: Owen G. Dunn Co., 1978), 6–7.

38. Iredell to Hannah Iredell, November 11, 1791, NCAH.

39. McRee, 2:439 (Iredell to Hannah Iredell, February 13, 1795), 440 (same,

February 20, 1795), 575 (same, May 16, 1799); Iredell to Hannah Iredell: November 5, 1792; December 7, 1795; April 8, 1796; June 1, 1796; August 3, 1796, all NCAH; Iredell to Helen (Nelly) Blair Tredwell, March 7, 1795, NCAH.

40. Copy of Iredell opinion in *United States v. Joseph Ravara*, July 1793, Pa. Circuit Court, U.S. Circuit Court Papers, NCAH.

41. McRee, 2:395 (Iredell to Hannah Iredell, May 27, 1793); Iredell to Hannah Iredell: April 6, 1791; April 9, 1791; December 2, 1795; May 31, 1797, all NCAH.

42. Iredell to Michael Payne, December 11, 1793, NCAH.

43. Marcus, 3:68 (Blair to Iredell, September 14, 1795), 69 n.5, 92 (ed. essay), 185–86 (Iredell to Hannah Iredell, May 31, 1797), 323 (ed. essay), 380–81 (Washington to Iredell, August 20, 1799) (also in McRee, 2:583), 389 (same, October 20, 1799), 390 n.1; McRee, 2:571 (Iredell to Hannah Iredell, April 11, 1799); Sitgreaves to Iredell, August 2, 1791, NCAH; Iredell to Hannah Iredell, May 25, 1797, NCAH (in McRee, 2:513 in part, but with pertinent parts omitted).

44. Marcus, 2:335 (Iredell to Arthur Iredell, November 30, 1792); Iredell to Hannah Iredell, May 25, 1797, NCAH.

45. Marcus, 2:336 (*National Gazette*, New Bern, N.C., December 11, 1792), 337 (Davie to Iredell, December 16, 1792), 3:299 (Minutes, Circuit Court for the District of Pennsylvania, October 11, 1798), 301 (Minutes, Circuit Court for the District of South Carolina, October 25, 1798), 316–17 (Washington to Iredell, December 5, 1798).

46. Iredell to Thomas Jefferson, March 19, 1793, and to Edmund Randolph, February 13, 1794, NCAH.

CHAPTER 17

Great Civilities and Distinction

1. McRee, 2:296 (Iredell to Hannah Iredell, September 14, 1790), 443 (same, May 7, 1795); Iredell to Hannah Iredell, January 29, 1797, Duke.

2. Iredell to Hannah Iredell, September 23, 1792, NCAH (in McRee, 2:360, in part).

3. Iredell to Hannah Iredell, May 27, 1795, NCAH.

4. McRee, 2:443 (Iredell to Hannah Iredell, April 15, 1795) (also in Marcus, 3:25).

5. Iredell to Hannah Iredell, September 7, 1791, NCAH.

6. McRee, 2:363 (Iredell to Hannah Iredell, October 7, 1792), 372 (same, November 1, 1792).

7. McRee, 2:285 (Maclaine to Iredell, March 31, 1790), 288 n.† (Pollok); Pollok to Iredell, May 20, 1790, Duke; Hay to Iredell, November 1, 1790, Duke.

8. McRee, 2:289 (Iredell to Hannah Iredell, May 23, 1790); Iredell to Hannah Iredell, May 4, 10, 12, 28, June 7, 18, 1790, NCAH; May 6, 1790, Duke.

9. Iredell to Hannah Iredell, May 31, 1790, Duke.

10. McRee, 2:290 (Iredell to Hannah Iredell, June 7, 1790); Iredell to Hannah Iredell: May 29, 1790, Duke; June 18, 1790, NCAH.

11. McRee, 2:299 (Iredell to Hannah Iredell, October 30, 1790), 346 (same, April 19, 1792); Iredell to Hannah Iredell, October 13, 21, 1791, NCAH.

12. McRee, 2:356 (Iredell to Hannah Iredell, May 10, 1792); Iredell to Hannah Iredell: April 28, 1792; May 15, 1792 (in McRee, 2:357, in part); May 28, 1792, NCAH.

13. Marcus, 2:308 (Iredell to Hannah Iredell, October 11, 1792), 318 (same, October 21, 1792), 329 (list), 330 (Iredell to Hannah Iredell, November 5, 1792); McRee, 2:373 n.* (list), 374 (Iredell to Arthur Iredell, November 30, 1792) (also in Marcus, 2:335); Iredell to Hannah Iredell: October 7, 1792; October 11, 1792; November 1, 1792, NCAH.

14. Marcus, 3:27 (Iredell to Hannah Iredell, April 21, 1795); Iredell to Hannah Iredell, April 7, 1795, and to Helen (Nelly) Blair Tredwell, May 27, 1795, NCAH.

15. Marcus, 3:273 (Iredell to Hannah Iredell, May 18, 1798); McRee, 2:456 (Iredell to Hannah Iredell, November 27, 1795), 527 (same, May 11, 1798); Iredell to Hannah Iredell, April 28, 1794 and May 5, 1798, NCAH.

16. Marcus, 2:4 (ed. essay quoting *Columbian Centinel*, Boston, May 14, 1791); McRee, 2:494 (Iredell to Hannah Iredell, March 3, 1797); Iredell to Hannah Iredell, May 20, 1791, NCAH; White, "Working Life," 6.

17. Hannah Iredell to Anna Iredell, February 12, 1797, NCAH.

18. McRee, 2:288 (Iredell to Hannah Iredell, May 10, 1790); Iredell to Hannah Iredell, February 3, 1796, NCAH.

19. McRee, 2:385 (Iredell to Hannah Iredell, May 16, 1793), 394 (same, May 20, 27, 1793); Iredell to Hannah Iredell: September 25, 1792, NCAH; April 15, 1795, Duke; June 22, 1795, NCAH.

20. McRee, 2:363–64 (Iredell to Hannah Iredell, October 11, 1792), 373 (same, November 5, 1792) (also in Marcus, 2:330), 446 (same, June 5, 1795), 447 (same, June 12, 1795). As to Mrs. Cabot, see Marcus, 3:56 n.1.

21. Iredell to Hannah Iredell: October 2, 1791, NCAH; May 16, 1793, NCAH; February 20, 1795, NCAH; June 5, 1795, NCAH (in McRee, 2:446, in part); April 21, 1797, Duke; April 11, 1799, NCAH.

22. McRee, 2:300 (Iredell to Hannah Iredell, October 30, 1790), 548 (same, March 7, 1799); Iredell to Hannah Iredell: October 13, 1792, May 18, 1795, February 24, 1797, NCAH; Iredell to Helen (Nelly) Blair Tredwell, May 27, 1795, March 10, 1797, NCAH; Iredell to Samuel Tredwell, March 10, 1797, NCAH. The May 18, 1795, letter is in McRee, 2:444, in part and with alterations; the March 10, 1797, letter is in McRee, 2:496, again in part with alterations (including lifting it from a letter to Helen (Nelly) Blair Tredwell and inserting it in one to Samuel Tredwell). In the first, McRee has Iredell dancing "till after two" rather than "till half after two" as in the original; in the second, Iredell dances until 10:00 p.m., not 1:00 a.m. as in the original. McRee published in the Victorian era and apparently was concerned about revealing the full extent of his subject's late-hours frivolity.

23. McRee, 2:439 (Iredell to Hannah Iredell, February 5, 1795), 456 (same, November 27, 1795), 493 (same, February 17, 1797), 494 (same, February 24, 1797). On another occasion Iredell spoke of having been unable to attend two plays in Boston but intending to go to one that night. *Ibid.*, 2:446 (same, June 5, 1795).

24. Marcus, 2:92 (Iredell to Hannah Iredell, September 14, 1790), 92 n.1, 162 (Iredell to Hannah Iredell, May 9, 1791), 162 n.1, 372 (Iredell to Hannah Iredell, May 5, 1793); McRee, 2:297 (Iredell to Hannah Iredell, September 15, 1790), 363 (same, October 7, 1792), 372 (same, October 25, 1792); Iredell to Hannah Iredell, March 21, 1799, NCAH.

25. Marcus, 2:326 (Iredell to Hannah Iredell, November 1, 1792) (also in McRee, 2:372–73), 327–28 (Iredell to Adams, November 4, 1792).

26. Casto, 90, 95; James Haw, "John Rutledge: Distinction and Declension," in Scott D. Gerber, ed., *Seriatim: The Supreme Court Before John Marshall* (New York: New York University Press, 1998), 87–88; Kermit L. Hall, ed., *The Oxford Companion to the Supreme Court of the United States* (New York: Oxford University Press, 1992), 750–51; Iredell to Hannah Iredell, May 11, 12, 18, 1798, NCAH.

27. McRee, 2:394 (Iredell to Hannah Iredell, May 27, 1793), 395 (ed. essay); Iredell to Samuel Johnston, May 29, 1793, Hayes Collection, SHC (original unclear in places; gaps filled from typescript in file marked "Iredell, James," Miscellaneous Manuscripts Collection, Manuscripts Division, Library of Congress, Washington, D.C.). See Beveridge, 2:188–89; William C. Bruce, *John Randolph of Roanoke 1773–1833* (New York: G.P. Putnam's Sons, 2 vols., 1922), 1:146; George Morgan, *Patrick Henry* (Philadelphia: J.P. Lippincott Co., 1929), 390–91; van Santvoord, 371–72; William W. Henry, *Patrick Henry: Life, Correspondence and Speeches* (New York: Charles Scribner's Sons, 2 vols., 1891), 2:473–75.

28. Beveridge, 2:187–88; Irwin S. Rhodes, *The Papers of John Marshall: A Descriptive Calendar* (Norman: University of Oklahoma Press, 1969), 1:480–81; van Santvoord, 371.

29. Marcus, 2:480 (John G. Guignard to Iredell, August 22, 1794), 481 n.1; Resolution of the Grand Jury (Circuit Court, June 1798 Term) at Raleigh, June 4, 1798, NCAH.

30. Marcus, 3:37 (Roger Griswold to Fanny Griswold, April 28, 1795), 47 (Iredell to Hannah Iredell, May 18, 1795) (also in McRee, 2:444–45); Iredell to Helen (Nelly) Blair Tredwell, May 27, 1795, NCAH. As to Cutler's probably being a Loyalist, see McRee, 2:445 (Iredell reference to "the little cloud on [Cutler's] political character during the war").

31. Marcus, 3:493 (circuits); McRee, 2:571 (Iredell to Hannah Iredell, April 11, 1799), 579–80 (ed. essay); Nash, 69–70.

CHAPTER 18

The Most-Serious Mortifications

1. A diligent search by the present author revealed no evidence of Iredell's presence there, and a subsequent letter to the author, co-signed by the archivist and the librarian of the Sussex Archaeological Society, states: "I have again been through all possible sources for information about this elusive Iredell but without success." Kenneth Dickins, archivist, and Joyce Crow, home librarian, Sussex Archaeological Society, Lewes, East Sussex, England, to the author, September 10, 1991 (in author's

files). The author visited Lewes on July 24, 1991. The foregoing is drawn from local publications, conversations with residents, and the author's personal observations and recollections. A helpful publication is Colin Brent, *Historic Lewes and its Buildings* (Lewes Town Council Official Guide; no date shown); see also Mark Girouard, *The English Town: A History of Urban Life* (New Haven: Yale University Press, 1990), 294 (Pl. 403), 295. For commentary on Paine and his Lewes experience, see Arthur Iredell to Iredell, May 3, 1791, NCAH (in McRee, 2:332, but with editorial liberties).

2. Higginbotham, 1:xxxvii (ed. essay), 36 n.4, 72 n.4, 105 (Iredell to Francis Iredell, Sr., July 20, 1772), 167–68 (Arthur Iredell to Iredell, November 17, 1773), 235 n.3, 2:473 (Iredell to Margaret Iredell, December 31, 1783); McRee, 1:5 (list of siblings).

3. Iredell to Arthur Iredell, February 16, 1784, NCAH; Arthur Iredell to Iredell, February 18, 1784, NCAH; Iredell to Thomas Iredell (uncle), February 11, 1784, NCAH; Iredell to Catherine Macartney, June 15, 1784, NCAH; McRee, 2:261–62 (Iredell to Lord Macartney, July 15, 1789).

4. McRee, 2:102 (Iredell to Thomas Iredell (uncle), May 28, 1784); Arthur Iredell to Iredell, February 18, 1784, and July 31, 1785, NCAH; Alexander Diack to Iredell, September 3, 1784, Duke; William Blair to Helen (Nelly) Blair, September 12, 1784, NCAH.

5. Arthur Iredell to Iredell: February 18, 1784; November 27, 1784; April 30, 1785; February 21, 1786; December 4, 1787; December 2, 1788; May 5, 1789; October 6, 1789; June 1, 1790; August 3, 1790, NCAH.

6. Iredell to Margaret Iredell, January 22, 1785; to Thomas Iredell (uncle), February 19, 1785; to Arthur Iredell, March 6, 1785, NCAH.

7. Marcus, 2:99 (Sarah Jay to John Jay, October 7, 1790), 99 n.2, 101 (minutes, Circuit Court for the District of Georgia, October 15, 1790), 101 n.2, 102–03 (minutes, Circuit Court for the District of South Carolina, October 25, 1790), 103 (Iredell to Hannah Iredell, October 30, 1790); McRee, 2:297 (ed. note); Iredell to Thomas Iredell (uncle), March 8, 1790, NCAH; Arthur Iredell to Iredell, July 27, 1790, NCAH; Hannah Iredell to Samuel Tredwell, September 27, 1790, NCAH; Hannah Iredell to Iredell, November 7, 1790, Duke.

8. Hannah Iredell to Samuel Tredwell, September 27, 1790; Iredell to Hannah Iredell: September 28, October 3, 8, 1790; Arthur Iredell to Iredell: November 30, 1790, January 4, 1791; NCAH.

9. Hannah Iredell to Samuel Tredwell, September 27, 1790; Hannah Iredell to Iredell, October 21, 1790; Arthur Iredell to Thomas Iredell (brother), April 5, 1791; Arthur Iredell to Iredell, May 3, 1791; Iredell to Thomas Iredell (uncle), July 6, 1791; Iredell to Hannah Iredell, October 29, 1791, NCAH.

10. Iredell's letter to Arthur has not been found, but its tenor is quite clear from Arthur's reply. Arthur Iredell to Iredell, August 1, 1791, NCAH.

11. Iredell to Hannah Iredell: September 11, 25, October 29, 1791, NCAH.

12. Arthur Iredell to Iredell, December 6, 1791, and Iredell to Arthur Iredell, January 10, 1792, NCAH.

13. Thomas Iredell (brother) to Iredell, February 10, 1792, and Arthur Iredell to Iredell, March 5, 1792, NCAH.

14. Marcus, 2:538 (circuit assignment); Iredell to Hannah Iredell: April 8, 28, June 22, October 13, 1792, NCAH.

15. Iredell's correspondence is replete with references to these visits and his mother's health; see, e.g., Iredell to Hannah Iredell: August 3, 8, 11, 1794, NCAH; February 13, March 13, July 17, 1795, NCAH; February 10, March 11, April 20, April 22, 1796, NCAH; May 16, 1796, Duke; February 17, March 18, 1797, Duke; March 15, August 16, 1797, NCAH; February 5, 1798, NCAH; March 7, 21, 28, 1799, NCAH; Iredell to Annie Iredell and to James Iredell, Jr., both February 17, 1797, NCAH. Only two and one-half months before Iredell's death, Justice Wilson's widow wrote Iredell expressing disappointment over not seeing him the previous Sunday, saying: "I thought if you had a day to spare, you would divide it between your mother and us." McRee, 2:581 (Hannah Wilson to Iredell, August 7, 1799).

16. Arthur Iredell to Iredell: July 31, 1792; January 3, 1793; September 1, 1795, NCAH.

17. Johnston to Iredell, May 8, 1797, NCAH; Iredell to Arthur Iredell: October 7, 1797, James Iredell Association, Inc., Edenton, N.C.; October 8, 1797, NCAH; Johnston to Joseph Anthony & Co., December 26, 1800, and Joseph Anthony & Co. to Johnston, April 30, 1801, SHC; Johnston to Arthur Iredell, July 25 and November 6, 1801, April 8, 1802, March 1803 (exact date not shown), SHC; Johnston to (illegible), January 7, 1803, and to William Cathcart, June 2, 1807, SHC; accounting of Johnston's expenses for elder Mrs. Iredell, April 22, 1807, Hayes Collection, SHC; Sykes, 10–14. In 1795 Iredell had noted an increase of fifty cents a week in his mother's keep, which he was "not surprised at, for everything has risen enormously." Iredell to Hannah Iredell, July 17, 1795, NCAH.

18. Marcus, 2:99 n.2; Arthur Iredell to Iredell, September 1, 1795, NCAH; Iredell to Hannah Iredell, April 25, 1799, NCAH; Benjamin Dungan to Hannah Iredell, January 20 and August 1, 1800, Duke; Samuel Johnston to (illegible), January 7, 1803, and to Arthur Iredell, March 1803 (exact date not shown), SHC.

19. Arthur Iredell to Iredell, February 18, 1784, and to Hannah Iredell, April 9, 1784, NCAH.

20. Iredell to Thomas Iredell (uncle), February 19, 1785; Iredell to Arthur Iredell, January 22, 1785; Arthur Iredell to Iredell, April 30, 1785, NCAH.

21. McRee, 2:92 (Iredell to Arthur Iredell, February 16, 1784); Iredell to Thomas Iredell (uncle), February 11, 1784, NCAH; Diack to Iredell, September 3, 1784, Duke; William Blair to Helen (Nelly) Blair, September 12, 1784, NCAH; Iredell to Henry E. McCulloh, September 26, 1784, NCAH.

22. Iredell to Margaret Iredell, January 22, 1785; Iredell to Thomas Iredell (uncle), February 19, 1785; Iredell to Arthur Iredell, March 6, 1785; Arthur Iredell to Iredell, February 21, 1786, NCAH.

23. Iredell to Richard B. Caswell, May 26, 1785, Governors Papers, 1785, NCAH; *Heads of Families at the First Census of the United States Taken in the Year 1790: North Carolina* (Washington: Government Printing Office, 1908), 19.

24. Iredell to Margaret Iredell, January 22, 1785, NCAH; Helen (Nelly) Blair to Iredell, February 3, 1787, Duke. As to Tom's service as master and clerk, see sub-

poena from Edenton Superior Court, November 1788 Term, Duke; documents signed by Thomas Iredell as clerk in Cupola House Papers, SHC.

25. Jean Blair to Helen (Nelly) Blair, March 18, 29, 1785, and to Hannah Iredell, April 3, 8, 1785, NCAH; Penelope Dawson to Iredell, March 10, 1789, NCAH; Samuel Johnston to Iredell, February 25, 1790, NCAH, and March 6, 1790, Duke; Iredell to Thomas Iredell (uncle), March 8, 1790, NCAH.

26. Samuel Johnston to Iredell, March 11, 1790, and April 15, 1791, NCAH; Iredell to Arthur Iredell, January 10, 1792, NCAH; Thomas Iredell (brother) to Iredell, June 19, 1793, NCAH; Arthur Iredell to Mrs. Francis Iredell, April 30, 1793, NCAH; Arthur Iredell to Iredell, April 29, 1793; July 3, 1793; February 4, 1799, NCAH; Iredell to Hannah Iredell, March 7, 1798, NCAH. Iredell's "delicate" allusion may have been to a gambling habit; see Iredell to Hannah Iredell, April 21, 1797, Duke ("Tell my brother none of his lottery tickets are drawn — nor is the canal lottery yet — a vile imposition."). Arthur came to depend on Iredell for information about Tom; in 1796 he reported to Iredell that his own correspondence with Tom had been "long discontinued." Arthur Iredell to Iredell, May 11, 1796, NCAH.

27. Arthur Iredell to Iredell: February 18, 1784; January 29, 1786; December 5, 1786; July 2, 1787; September 20, 1787, NCAH. See Higginbotham, 1:xxxi (ed. essay).

28. Arthur Iredell to Iredell: January 29, February 21, September 5, December 5, 1786, NCAH.

29. Marcus, 3:161 (Iredell to Oliver Ellsworth, April 10, 1797), 161 n.4; Iredell to Hannah Iredell, April 7 and May 4, 1797, NCAH; Johnston to Iredell, May 6, 1797, NCAH (in McRee, 2:503, but with alterations and omissions); Iredell to Rev. James Abercrombie, no date shown, Ferdinand Dreer Collection, Historical Society of Pa., Philadelphia, Pa.

30. Arthur Iredell to Iredell, April 5 and May 3, 1791, NCAH.

31. Iredell to Arthur Iredell, February 16, 1784, and January 22, 1785, NCAH; Arthur Iredell to Iredell, December 4, 1797, NCAH. See Higginbotham, 1:xxxii (ed. essay).

32. McRee, 2:344 (Arthur Iredell to Iredell, March 5, 1792); Arthur Iredell to Iredell: August 5, 1788; October 4, 1791; April 5, 1796 (from "near Lewes"); May 11, 1796, NCAH.

33. Arthur Iredell to Iredell: May 1, 1786; May 5, 1789; March 5, 1793; November 5, 1793, NCAH; Mrs. Arthur Iredell to Mrs. James Iredell, June 22, 1794, NCAH.

34. Marcus, 1(#2):710 (Arthur Iredell to Iredell, May 5, 1790); McRee, 2:268 (same, October 6, 1789); Arthur Iredell to Iredell: February 2, 1790; March 5, 1792; July 31, 1792; April 29, 1793, NCAH. See also Anna Iredell (Arthur's wife) to Hannah Iredell, April 2, 1793, NCAH ("Mr. Iredell almost idolizes his brother.").

35. McRee, 2:399 (Arthur Iredell to Iredell, September 3, 1793); Arthur Iredell to Iredell, September 1, 1795, NCAH. The author bases the conclusion that the opinion mentioned was *Chisholm* on the letter's proximity to that decision.

36. Iredell to Arthur Iredell, February 16, 1784, and March 6, 1785, NCAH;

Arthur Iredell to Hannah Iredell, February 25, 1784, Duke; Mrs. Arthur Iredell to Hannah Iredell, April 2, 1793, NCAH.

37. Arthur Iredell to Iredell, July 3, 1793, and June 23, 1794, NCAH; Iredell to Arthur Iredell, February 11, 1797, James Iredell Association, Inc., Edenton, N.C.; Iredell to Hannah Iredell, April 7, 1797 (two letters), and August 11, 1797, NCAH; Thomas Iredell (brother) to Iredell, July 28, 1797, NCAH. As to Arthur's performing clerical duties, see Sussex Archeological Collections, vols. XXVI at 83 and XXX at 73, 76–77, Sussex Archeological Society, Lewes, East Sussex, England. As to Arthur's death, see John Venn and J.A. Venn, eds., *Alumni Cantabrigienses: A Biographical List of All Known Students, Graduates, and Holders of Office at the University of Cambridge, from the Earliest Times to 1900* (Cambridge: At the University Press, 1947), 525; Gentleman's Magazine, vol. 75, pt. 1 (1805), 3:183.

CHAPTER 19

Felicitous Relationships

1. Higginbotham, 1:liv (ed. essay), 17 (McCulloh to Iredell, September 5, 1768), 34 (same, July 14, 1769), 64 (Macartney to Iredell, March 20, 1771).

2. Higginbotham, 1:86 (Iredell to Nathaniel Dukinfield, February 19, 1772), 180 (Iredell's Diary, November 11, 1772).

3. *Ibid.*, liv (ed. essay), 86–88 (Iredell to Nathaniel Dukinfield, February 19, 1772), 94 (Iredell to Hannah Johnston, ca. April 1, 1772), 96 (Iredell to Samuel Johnston, April 7, 1772), 123 (Iredell to Francis Iredell, Sr., October 22, 1772); see generally Watson, "Women," 7–8.

4. Higginbotham, 1:459 (Iredell to Hannah Iredell, August 19, 1777); Iredell to Hannah Iredell, July 18, 1788, NCAH.

5. Higginbotham, 2:107 (ed. note), 108–09 (Iredell to Hannah Iredell, September 7, 1779), 110 (same, September 9, 1779), 113 (same, October 1, 1779), 116 (same, October 17, 1779), 128 (same, November 21, 1779), 129 (same, November 25, 1779), 131 (same, December 1, 1779), 132 (same, December 2, 1779), 133 (same, December 8, 1779), 134–35 (ed. note).

6. Jean Blair (Hannah's sister) to Helen (Nelly) Blair (Hannah's niece), May 13, 1785; Helen (Nelly) Blair to Iredell, April 25, 1787; Iredell to Hannah Iredell, April 26, 1788, NCAH.

7. Iredell to Hannah Iredell: May 23, 1786; January 31, 1787; February 13, 1787; April 26, 1788, NCAH.

8. Hannah Iredell to Iredell, November 11, 1790, and Iredell to Hannah Iredell, November 15, 1790, NCAH.

9. Hannah Iredell to Helen (Nelly) Blair Tredwell, March 4, 1797, NCAH; Iredell to Hannah Iredell: March 3, 1796; March 24, 1797; March 29, 1797; April 14, 1797; April 28, 1797, NCAH.

10. Iredell to Hannah Iredell: July 8, 1795; February 28, March 14, April 25, May 2, 1799, NCAH.

11. McRee, 2:297 (Hannah Iredell to Iredell, September 15, 1790), 299 (same,

October 21, 1790) (full letter, NCAH), 346 (Iredell to Hannah Iredell, April 19, 1792); Hannah Iredell to Iredell, November 7, 1790, Duke; Iredell to Hannah Iredell, March 25, 1796, Duke. As to the Pinkneys, see Marcus, 2:261 nn.5, 6.

12. Davis, 21–22; McRee, 2:296 (Hannah Iredell to Iredell, September 15, 1790), 587 (ed. essay, quoting Bishop Charles Pettigrew); Spence, 63.

13. McRee, 1:37 (ed. essay) (name), 2:90 (Hooper to Iredell, February 12, 1784); Iredell to Thomas Iredell (uncle), February 19, 1785, NCAH.

14. Penelope Dawson to Helen (Nelly) Blair, October 22, 1784, Duke; Iredell to Nathaniel Dukinfield, January 9, 1785, Duke; Iredell to Thomas Iredell (uncle), February 19, 1785, NCAH.

15. Iredell to Hannah Iredell, October 15, 19, 24, 1784, NCAH; to Nathaniel Dukinfield, January 9, 1785, Duke; to Margaret Iredell, January 22, 1785, NCAH; to Thomas Iredell (uncle), February 19, 1795, NCAH.

16. Iredell to Thomas Iredell (uncle), December 4, 1794, NCAH.

17. Higginbotham, 1:107 (Iredell to Francis Iredell, Sr., July 20, 1772) (Hewes), 111 n.2 (Anne Isabella Johnston); Cadwallader Jones, *A Genealogical History* (Columbia, S.C.: Ye Bryan Printing Co., 1900), 61; McRee, 1:34 (ed. essay), 2:116 (ed. note); Mrs. A.J. Robertson (great-granddaughter of James Iredell), "A Sketch of Judge James Iredell," *The State*, Columbia, S.C., January 3, 1904, at 17; Hooper to Iredell, February 12, 1786, Duke; Helen (Nelly) Blair to Iredell: April 1786 (exact date not shown), NCAH; February 3, 1787, Duke; April 15, 1787, Duke; April 20, 1789, Duke.

18. Iredell to Hannah Iredell: April 6, 18, 1786; May 23, 24, 27, 1786; October 17, 1786, NCAH.

19. Iredell to Hannah Iredell: December 21, 1786; March 31, 1787; May 25, 27, 1787; November 28, 1787; November 23, 1788; October 27, 1791; November 11, 1791; February 28, 1799, NCAH. Iredell to Annie Iredell: March 6, 1795; January 21, 1796; March 18, 1796; April 7, 1797; February 28, 1799, NCAH.

20. McRee, 2:244 (ed. note); Blair to Iredell, May 29, 1788, NCAH.

21. Davie to Iredell, November 1788 (exact date not shown), Duke; Johnston to Iredell, November 14, 20, 1788, NCAH.

22. Iredell to Hannah Iredell, April 11, 25, 1789; Hannah Iredell to Iredell, October 31, 1790, NCAH. Tredwell to Hannah Iredell, November 1791 (exact date not shown), Duke.

23. Hannah Iredell to Helen (Nelly) Blair Tredwell, June 10, 1792, NCAH; Iredell to Hannah Iredell, November 1, 1792, NCAH (in McRee, 2:373, in part).

24. Iredell to Hannah Iredell, March 3, 1796, and February 28, 1799; to Master James Iredell, Jr., April 26, 1795, NCAH.

25. Iredell to Hannah Iredell, April 18, 1799, NCAH; James Johnston to Master James Iredell, Jr., April 18, 1799, NCAH.

26. Jones, *supra* note 17, at 63. McRee, 1:36–37 (ed. essay), 2:338 (ed. note), and notation in Iredell Papers, Duke (all regarding birth and name); Iredell to Arthur Iredell, January 10, 1792, NCAH; Thomas Iredell (brother) to Iredell, February 10, 1792, NCAH; Johnston to Iredell, April 3, 1792, Duke, and April 22, 1797, NCAH; Hannah Iredell to Helen (Nelly) Blair Tredwell, June 10, 1792, NCAH.

27. Iredell to Hannah Iredell: May 20, 1793; April 15, 1794; January 21, 1795;

January 20, 1797; February 24, 1797; January 18, 1799; February 28, 1799, NCAH. Iredell to Helen Iredell: August 6, 1796, Duke; February 17, 1797, NCAH; April 5, 1798, Duke.

28. Marcus, 2:65 (Iredell to Hannah Iredell, May 10, 1790); Iredell to Hannah Iredell, November 22, 1788, and September 20, 1792, NCAH.

29. Iredell to Thomas Iredell (uncle): July 6, 1791, and December 4, 1794, NCAH; November 29, 1795, James Iredell Association, Inc., Edenton, N.C.

30. Iredell to Hannah Iredell: May 20, 1791; April 7, 15, 19, 1794; August 11, 1794; February 20, 1795; February 24, 1797; April 7, 1797; May 31, 1797; April 11, 1799, NCAH. Iredell to Annie Iredell, April 7, 1795, and to Annie, James, and Helen Iredell, April 22, 1796, NCAH.

31. Hannah Iredell to Iredell, November 11, 1790, and Iredell to Hannah Iredell, April 28, 1794, NCAH; Iredell to Johnston, May 29, 1793, Miscellaneous Manuscripts, Iredell Collection, Manuscripts Division, Library of Congress, Washington, D.C. (see also SHC).

32. McRee, 2:449 (ed. note); Thomas Iredell (brother) to Iredell, July 28, 1797, NCAH; Iredell to Hannah Iredell, July 31 and August 16, 1797, NCAH; John Metcalf to Iredell, November 7, 1797, Duke.

33. Iredell to McCulloh, July 11, 1789, NCAH; to Butler, July 25, 1789, NCAH; to Annie Iredell, July 17, 1795, NCAH; to Hannah Iredell: April 8, 1792, NCAH; June 5, 1795, NCAH; March 25, 1796, Duke; January 29, 1797, Duke.

34. Iredell to Helen Iredell, March 10, 1795, NCAH; to Annie Iredell, March 10, July 17, 1795, NCAH; to Hannah Iredell: March 6, 10, 13, 1795; July 18, 1795; April 7, 1797, NCAH.

35. McRee, 2:587 (ed. essay, funeral oration); Iredell to Hannah Iredell, November 29, 1789, NCAH.

36. E.g., Marcus, 2:65 (Iredell to Hannah Iredell, May 10, 1790); Iredell to Hannah Iredell: May 24, 1786; December 21, 1786; April 22, 1787; January 20, 1797; NCAH.

37. Spence, 62; Sykes, 49 (document regarding Annie "in her brother James's handwriting"); handwritten document in "Miscellany" file, Duke; Samuel Johnston to Iredell, December 4, 1798, NCAH; Helen (Nelly) Blair to James Iredell (Jr.), February 3, 1827, Duke.

38. Hannah Iredell to Helen Iredell, March 1825 (?) (and notations on typescript thereof) and May 30, 1825, Duke.

39. McRee, 1:1 (ed. essay); Helen Iredell to Hannah Iredell, April 12, 1825, Duke; Dr. James I. Chaplin to James Iredell (Jr.), May 7, 1825, Duke.

40. Sykes, 109–13; Max R. Williams, "The Johnston Will Case: A Clash of Titans," North Carolina Historical Review 67 (1990): 193, 218, 218 n.79; Will of Hannah Iredell, Book A, page 1257, Chowan County, N.C., Registry (original now in NCAH). The author has also drawn here on family materials provided to him by Harvey Johnson of Raleigh, North Carolina, an Iredell great-great-great-grandson (in author's files).

41. McRee, 2:503 (Johnston to Iredell, May 3, 1797); Johnston to Iredell, June 30, 1799, NCAH.

42. J.G. deRoulhac Hamilton, ed., *The Papers of Thomas Ruffin* (Raleigh, N.C.: Edwards & Broughton, 4 vols., 1918–20), 1:21, 37; Roscoe Pound, *The Formative Era of American Law* (Boston: Little, Brown & Co., 1938), 4, 30 n.2; Beth Crabtree, "Iredell, James, Jr.," in Powell, *DNCB*, 3:255.

43. Hamilton, *supra* note 42, at 1:183 n.3 (succeeding Ruffin), 4:258 n.1 (University of North Carolina trustee); Henderson, 2:648 (legal education); Johnson, 288–89 (same); Lefler and Newsome, 382 (same); Beth Crabtree, "Iredell, James, Jr.," in Powell, *DNCB*, 3:255 (general); J.P. Boyd, "James Iredell, Junior, As a Student at Princeton College," *The Charlotte Observer*, Charlotte, N.C., October 9, 1927, sec. 3, at 12; file marked "Legal Papers," Duke. For an example of James' signature, see "Memorial to the Congress of the United States from the Citizens of the Town of Edenton," December 16, 1807, "Miscellany" file, Duke.

44. Jones, *supra* note 17, at 69; Hannah Iredell to Helen (Nelly) Blair Tredwell, November 15, 1791, NCAH; James Iredell Association Newsletter, Edenton, N.C., June 1993 (copy in author's files).

45. Spence, 63; H.G. Jones, "Ex-Governor's Bible Tells Family's Story," *Hickory Daily Record*, Hickory, N.C., January 23, 1974, at 10A; William D. Valentine Diaries, entry for April 15, 1853, SHC.

46. McRee, 2:399 (Iredell to Helen (Nelly) Blair Tredwell, August 12, 1793); Hannah Iredell to Iredell, October 31, 1790, and to Helen (Nelly) Blair, February 27, 1791, NCAH.

47. Iredell Will, Will Book B at 142, Chowan County Registry, Edenton, N.C. (original now in NCAH); James C. Johnston to Griffith J. McRee, December 14, 1857, McRee Papers, SHC; Iredell to Hannah Iredell: February 28, 1799; April 25, 1799; May 2, 1799, NCAH; Memorandum to Iredell House File from William J. McCrea and Terry Harper, regarding Dendrochronology Report and Architectural Analysis, June 30, 1993, Department of Cultural Resources, Raleigh, N.C. (copy in author's files; the author served as a consultant on this project).

48. Iredell house materials, NCAH; Mary Ann Coffey, "Women's Daring is Remembered," Chowan Herald, Edenton, N.C., September 28, 1995, at 4–5A; letter from Cornelia J. Privott, President of James Iredell Association, Inc., July 1, 1965, Duke (copy); pamphlet, "Edenton's Historic James Iredell House," NCC; Act of Apr. 11, 1951, ch. 788, 1951 N.C. Sess. Laws 779–80; Iredell family materials from Harvey Johnson, Raleigh, N.C. (in author's files).

49. McCulloh to Iredell, April 28, 1784, and July 25, 1785, Duke; Iredell to McCulloh, September 26, 1784, NCAH, and January 6, 1785, Duke.

50. George Blair to Iredell, February 27, 1799, NCAH; Robert Lenox to Iredell, March 2, 20, 1799, Duke; Iredell to Hannah Iredell, March 7, 21, 1799, NCAH; Iredell to Mrs. Gray (?), September 6, 1799, NCAH.

51. Higginbotham, 2:389 (Iredell to Helen (Nelly) Blair, April 10, 1783), 407 (Iredell to Hannah Iredell, May 26, 1783); Iredell to Helen (Nelly) Blair, October 18, 1785, Duke; Iredell to Hannah Iredell, September 29, 1786, Duke; Helen (Nelly) Blair to Hannah Iredell, May 18, 1785, Duke, and July 19, 1792, NCAH; Helen (Nelly) Blair to Iredell, April 17, 1786, NCAH.

52. Higginbotham, 1:461 (Iredell to Helen (Nelly) Blair, September 3, 1777);

Jean Blair to Helen (Nelly) Blair, March 21, 1785, NCAH; see generally Watson, "Women," 2–4, 12.

53. McRee, 2:256 (Iredell to the Misses Blair, March 15, 1789); Helen (Nelly) Blair to Iredell, April 20, 1789, Duke.

54. Jean Blair to Helen (Nelly) Blair, August 18, 1787, Duke; Helen (Nelly) Blair Tredwell to Hannah Iredell, June 22, 1790, NCAH, and September 26, 1790, Duke.

55. Iredell to Dr. Tredwell, July 31, 1792, NCAH; to Samuel Tredwell, March 30, 1797, NCAH; to Hannah Iredell, May 25, 1797, NCAH (in McRee, 2:513, but with alterations); Helen (Nelly) Blair Tredwell to Iredell, March 4, 1797, NCAH.

56. Johnston to Iredell, August 1, 1795; to Hannah Iredell, June 21, 1798, NCAH.

57. McRee, 2:396 (Johnston to Iredell, June 10, 1793), 441 (Iredell to Hannah Iredell, March 30, 1795); Johnston to Hannah Iredell, May 26, 1793, NCAH; Johnston to Iredell, April 20, 1799, NCAH; Iredell to Hannah Iredell: April 22, 1796, NCAH; April 4, 1799, Duke; May 2, 1799, NCAH.

58. Johnston to Iredell, July 28, 1798, and June 30, 1799, NCAH; Iredell to Hannah Iredell, May 11, 1799, NCAH. For other evidence of the special relationship between Iredell and James Johnston, see the following: Iredell to Hannah Iredell, March 25, 1796, Duke; same, May 3, 1796, NCAH; Iredell to Samuel Tredwell, March 30, 1797, NCAH; Iredell to Hannah Iredell, April 21, 1797, Duke; same, April 4, 1799, Duke; Samuel Johnston to Hannah Iredell, April 23, 1799, NCAH; same, May 10, 1799, NCAH; Samuel Johnston to Iredell, May 18, 1799, NCAH; same, May 25, 1799, NCAH; Iredell to Hannah Iredell, June 5, 1799, NCAH.

59. Higginbotham, 1:88 n.1 (Dawson biographical sketch), 107 (Iredell to Francis Iredell, Sr., July 20, 1772); Penelope Dawson to Hannah Iredell, undated typescripts, Duke; Watson, "Women," 13.

60. See generally Alden, 343–44 (mentions numerous leaders of period, including Iredell); Joseph J. Ellis, *American Sphinx: The Character of Thomas Jefferson* (New York: Alfred A. Knopf, 1997), 144–52, 263–73 (Jefferson); John C. Miller, *The Wolf by the Ears: Thomas Jefferson and Slavery* (New York: Free Press, 1977) (Jefferson); Smith, *Patriarch*, 203–04, 209, 258, 302, 305–06, 345–46 (Washington). As to Iredell, see Johnson, 561; Lefler and Newsome, 415; Lefler and Stanford, 260; Powell, 297.

61. Act of May 9, 1777, ch. VI, 1777 N.C. Sess. Laws, reprinted in Iredell, 288–89 (also in Clark, 24:14–15); Jesse Copeland and Iredell affidavits, Edenton Superior Court records (1778 and 1779 folders), NCAH. See Jeffrey J. Crow, *The Black Experience in Revolutionary North Carolina* (Raleigh: N.C. Division of Archives and History, 1977), 62–63; Waldrup, 145–46.

62. Elliot, 4:100–01; Higginbotham, 1:264 (Iredell's "To The Inhabitants of Great Britain"); McRee, 2:212–13 (Iredell's "Answers").

63. See "List of the Number of Persons in the Family of James Iredell in the Town of Edenton," dated February 8, 1786, in file marked "James Iredell, Sr. — miscellaneous," NCAH (reference to fourteen slaves). The Iredell papers are replete with references to assistance from his slaves, and the wills of Iredell and his wife suggest that both died owning slaves. As to manumission, see text *infra* and, e.g., Lefler and Stanford, 251; Marcus, 2:446 n.1.

64. *State Gazette of North Carolina*, Edenton, N.C., August 13, 1789, at 4.

65. Higginbotham, 1:452 n.1, 2:284 (Iredell to Hannah Iredell, August 29, 1781), 292–93 (same, September 11, 1781), 342 (same, May 17, 1782), 345 (same, June 3, 1782), 362 (same, November 20, 1782).

66. Marcus, 2:101 n.1, 446 n.1; Iredell to Hannah Iredell: October 14, 1790; April 6, 1791; April 28, 1792, NCAH.

67. Marcus, 2:348 (Iredell to Hannah Iredell, April 2, 1793); McRee, 2:359 (same, September 23, 1792).

68. Helen (Nelly) Blair to Iredell, May 29, 1788, NCAH, and June 13, 1789, J. Duke.

69. McRee, 2:427 n.*, 520 n.*; Samuel Johnston to Hannah Iredell, September 27, 1790, NCAH; Iredell to Hannah Iredell: August 3, 1794; February 13, 1795 (in McRee, 2:439, in part); February 5, 1798, NCAH; James C. Johnston to Griffith J. McRee, December 14, 1857, McRee Papers, SHC. A "Taxable List of James Iredell, 1796," file marked "James Iredell, Sr. — Accounts, Property," NCAH, contains a list of Iredell's slaves; while the list is largely illegible, it is clear that Peter is not mentioned, thus indicating prior manumission.

70. Iredell to Hannah Iredell: July 29, 1796; January 21, 1796; January 20, 1797; May 1, 1798; May 5, 1798, NCAH.

71. Marcus, 2:446 (Iredell to Hannah Iredell, April 15, 1794); Iredell to Hannah Iredell: January 21, 1795, NCAH; April 7, 1795, NCAH; April 15, 1795, Duke; May 27, 1795, NCAH.

72. Higginbotham, 1:32–33 (Thomas Iredell to Iredell, July 10, 1769), 53 (same, July 2, 1770).

73. Arthur Iredell to Iredell: January 3, 1797, NCAH; February 5, 1797, NCAH; February 17, 1797, NCAH; June 14, 1797, NCAH; September 5, 1797, NCAH; November 7, 1798, Duke. Iredell to Hannah Iredell: April 7 (two letters), 14, and August 11, 1797, NCAH. Iredell to Arthur Iredell, October 8, 1797, NCAH. Bill of sale, NCAH. The matter must have weighed heavily on Iredell's mind, for his second letter to Hannah of April 7, 1797, essentially reiterates what he said in the first. It is clear that there were two distinct letters because in the second, Iredell refers to having written her that morning.

74. McRee, 2:587 (ed. essay quoting Bishop Charles Pettigrew's funeral oration).

CHAPTER 20

Friends, Finances, Faith, Fun, Foibles

1. McRee, 2:587 (ed. essay quoting Bishop Pettigrew's funeral oration).

2. *Ibid.*, 426 (ed. note; original letter not found), 584 (Davie to Iredell, September 18, 1799); Thomas Cox to Iredell, July 18, 1799, Duke; Griffin to Iredell, August 25, 1799, Duke.

3. Iredell to Hamilton, March 1, 1793, NCAH.

4. McRee, 2:334 (Sitgreaves to Iredell, August 2, 1791); Johnston to Iredell, October 11, 1790, NCAH; John Brownrigg to Iredell, October 18, 1790, NCAH; J.

Read, Jr., to Iredell, March 14, 1799, Duke. For another request for such assistance, see Robert Black to Iredell, October 5, 1790, NCAH.

5. McRee, 2:306 (ed. note; original Lenox to Iredell letter not found); Baron von Poellnitz to Iredell, April 22, 1784, Duke (as to Poellnitz, see Higginbotham, 2:349 n.1); William R. Davie to Iredell, August 6, 1787, Duke; Samuel Johnston to Iredell, April 10, 1793, NCAH; Thomas Iredell (brother) to Iredell, June 19, 1793, NCAH; Iredell to Samuel Tredwell, August 9, 1793, NCAH.

6. E.g., Iredell to Hannah Iredell, October 2, 1791, and July 31, 1797, NCAH; document captioned "Judge Iredell, Edenton May 1799," Arthur Jones Papers, NCAH (dining invitation).

7. McRee, 2:574 (Iredell to Hannah Iredell, May 11, 1799), 577 (Davie to Iredell, June 17, 1799), 580 (John Steele to Iredell, August 5, 1799), 584 (Davie to Iredell, September 18, 1799); Davie to Iredell, September 4, 1795, Marshall Delaney Haywood Papers, NCAH. As to the county, see William S. Powell, *The North Carolina Gazetteer* (Chapel Hill: University of North Carolina Press, 1968), 136.

8. Higginbotham, 1:244–45 (Hooper to Iredell, August 5, 1774), 2:29–30 (Iredell to Hannah Iredell, June 4, 1778); McRee, 2:259 (Ann Hooper to Iredell, June 2, 1789), 300 (Iredell to Ann Hooper, November 6, 1790); Iredell to Hannah Iredell: April 10, 1783, NCAH; April 8, 1784, NCAH; October 5, 1785, NCAH; April 18, 1786, NCAH; June 9, 1799, Duke. See Watson, "Women," 13.

9. McRee, 2:119 (Iredell to Dukinfield, January 7, 1785), 130 (Iredell to Helen (Nelly) Blair, October 18, 1785), 326 (Iredell to John Hay, April 14, 1791), 476 (Iredell to Miss Gray, June 1796) (exact date not shown); William R. Davie to Iredell, September 7, 1789, Duke; John Haywood to Iredell, June 18, 1792, Duke. See W.B. Grove to Iredell, January 31, 1791, Duke (informing of Archibald Maclaine's death).

10. Marcus, 2:540 (circuit assignments); McRee, 2:430 (Iredell to Wilson, November 24, 1794), 431 (William R. Davie to Iredell, December 15, 1794) (also in Marcus, 2:499); Iredell to Hannah Iredell, May 6, 16, 1791, NCAH.

11. Marcus, 2:408–10 (John Quincy Adams to Thomas Boylston Adams, June 23, 1793); Smith, *Wilson*, 212, 361–66.

12. Marcus, 3:151–52 (ed. essay), 223 (Wilson to Bird Wilson, September 6, 1797), 231 (same, December 17, 1797), 232 (Wilson to Joseph Thomas, December 17, 1797), 266 (same, May 12, 1798), 281 (Hannah Wilson to Bird Wilson, July 28, 1798); Smith, *Wilson*, 383–87; Lewis Burd Walker, ed., *The Burd Papers: Selections from Letters Written by Edward Burd, 1763–1828* (Pottsville, Pa.: Standard Publishing, 1899), 191–92 (Edward Burd to Jasper Yeates, August 4, 1796).

13. Marcus, 3:492–93 (circuit assignment); McRee, 2:494 (Iredell to Hannah Iredell, February 24, 1797), 516 (same, August 11, 1797) (also in Marcus, 1(#2):856–57), 527 (same, May 11, 1798); Iredell to Hannah Iredell, February 5, 8, and April 5, 1798, NCAH.

14. Marcus, 3:283–84 (Iredell to Hannah Iredell, August 6, 1798) (also in McRee, 2:533–34, but McRee incorrectly says $6,000 rather than $60,000); Johnston to Iredell, July 28, 1798, NCAH (in McRee, 2:532, but with alterations); Thomas Iredell (brother) to Iredell, August 17, 1798, NCAH.

15. Marcus, 3:287–88 (Iredell to Bird Wilson, September 1, 1798), 301 (Iredell

to William Cushing, October 28, 1798) (original in Cushing Family Papers, Massachusetts Historical Association, Boston, contains additional minor detail); McRee, 2:534 (Iredell to Miss Gray, Hannah Wilson's sister, August 25, 1798); file marked "James Iredell, Sr., Miscellaneous Papers, Estate of James Wilson, 1798," NCAH (and see Iredell to Hannah Iredell, February 28, 1799, NCAH). For the conflicting accounts, see Campbell, 49 (Iredell's home); van Santvoord, 291–92 (same); Smith, *Wilson*, 388 (Horniblow's). A recent biography of John Marshall perpetuates the apparently erroneous assertion that Wilson died at Iredell's home. Jean Edward Smith, *John Marshall: Definer of a Nation* (New York: Henry Holt and Company, 1996), 599 n.60.

16. Marcus, 1(#1):49 n.17 (citing *Washington Daily News*, Washington, N.C., August 18, 1976); William MacLean, Jr., in Burton A. Konkle, *James Wilson and The Constitution* (Philadelphia: Law Academy, 1907), 3–4; Spence, 62.

17. Marcus, 1(#1):124–36 (ed. essay, correspondence, etc., regarding Washington's appointment), 1(#2):868–69 (Bushrod Washington to George Washington, October 19, 1798, and George Washington to Bushrod Washington, October 24, 1798), 928 (John Marshall to Joseph Story, 1827) (exact date not shown), 3:286 (Iredell to Pickering, August 25, 1798), 493 (circuit assignment); Smith, *Patriarch*, xx.

18. Marcus, 3:288 n.3; McRee, 2:534 (Iredell to Miss Gray, August 25, 1798), 546 (Iredell to Hannah Wilson, February 16, 1799); Iredell to Bird Wilson, September 24, 1798, James A. Montgomery Papers, Historical Society of Pa., Philadelphia, Pa.; Bird Wilson to Iredell, October 22, 1798, NCAH; Samuel Johnston to Iredell, December 14, 1798, NCAH (shows Mrs. Wilson still in Edenton almost four months after Wilson's death); Iredell to Hannah Iredell: January 18, 22, February 28, March 7, 14, April 11, 1799, NCAH.

19. Marcus, 3:289 (Hannah Wilson to Bird Wilson, September 1, 1798); McRee, 2:536 (William White to Iredell, date not shown), 537 (William Rawle to Iredell, September 26, 1798), 539 (Cushing to Iredell, November 9, 1798); Bird Wilson to Iredell, October 22, 1798, NCAH; Hannah Wilson to Hannah Iredell, July 12, 1799, NCAH.

20. See the following letters in the Konkle Papers, SHC: Henry M. London to Konkle, March 2, 7, 1935; Charles W. Tillett, Jr., to Konkle, March 20, 1935; I.M. Bailey to Konkle, April 1, 1935 (London, Tillett, and Bailey were officers of the North Carolina Bar or the North Carolina Bar Association); Alexander B. Andrews (member, North Carolina Society of the Sons of the Revolution) to Konkle, September 11, 1934; Mrs. James Iredell IV to Konkle, August 16, 1934; Martha S. Iredell to Konkle, August 15, 21, 1934. The material on the Iredell portrait is from a Photographic Record of Portraits file at the United States Supreme Court Building, Washington, D.C., and information gleaned during the author's visit to the Court on May 3, 1993. See generally, regarding the Wilson-Iredell relationship, Hampton L. Carson, "James Wilson and James Iredell. A Parallel and A Contrast," The Pennsylvania Magazine of History and Biography 45 (1921): 1–33.

21. McRee, 2:56 (Iredell to Arthur Iredell, July 30, 1783); Gordon S. Wood, *The Radicalism of the American Revolution* (New York: Vintage Books, 1991), 287;

Martha Dozier, "James Iredell — A Character Sketch," North Carolina Law Journal 1 (1900): 197, 201–02; William C. Pool, "An Economic Interpretation of the Ratification of the Federal Constitution in North Carolina: Part I, The Hillsboro Convention — Background and Economic Interests of the Federalists," North Carolina Historical Review 27 (1950): 119, 139; Higginbotham 2:273–74 (Iredell to Governor Thomas Burke, August 12, 1781); List of the Taxable Property of James Iredell, 1787, NCAH.

22. Iredell to Hannah Iredell: April 23, 1784; April 18, 20, 21, 1786; May 19, 1787; October 21, 1788; April 20 and September 25, 1789, NCAH; Helen (Nelly) Blair to Iredell, May 29, 1788, NCAH.

23. Iredell to Margaret Iredell, January 22, 1785, and to Arthur Iredell, same date, NCAH.

24. Iredell to Secretary of the Treasury (Alexander Hamilton), April 26, 1790, NCAH; Thomas Iredell (brother) to Iredell, February 10, 1792, NCAH; *State Gazette of North Carolina*, Edenton, N.C., May 8, 1790, at 3; document dated November 19, 1795, NCAH, and one dated January 20, 1797, in file marked "James Iredell, Sr. — Miscellaneous," NCAH.

25. Marcus, 1(#2):698 (John Swann to Iredell, March 5, 1790), 700 (Iredell to Thomas Iredell (uncle), March 8, 1790); Nathaniel Dukinfield to Iredell, May 12, 1791, Duke.

26. Johnston to Iredell, March 21, 1790, NCAH, and May 9, 1790, Duke; Hannah Iredell to Iredell, October 21, 31, 1790, NCAH. See Walter Sikes, "James Iredell," in *Wake Forest Historical Society Papers* (Raleigh: Edwards & Broughton, 1899), No. 1, at 57.

27. Iredell to Hannah Iredell: April 9, 11, 1791; April 2, 21, 1795; March 3, 11, 1796; March 3, 17, 1797; May 4, 1797; February 28 and April 11, 1799, NCAH; Iredell to Helen (Nelly) Blair Tredwell, August 12, 1793, NCAH; Arthur Iredell to Iredell, June 23, 1794, NCAH; Iredell to Thomas Iredell (uncle), December 4, 1794, NCAH; Iredell to George Simpson, cashier of the Bank of the United States, May 22, 1795, Etting Collection, Historical Society of Pa., Philadelphia, Pa.

28. Marcus, 1(#2):699 n.2; Sykes, 23; Iredell to Hannah Iredell, February 9, 1797, NCAH; Johnston to Arthur Iredell, October 30, 1799, SHC.

29. Higginbotham, 1:11 (Iredell's "Essay on Religion," ca. 1768), 11 n.1, 37, 39 (Iredell's "Essay on Religion," September 17, 1769), 68 (Iredell to Francis Iredell, Jr., June 15, 1771), 173 (Iredell's Diary, August 23, 1770). On the state of religious life at the time, see Bernard Bailyn, *Faces of Revolution: Personalities and Themes in the Struggle for American Independence* (New York: Alfred A. Knopf, 1990), 192; Samuel S. Hill, Jr., *Southern Churches in Crisis* (New York: Holt, Rinehart and Winston, 1966), 52–56; Lefler and Newsome, 122–32; McRee, 1:149 (ed. essay); Price, 426–27.

30. Higginbotham, 1:143 (Penelope Dawson to Samuel Johnston, ca. 1773), 177 (Iredell's Diary, August 27, 1770) (also in McRee, 1:70), 195 (Iredell's Diary, December 13, 1772), 203 (same, December 30, 1772), 208 (same, January 17, 1773).

31. McRee, 2:586 (ed. essay); Bennett H. Wall, "Charles Pettigrew, First Bishop-

Elect of the North Carolina Episcopal Church," North Carolina Historical Review 28 (1951): 15, 18 n.18.

32. Iredell to Hannah Iredell, October 2, 1791, and October 7, 1792, NCAH.

33. McRee, 2:289 (Iredell to Hannah Iredell, May 23, 1790), 346 (same, April 19, 1792), 522 (same, May 1, 1798); Iredell to Hannah Iredell: September 19, 1790; September 6, 1791; September 25, 1792; May 5, 1793; August 3, 1794, NCAH.

34. McRee, 2:374 (Iredell to Arthur Iredell, November 30, 1792), 461 (Iredell to Hannah Iredell, February 25, 1796), 463 (same, March 3, 1796), 475 (same, April 15, 1796).

35. *Ibid.*, 289 (Iredell to Hannah Iredell, May 23, 1790), 361 (same, September 30, 1792); Iredell to Hannah Iredell, May 16, 1793, NCAH.

36. McRee, 2:119 (Iredell to Nathaniel Dukinfield, January 7, 1785), 326 (Iredell to John Hay, April 14, 1791), 587 (ed. essay quoting Pettigrew's funeral oration).

37. Higginbotham, 2:66 (Iredell to Hannah Iredell, January 16, 1779); McRee, 2:371 (Iredell to Hannah Iredell, October 13, 1792); Iredell to Hannah Iredell, June 22, 1792, NCAH; Johnston to Iredell, December 25, 1796, NCAH.

38. McRee, 2:218 (Hannah Iredell to Margaret Iredell, January 31, 1788), 362 (Iredell to Hannah Iredell, October 4, 1792); Elizabeth Hogg Huske to Helen (Nelly) Blair, June 2, 1784, Duke; Iredell to Hannah Iredell, November 24, 1785, NCAH.

39. McRee, 2:439 (Iredell to Hannah Iredell, February 5, 1795), 441 (same, March 30, 1795), 446 (same, June 5, 1795), 456 (same, November 27, 1795), 493 (same, February 17, 1797), 494 (same, February 24, 1797); Iredell to Hannah Iredell: May 23, 27, 1787; April 22, 1796; March 14, 1799, NCAH. See Alonzo T. Dill, Jr., "Eighteenth Century New Bern Part VIII," North Carolina Historical Review 23 (1946): 495, 524–25.

40. Smith, *Patriarch*, 5 (Washington); Iredell to Hannah Iredell, April 21, 1786, NCAH.

41. McRee, 2:571 (Iredell to Hannah Iredell, April 11, 1799).

42. Marcus, 3:273 (Iredell to Hannah Iredell, May 19, 1798); McRee, 2:523 (Iredell to Hannah Iredell, May 8, 1798) (also in Marcus, 3:263–64), 527 (same, May 11, 1798) (also in Marcus, 3:264).

43. Iredell to Butler, March 14, 1784, NCAH.

44. Iredell to Blair, September 15, 1785, NCAH.

45. Hannah Iredell to Helen (Nelly) Blair Tredwell, July 22, 1793, NCAH.

CHAPTER 21

King of Terrors and Terror of Kings

1. Robert M. Miller, *Harry Emerson Fosdick: Preacher, Pastor, Prophet* (New York: Oxford University Press, 1985), 570.

2. Higginbotham, 1:194–95 (Iredell's Diary, December 13, 1772); McRee, 1:66 (same, August 23, 1770).

3. McRee, 1:72 (Iredell's Diary, September 7, 1770), 96 (Iredell to Margaret Iredell, October 3, 1771).

4. *Colds*: Marcus, 3:84 (Iredell to Hannah Iredell, December 2, 1795); McRee, 2:114 (same, November 20, 1784); Iredell to Hannah Iredell: April 24, 1785; October 19, 1785; April 21, 1786; May 30, 1787; November 23, 1788; April 28, 1789; November 26, 1789; June 5, 1795; November 29, 1797, all NCAH.

Fevers: McRee, 1:71 (Iredell's Diary, August 28, 1770), 2:346 (Iredell to Hannah Iredell, April 19, 1792); Iredell to Hannah Iredell: October 23, 1786, Duke; September 16, 1791, Duke; June 22, 1792, NCAH.

Intestinal Complaints: Iredell to Hannah Iredell: November 18, 1784; November 22, 1787; July 31, 1797; August 3, 1797; April 17, 1798, all NCAH.

Stomach Disorders: McRee, 2:438 (Iredell to Hannah Iredell, January 28, 1795); Iredell to Hannah Iredell, January 28, 1798, NCAH.

Rheumatism: M. McKenzie to Iredell, April 21, 1790; Iredell to Hannah Iredell, May 6, 1790; Samuel Johnston to Iredell, May 9, 1790, all Duke.

Eye Inflammation: Samuel Johnston to Hannah Iredell, April 28, 1796, Duke; Iredell to Hannah Iredell: May 3, 1796, NCAH; May 6, 1796, Duke; May 16, 1796, Duke; June 1, 1796, NCAH.

Cholera Morbus: McRee, 2:70–71 (ed. note).

5. Higginbotham, 2:3 (Iredell to Hannah Iredell, January 14, 1778); Iredell to: John Williams, December 10, 1781, Judge John Williams Papers, SHC; H.E. McCulloh, June 15, 1784, NCAH; Arthur Iredell, January 22, 1785, NCAH; Hannah Iredell, October 10, 1786, NCAH; H.E. McCulloh, September 7, 1787, NCAH.

6. Marcus, 2:79 (Iredell to Hannah Iredell, June 18, 1790) (salts, tartar, bitters), 378 (same, May 16, 1793) (bark), 3:122 (same, May 3, 1796) (blooding); Iredell to Hannah Iredell: May 20, 1785 (bitters); September 29, 1785 (snake root); May 27, 1787 (rhubarb, magnesia); July 16, 1788 (bitters); October 3, 1790 (bitters, bark); July 31, 1797 (bark, cream tartar, chicken water, paregoric), all NCAH. For a detailed account of a new extract of bark, see William Saunders to Guy's Hospital, February 11, 1790, Duke (copy in Iredell's hand).

7. Higginbotham, 2:397 (Butler to Iredell, May 5, 1783); McRee, 2:94 (Iredell to Butler, March 14, 1784).

8. McRee, 2:83 (Hooper to Iredell, January 4, 1784), 96 (same, March 18, 1784); Elizabeth Hogg to Helen (Nelly) Blair, April 12 and June 2, 1784, Duke; James Hogg to Iredell, September 14, 1784, Duke; Hooper to Iredell, July 6, 1785, Emmet Collection, New York Public Library, New York, N.Y.; John Stokes to Iredell, March 29, 1789, Gratz Collection, Historical Society of Pa., Philadelphia, Pa.

9. McRee, 2:97 (Iredell to Hannah Iredell, April 8, 1784), 140 (Hooper to Iredell, August 1, 1786), 264 (Butler to Iredell, August 11, 1789), 399 (ed. note); Iredell to Hannah Iredell, April 8, 17, 1784, NCAH; Helen (Nelly) Blair to Iredell, April 14, 1784, NCAH; unsigned letter to Iredell, penciled date September (?), 1784, Duke (probably from William Hooper; it appears to be in his handwriting, and it has a reference to "my Betsy," which was the name of a Hooper daughter).

10. Higginbotham, 1:171 (Iredell's Diary, August 23, 1770); McRee, 2:396 (Samuel Johnston to Iredell, June 10, 1793); Iredell to Hannah Iredell, May 27, 1785, NCAH; Helen (Nelly) Blair to Iredell, May 26, 1786, NCAH; Samuel John-

ston to Hannah Iredell, April 29, 1797, NCAH; James C. Johnston to Griffith J. McRee, December 14, 1857, McRee Papers, SHC.

11. McRee, 2:130–31 (Samuel Cutler to Iredell, December 13, 1785) (regarding Cutler, see Marcus, 3:47 n.2); Jean Blair to Hannah Iredell, April 8, 1785, NCAH.

12. McRee, 2:106 (Hooper to Iredell, July 8, 1784); Dukinfield to Iredell, August 24, 1787, and February 13, 1788, Duke; Arthur Iredell to Iredell, September 21, 1787, and January 5, 1795, NCAH.

13. Hannah Iredell to Iredell, May 11, 1790, and Samuel Johnston to Iredell, June 30, 1799, NCAH.

14. McRee, 2:291–92 (Butler to Iredell, July 5, 1790); Johnston to Iredell, March 18, 1790, Duke; Response to Iredell's address to Grand Jury of North Carolina, June 2, 1794, in file marked "Legal Papers 1789–1799," Duke.

15. Iredell to Hannah Iredell, July 18, 1788, and July 18, 1795, NCAH.

16. McRee, 2:101 (Iredell to Thomas Iredell (uncle), May 28, 1784); Iredell to Hannah Iredell, October 10, 1786, and April 23, 1784, NCAH; Iredell to W. John Cameron, September 1, 1787, NCAH.

17. Marcus, 2:318 (Iredell to Hannah Iredell, October 21, 1792); McRee, 2:573 (same, May 11, 1799); Iredell to Hannah Iredell: June 18, 1790; September 6, 1791; October 7, 25, 1792; May 3, 20, 1793; March 13, 1795, all NCAH; Iredell to Helen (Nelly) Blair Tredwell, July 30, 1793, NCAH.

18. Marcus, 2:237 (ed. essay), 335 (Iredell to Arthur Iredell, November 30, 1792) (also in McRee, 2:373), 442 (Iredell to Edmund Randolph, February 13, 1794), 3:323 (ed. essay); McRee, 2:405 (ed. note); Iredell to John Jay, January 21, 1794, NCAH; Iredell to Mrs. Gray, September 6, 1799, NCAH. See also 3 U.S. (3 Dall.) 412 (1799) (reporter's note); 4 U.S. (4 Dall.) 1 n.* (1799) (reporter's note).

19. Chase to Iredell, April 28, 1799, Duke; Paterson to Iredell, December 3, 1797, and April 27, 1799, Duke.

20. Goebel, 553; McRee, 2:583 (Washington to Iredell, August 20, 1799) (also in Marcus, 3:380); file captioned "James Iredell, Sr. — U.S. Supreme Court Papers, Miscellaneous Materials, The Chief Justice and the Associate Justices . . . to the Congress," NCAH. Numerous accounts state the obvious conclusion that circuit duty undermined Iredell's health. See, e.g., the following: Ashe, 2:202; Friedman and Israel, 128–29; Henderson, 1:484; Marcus, 3:323 (ed. essay); Virginius Dabney, ed., *The Patriots: The American Revolution Generation of Genius* (New York: Atheneum, 1975), 140; Shnayerson, 74.

21. Marcus, 1(#2):876 n.1 (following Bushrod Washington to Iredell, August 20, 1799), 878 (*North-Carolina Minerva*, Raleigh, N.C., October 29, 1799), 878 n. (following *North-Carolina Minerva*, October 29, 1779, obituary) (citing *City Gazette*, Charleston, S.C., November 7, 1799; *Federal Gazette*, Baltimore, Md., November 8, 1799; and *Commercial Advertiser*, New York, N.Y., November 12, 1799), 879 (Samuel Johnston to Arthur Iredell, October 30, 1799); McRee, 2:550 (Iredell to Hannah Iredell, March 28, 1799); Iredell to Hannah Iredell: March 7, 1799, NCAH; April 4, 1799, Duke; April 11, 1799, NCAH; May 2, 11, 16, 19, 1799, NCAH; June 5, 1799, NCAH; June 9, 1799, Duke.

22. Iredell to Johnston, February 28 and March 7, 1799, Hayes Collection, SHC

(handwriting); Johnston to Hannah Iredell: May 10, July 23, 27, 1799, NCAH; Johnston to Iredell, August 13, 1799, NCAH.

23. McRee, 2:574 (Iredell to Hannah Iredell, May 11, 1799), 580 (ed. note); Iredell to Hannah Iredell, March 7 and May 11, 1799, NCAH; see Herndon, 295 (original letter Iredell to Mrs. James Wilson, August 7, 1799, cited by Herndon, not found).

24. Iredell to Annie Iredell, May 29, 1799, NCAH; Hannah Wilson to Iredell, August 7, 1799, NCAH (in McRee, 2:581, but somewhat altered).

25. Charles Dickens, *Hard Times* (New York: Oxford University Press, 1989 ed.), 95 ("Old Time"); Higginbotham, 2:423 (Arthur Iredell to Iredell, July 28, 1783) (quoting their uncle); John Miller to Iredell, August 8, 1799, Duke.

26. Marcus, 1(#2):880 (Steele to John Haywood, November 13, 1799), 881 (same, November 21, 1799), 881 n.1 (following John Steele to John Haywood, November 21, 1799); Iredell to an unnamed client, January 5, 1791, NCAH; Iredell to (?) (recipient's name torn off), January 29, 1786, NCAH ("I admire Alfred Moore."); Samuel Johnston to Iredell: November 21, 1798; April 13, 20, 1799, NCAH.

27. Marcus, 1(#2):879 (Samuel Johnston to Arthur Iredell, October 30, 1799); bills and document dated May 16, 1801 regarding settlement of Iredell's accounts, Hayes Collection, SHC.

28. Anthony to Iredell, November 6, 1799, and to Johnston, November 14, 1799, Hayes Collection, SHC. Regarding Fenno's paper, see John L. Brooke, "Ancient Lodges and Self-Created Societies: Voluntary Association and the Public Sphere in the Early Republic," in Ronald Hoffman and Peter J. Albert, eds., *Launching the "Extended Republic": The Federalist Era* (Charlottesville: University Press of Virginia, 1996), 310; Smith, *Patriarch*, 99.

29. McRee, 2:590 (grave monument inscription); draft of inscription in file marked "James Iredell, Sr. — Miscellaneous Papers," NCAH.

30. Fitzpatrick, 31:360 (Washington to Knox, September 8, 1791); McRee, 2:264 (Butler to Iredell, August 11, 1789); Johnston to Iredell, July 21, 1797, NCAH. On Washington's fatalistic attitude toward death, see also Smith, *Patriarch*, 156, 316, 345.

CHAPTER 22

A Parting Assessment

1. Elliot, 4:14; William Shakespeare, *The Tragedy of Hamlet, Prince of Denmark* (New Haven: Yale University Press, 1947, Brooke and Crawford, eds.), act 3, scene 2, at 92; Davie to Iredell, August 2, 1791, and May 25, 1792, Duke; Maclaine to Iredell, January 20, 1789, NCAH.

2. McRee, 2:218 (Elizabeth Williams to Iredell, February 9, 1788); Penelope Dawson to Helen (Nelly) Blair, October 22, 1784, Duke; Stokes to Iredell, March 27, 1787, Duke; Johnston to Iredell, October 11, 1790, NCAH; Helen (Nelly) Blair Tredwell to Hannah Iredell, November 1791 (exact date not shown), Duke.

3. Arthur Iredell to Iredell, January 4 and February 1, 1791, NCAH.

4. Higginbotham, 2:283 (Hooper to Iredell, August 28, 1781); Marcus, 2:413 (Paterson to Iredell, July 4, 1793); McRee, 2:248 (Williamson to Iredell, January 5, 1789), 263–64 (Butler to Iredell, August 11, 1789), 544–45 (Rev. Adam Boyd to Iredell, February 8, 1799).

5. Marcus, 1(#2):879 (Johnston to Arthur Iredell, October 30, 1799); McRee, 2:586–87 (funeral oration).

6. Swain to Griffith J. McRee, August 18, 1857, and (illegible) to McRee, December 10, 1857, McRee Papers, SHC.

7. Henderson, 2:681 (historian); Higginbotham, 1:xxxii (editor); Nash, 59, 70 (commentator).

8. Peele, 72.

9. Nash, 58.

10. G.B. Johnston, "Life and Character of James Iredell," North Carolina University Magazine 8 (no. 7) (March 1859): 302, 304.

11. Julian P. Boyd, to the Editor, William and Mary Quarterly 8 (Third Series, 1951): 317, 319; Bernard Bailyn, Faces of Revolution: Personalities and Themes in the Struggle for American Independence (New York: Alfred A. Knopf, 1990), 230 (repeated verbatim in Bernard Bailyn, The Ideological Origins of the American Revolution (Cambridge: Belknap Press at Harvard University Press, 1992), 328).

12. Carson, 154–55.

13. Andrew C. McLaughlin, The Courts, the Constitution and Parties (Chicago: University of Chicago Press, 1912), 74 n.1.

14. Van Santvoord, 61 n.*.

15. Johnson, 821.

16. Davis, 32; see also Campbell, 57 ("the ablest constitutional lawyer on the court").

17. Connor, "James Iredell," 253.

18. Henry J. Abraham, Justices and Presidents: A Political History of Appointments to the Supreme Court (New York: Oxford University Press, 3rd ed., 1992), 75.

19. Robert J. Wagman, The Supreme Court: A Citizen's Guide (New York: Pharos Books, 1993), 194.

20. Higginbotham, 2:xvii (quoting letter from Oliver W. Holmes to Christopher Crittenden, January 23, 1962, NCAH) (Frankfurter); William H. Hoyt, ed., The Papers of Archibald D. Murphey (Raleigh: E.M. Uzzell & Co., 1914), 1:366 (John Marshall to Archibald D. Murphey, October 6, 1827); Jim L. Sumner, " 'Let Us Have a Big Fair': The North Carolina Exposition of 1884," North Carolina Historical Review 69 (1992): 57, 71–72.

21. Robinson, 151.

22. William G. Brown, The Life of Oliver Ellsworth (New York: Macmillan Co., 1905), 240.

23. George Morgan, Patrick Henry (Philadelphia: J.B. Lippincott Co., 1929), 390.

24. Walter Sikes, "James Iredell," Wake Forest Historical Society Papers 1 (1899): 53, 57–58.

25. Arthur M. Schlesinger (Sr.), The Birth of the Nation: A Portrait of the American People on the Eve of Independence (New York: Alfred A. Knopf, 1968), 247.

26. Davis, 33 ("models"); McRee, 1:109 (Iredell to Hannah Johnston, April 19, 1772); Weeks, 251 (best letter-writer).

27. William K. Boyd, *History of North Carolina: The Federal Period, 1783–1860* (Spartanburg, S.C.: Reprint Co., 1973) (original ed., 1919), 385 (invaluable); Henderson, 1:418 (illuminate).

28. David Lowry Swain to James J. Iredell (Iredell's grandson), August 8, 1856, Swain Papers, and James J. Iredell to Griffith J. McRee, August 16, 1856, McRee Papers, SHC. See Higginbotham, 1:xxvi (ed. essay); Houston G. Jones, *For History's Sake: The Preservation and Publication of North Carolina History 1663–1903* (Chapel Hill: University of North Carolina Press, 1966), 165 n.130.

29. The conclusion is the author's, based on his own study; for the same view, see Julian P. Boyd, to the Editor, William and Mary Quarterly 8 (Third Series, 1951): 317 (passim).

30. Marcus, 2:4, 6:2; Linda Greenhouse, "Riding Circuit With Swamps and Yellow Fever," *The New York Times*, New York, N.Y., November 2, 1990, at B5.

31. Aubrey L. Brooks and Hugh T. Lefler, eds., *The Papers of Walter Clark* (Chapel Hill: University of North Carolina Press, 1948), 1:27 (Clark to his mother, August 15, 1860), 32 (same, August 25, 1860); Willis P. Whichard, "A Place for Walter Clark in the American Judicial Tradition," North Carolina Law Review 63 (1985): 287, 290–91; Richard F. Gibbs, "Now and Then," *The News and Observer*, Raleigh, N.C., February 24, 1974, sec. 4, at 3 (Ervin).

32. Battle, 2:321, 426; Dean Hair, "Statue Honoring Founding Trustees Dedicated," *The Daily Tar Heel*, Chapel Hill, N.C., July 6, 1995, at 3.

33. *Report of the Forty-Third Annual Meeting of the American Bar Association* (Baltimore: Lord Baltimore Press, 1920), 165; see Nash, 71.

34. *The Chowan Herald*, Edenton, N.C., January 25, 1940, at 1, 4; February 1, 1940, at 1; February 8, 1940, at 1; see Herndon, 337.

35. Iredell Meares to Connor, September 20, 1919; Connor to Gen. Francis S. Iredell, November 22, 1919; H.S. Iredell to Connor, December 20, 1919, Connor Papers, SHC.

36. The Library of Congress Information Bulletin, vol. 9, No. 38, September 18, 1950. The incorrect date is at McRee, 2:590.

37. Higginbotham, 1:79 (Iredell to Margaret Iredell, October 3, 1771); Steven P. Halbrook, "What the Framers Intended: A Linguistic Analysis of the Right to 'Bear Arms'," Law and Contemporary Problems 49 (1986): 151, 155. Higginbotham suggests, probably correctly, that Iredell was referring to no longer fearing the Regulators but needing protection during his law-practice travels. Higginbotham, 1:82 n.4.

38. The original Chowan County Courthouse in Edenton, N.C., is still used for certain court proceedings. See generally Marc D. Brodsky, *The Courthouse at Edenton: A History of the Chowan County Courthouse of 1767* (Edenton, N.C.: Chowan County, 1989). The Phi Alpha Delta Legal Fraternity, Norman Adrian Wiggins School of Law, Campbell University, Buies Creek, N.C., is named for Iredell and presents an annual James Iredell Award for significant contributions to the legal profession and the law school. There are Iredell streets, e.g., in Durham and Raleigh, North Carolina. As to the award, see *North Carolina Lawyers Weekly*, September 14,

1992, at 5. As to the Institute, see "One Common Interest" (Raleigh, N.C.: North Carolina Commission on the Bicentennial of the U.S. Constitution, April 1989), III:12.

39. Professor David A.J. Richards, in *Hearings Before the Committee on the Judiciary, United States Senate, One Hundredth Congress, First Session, on the Nomination of Robert H. Bork to be Associate Justice of the Supreme Court of the United States* (Washington: Government Printing Office, 1987), 1578–80. For Iredell's argument at Hillsborough, see Elliot, 4:148–49.

40. 144 Cong. Rec. S10,111 (daily ed. Sept. 9, 1998) (statement of Sen. Byrd) (see Elliot, 4:113); 145 Cong. Rec. S293–94 (daily ed. Jan. 16, 1999) (statement of Rep. Canady); Robert H. Bork, "Read the Constitution: It's Removal or Nothing," *The Wall Street Journal*, February 1, 1999, A21

41. See, e.g., Robert Cowley, ed., *What If?: The World's Foremost Military Historians Imagine What Might Have Been* (New York: G.P. Putnam's Sons, 1999); History Book Club Review, Midsummer 1998, inviting readers to submit "alternate" history essays to the Club's annual essay contest.

42. The originals are in the Iredell Papers, SHC. For commentary, see Henderson, 1:613–14; McRee, 2:458; Weeks, 250–51.

43. Cushing was almost sixty-nine—almost twenty years older than Iredell would have been—in late 1800 when Ellsworth resigned. See Kermit L. Hall, ed., *The Oxford Companion to the Supreme Court of the United States* (New York: Oxford University Press, 1992), 213. As to his poor health, his unpopularity, and Marshall's view, see McRee, 2:460 (Iredell to Hannah Iredell, February 19, 20, 1796), and James R. Perry, "Supreme Court Appointments, 1789–1801: Criteria, Presidential Style, and the Press of Events," Journal of the Early Republic 6 (1986): 371, 385–86, 396, 404. For Plumer quote, see Warren, *History*, 139; Plumer to Jeremiah Smith, February 19, 1796, Plumer Papers, Manuscripts Division, Library of Congress, Washington, D.C.

44. Marcus, 1(#2):906–07 (John Adams to Thomas B. Adams, December 23, 1800), 907 (Abigail Adams to Thomas B. Adams, December 25, 1800); see Perry, *supra* note 43, at 403–04.

45. Beveridge, 2:554–55.

46. Jim Schlosser, "N.C. scholar's views resurrected to criticize Bork," *Greensboro News & Record*, Greensboro, N.C., October 3, 1987, at D1.

47. For similar conclusions, see Ashe, 2:201; Connor, "James Iredell," 253.

48. William Shakespeare, *The Tragedy of Julius Caesar* (New Haven: Yale University Press, 1919, Mason, ed.), act 2, scene 2, at 36.

49. Albert P. Blaustein and Roy M. Mersky, *The First One Hundred Justices: Statistical Studies on the Supreme Court of the United States* (Hamden, Conn.: Archon Books, 1978), 38–39; Albert P. Blaustein and Roy M. Mersky, "Rating Supreme Court Justices," American Bar Association Journal 58 (November 1972): 1183.

50. Connor, "James Iredell," 225.

51. John P. Reid, *Chief Justice: The Judicial World of Charles Doe* (Cambridge: Harvard University Press, 1967), 436.

52. See Davis, 33.

53. For the same conclusion, see Berger, *Writings,* 129 ("one of the great Founders"), 184 ("one of the ablest of the Founders"), and Raoul Berger, "Original Intent: The Rage of Hans Baade," North Carolina Law Review 71 (1993): 1151, 1156 ("one of the ablest Founders").

54. See Smith, *Wilson,* 394.

Repository Symbols

Duke	Iredell Papers, Manuscripts Department, Perkins Library, Duke University, Durham, North Carolina
NCAH	State Archives, Division of Archives and History, North Carolina Department of Cultural Resources, Raleigh, North Carolina
NCC	North Carolina Collection, Wilson Library, University of North Carolina at Chapel Hill, Chapel Hill, North Carolina
SHC	Southern Historical Collection, Wilson Library, University of North Carolina at Chapel Hill, Chapel Hill, North Carolina

Short Titles

The following list includes all short titles and abbreviations used in this book:

Abbot and Twohig	W.W. Abbot and Dorothy Twohig, eds., *The Papers of George Washington* (Presidential Series) (Charlottesville: University Press of Virginia, 7 vols., 1987–98).
Alden	John Richard Alden, *The South in the Revolution, 1763–1789* (Baton Rouge: Louisiana State University Press, 1957).
Ashe	Samuel A. Ashe, *Biographical History of North Carolina: From Colonial Times to the Present* (Greensboro, N.C.: Charles L. Van Noppen, 8 vols., 1905–17).
Baker	William Spohn Baker, *Washington After the Revolution MDCCLXXXIV-MDCCXCIX* (Philadelphia: J.B. Lippincott Co., 1898).
Bates	Ernest Sutherland Bates, *The Story of the Supreme Court* (Indianapolis: Bobbs-Merrill Co., 1936).
Battle	Kemp P. Battle, *History of the University of North Carolina.* Vol. 1, *From 1789 to 1868*; vol. 2, *From 1868 to 1912* (Raleigh: Edwards & Broughton, 1907–12).

Berger, Government	Raoul Berger, *Government by Judiciary: The Transformation of the Fourteenth Amendment* (Cambridge: Harvard University Press, 1977).
Berger, Writings	Raoul Berger, *Selected Writings on the Constitution* (Cumberland, Va.: James River Press, 1987).
Beveridge	Albert J. Beveridge, *The Life of John Marshall*; vol. 2, *Politician, Diplomatist, Statesman, 1789–1801;* vol. 3, *Conflict and Construction, 1800–1815* (Boston: Houghton Mifflin Co., 1916–19).
Campbell	Tom W. Campbell, *Four Score Forgotten Men: Sketches of the Justices of the U.S. Supreme Court* (Little Rock, Ark.: Pioneer, 1950).
Carson	Hampton L. Carson, *The Supreme Court of the United States: Its History* (Philadelphia: John Y. Huber Co., 1891).
Casto	William R. Casto, *The Supreme Court in the Early Republic: The Chief Justiceships of John Jay and Oliver Ellsworth* (Columbia: University of South Carolina Press, 1995).
Cheney	John L. Cheney, Jr., ed., *North Carolina Government 1585–1974: A Narrative and Statistical History* (Raleigh: North Carolina Department of the Secretary of State, 1975).
Cibes	William J. Cibes, Jr., "Extra-Judicial Activities of Justices of the United States Supreme Court, 1790–1960." Ph.D. diss., Princeton University, 1975. Ann Arbor, Mich.: University Microfilms, 1992.
Clark	Walter Clark, ed., *The State Records of North Carolina*. 16 vols., numbered 11–26. Goldsboro, N.C.: Nash Bros., Book and Job Printers, 1907; Winston, N.C.: M.I. and J.C. Stewart, Printers to the State, 1896.
Connor, "James Iredell"	Henry G. Connor, "James Iredell: Lawyer, Statesman, Judge. 1751–1799," University of Pennsylvania Law Review 60 (1912): 225.
Connor, History	R.D.W. Connor, *History of North Carolina*. 6 vols. Chicago: Lewis Publishing Co., 1919.
Connor, Rebuilding	R.D.W. Connor, *North Carolina: Rebuilding an Ancient Commonwealth*. 4 vols. Chicago: American Historical Society, 1928–29.
Crow	Jeffrey J. Crow, *A Chronicle of North Carolina During the American Revolution, 1763–1789* (Raleigh: North Carolina Division of Archives and History, 1975).
Currie	David P. Currie, *The Constitution in the Supreme Court: The First Hundred Years, 1789–1888* (Chicago: University of Chicago Press, 1985).

Davis

Junius Davis, *Alfred Moore and James Iredell, Revolutionary Patriots, and Associate Justices of the Supreme Court of the United States.* Booklet. Raleigh, N.C.: North Carolina Society of the Sons of the Revolution, Edwards & Broughton, 1899.

Dillon

John F. Dillon, comp. and ed., *John Marshall: Life, Character and Judicial Service.* 3 vols. Chicago: Callaghan & Co., 1903.

Dougherty

John H. Dougherty, *Power of Federal Judiciary over Legislation* (New York: G.P. Putnam's Sons, 1912).

Elliot

Jonathan Elliot, ed., *The Debates in the Several State Conventions on the Adoption of the Federal Constitution.* 5 vols. Philadelphia: J.B. Lippincott Co., 1907.

Fitzpatrick

John C. Fitzpatrick, ed., *The Writings of George Washington from the Original Manuscript Sources, 1745–1799.* 39 vols. Washington: Government Printing Office, 1931–44.

Fordham, "Political Ideas"

Jefferson B. Fordham, "Political Ideas of James Iredell." Unpublished master's thesis, Department of History and Government, University of North Carolina, Chapel Hill, 1929.

Fordham, "Iredell's Dissent"

Jefferson B. Fordham, "Iredell's Dissent in *Chisholm v. Georgia:* Its Political Significance," North Carolina Historical Review 8 (1931): 155.

Friedman and Israel

Leon Friedman and Fred L. Israel, eds., *The Justices of the United States Supreme Court 1789–1969: Their Lives and Major Opinions.* Vol. 1. New York and London: Chelsea House in association with R.R. Bowker Co., 1969.

Gillespie and Lienesch

Michael A. Gillespie and Michael Lienesch, eds., *Ratifying the Constitution* (Lawrence: University Press of Kansas, 1989).

Goebel

Julius Goebel, Jr., *History of the Supreme Court of the United States.* Vol. 1, *Antecedents and Beginnings to 1801.* New York: Macmillan Co., 1971.

Haines, *Role of Supreme Court*

Charles Grove Haines, *The Role of the Supreme Court in American Government and Politics.* Vol. 1, *1789–1935.* Berkeley: University of California Press, 1944.

Henderson

Archibald Henderson, author and ed., *North Carolina: The Old North State and the New.* 5 vols. Chicago: Lewis Publishing Co., 1941.

Herndon

Nettie Southworth Herndon, "James Iredell," unpublished Ph.D. diss., Duke University, 1944.

Higginbotham

Don Higginbotham, ed., *The Papers of James Iredell.* 2 vols. Raleigh: Division of Archives and History, North Carolina Department of Cultural Resources, 1976.

Holt, "'The Federal Courts Have Enemies'"	Wythe Holt, "'The Federal Courts Have Enemies in All Who Fear Their Influence on State Objects': The Failure to Abolish Supreme Court Circuit-Riding in the Judiciary Acts of 1792 and 1793," Buffalo Law Review 36 (1987): 301.
Holt, "To Establish Justice"	Wythe Holt, "'To Establish Justice': Politics, the Judiciary Act of 1789 and the Intervention of the Federal Courts," Duke Law Journal 1989: 1421.
Holton	Quinton Holton, "History of the Case of *Bayard v. Singleton*." Unpublished master's thesis, University of North Carolina, Chapel Hill, 1948.
Iredell	James Iredell, *Laws of the State of North Carolina* (Edenton, N.C.: Hodge & Wills, 1791).
Jay	Stewart Jay, *Most Humble Servants: The Advisory Role of Early Judges* (New Haven: Yale University Press, 1997).
Johnson	Guion G. Johnson, *Ante-Bellum North Carolina: A Social History* (Chapel Hill: University of North Carolina Press, 1937).
Lefler	Hugh T. Lefler, ed., *A Plea for Federal Union: North Carolina, 1788* (Charlottesville: McGregor Library, University of Virginia, 1947).
Lefler and Newsome	Hugh T. Lefler and Albert R. Newsome, *North Carolina: The History of a Southern State* (Chapel Hill: University of North Carolina Press, 1954).
Lefler and Powell	Hugh T. Lefler and William S. Powell, *Colonial North Carolina: A History* (New York: Charles Scribner's Sons, 1973).
Lefler and Stanford	Hugh T. Lefler and Patricia Stanford, *North Carolina* (New York: Harcourt Brace Jovanovich, 2nd ed., 1972).
Levy	Leonard W. Levy, *Original Intent and the Framers' Constitution* (New York: Macmillan, 1988).
Marcus	Maeva Marcus, ed., *The Documentary History of the Supreme Court of the United States*. Vols. 1–6. New York: Columbia University Press, 1985–98.
Marcus and Van Tassel	Maeva Marcus and Emily Field Van Tassel, "Judges and Legislators in the New Federal System, 1789–1800," in Robert A. Katzmann, ed., *Judges and Legislators: Toward Institutional Comity* (Washington, D.C.: The Brookings Institution, 1988).
McRee	Griffith J. McRee, ed., *Life and Correspondence of James Iredell*. 2 vols. New York: Appleton and Co., 1857–58.
Miller	Samuel F. Miller, *Lectures on the Constitution of the United States* (New York: Banks & Bros., 1891).
Nash	Frank Nash, "An Eighteenth Century Circuit Rider" (Raleigh: Edwards & Broughton, 1922) (Proceedings of the Twentieth

and Twenty-First Annual Sessions of the State Literary and
Historical Association of North Carolina, North Carolina
Historical Commission Bulletin No. 28).

Newsome   Albert R. Newsome, "North Carolina's Ratification of the
Federal Constitution," North Carolina Historical Review 17
(1940): 287.

Orth, "Fee   John V. Orth, "Does the Fee Tail Exist in North Carolina,"
Tail"   Wake Forest Law Review 23 (1988): 767.

Orth, "The   John V. Orth, "The Truth About Justice Iredell's Dissent in
Truth"   *Chisholm v. Georgia* (1793)," North Carolina Law Review 73
(1994): 255.

Peele   William J. Peele, *Lives of Distinguished North Carolinians*
(Raleigh: N.C. Publishing Society, 1898).

Powell, *DNCB*   William S. Powell, ed., *Dictionary of North Carolina Biography*.
6 vols. to date. Chapel Hill, N.C.: University of North Carolina
Press, 1979–96.

Powell   William S. Powell, *North Carolina Through Four Centuries*
(Chapel Hill, N.C.: University of North Carolina Press, 1989).

Pratt   Walter F. Pratt, Jr., "Law and the Experience of Politics in Late
Eighteenth-Century North Carolina: North Carolina Considers
the Constitution," Wake Forest Law Review 22 (1987): 577.

Price   William S. Price, Jr., " 'There Ought to Be a Bill of Rights':
North Carolina Enters a New Nation," in Patrick T. Conley and
John P. Kaminski, eds., *The Bill of Rights and the States: The
Colonial and Revolutionary Origins of American Liberties*
(Madison, Wis.: Madison House, 1992).

Robinson   Blackwell P. Robinson, *William R. Davie* (Chapel Hill:
University of North Carolina Press, 1957).

Saunders   William L. Saunders, ed., *The Colonial Records of North
Carolina* (Raleigh: Josephus Daniels, 1890).

Shnayerson   Robert Shnayerson, *The Illustrated History of the Supreme Court
of the United States* (New York: Harry N. Abrams, 1986).

Smith, *Adams*   Page Smith, *John Adams*. Vol. 2, *1784–1826.* Garden City,
N.Y.: Doubleday & Co., 1962.

Smith, *Wilson*   Charles Page Smith, *James Wilson, Founding Father: 1742–
1798* (Chapel Hill: University of North Carolina Press, 1956).

Smith,   Richard Norton Smith, *Patriarch: George Washington and the
Patriarch   New American Nation* (Boston: Houghton Mifflin Co., 1993).

Spence   Wilma Cartwright Spence, *Tombstones and Epitaphs of Northeastern North Carolina* (Baltimore: Gateway Press, Inc., 1973).

Sykes   John Sykes, "The James Iredell House: An Examination of
                 Documentary Evidence Relating to the Present Structure and the
                 Iredell Family." Historic Sites Library, North Carolina Depart-
                 ment of Cultural Resources, Raleigh, North Carolina, 1992.

Trenholme   Louise Irby Trenholme, *The Ratification of the Federal
                 Constitution in North Carolina* (New York: Columbia University
                 Press, 1932).

van Santvoord   George van Santvoord, *Sketches of the Lives, Times and Judicial
                 Services of the Chief Justices of the Supreme Court of the United
                 States* (Albany, N.Y.: Weare C. Little & Co., 2nd ed., 1882).

Waldrup   John Charles Waldrup, "James Iredell and the Practice of Law in
                 Revolutionary Era North Carolina." Ph.D. diss., University of
                 North Carolina at Chapel Hill, 1985. Ann Arbor, Mich.:
                 University Microfilms, 1985.

Warren,   Charles Warren, *The Supreme Court in United States History.*
History   Vol. 1, 1789–1821. Boston: Little, Brown & Co., 1922.

Warren, "New   Charles Warren, "New Light on the History of the Federal
Light"   Judiciary Act of 1789," Harvard Law Review 37 (1923): 49.

Watson,   Alan D. Watson, "States' Rights and Agrarianism Ascendant,"
"State's   in Patrick T. Conley and John P. Kaminski, *The Constitution
Rights"   and the States: The Role of the Original Thirteen in the Framing
                 and Adoption of the Federal Constitution* (Madison, Wis.:
                 Madison House, 1988).

Watson,   Alan D. Watson, "Women in Colonial North Carolina: Over-
"Women"   looked and Underestimated," North Carolina Historical Review
                 58 (1981): 1.

Weeks   Stephen B. Weeks, "Libraries and Literature in North Carolina
                 in the Eighteenth Century," in *Annual Report of the American
                 Historical Association, 1895* (Washington: Government Printing
                 Office, 1896), 169.

White, *AJT*   G. Edward White, *The American Judicial Tradition: Profiles of
                 Leading American Judges* (New York: Oxford University Press,
                 expanded ed. 1988).

White,   G. Edward White, "The Working Life of the Marshall Court,"
"Working Life"   Virginia Law Review 70 (1984): 1.

Wood   Gordon S. Wood, *The Creation of the American Republic 1776–
                 1787* (Chapel Hill: University of North Carolina Press, 1969).

Yarborough   Kemp Plummer Yarborough, "*Chisholm v. Georgia*: A Study of
                 the Minority Opinion." Ph.D. diss., Columbia University, 1963.
                 Ann Arbor, Mich.: University Microfilms, 1991.

Table of Cases

Index

Page references in italics refer to illustrations.